Development and Underdevelopment

FIFTH EDITION

Development and Underdevelopment

The Political Economy of Global Inequality

EDITED BY
Mitchell A. Seligson
John T Passé-Smith

LYNNE
RIENNER
PUBLISHERS

BOULDER
LONDON

Published in the United States of America in 2014 by
Lynne Rienner Publishers, Inc.
1800 30th Street, Boulder, Colorado 80301
www.rienner.com

and in the United Kingdom by
Lynne Rienner Publishers, Inc.
3 Henrietta Street, Covent Garden, London WC2E 8LU

Library of Congress Cataloging-in-Publication Data
Seligson, Mitchell A.
    Development and underdevelopment : the political economy of global inequality /
by Mitchell A. Seligson and John T Passé-Smith. — 5th Edition.
        p. cm.
    Includes bibliographical references and index.
    ISBN 978-1-62637-031-9 (alk. paper)
    1. Developing countries—Economic conditions. 2. Economic development.
3. Income distribution. 4. Capitalism. 5. Economic history—1945–   6. Social
history—1945–   I. Passé-Smith, John T II. Title.
    HC59.7.D4453 2014
    320.967—dc23

                                                          2013019990

British Cataloguing in Publication Data
A Cataloguing in Publication record for this book
is available from the British Library.

Printed and bound in the United States of America

  The paper used in this publication meets the requirements
of the American National Standard for Permanence of
Paper for Printed Library Materials Z39.48-1992.

5 4 3 2 1

For the grandchildren:
Maya, Dalia, and Tamar Levanon

and

For Mary Sue

Contents

Preface

THE RAPIDLY ADVANCING FIELD OF DEVELOPMENT STUDIES HAS PRO-
duced new and in some cases revolutionary understandings of the factors that
explain why some nations have become so rich while others have lagged woe-
fully behind. This new edition of *Development and Underdevelopment* reflects
these changes in our thinking. More than two-fifths of the readings included
here are new to this edition. At the same time, the volume maintains a bedrock
of studies that lay the foundations for the new advances. The many instructors
who have used previous editions of the book will find much that is familiar,
but they can also be confident that the most recent developments in the field
are covered—and in a somewhat reorganized format that is, we hope, more
user-friendly for students.

The book is about the international gap in wealth between rich and poor
nations and the domestic gap in wealth between rich and poor people. When
did those gaps begin? What is their cause? Are they widening or narrowing?
Most important, perhaps, is the attempt by several of the authors in this new
edition to attempt to answer the question, How can the gap between rich and
poor be narrowed? Even though many had hoped that the end of the Cold War
would bring about the end of conflict—the "end of history," as Francis
Fukuyama termed it—we now know that hope was premature. Civil wars and
international conflicts mark our own time, just as they did during the Cold
War. As we write these words, the Arab Spring, in which long-standing authoritarian rulers have been deposed by popular uprisings, is still unfolding, and
nations that threw off dictators have been plunged into protracted civil wars.
The causes of these uprisings and the violence that has accompanied them are
closely linked to the problems of growth and inequality that are the focal
points for this volume.

The first edition of the book, published in 1984 as *The Gap Between Rich and Poor,* grew out of a seminar taught by Mitch Seligson at the University of Arizona. In preparing for the seminar while on sabbatical at the University of Essex, he recognized that there was a great deal of impressive research addressing the questions posed above, and he attempted to organize that material for his graduate students. Although there were a number of collections that at that time examined political and economic development, none directly addressed the questions he sought to answer. In addition, the then most recent theoretical and empirical research was absent from those volumes.

When the seminar was taught for the first time, the students attending it helped to refine the thinking that went into its preparation. One of those students, John Passé-Smith, was so stimulated by the subject matter that he wrote his doctoral dissertation on it. When Seligson was about to begin another sabbatical, Passé-Smith suggested that a new edition of the volume be developed to incorporate the latest scholarship on the problem of the dual gaps between rich and poor. Hence this collaborative effort emerged, with Seligson and Passé-Smith serving as coeditors for every edition thereafter.

This new edition begins with a reorganized Part 1, which presents strong evidence of the international and domestic gaps between rich and poor. A revised Part 2 describes the emergence of the international gap in wealth over the long term. These studies trace the gap back over centuries, even thousands of years, and attempt to explain when, where, and why it emerged. Part 3, which addresses the domestic gap between rich and poor, has three new chapters to focus more directly on the status of the "bottom billion."

Turning to explanations of the gaps, Part 4 focuses on the so-called convergence thesis. It begins with W. W. Rostow's classic work on the stages of economic growth, which implies that eventually all countries will pass through these stages and become rich. This thesis is then partially supported but partially refuted by William J. Baumol.

Part 5, on the impact of culture on development, which underwent a major revision in the last edition, is presented here in largely the same form. The classic contributions of David C. McClelland and Lawrence E. Harrison are retained, along with the recent empirical test of Jim Granato, Ronald Inglehart, and David Leblang.

Dependency and world systems theory is covered in Part 6, which now includes a modern statement from the father of dependency theory, Fernando Enrique Cardoso.

Part 7 focuses squarely on institutions, opening with Mancur Olson's fascinating "Big Bills Left on the Sidewalk" article, which makes a strong case that poor countries are poor because they have the wrong institutions and policies. This section also includes the classic work by Michael Lipton on urban bias and the newer work on the impact of democracy on growth by Adam Przeworski and Fernando Limongi. After the contribution by Nancy Birdsall and Richard Sabot, which offers comparisons of Latin America and Asia, the section ends with a critique of the institutions approach by Jared Diamond.

A substantially revised Part 8 now includes research by several scholars that helps to explain what natural resource abundance (the "resource curse"), climate change, and health have to do with the gap.

We are indebted to numerous people for helping us to prepare the manuscript for this edition. Mary Sue Passé-Smith offered invaluable advice and support. At Vanderbilt, Professor Seligson is grateful for the many helpful suggestions made by the graduate and undergraduate students in his Politics of Global Inequality classes. Finally, we would like to thank the many authors and publishers who so kindly granted permission for their works to appear here.

—Mitchell A. Seligson and John T Passé-Smith

Development and Underdevelopment

1

The Dual Gaps: An Overview of Theory and Research

Mitchell A. Seligson

THE TWENTY-FIRST CENTURY HAS BROUGHT WITH IT A RISING CONCERN over rapidly increasing income and wealth inequality worldwide. In the United States, income inequality has risen so steeply and so rapidly that political debates often reference the so-called one-percenters—the top 1 percent of the income distribution. In Europe, protest marches frequently turn violent as the unemployed and those who have suffered from widespread austerity programs demand that the rich pay more in taxes to help alleviate the burdens faced by the rest. From a global perspective, as this book shows in considerable detail, there are wide gaps between rich nations and poor nations, and between rich people and poor people within many nations. But why should we care? If we read works in classical economic theory, we will find assertions that in the end, we will all be rich. According to W. W. Rostow's thesis, for example, in his widely read book *The Stages of Economic Growth,*[1] economic underdevelopment is only a stage that nations pass through on their way to becoming rich. But the data we have at hand tell a different story.

The income gap between rich and poor countries has grown dramatically since World War II and shows few signs of shrinking. In 1950 the average per capita income (in 1980 US dollars) of low-income countries was $164, whereas the per capita income of the industrialized countries averaged $3,841, yielding an absolute income gap of $3,677. Thirty years later, in 1980, average per capita income in the poor countries had risen to only $245, whereas that in the industrialized countries had soared to $9,648, yielding an absolute gap in 1980 of $9,403. For this period, then, there is clear evidence to support the old adage that "the rich get richer." It is not true, however, that the poor get poorer, not literally anyway, but this would be a perverse way of looking at these data. A more realistic view of the increases in "wealth" in the poor countries would show that in this thirty-year period, the average income increased by an average of only $2.70 a year, less than what a US resident might have spent for lunch at a neighborhood fast-food restaurant. And in terms of relative wealth, the poor countries certainly did get poorer: the total income (gross national product [GNP]) of the low-income countries declined from 4.3 percent of the income earned by the industrialized countries in 1950 to a mere 2.5 percent by 1980.

The growth in the gap has continued on into the new century. By 2001 the gap was wider than ever, according to the World Bank. In that year the low-income countries averaged only $430 in gross national income (GNI, the revised term for gross national product) in current dollars, whereas the high-income countries averaged $26,710, yielding an astounding gap of $26,280. The relative gap grew even wider by 2011 compared to 1980, with the GNI of the low-income countries equal to only 1.4 percent of the GNI of the industrialized countries, meaning that, since 1950, the relative gap between rich and poor countries widened by 60 percent.[2] In the appendix to this book, we provide the 2011 GNI per capita data showing that the trend continues. The average income of the low-income countries was $571 per capita in 2011, compared to an average of $41,274 for the high-income advanced industrial countries.

One might suspect that these data do not reflect the general pattern of growth found throughout the world but may be excessively influenced by the disappointing performance of a few "basket case" nations. That suspicion is unfounded. The low-income countries comprise 817 million people living in thirty-six nations.[3] Moreover, it is incorrect to speculate that the world's poor countries are all in Africa; a number are in Asia and one (Haiti) is in the Americas. One notch up from the poorest countries are what the World Bank classifies as "lower middle income" countries, where GNI per capita is only $1,772. In those countries reside 2.5 billion people out of the world's 7 billion. The poor and lower-middle-income countries together total 3.3 billion of the world's population. It is also incorrect to speculate that, because the growth rates of some poor and lower-middle-income countries have recently outperformed those of the industrialized countries, the gap will soon be narrowed. In Chapter 2, John Passé-Smith tells us that it could take Pakistan's 152 million people 1,152 years to close the gap. Even in the "miracle countries" such as China, where growth rates have been far higher than in the industrialized countries, the gap will take sixty-four years to close on the unrealistic assumption that China could maintain its present level of growth for many decades to come.

There is another gap separating rich from poor: many developing nations have long experienced a growing gap between their own rich and poor citizens, as the chapters in Part 3 of this volume demonstrate. Many poor people who live in poor countries, therefore, are falling farther behind not only the world's rich, but also the more affluent citizens in their own countries. The world's poor, therefore, find themselves in double jeopardy.

The consequences of these yawning gaps can be witnessed every day. In the international arena, tensions between the "haves" and "have-nots" dominate debate at the United Nations and in other international forums. The poor countries are demanding better treatment from the rich nations of the world. The industrialized countries have responded with foreign aid programs that, because of limited funds, have not reversed the trends in growing worldwide inequality. Within many developing countries, domestic stability is frequently tenuous at best, as victims of the domestic gap between rich and poor (along with their sympathizers) seek redress through violent means. Political violence, civil wars, and other insurgencies have many causes, but, as shown by Edward Muller and Mitchell Seligson in Chapter 13 of this volume, one root cause can be traced to domestic inequality. In the final analysis, this may lie at the root of the rise of global terrorism in the twenty-first century.

Thinking and research on the international and domestic gaps between rich and poor have been going through a protracted period of debate that can be traced back to the end of World War II. The war elevated the United States to the position of world leader, and in that position the nation found itself confronted with a Western Europe in ruins. The motivations behind the Marshall Plan, which sought to rebuild Europe, are debated to this day, but two things remain evident: unprecedented amounts of aid were given, and the expected results were rapidly achieved. War-torn industries were rebuilt, new ones were begun, and economic growth quickly resumed. Similarly, Japan, devastated by conventional and nuclear attack, was able to rebuild its economy and become a world leader in high-technology industrial production.

The successful rebuilding of Europe and Japan encouraged many to believe that similar success would meet efforts to stimulate growth in the developing world. More often than not, however, such efforts have failed or fallen far below expectations. Even when programs have been effective and nations have seemed well on the way toward rapid growth, many of them nonetheless continued to fall farther and farther behind the wealthy countries. Moreover, growth almost inevitably seemed to be accompanied by a widening income gap within the developing countries. We have seen an important reversal of this worldwide trend, however, in Asia, where poor nations have grown rapidly while income inequality has not worsened and in some cases has even improved. The lessons of Asia, therefore, are important ones. Thus, even well into the new century, the world is still confronted by what Paul Collier refers to as the "bottom billion."[4]

As a result of these experiences, an impressive volume of research on explaining the "gap" question has been generated, and we have attempted to include some of the very best of it in this volume. The authors collected here present a wide-ranging treatment of the thinking that is evolving on the subject of the international and domestic gaps between rich and poor. Their studies are not confined to a single academic discipline or geographic area. Rather, their work, as presented in the chapters here, reflects a variety of fields, including anthropology, economics, political science, psychology, and sociology.

The volume is organized to first present the reader with a broad picture that defines the international and domestic gaps between the rich and the poor. This picture is contained in Part 1 of the volume. Part 2 takes the long-term view, going back in some cases thousands of years to attempt to locate the point in time when the gap between rich and poor began. Part 3 looks at the domestic income inequality gap. Part 4 explores the classic explanation for closing the gap and the convergence/divergence thesis. The remaining parts attempt to explain the existence of the gaps, with Part 5 looking at culture, Part 6 looking at dependency and world systems, Part 7 focusing on institutions, and Part 8 exploring the impact of natural resources and climate change.

Part 1, "Is There a Gap Between Rich and Poor Countries?" presents a broad overview of the facts of the international gap. The chapters here show that the gap between rich and poor countries is wide and growing. John Passé-Smith (Chapter 2) and Robert Hunter Wade (Chapter 3) show that even though some countries manage to narrow the gap, most do not. Glenn Firebaugh (Chapter 4), weighting the data by the population sizes of countries, finds that the gap is neither growing nor shrinking but is in fact remaining quite stable. These findings are robust, as Passé-Smith shows in Chapter 5, even when the newer way of calculating per capita incomes, called purchasing power parity, is used. Part 1 concludes with Abhijit Banerjee and Esther Duflo (Chapter 6) asking the important question: How does one live on less than a dollar a day?

Part 2, "Historical Origins of the Gap," takes the long-term view. Angus Maddison (Chapter 7) has collected the longest time-series of world wealth of any scholar. He shows that the gap is anything but a recent phenomenon, having widened significantly since the 1800s. Jared Diamond (Chapter 8) takes an even longer-range view, looking back at the impact of geography on the emergence of civilization and economic development. Diamond's emphasis on geography, climate, and other natural conditions is disputed by two teams of scholars (Chapters 9 and 10). The emphasis in this work is that it is institutions rather than geography that matter. The age of imperialism established different kinds of institutions in the colonized parts of the world, some focused on extraction of resources while others were focused on building a state in which property rights and rule of law were firmly established. According to the argument, conditions confronted by colonial settlers strongly determined the kinds of institutions that were put in place, and those institutions determined, over the centuries, the rate of economic growth, ending with some nations being very rich and others very poor. Peter Blair Henry and Conrad Miller (Chapter 11) argue that Jamaica and Barbados, while having similar historical experiences and institutions, have experienced very different growth trajectories. They assert that the distinguishing factor is policy, not geography or institutions, that determines variation in rates of economic growth.

Part 3, "The Other Gap: Domestic Income Inequality," examines domestic inequality. Nobel Prize winner Simon Kuznets (Chapter 12) sees widening domestic income inequality as an almost inevitable by-product of development. Kuznets traces a path that seems to have been followed quite closely by nations that have become industrialized. The process begins with relative domestic equality in the distribution of income. The onset of industrialization produces a significant shift in the direction of inequality and creates a widening gap. Once the industrialization process matures, however, the gap is again reduced. This view was certainly held by those who still regard the Marshall Plan as the model for the resolution of world poverty. Inequality has consequences. Edward Muller and Mitchell Seligson (Chapter 13) show that domestic income inequality is linked to violence in the form of insurgency and thus that there are real societal costs to pay beyond any ethical ones. Isabel Ortiz and Matthew Cummins (Chapter 14) show how difficult it will be for the gap to be closed for the poorest countries—that is, the "bottom billion." According to their calculations, it will take 800 years, at the current rate of growth, for those countries to catch up. Andrew Berg and Jonathan Ostry (Chapter 15) warn that inequality may cause a short-term growth spurt, but in the long run high levels of inequality bring unrest and, potentially, political instability. Contrary to many previous studies, their analysis suggests that equality does not slow growth. The authors paraphrase and invert the famous remark of President John Kennedy, "a rising tide lifts all boats," concluding that "helping raise the smallest boats may help keep the tide rising for all craft, big and small." Part 3 ends with the work of Martin Ravallion (Chapter 16), which heaps more pessimism onto the equation. He finds that while middle-income countries have the capacity to tax their way to greater equality in the distribution of wealth, the poorest countries do not.

A more optimistic perspective is demonstrated in Part 4, "The Classical Thesis: Convergence or Divergence?" According to this thesis, even though Kuznets may have been right regarding the long run, both rich and poor countries will follow the same stages of growth. W. W. Rostow's classic work on the stages of economic growth (Chapter 17) leads to the conclusion that all countries will eventually converge. William Baumol (Chapter 18) provides evidence of this convergence when he reports on a study of countries over a 110-year period. However, he notes that there is a "convergence club," and that not all countries are "members." For those excluded countries, convergence between rich and poor becomes an ever-receding dream. This part of the book concludes by returning to the pessimism of the prior sections. J. Bradford DeLong (Chapter 19) shows that convergence theory is illusory, as convergence occurs only when the sample of countries selected includes those that have already converged. When this "selection bias" is dropped, and a broader sample of countries is included, the widening gap is again the norm.

Explanations for the great gaps have often focused on variation in national culture. We have all heard the expressions, "Germans are so industrious, that is why they are rich," or "the Japanese work so hard, it is no wonder that they are so wealthy." Part 5 of this volume, "Culture and Underdevelopment," presents evidence for and against the role of culture. Specifically, the cultural values associated with industrialization are seen as foreign to many developing nations, which apparently are deeply attached to more traditional cultural values. According to the cultural thesis, punctuality, hard work, achievement, and other "industrial" values are the keys to unlocking the economic potential of poor countries. Most adherents of this perspective believe that such values can be inculcated through deliberate effort. For example, this is the thesis of David McClelland (Chapter 20), who writes about the importance of high "N-achievement" for growth. Lawrence Harrison has written extensively on this thesis, and here (Chapter 21) he makes a broad case that values matter most in development. Others argue that values will emerge naturally as the result of a worldwide process of diffusion of those values that are functional for development. This perspective has been incorporated into a more general school of thought focusing on the process called "modernization." Development occurs, and the international gap is narrowed, when a broad set of modern values *and* institutions is present. Jim Granato, Ronald Inglehart, and David Leblang (Chapter 22) present strong quantitative evidence for the importance of culture, showing that McClelland was right about the achievement motive driving development.

In marked contrast to the convergence theory and the cultural perspectives on the gap, which suggest that the phenomena of rich and poor disparity can be transitory, a third school of thought comes to rather different conclusions, as explored in Part 6, "Dependency and World Systems Theory: Still Relevant?" The scholars who support this approach—known as *dependentistas*—observe that the economies of the developing nations have been shaped in response to forces and conditions established by the industrialized nations, and that their development has been both delayed and dependent as a result. The *dependentistas* conclude that the failure of poor countries is a product of the distorted development brought on by dependency relations. In Part 6 the dependency and world-systems perspectives are presented by the major writers in the field, and refuted by others based on careful studies of large datasets. The classic article in the field, by Andre Gunder Frank (Chapter 23), begins this section. Next, Heather-Jo Hammer and John Gartrell (Chapter 24), in a case study of Canada, suggest that dependency is a problem not only for the developing world but also for some parts of the industrialized world. The section concludes with a paper by Fernando Henrique Cardoso (Chapter 25), the founder of dependency thinking and former president of Brazil, who offers a broad picture on the evolution of dependency thinking in the context of the globalizing world.

Part 7, "The Role of Institutions," presents what has become the dominant paradigm for economists in explaining the gaps, focusing attention on the role of states within the third world. As socialist economies throughout the world proved incapable of keeping up with the capitalist industrialized countries, international development agencies focused their attention on the need for institutional and policy reforms within the third world. This attention brought with it a host of neoliberal policy prescriptions, including privatization, trade liberalization, and the ending of import substitution industrialization (ISI) policies. The collapse of the Soviet Union and the socialist states of Eastern Europe, along with the entry of China into the world economy as a major player, has reinforced this tendency. According to the perspective that focuses on institutions, failures of state policy to provide property rights and the rule of law are largely responsible for the gaps. This is the thesis argued by Mancur Olson Jr. (Chapter 26), whose paper "Big Bills on the Sidewalk" has become a classic in the field. One way policies become distorted is as a result of "urban bias," as explored by Michael Lipton (Chapter 27). From this perspective, there are numerous policies in the third world that favor the cities over the countryside, with the result that growth is slowed and the gap between rich and poor nations widens.

Because of the dramatic increase in the number of democratic governments in recent years, the connection between democracy on the one hand and growth and inequality on the other has become a major topic for research. Some have argued that democratic political systems are less capable than their authoritarian counterparts of setting a clear economic agenda, whereas others have argued that democracies not only are good for growth, but also are inherently egalitarian in nature and hence help reduce the domestic gap between rich and poor. Adam Przeworski and Fernando Limongi (Chapter 28) present the evidence in this debate. On the other hand, Nancy Birdsall and Richard Sabot (Chapter 29) focus less on institutions and more on human capital, specifically education, as the key to growth. An even broader perspective is taken by world-famous geographer Jared Diamond (Chapter 30), who argues that while institutions no doubt matter, it is geography that matters more. Diamond's chapter also relates directly to the studies on natural resources, to which we next turn.

Part 8, "Natural Resources, Climate Change, and the Gap," is an entirely new section of this book. Here we look at various physical factors that might influence the emergence and persistence of the gap between rich and poor. One of the most important areas of research has been on the so-called resource curse—that is, the growth problem faced by countries that are well endowed with highly valuable commodities such as petroleum, gold, or diamonds. Paul Collier and Benedikt Goderis (Chapter 30) explain why resource-rich countries tend to grow very slowly. As a result of variation in climates worldwide, some countries suffer from high disease levels. Christopher Eppig, Corey Fincher, and Randy Thornhill (Chapter 32) show that those countries that suffer from high levels of parasites also suffer from a lower level of average cognitive ability in their populations, which presumably inhibits economic growth. Finally, Melissa Dell, Benjamin Jones, and Benjamin Olken (Chapter 33) look at the ill effects of climate change on economic growth. In Part 9, to conclude the book, Mitchell Seligson (Chapter 34) looks to the future and explores areas for further research.

It is hoped that readers of this volume will come away from it with a clear sense of the causes of the gaps between the rich and poor. It is hoped that some of these readers might someday help in implementing the "cure."

Notes

1. W. W. Rostow, *The Stages of Economic Growth: A Non-Communist Manifesto* (Cambridge, UK: Cambridge University Press, 1960).

2. Data from World Bank, *World Development Report 2003* (New York: Oxford University Press, 2003), pp. 234–235; and www.data.worldbank.org.

3. Data taken from www.data.worldbank.org.

4. Paul Collier, *The Bottom Billion: Why the Poorest Countries Are Falling Behind and What Can Be Done About It?* (Oxford: Oxford University Press, 2007).

Part 1

Is There a Gap Between Rich and Poor Countries?

2

Characteristics of the Income Gap Between Countries, 1960–2010

John T Passé-Smith

The purpose of this chapter and this section of the book is to take stock of global economic growth in order to establish the long-term characteristics of the gap between the rich and poor within countries as well as between the rich and poor countries themselves. Much of the rest of the book presents the various arguments for why the gap exists and the policies that governments could follow in hopes of reducing the gap. In years past, the existence of the gap was more or less accepted as fact, but as the reader will see, this is no longer the case. Also, with the extraordinary growth experienced by countries such as China, Korea, Singapore, and Botswana, the characteristics of the gap are changing. This chapter gives the reader an understanding of the characteristics of the gap between rich and poor countries and a starting point for understanding the impact of using different measures of the gap as presented throughout the book. World economic trends are presented in four sections that review global rates of growth, the absolute gap, the relative gap, and country mobility.

Rates of Economic Growth

Following Western Europe's rapid recovery after World War II, the governments of the industrialized countries turned their attention to aiding third world nations in their development efforts. In the 1950s and early 1960s, economic growth became the centerpiece of economists' development plans. To that end, the United Nations declared the 1960s the "Development Decade" and set a goal of 6 percent annual growth as necessary to raise the poverty-stricken to a decent standard of living within a reasonable time frame (Dube 1988: 2–3). Early analysis of economic trends by David Morawetz (1977) indicated that although the whole world had experienced relatively rapid growth, the gap between the high-income and the poor countries had widened. While the millennial development goals are much more expansive than a 6 percent growth target, underlying this effort is the same desire to help the poor lift themselves out of poverty. This chapter examines the growth of countries between 1960 and 2010 to determine if the gap between rich and poor has lessened or continued to widen, as found by Morawetz.

Data for this chapter were obtained from the World Bank's *World Development Indicators*.[1] Growth rates were computed using the regression method described by the World Bank in its *World Development Report* (1988: 288–289).[2] The income groupings and regional designations were also borrowed from the World Bank's *World Development Indicators*.[3] All measures of gross domestic products per capita (GDP/pc) are in constant US dollars with a base year of 2000. The cutoffs for the income groups were computed from those defined by the World Bank. In the analysis offered here, high-income countries are those with a GDP/pc of $9,567 and higher; upper-middle-income countries have a GDP/pc of between $3,099 and $9,566; lower-middle-income countries have a GDP/pc of between $784 and $3,098; and the poor countries are those with a GDP/pc of $783 or less.[4]

In the previous edition of this volume, I reported that the countries of the world (for which we have data) grew at an annual average rate of 1.61 percent between 1960 and 2005. With five more years of growth, the percentage has remained largely the same, at 1.64 percent (see Table 2.1). With each new edition of this volume adding approximately five more years of growth, it becomes ever more remarkable that this growth rate includes *all* of the countries in the world. As I have reminded the reader many times now, when Simon Kuznets (1972: 19) lauded the countries that had become rich by the 1950s

Table 2.1   Annual Average Percentage Growth Rates by World Bank Income Grouping, 1960–2010 (*N* in parentheses)

	1960–2010	1960–1969	1970–1979	1980–1989	1990–1999	2000–2010
World	1.64 (94)	2.85 (96)	2.50 (119)	0.96 (142)	0.97 (183)	2.92 (176)
High income	2.22 (9)	3.60 (9)	2.20 (23)	1.40 (35)	1.94 (40)	1.46 (35)
Upper-middle income	2.07 (17)	4.21 (18)	3.29 (21)	1.70 (26)	1.48 (33)	2.97 (33)
Lower-middle income	2.18 (26)	3.55 (27)	3.36 (33)	0.70 (42)	0.20 (56)	3.49 (49)
Poor	1.64 (42)	1.66 (42)	1.59 (42)	0.35 (39)	0.72 (54)	3.29 (59)

Source: Computed from World Bank, *World Development Indicators, 2012* (Washington, DC, 2012).

(largely Western European countries, the United States, Canada, Japan, and Australia) for their long century of 1.6 percent growth, that average growth rate included only those rich countries.[5] For the fifty-one-year period of 1960 to 2010, fifty of the ninety-four countries for which there were data over the entire period maintained growth rates of 1.6 percent or higher.

Examining Table 2.1 a bit further reveals that the eras commonly associated with the global debt crisis and the Asian currency crisis, the 1980s and 1990s respectively, were periods of global economic slowdown. The 1980s saw global growth plummet to 0.96 percent, down from 2.5 percent in the 1970s. Growth during the 1990s remained below the 1 percent mark. The turn of the century brought new hope for the future, with growth rates for over 175 countries averaging 2.92 percent, the highest of any decade in the study.

For the period as a whole, the high-income countries had the highest growth rates. The annual average growth rate of high-income countries was 2.22 percent. The lower-middle-income countries attained the second highest growth rate, at 2.18 percent, while the upper-middle-income countries averaged just over 2 percent growth between 1960 and 2010. The GDPs per capita of the poorest countries grew at a respectable 1.64 percent. For the entire fifty-one-year period, the pattern of growth found in Table 2.1 contradicts the predictions offered by convergence theorists, such as William Baumol (see Chapter 18), who assert that the gap between rich and poor will disappear over the long run. They argue that the poorer countries have the highest growth potential and that, as this potential is realized, the gap will dissolve. Of course, if convergence in its purest form were occurring today, the growth rates of the poorest countries would be the highest, followed by the middle-income countries, with the high-income countries exhibiting the lowest growth rates.

In his 1982 study of world growth, Robert Jackman discovered what he termed the "modified Matthew effect" (1982: 175). In the Bible, the Book of Matthew contains a reference to the continued accumulation of wealth by the rich and the further impoverishment of the poor; by the "modified Matthew effect," Jackman meant that both the high-income and middle-income countries were growing richer (in fact the middle-income countries were growing more rapidly than the high-income countries), while the poor countries remained roughly constant rather than falling farther behind. Convergence theorists later made reference to such a pattern, which they referred to as "modified convergence." Here the countries predicted to converge—the so-called convergence club—did not include the poorest countries, which, the theorists argued, lacked the human capital to take advantage of the high-growth potential of club members (see Abramovitz 1986).

Table 2.1 breaks down the annual average rates of growth for the high-income, upper-middle-income, lower-middle-income, and poor countries by decades. In the previous edition of this volume, I found a pattern consistent with the modified version of the "Matthew effect" (modified convergence) in every single decade. However, with the addition of more countries' data, five more years of data added, and the refining of the data that is the ongoing job of the World Bank, that finding has dissolved. For the period as a whole, 1960 to 2010, the high-income countries were the fastest-growing countries, with the middle-income countries slightly behind and the poor countries having the lowest rates of growth. Globally the 1960s was the second-fastest decade for economic growth for the period under investigation. During this decade, a version of the modified Matthew effect takes place. The growth rate of the high-income countries (3.6 percent) is exceeded by that of the upper-middle-income countries (with the lower-middle-income countries only very slightly behind the high-income), with the poor countries remaining in the 1.6 percent range. A similar pattern emerges for the 1970s, although the growth rates for all income groups are lower than in the 1960s. A period of divergence takes shape in the 1990s, where the higher the income level, the higher the economic growth rate. That is followed by a decade of convergence, where the lower the income level, the higher the growth rate.

Table 2.2 shows that the percentage of people living in the wealthiest countries in the world is relatively small and rather stable. The percentage of the world population living in high-income countries was 10.3 percent in 1960. That percentage climbs to 18.7 by 1980 and then declines and remains relatively constant at 15.6 percent between 1990 and 2010. At the other end of the spectrum, those living in the poor countries constituted 65 percent of the world's population in 1960, with the percentage declining slightly to 58.9 about three decades later. Interestingly, the percentage of people living in the poor countries drops dramatically to about 40 percent in 2000 and remains relatively constant through 2010. Examining the percentage of population in the lower-middle-income countries reveals that this group of countries experienced a dramatic increase in population at the same time that the population of

Table 2.2　World Population and Percentage of World Population by World Bank Income Grouping, 1960–2010 (*N* in parentheses)

	1960	1970	1980	1990	2000	2010
World population (billions)	2.42 (96)	3.12 (11)	3.85 (142)	5.14 (183)	5.98 (193)	6.65 (176)
High income	10.3 (9)	18.7 (23)	18.7 (35)	15.6 (40)	15.5 (47)	15.5 (37)
Upper-middle income	13.4 (18)	7.0 (21)	10.1 (26)	10.1 (33)	9.4 (35)	11.1 (39)
Lower-middle income	11.3 (27)	12.5 (33)	10.7 (42)	15.5 (56)	34.7 (51)	35.2 (49)
Poor	65.0 (42)	61.8 (42)	60.6 (39)	58.9 (54)	40.4 (60)	38.2 (51)

Source: Computed from World Bank, *World Development Indicators, 2012* (Washington, DC, 2012).

the poor countries diminished. The decline of the poor countries and the increase of the lower-middle-income groups reflect the economic success of China. Other than China's obvious and substantial impact on the numbers, it is remarkable how stable the populations of the income groups are.

When examining the geographic distribution of economic growth, it is clear that all regions of the world experienced reasonably high levels of growth at one time or another between 1960 and 2010. The decade of fastest growth was the most recent (2000 to 2010). That is particularly interesting in that the data discussed earlier show that the high-income countries were the slowest-growing group (see Table 2.1). Table 2.3 reports annual average economic growth by region. The table shows that the South Asia region, which includes India and Pakistan (see the complete list of countries in each region at the bottom of the table), grew the fastest of any region, with an annual average growth rate of 4.7 percent for the decade. Even sub-Saharan Africa expanded at an annual average rate of 2.27 percent between 2000 and 2010. The slowest growth for this decade was recorded by North America (Bermuda, Canada, and the United States), at 1.09 percent. East Asia and the Pacific tended to maintain the most stable and strongest growth rate throughout the entire period, even though this was not necessarily the fastest-growing region each decade. The so-called lost decade of the 1980s was the slowest decade of growth. Every single region of the world experienced lower growth rates than in the previous decade, except South Asia, which more than doubled its rate of growth. The 1990s was the second slowest decade of growth, but there was much more regional variation. It could be that the Asian currency crisis of the late 1990s dampened growth sufficiently to keep the global average rate down. Most regions of the world were beginning to rebound from the 1980s, experiencing higher growth rates. However, Europe and Central Asia, and East Asia and the Pacific, had lower rates of growth in the 1990s than in the 1980s.

Turning from income groups and regions to individual countries, Table 2.4 highlights the ten fastest- and slowest-growing countries. As mentioned earlier, economic growth between 1960 and 2010 was remarkably high and extensive in terms of the participation. This is apparent in the list of the ten fastest-growing countries. Five of the top ten fastest-growing countries (China, Botswana, Thailand, Indonesia, and Sri Lanka) are from the poor income group, and the remaining five are from the lower-middle-income group (the Republic of Korea, Singapore, Hong Kong, Malaysia, and Portugal). The fastest-growing countries in the world between 1960 and 2010 grew at an annual average rate of from 3.18 percent (Sri Lanka) to 7.25 percent (China). As can be seen in Tables 2.3 and 2.4, Asia is well represented in the list of fastest-growing countries.

Unfortunately one region of the world dominates the list of the slowest-growing countries. Of the ten slowest-growing countries in the world between 1960 and 2005, only two are not from Africa (Nicaragua and Venezuela). The

Table 2.3 Annual Average Gross Domestic Product per Capita Growth Rates by World Bank Geographic Region Grouping, 1960–2010 (N in parentheses)

	1960–2010	1960–1969	1970–1979	1980–1989	1990–1999	2000–2010
World	1.64 (94)	2.85 (96)	2.50 (119)	0.96 (142)	0.97 (183)	2.92 (176)
Europe and Central Asia[a]	2.47 (16)	4.15 (16)	3.04 (26)	2.10 (33)	–0.41 (52)	3.93 (49)
North America[b]	2.10 (3)	4.10 (3)	2.96 (3)	1.75 (3)	2.06 (3)	1.09 (3)
East Asia and Pacific[c]	3.69 (12)	4.13 (12)	3.51 (15)	2.48 (18)	2.24 (28)	3.02 (27)
Latin America and Caribbean[d]	1.45 (24)	2.50 (25)	2.13 (27)	0.68 (33)	2.01 (34)	2.51 (32)
Middle East and North Africa[e]	2.17 (5)	4.52 (6)	4.99 (10)	–0.63 (13)	1.38 (16)	1.57 (13)
South Asia[f]	2.25 (5)	2.49 (5)	1.00 (5)	2.32 (5)	3.25 (6)	4.70 (7)
Sub-Saharan Africa[g]	0.26 (29)	1.50 (29)	1.35 (33)	–0.23 (37)	0.44 (44)	2.27 (45)

Source: Computed from World Bank, *World Development Indicators, 2012* (Washington, DC, 2012).

Notes: a. Europe and Central Asia: Albania, Andorra, Armenia, Austria, Azerbaijan, Belarus, Belgium, Bosnia and Herzegovina, Bulgaria, Channel Islands, Croatia, Cyprus, Czech Republic, Denmark, Estonia, Faeroe Island, Finland, France, Georgia, Germany, Gibraltar, Greece, Greenland, Hungary, Iceland, Ireland, Isle of Man, Italy, Kazakhstan, Kosovo, Kyrgyz Republic, Latvia, Liechtenstein, Lithuania, Luxembourg, Macedonia, Moldova, Monaco, Montenegro, Netherlands, Norway, Poland, Portugal, Romania, Russia, San Marino, Serbia, Slovak Republic, Slovenia, Spain, Sweden, Switzerland, Tajikistan, Turkey, Turkmenistan, Ukraine, United Kingdom, Uzbekistan.

b. North America: Bermuda, Canada, United States.

c. East Asia and Pacific: American Samoa, Australia, Brunei, Cambodia, China, Fiji, French Polynesia, Guam, Hong Kong, Indonesia, Japan, Kiribati, Laos, Macao, Malaysia, Marshall Islands, Micronesia, Mongolia, Myanmar, New Caledonia, New Zealand, Palau, Papua New Guinea, Philippines, Samoa, Singapore, Solomon Islands, South Korea, Thailand, Timor-Leste, Tonga, Tuvalu, Vanuatu, Vietnam.

d. Latin America and Caribbean: Antigua and Barbuda, Argentina, Aruba, Bahamas, Barbados, Belize, Bolivia, Brazil, Cayman Islands, Chile, Colombia, Costa Rica, Cuba, Curacao, Dominica, Dominican Republic, Ecuador, El Salvador, Grenada, Guatemala, Guyana, Haiti, Honduras, Jamaica, Mexico, Nicaragua, Panama, Paraguay, Peru, Puerto Rico, St. Kitts and Nevis, St. Lucia, St. Martins, St. Vincent and Grenadines, Suriname, Trinidad and Tobago, Turks and Caicos, Uruguay, Venezuela, Virgin Islands.

e. Middle East and North Africa: Algeria, Bahrain, Djibouti, Egypt, Iran, Iraq, Israel, Jordan, Kuwait, Lebanon, Libya, Malta, Morocco, Oman, Qatar, Saudi Arabia, Syria, Tunisia, United Arab Emirates, West Bank, Yemen.

f. South Asia: Afghanistan, Bangladesh, Bhutan, India, Maldives, Nepal, Pakistan, Sri Lanka.

g. Sub-Saharan Africa: Angola, Benin, Botswana, Burkina Faso, Burundi, Cameroon, Cape Verde, Central African Republic, Chad, Comoros, Democratic Republic of Congo, Republic of Congo, Côte d'Ivoire, Equatorial Guinea, Eritrea, Ethiopia, Gabon, Gambia, Ghana, Guinea, Guinea-Bissau, Kenya, Lesotho, Liberia, Madagascar, Malawi, Mali, Mauritania, Mauritius, Mayotte, Mozambique, Namibia, Niger, Nigeria, Rwanda, São Tomé and Príncipe, Senegal, Seychelles, Sierra Leone, Somalia, South Africa, South Sudan, Sudan, Swaziland, Tanzania, Togo, Uganda, Zambia, Zimbabwe.

Table 2.4   The Ten Fastest- and Slowest-Growing Countries, 1960–2010

Rank	Country	Economic Growth Rate, 1960–2010 (%)	Income Group in 1960
Fastest-growing countries			
1	China	7.25	Poor
2	Botswana	6.51	Poor
3	Republic of Korea	5.90	Lower-middle income
4	Singapore	5.65	Lower-middle income
5	Hong Kong	4.95	Lower-middle income
6	Thailand	4.66	Poor
7	Malaysia	3.97	Lower-middle income
8	Indonesia	3.95	Poor
9	Portugal	3.19	Lower-middle income
10	Sri Lanka	3.18	Poor
Slowest-growing countries			
1	Liberia	−4.58	Poor
2	Democratic Republic of Congo	−3.26	Poor
3	Niger	−1.68	Poor
4	Madagascar	−1.36	Poor
5	Zambia	−1.25	Poor
6	Nicaragua	−1.15	Lower-middle income
7	Central African Republic	−1.03	Poor
8	Côte d'Ivoire	−0.60	Poor
9	Sierra Leone	−0.46	Poor
10	Venezuela	−0.44	Upper-middle income

Source: Computed from World Bank, *World Development Indicators, 2012* (Washington, DC, 2012).

slowest-growing countries all experienced negative growth, ranging from –0.44 percent per year in Venezuela to –4.58 percent in Liberia. Only two of the slowest-growing countries came from income groups other than the poor: Nicaragua (lower-middle income) and Venezuela (upper-middle income).

The Absolute Gap

The absolute gap is the difference between the mean GDP/pc of a set of high-income countries and that of poorer countries or groups of countries. Simon Kuznets (1972) reported in the 1970s that one of the major trends over the previous 100 to 125 years was that the absolute gap widened very slowly up until World War II and then began to accelerate. David Morawetz (1977) later found that, indeed, the absolute gap was growing wider. Morawetz showed that the absolute gap between Organization for Economic Cooperation and Development (OECD) countries and developing countries between 1950 and 1975 had more than doubled. Neither the developing countries as a group nor any of the geographic regions reported by Morawetz were able to achieve a narrowing of the absolute gap.

The top graph of Figure 2.1 shows the GDP/pc of the high-, upper-middle, lower-middle, and low-income groups, and the bottom graph depicts the absolute gap. It would appear from this figure that the rate of increase is roughly similar to that found by Kuznets and Morawetz. The data presented in Table 2.5 confirm that the absolute gap between the high-income countries and the low-income countries (between 1960 and 2010) grows 2.1 times larger. This gap expands 2.1 times for the lower-middle-income countries and 3.1 times between the high-income and the upper-middle-income countries.

The 1980s and 1990s were the slowest decades for economic growth (for the period under examination), and it would appear that the absolute gap was affected by the slower growth. In the bottom graph of Figure 2.1, the absolute gap grows quickly during the 1960s and 1970s, when global economic growth was robust; however, during the 1980s the gap appears to flatten out. This is confirmed by the data in Table 2.5. While the absolute gap may be increasing during the 1980s, the widening seems noticeably slower. This continues on until about 1993, when the rate begins to accelerate and continues to do so until the beginnings of the global financial crisis around 2007.

Whether the rate of increase temporarily slowed or not, the overall conclusion is that the absolute gap grew wider. The data presented in Table 2.5 show that in 1960 the absolute gap between the rich and the upper-middle-income countries was $6,454, and by 2010 it had widened to $20,128. This represents an annual average increase of $268 per year. The gap is expanding for the lower-middle-income and poor countries as well. The absolute gap between the rich and the poor countries stood at $12,149 in 1960, and grew 2.1 times larger, to $25,386, by 2010. Thus the current data confirm what Kuznets (1972) and Morawetz (1977) found in earlier studies—that the absolute gap is growing wider. Figure 2.1 shows that the absolute gap begins a sharp reversal in about 2007. It is really too soon to draw any conclusions about this. Should this trend continue, it would mark a historic reversal in global inequality. Unfortunately, it is probably more likely that once the current financial crisis is resolved, and once economic growth in high-income countries recovers, the absolute gap will resume its expansion.

If this analysis of the absolute gap is correct, it appears to suggest that no matter how well countries perform economically, they will never catch up to the rich. That said, the only real criterion for catching up is that the nonrich country sustain a growth rate higher than that of the rich. In 2010 the high-income countries had a mean GDP/pc of $25,807 and an annual average growth rate of 2.22 percent. I took the nonrich countries that had a growth rate higher than 2.22 percent and projected their GDP/pc, and that of the rich countries, into the future by assuming that both groups would be able to sustain the growth rate they had achieved during the 1960–2010 period. Table 2.6 identifies the sixteen countries whose growth rates are higher than the mean growth

Figure 2.1   GDP/pc by Income Group and the Absolute Gap, 1960–2010

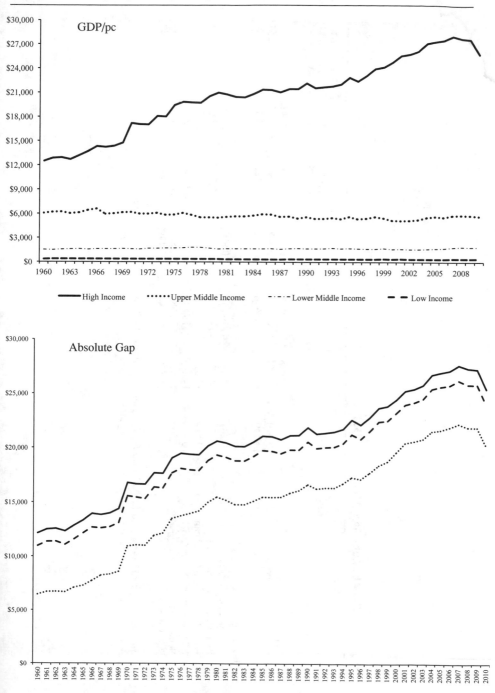

Table 2.5   The Absolute Gap, 1960–2010 (US$)

	1960	1970	1980	1990	2000	2010	Average Annual Increase
Income group							
Upper-middle income	6,454	10,968	15,448	16,608	19,591	20,128	268
Lower-middle income	10,979	15,564	19,321	20,538	23,194	23,951	254
Poor	12,149	16,795	20,596	21,858	24,421	25,386	260
Absolute gap by region							
East Asia and Pacific	10,241	14,886	19,015	20,801	23,258	23,969	269
Europe and Central Asia	6,990	11,970	17,010	19,193	22,754	22,653	307
Latin America and Caribbean	10,514	14,519	17,751	18,942	20,920	21,277	211
Middle East and North Africa	10,900	14,248	18,813	18,933	22,006	22,728	232
South Asia	12,307	16,919	20,685	21,857	24,033	24,530	240
Sub-Saharan Africa	11,989	16,559	20,144	21,439	23,906	24,576	247

Source: Computed from World Bank, *World Development Indicators, 2012* (Washington, DC, 2012).
Note: See Table 2.3 for definitions of region groupings.

rate for the high-income countries, and shows how long it will take them to catch up to the rich. Only four countries—Botswana, China, Thailand, and Malaysia—have the opportunity to catch up to the rich within a century. Three more countries (Seychelles, Indonesia, and St. Vincent and the Grenadines) would catch up in the following century. As difficult as it is, the easy part is growing faster than the rich countries; the hard part is continuing to grow faster for as long as it takes to catch up. Alas, catching up could take hundreds if not thousands of years if the nonrich countries are relatively poor and their growth rates are only slightly faster than those of the rich.

Care should be taken when using the absolute gap as a measure of the success or failure of a country's development policies. Because of the peculiar pattern exemplified by countries that are in the process of closing the gap, one could mistake success for failure. In fact, a country can actually be in the process of closing the gap on the rich while at the same time their absolute gap is worsening. Using Indonesia as an example, Table 2.6 shows that in 2010 it had a GDP/pc of $1,144 and an annual average growth rate of 3.95 percent (between 1960 and 2010). Indonesia is one of the sixteen countries that can close the gap. One might assume that this would mean that the absolute-gap score for Indonesia would creep very slowly but ever closer to zero. Figure 2.2 traces Indonesia's absolute-gap score and shows that at the current rate of

Table 2.6   Closing the Absolute Gap

Rank	Country	2010 GNP/pc (2000 US$)	Annual Average Growth Rate, 1960–2010 (%)	Number of Years Until the Gap Is Closed
1	Botswana	4,189	6.51	45
2	China	2,425	7.25	53
3	Thailand	2,713	4.66	97
4	Malaysia	5,185	3.97	97
5	Seychelles	8,614	2.87	182
6	Indonesia	1,144	3.95	189
7	St. Vincent and Grenadines	4,885	3.15	191
8	Belize	3,546	3.11	237
9	Egypt	1,976	3.10	312
10	Chile	6,334	2.69	330
11	Sri Lanka	1,296	3.18	332
12	Dominican Republic	4,049	2.82	332
13	India	787	3.01	473
14	Turkey	5,349	2.37	1,303
15	Pakistan	669	2.40	2,520
16	Lesotho	496	2.36	3,829

Source: Computed from World Bank, *World Development Indicators, 2012* (Washington, DC, 2012).

Note: For comparison, a "high-income" country is defined as having a 2010 GNP per capita of US$25,807, and an annual average growth rate for 1960–2010 of 2.22 percent.

Figure 2.2 The Absolute Gap Between High-Income Countries and Indonesia

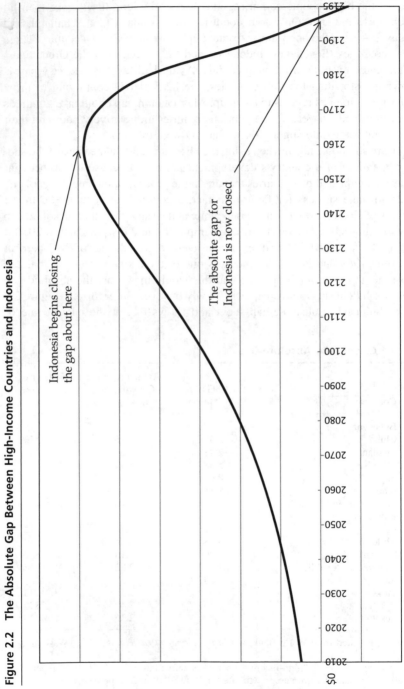

growth (of Indonesia as well as the rich), the absolute-gap score will not stop growing larger for another 151 years. While the number of years that the absolute gap continues to widen is dependent upon the size of the country's GDP/pc and its growth rate, nearly all countries experience this pattern. This is due to what Morawetz called the "algebra of the gap."

The absolute gap between high-income and poor countries will not actually close until the ratio of their GDPs per capita is equal to the inverse ratio of their growth rates. A relatively simple way to determine if a non-high-income country can immediately narrow the absolute gap is to divide the growth rate of the high-income country by the ratio of the non-high-income country's GDP/pc to the high-income country's gross national product per capita (GNP/pc). This equation yields the growth rate that the non-high-income country must exceed in order to begin closing the absolute gap immediately. If, for example, the high-income countries have a mean GDP/pc of $8,000 and a growth rate of 2 percent, a nonrich country with a GDP/pc of $1,000 must exceed a growth rate of 16 percent in order to begin narrowing the absolute gap that year. Very few countries are able to achieve or maintain such a rate of economic expansion for very long.

The Relative Gap

The relative gap measures the GDP/pc of the poor or middle-income groups as a percentage of that of the high-income countries. Morawetz (1977) reported that the developing countries had narrowed the relative gap by about half a percentage point between 1950 and 1975. He added that since it was nearly impossible to narrow the absolute gap, it was not a goal that any rational policymaker would set for their country. Narrowing the relative gap, however, is not exactly easy, but it is attainable, thereby making it a more accessible development goal.

Table 2.7 reports the relative gap by income group and geographic region. It shows that for all three income groups, GDP/pc expressed as a percentage of GDP/pc of the high-income countries worsened each decade until 2000 and then improved slightly in 2010. The upper-middle-income group's GDP/pc expressed as a percentage of the GDP/pc of the rich shrank from 48.39 percent in 1960 to 21.03 percent in 2000, and then increased to 22.01 percent in 2010. The relative gap for the lower-middle-income group declined from 12.21 percent in 1960 to 6.51 percent in 2000 and then in 2010 improved to 7.19 percent of the per capita income of the high-income countries. Even the poor countries' relative gap compared to the rich improved by 2010, to a score of 1.63 percent, having begun at 2.85 percent in 1960 and falling to 1.57 in 2000. In other words, the relative gap between high-income countries and each of the income groups worsened overall, but there was a slight reversal for all groups in 2010.

Table 2.7 The Relative Gap, 1960–2010 (percentages)

	1960	1970	1980	1990	2000	2010
Income group						
Upper-middle income	48.39	36.13	26.31	25.29	21.03	22.01
Lower-middle income	12.21	9.37	7.83	7.62	6.51	7.19
Poor	2.85	2.20	1.75	1.68	1.57	1.63
Relative gap by region						
East Asia and Pacific	18.11	13.31	9.29	6.44	6.15	7.12
Europe and Central Asia	44.11	30.30	18.86	13.67	8.29	12.22
Latin America and Caribbean	15.92	15.46	15.32	14.79	15.68	17.55
Middle East and North Africa	12.84	17.03	10.25	14.84	11.30	11.93
South Asia	1.59	1.48	1.33	1.69	3.13	4.95
Sub-Saharan Africa	4.14	3.57	3.91	3.56	3.64	4.77

Source: Computed from World Bank, *World Development Indicators, 2012* (Washington, DC, 2012).
Note: See Table 2.3 for definitions of region groupings.

Even though the relative gap by income group shows that each of the income groups' relative gap worsened over time, examination of the geographic regions is a bit more hopeful and interesting. Three of the six geographic regions actually closed the relative gap over the fifty-one-year period. In 1960, Latin America's mean GDP/pc was 15.92 percent of the GDP/pc of the high-income countries. Its relative-gap percentage weakened very slightly each decade through 2000 and then, in 2010, Latin America's GDP/pc as a percentage of the GDP/pc of the high-income group increased to 17.55 percent. South Asia's relative gap improved from 1.59 to 4.95 percent over the same period. Sub-Saharan Africa also improved, with its relative gap increasing from 4.14 to 4.77 percent. It may be that the current global financial crisis is the culprit and that, when it comes to an end, this trend too will end. However, in these three regions, as well as in the Middle East and North Africa, the relative gap is rather stable through time.

Is an improvement in the relative gap really meaningful when the absolute gap is opening so widely? In other words, has the economic growth in non-high-income countries, though not sufficient to close the absolute gap, really meant an improvement in living standards in the developing world? One way to answer this question is to examine the World Bank's measure of living standards, the Human Development Index (HDI). The HDI is a composite index of the standard of living in a country as measured by three different aspects of human development: health, knowledge, and wealth. Health is measured by the life expectancy of the people in a country; knowledge is measured by the levels of literacy and school enrollment; and wealth is measured by a purchasing power parity (PPP)–converted GDP.

Table 2.8 presents the standard of living of the four income groups as measured by the HDI. It shows that as countries grow richer, their standard of living improves. Without fail, each income group measures higher on the HDI scale than the next-lower income group. The table also shows that each of the four income groups has improved its standard of living over time. In 1980 the Human Development Index for the world was 0.536. The index slowly but steadily improves over each five-year period until 2010, when the global HDI reaches 0.655. Even the poor, starting out in 1980 with an HDI of 0.333, improve their standard of living, to 0.448 in 2010. The unfortunate point, and one that is reinforced periodically through television images of extreme poverty and starvation in the poor countries, is that the HDI for the poor countries in 2010 is *lower* than the HDI for the lower-middle-income countries in 1980.

Like the income groups, the geographic regions show a similar improvement in HDI scores over time. With the exception of the Europe and Central Asia region, whose HDI dropped from 0.756 in 1990 to 0.744 in 1995 before resuming its improvement, all geographic regions improved their standard of living as measured by the Human Development Index in each time interval. The HDI scores suggest that the improvement in the relative gap that countries

Table 2.8   **Average Human Development Index by World Bank Income Grouping, 1980–2010 (*N* in parentheses)**

	1980	1985	1990	1995	2000	2005	2010
World HDI average	0.536	0.557	0.582	0.603	0.617	0.638	0.655
	(101)	(109)	(118)	(132)	(149)	(168)	(169)
HDI by income group							
High income	0.754	0.781	0.801	0.826	0.841	0.858	0.870
	(26)	(24)	(26)	(28)	(34)	(35)	(34)
Upper-middle income	0.636	0.666	0.680	0.705	0.717	0.732	0.740
	(16)	(19)	(21)	(23)	(28)	(33)	(38)
Lower-middle income	0.495	0.536	0.583	0.602	0.606	0.642	0.656
	(29)	(33)	(34)	(38)	(39)	(49)	(46)
Poor	0.333	0.353	0.372	0.403	0.410	0.422	0.448
	(30)	(32)	(37)	(43)	(48)	(51)	(51)
HDI by region							
Europe and	0.729	0.746	0.756	0.744	0.773	0.787	0.803
Central Asia	(20)	(22)	(28)	(39)	(40)	(47)	(51)
North America	0.827	0.844	0.864	0.877	0.888	0.897	0.908
	(2)	(2)	(2)	(2)	(2)	(2)	(2)
East Asia and Pacific	0.579	0.603	0.604	0.623	0.643	0.670	0.687
	(14)	(16)	(18)	(19)	(24)	(25)	(27)
Latin America and							
Caribbean	0.556	0.577	0.597	0.622	0.653	0.680	0.707
	(23)	(24)	(24)	(24)	(26)	(28)	(32)
Middle East and							
North Africa	0.567	0.601	0.629	0.637	0.669	0.680	0.699
	(14)	(14)	(14)	(15)	(15)	(20)	(21)
South Asia	0.331	0.361	0.388	0.409	0.451	0.499	0.532
	(6)	(6)	(6)	(6)	(7)	(7)	(8)
Sub-Saharan Africa	0.344	0.364	0.382	0.390	0.406	0.424	0.448
	(27)	(30)	(31)	(31)	(39)	(45)	(46)

Source: Computed from World Bank, *World Development Indicators, 2012* (Washington, DC, 2012).
Note: See Table 2.3 for definitions of region groupings.

have achieved has also meant an improvement in the standard of living. Morawetz was right in saying that policymakers should prefer establishing development goals around relative-gap rather than absolute-gap measures. And if they do achieve improvements in the relative-gap score, they can be reasonably assured that this improvement will bring with it an improved standard of living.

Country Mobility

This section identifies those countries that have successfully moved up into the higher-income groups and those that have moved down. I also ranked countries by GDP/pc in 1970 and 2010 to determine which countries have experienced the most and the least success in moving up and down the rankings. In terms of upward mobility across income groups, the record between 1970 and 2010 is mixed.[6] Table 2.9 summarizes the movement of countries across income groups. Of the 109 countries in the sample, 64 remained in the same income group in 2010 that they occupied in 1970. Unfortunately, 30 of the countries that were in the low-income group in 1970 remained in the low-income group in 2010. However, 13 countries joined the high-income group by 2010, and 18 joined the upper-middle-income group by 2010. Between 1970 and 2010, 11 countries that had been in the low-income group moved up to the lower-middle-income group. It is rather remarkable that even with the debt crisis, currency crisis, and current global financial crisis, only three countries dropped into a lower-income group: Côte d'Ivoire, Kiribati, and Liberia, which moved from the lower-middle-income group to the low-income group.

Another way of examining improvement in a country's position in the world economy is to examine its mobility in GDP per capita rankings. Table 2.10, which highlights the ten most upwardly and downwardly mobile countries, shows that there was quite a bit of movement in GDP/pc rankings between 1970 and 2010. The country that achieved the highest jump in the rankings was China, which moved up from a rank of 108 in 1970 to 58 in 2010, an increase of 50. China's jump in the rankings is even more impressive when considering the fact that, of the top ten countries in terms of upward movement in the rankings of GDP/pc, China was originally ranked next to last. In fact, it was ranked as one of the poorest countries in the world. Botswana moved up the rankings 36 places, from 83 in 1970 to 47 in 2010. Dominating the group of the top ten upward movers are some of the countries referred to as the Asian newly industrializing countries (NICs). On the other side of the ledger, six of the ten most downwardly mobile countries were African. In 1970, Liberia had

Table 2.9 Mobility Across Income Groups, 1970 and 2010 (number of countries)

	Remained in Same Income Group from 1970 to 2010	Joined from the High Income	Joined from the Upper-Middle Income	Joined from the Lower-Middle Income	Joined from the Low Income
High income	18	—	11	2	0
Upper-middle income	6	0	—	17	1
Lower-middle income	10	0	0	—	11
Low income	30	0	0	3	—

Source: Computed from World Bank, *World Development Indicators, 2012* (Washington, DC, 2012).

Table 2.10   Mobility in Rankings of GDP per Capita, 1970–2010

Rank	Country	1970	2010	Difference
Upwardly mobile countries				
1	China	108	58	+50
2	Botswana	83	47	+36
3	India	101	77	+24
4	Thailand	79	56	+23
5	Indonesia	98	75	+23
6	Hong Kong	28	6	+22
7	Singapore	29	8	+21
8	South Korea	45	24	+21
9	Malta	47	29	+18
10	Malaysia	60	42	+18
Downwardly mobile countries				
1	Liberia	67	107	–40
2	Democratic Republic of Congo	87	109	–22
3	Kiribati	56	78	–22
4	Nicaragua	54	76	–22
5	Madagascar	82	102	–20
6	Central African Republic	84	103	–19
7	Côte d'Ivoire	65	83	–18
8	Niger	88	105	–17
9	Jamaica	34	51	–17
10	Bahamas	5	22	–17

Source: Computed from World Bank, *World Development Indicators, 2012* (Washington, DC, 2012).

the 67th largest GDP/pc in the world, but by 2010 it had the 107th largest, a drop of 40 places in the rankings.

Conclusions

If scholars such as Simon Kuznets (1972) and David Morawetz (1977) are correct, the worldwide economic growth experienced since World War II is unprecedented. Between 1850 and 1950, the countries considered high income in 1950 experienced economic expansion averaging 1.6 percent. Between 1960 and 2010, the economy of the entire world grew at an annual average rate of 1.64 percent. In the decades of the 1960s and the 1970s, the world averaged 2.85 and 2.50 percent economic growth respectively. This extended period of rapid growth caused post–World War II generations to become accustomed to rapid growth, leading many people to believe that it was inevitable. The 1980s, with the debt crisis, and the 1990s, with the currency crisis, drove growth rates down and dampened expectations, but the new century witnessed the return of rapid growth. Between 2000 and 2010, the world economy grew at an impressive average rate of 2.92 percent and, perhaps even more striking and hopeful, the economies of the poor countries grew at rates averaging 3.29 percent annually. This feat is made even more impressive when one realizes that the high-income countries had the lowest rate of economic expansion. The world's growth rate was being driven by the economic growth of nonrich countries. However, historical examination of growth rates instructs us that economic growth is not inevitable. Kuznets (1972) and Morawetz (1977) both concluded that, over time, countries likely experience periods of expansion followed by long periods of stagnation or contraction.

Second, the data here indicate that the gap between the rich and the nonrich has not closed. The absolute gap between high-income and the non-high-income countries has grown steadily since 1960. For the upper-middle-income countries, the absolute gap grew from $6,454 to $20,128. The gap between the rich and the lower-middle-income countries expanded from $10,979 in 1960 to $23,951 in 2010, and the gap for the poor widened from a deficit of $12,149 to $25,386. On average, the absolute gap widened $268 for the upper-middle-income countries, $254 for the lower-middle-income countries, and $260 for the poor countries every year.

The relative gap showed a much more hopeful pattern. Even though none of the nonrich income groups were able to increase their percentage of GDP/pc of the rich, all three nonrich income groups were able to close the relative gap between 2000 and 2010. As discussed earlier, this could be a result of the current global financial crisis weakening the economic performance of the richer countries more than that of the developing countries. In terms of the geographic regions, three of the six were also able to close the relative gap between 1960 and 2010. Other regions did lose ground to the rich, but still there are hopeful signs. As Morawetz suggested, if policymakers are trying to determine whether to use the absolute gap or the relative gap as a goal for development policies, they should consider that closing the relative gap, though not easy, is possible. The same cannot be said for the absolute gap.

Third, this analysis of income groups would have proven irrelevant if the percentage of the world's population in the lowest income group was small or had fallen significantly. Unfortunately, such was not the case. Overall, the income groups remained remarkably stable as a percentage of the world's population. The only departure from this conclusion revolves around the movement of one country from the poor group into the lower-middle-income group. When China moved from the poor to the lower-middle-income group, the percentage distributions of those two categories changed substantially. Between 1960 and 1990, the lower-middle-income group held about 10 to 15 percent of the world's population, but the percentage jumped to 34.7 in 2000 with the entry of China. Likewise, the poor group constituted about 60 to 65 percent of the world's population between 1960 and 1990, but that percentage dropped to

40.4 in 2000 after China moved from the poor to the lower-middle-income group. While these measures do not represent income inequality within countries, they still constitute a very positive sign, in that the proportion of the world's population living in countries with a GDP/pc of less than $783 dropped from 65 percent in 1960 to 38.2 percent in 2010. Further, while these data do not show standard of living, Table 2.8, which reports HDI scores by income group, shows that upward movement from one income group to the next does mean an improvement in the standard of living.

Fourth, the number of high-income countries increased from nine in 1960 to thirty-five in 2010. While this may sound tremendously impressive, Table 2.2 shows that the high-income population as a proportion of world population increased only from 10.3 percent in 1960 to 15.5 percent in 2010. Thirteen countries joined the high-income group during the fifty-one-year period under investigation, and eighteen moved up into the upper-middle-income category, as shown in Table 2.9. Twelve countries escaped the poor category between 1970 and 2010, even though thirty remain, and these thirty constitute over a third of the world's population.

Finally, as Table 2.6 shows, it appears that only sixteen countries can close the gap with the high-income countries, and only four of those can do so within the next century: Botswana (45 years), China (53 years), Thailand (97 years), and Malaysia (97 years). If growth rates remain similar to those of the entire fifty-one-year period, Botswana will be the first African country to join the high-income countries, in 2055.

Notes

1. See http://databank.worldbank.org/ddp/home.do.
2. The World Bank's income groups were offered in current gross national incomes per capita as of 2010. Since I am analyzing GDP/pc (in 2000 US dollars), I had to convert the income categories. To convert the income breaks to constant 2000 GDP per capita figures, I calculated each current dollar GNI/pc income break as a percentage of US GNI/pc. I then used that percentage to calculate an income break in GDP/pc constant dollars.
3. See the "Tables, Quick Reference" section at http://data.worldbank.org/about/country-classifications/country-and-lending-groups where the technical notes offer "classification of economies by income and region." The growth rates are calculated by the regression method described in the World Bank's 1988 *World Development Report* (Oxford: Oxford University Press, 1988). The least-squares method finds the growth rate by fitting a least-squares trend line to the log of the gross national product per capita. This takes the equation form of $X_t = a + bt + e_t$ where x equals the log of the GNP/pc, a is the intercept, b is the parameter to be estimated, t is time, and e is the error term. The growth rate, r, is the [antilog (b)] − 1. For further information, see the 1988 *World Development Report,* pp. 288–289. For a discussion of different methods of computing growth rates, see Robert Jackman, "A Note on the Measurement of Growth Rates in Cross-National Research," *American Journal of Sociology* 86 (1980): 604–610.

4. The regional categories were drawn from the World Bank's 2012 *World Development Indicators* online dataset, available at http://data.worldbank.org/about/country-classifications/country-and-lending-groups.

5. Kuznets defined high-income countries as those with a GNP/pc greater than $1,000 (in 1965 US dollars). A "narrow" definition of the poor countries set the GNP/pc cutoff point at $120 or less. For his more broadly defined poor category, Kuznets raised the cutoff point to $300. The middle-income group varied according to Kuznets's choice of the narrowly or broadly defined poor group in any particular example. Kuwait and Qatar were excluded because of the fact that their growth had been dependent upon a single commodity and did not reflect diversified growth. Puerto Rico was excluded because its GNP/pc was so tightly connected to the United States. Japan was included in the high-income group even though its GNP/pc was below the cutoff point because it had managed tremendous growth with very few natural resources. Thus its growth was achieved through diversified development of the economy. For further information on how Kuznets defined his income groups, see "The Gap: Concept, Measurement, Trends" in G. Ranis, ed., *The Gap Between Rich and Poor Nations* (London: Macmillan, 1972).

6. Here, I shifted the time frame from 1960–2010 to 1970–2010 to include more countries in the analysis of mobility.

References

Dube, S. C. 1988. *Modernization and Development: The Search for Alternative Paradigms.* London: Zed.

Durning, A. B. 1990. "Ending Poverty." In L. Starke, ed., *State of the World, 1990.* New York: Norton.

International Monetary Fund. 1984. *International Financial Statistics: Supplement on Output Statistics.* No. 8. Washington, DC.

Jackman, R. W. 1980. "A Note on the Measurement of Growth Rates in Cross-National Research." *American Journal of Sociology* 86: 604–610.

———. 1982. "Dependence on Foreign Investment and Economic Growth in the Third World." *World Politics* 34: 175–197.

Kahn, H. 1979. *World Economic Development: 1979 and Beyond.* Boulder: Westview.

Kuznets, S. 1972. "The Gap: Concept, Measurement, Trends." In G. Ranis, ed., *The Gap Between Rich and Poor Nations.* London: Macmillan.

———. 1979. *Growth, Population, and Income Distribution.* New York: Norton.

———. 1984. "Economic Growth and Income Inequality." In M. A. Seligson, ed., *The Gap Between Rich and Poor.* Boulder: Westview.

Lipton, M. 1977. *Why the Poor People Stay Poor: A Study of Urban Bias in World Development.* London: Temple Smith.

———. 1989. *New Seeds and Poor People.* London: Unwin Hyman.

Morawetz, D. 1977. *Twenty-five Years of Economic Development: 1950–1975.* Washington, DC: World Bank.

World Bank. 1988, 1990. *World Development Report.* Oxford: Oxford University Press.

———. 1992. *The World Tables, 1992.* Washington, DC.

———. 2000. *World Development Indicators, 2000.* Washington, DC, 2000.

3

The Rising Inequality of World Income Distribution

Robert Hunter Wade

*O*ne of the important debates surrounding the gap between rich and poor countries is what, if anything, a government should do. Robert Hunter Wade argues that conflicting conclusions about the gap have arisen in part due to the measure of inequality used, whether and how the measure is weighted, and the method of converting to a common currency. The varying recipes produce eight different measures of income inequality. Wade concludes that seven of the eight measures of inequality clearly show that the gap is worsening and the last suggests that the gap is stable. His warnings about the consequences of ignoring a worsening gap are amplified in Chapter 13 by Edward N. Muller and Mitchell A. Seligson, who tie income inequality to domestic political violence.

DOES IT MATTER WHAT IS HAPPENING TO WORLD INCOME DISTRIBUTION (among all 6.2 billion people, regardless of where they live)? Amartya Sen, the recent Nobel laureate in economics, warns that arguing about the trend deflects attention from the central issue, which is the sheer magnitude of inequality and poverty on a world scale. Regardless of the trend, the magnitude is unacceptable (Sen, 2001). He is right, up to a point. The concentration of world income in the wealthiest quintile (fifth) of the world's population is indeed shocking and cannot meet any plausible test of legitimacy. The chart [Figure 3.1] shows the distribution of world income by population quintiles. Ironically,

Reprinted with permission from *Finance and Development* 38, no. 4 (December 2001). Copyright © 2001 by the International Monetary Fund.

Figure 3.1   **Distribution of World GDP, 1989 (percent of total with quantities of population ranked by income)**

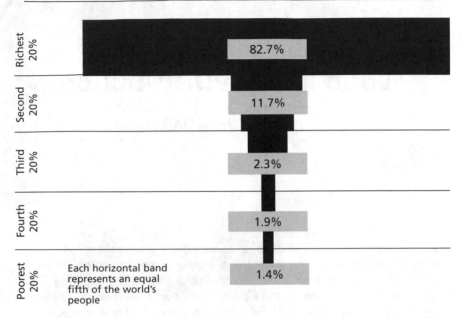

Source: United Nations Development Programme, *Human Development Report 1992* (New York: Oxford University Press for the UNDP, 1992).

it resembles a champagne glass, with a wide, shallow bowl at the top and the slenderest of stems below.

But still, the trend does matter. Many champions of free trade and free capital movements say that world income distribution is becoming more equal as globalization proceeds, and on these grounds they resist the idea that reducing world income inequality should be an objective of international public policy. Moreover, many theories of growth and development generate predictions about *changes* in world income distribution; testing them requires information about trends. Indeed, the neoliberal paradigm—which has supplied the prescriptions known as the Washington Consensus that have dominated international public policy about development over the past twenty years—generates a strong expectation that as national economies become more densely interconnected through trade and investment, world income distribution tends to become more equal. And it is a fair bet that if presented with the statement, "World income distribution has become more equal over the past twenty years" and asked to agree, agree with qualifications, or disagree, a majority of Western economists would say, "agree" or "agree with qualifications."

If they are right, this would be powerful evidence in favor of the "law of *even* development," which says that all national economies gain from more integration into international markets (relative to less integration), and lower-cost, capital-scarce economies (developing countries) are likely to gain *more* from fuller integration than higher-cost, capital-abundant economies (developed countries). Developing countries wishing to catch up with standards of living in the West should therefore integrate fully into international markets (by lowering tariffs, removing trade restrictions, granting privileges to *foreign* direct investment, welcoming foreign banks, enforcing intellectual property rights, and so on) and let the decisions of private economic agents operating in free markets determine the composition and volume of economic activities carried out within the national territory. This "integrationist" strategy will maximize their rate of development; put the other way around, their development strategy should amount to an integrationist strategy—the two things are really one and the same.

Fortunately, the self-interest of the wealthy Western democracies coincides with this integrationist strategy for developing countries, because as developing countries grow richer, their demand for Western products expands and their capacity to absorb their population growth at home also expands, reducing the pressure on the West created by surging immigration. The World Bank, the IMF [International Monetary Fund], the World Trade Organization (WTO), and the other global supervisory organizations are therefore well justified in seeking to enforce maximum integration on developing countries for the good of all.

What Does the Evidence Show?

Therefore, a lot is at stake in the question of whether world income distribution has become more, or less, equal over the past twenty years or so. It turns out that there is no single correct answer, because the answer depends on which combination of measures one adopts. It depends on (1) the measure of inequality (a coefficient like the Gini, or quintile or decile [tenth] ratios), (2) the unit of inequality (countries weighted equally, or individuals weighted equally and countries weighted by population), and (3) the method of converting incomes in different countries to a common numeraire (current market exchange rates or purchasing power parity exchange rates). Treating these as either/or choices yields eight possible measures, each with some plausibility for certain purposes. Then there is the further question of what kind of data is used—the national income accounts or household income and expenditure surveys.

My reading of the evidence suggests that none of the eight alternative measures clearly shows that world income distribution has become more equal over the past twenty years. Seven of the eight show varying degrees of *increasing inequality*. The eighth—the one that uses the Gini coefficient, countries weighted by population, and purchasing power parity—shows no significant change in world income distribution. This is because the Gini coefficient gives excessive weight to changes around the middle of the distribution and insufficient weight to changes at the extremes and therefore, in this case, gives more weight (than a decile ratio) to fast-growing China; the use of countries weighted by population has the same effect; and the use of purchasing power parity tends to raise low incomes more than high incomes, compared with market exchange rates. Hence this combination generates the least rise in inequality. But a recent paper by Dowrick and Akmal (2001) suggests that the Penn World Tables, on which most calculations of purchasing power parity are based (see Heston and Summers, 1991), contain a bias that makes incomes of developing countries appear higher than they are. The tables consequently *understate* the degree and trend of inequality. When the bias is corrected, even the most favorable combination of measures shows rising inequality of world income distribution over the past twenty years, although the trend is less strong than the trend based on any of the other possible combinations.

It is often said that purchasing power parity measures should always be preferred to market exchange rates and that countries should always be weighted by population rather than treated as equal units of observation. Certainly, purchasing power parity measures are better for measuring relative purchasing power, or relative material welfare, though the available data are not good enough for them to be more than rough-and-ready approximations, especially for China and, before the early 1990s, the countries of the former Soviet Union. But data problems aside, we may also be interested in income for other purposes. Indeed, for most of the issues that concern the world at large—such as migration flows; the capacity of developing countries to repay foreign debts and import capital goods; the extent of marginalization of developing countries in the world polity; and, more broadly, the economic and geopolitical impact of a country (or region) on the rest of the world—then we should use market exchange rates to convert incomes in different countries into a common numeraire. After all, the reason why many poor countries are hardly represented in international negotiations whose outcomes profoundly affect them is that the cost of hotels, offices, and salaries in places like New York, Washington, and Geneva must be paid in U.S. dollars, not in purchasing power parity–adjusted dollars. Using market exchange rates, the conclusion is clear: all four combinations of measures using market exchange rates show that world income distribution has become *much more unequal*.

Causes of Increasing Inequality

What are the causes of the rise in world income inequality? The theory is not exactly what one might call watertight; the causality is very difficult to establish. Differential population growth between poorer and richer countries is one cause. The fall in non-oil commodity prices—by more than half in real terms between

1980 and the early 1990s—is another, affecting especially the poorest countries. The debt trap is a third. Fast-growing middle-income developing countries, seeking to invest and consume more than can be covered by domestic incomes, tend to borrow abroad; and they borrow on terms that are more favorable when their capacity to repay is high and less favorable when—as in a financial crisis— their capacity to repay is low. We saw repeatedly during the 1980s and 1990s that countries that liberalized and opened their financial systems and then bor- rowed heavily—even if to raise investment rather than consumption—ran a sig- nificant risk of costly financial crisis. A crisis pulls them back down the world income hierarchy. Hence the debt trap might be thought of as a force in the world economy that is somewhat analogous to gravity.

Another basic cause is technological change. Technological change of the kind we have seen in the past two decades tends to reinforce the tendency for high-value-added activities (including innovation) to cluster in the (high-cost) Western economies rather than disperse to lower-cost developing countries. Sil- icon Valley is the paradigm: the firms that are pioneering the collapse of dis- tance themselves congregate tightly in one small space. Part of the reason is the continuing economic value of tacit knowledge and "handshake" relationships in high-value-added activities. Technological change might be thought of as dis- tantly analogous to electromagnetic levitation—a force in the world economy that keeps the 20 percent of the world's population living in the member coun- tries of the Organization for Economic Cooperation and Development (OECD) comfortably floating above the rest of the world in the world income hierarchy. If we have world economy analogues of gravity and electromagnetism, can the world economy analogue of relativity theory be far behind?

Consequences

Income divergence helps to explain another kind of polarization taking place in the world system, between a zone of peace and a zone of turmoil. On the one hand, the regions of the wealthy pole show a strengthening republican order of economic growth and liberal tolerance (except toward immigrants), with technological innovation able to substitute for depleting natural capital. On the other hand, the regions of the lower- and middle-income poles contain many states whose capacity to govern is stagnant or eroding, mainly in Africa, the Middle East, Central Asia, the former Soviet Union, and parts of East Asia. Here, a rising proportion of the people find their access to basic necessities re- stricted at the same time as they see others driving Mercedes.

The result is a large mass of unemployed and angry young people, mostly males, to whom the new information technologies have given the means to threaten the stability of the societies they live in and even threaten social sta- bility in countries of the wealthy zone. Economic growth in these countries often depletes natural capital and therefore future growth potential. More and more people see migration to the wealthy zone as their only salvation, and a few are driven to redemptive terrorism directed at the symbolic centers of the powerful.

Reorienting International Organizations

The World Bank and the IMF have paid remarkably little attention to global inequality. The Bank's *World Development Report 2000: Attacking Poverty* says explicitly that rising income inequality "should not be seen as negative," provided the incomes at the bottom do not fall and the number of people in poverty falls or does not rise. But incomes in the lower deciles of world income distribution have probably fallen absolutely since the 1980s; and one should not accept the Bank's claim that the number of people living on less than $1 a day remained constant at 1.2 billion between 1987 and 1998, because the method used to compute the figure for 1998 contains a downward bias relative to that used to compute the figure for 1987. Suppose, though, that the incomes of the lower deciles had risen absolutely and the number of people in absolute poverty had fallen, while inequality increased. The Bank's view that the rise in inequality should not be seen as a negative ignores the associated political instabilities and flows of migrants that—all notions of justice and fairness and common humanity aside—can harm the lives of the citizens of the rich world and the democratic character of their states.

The global supervisory organizations like the Bank, the IMF, the WTO, and the United Nations system should be giving the issue of global income inequality much more attention. If we can act on global warming—whose effects are similarly diffuse and long term—can we not act on global inequality? We should start by rejecting the neoliberal assumption of the Bretton Woods institutions over the past two decades, now powerfully reinforced by the emergent WTO, that development strategy boils down to a strategy for maximum integration of each economy into the world economy, complemented by domestic reforms to make full integration viable. The evidence on world income distribution throws this assumption into question—as does a lot of evidence of other kinds. International public policy to reduce world income inequality must include a basic change in the policy orientation of the World Bank, the IMF, and the WTO so as to allow them to sanction government efforts to impart directional thrust and nourish homegrown institutional innovations.

References

Dowrick, Steve, and Muhammad Akmal. 2001. "Explaining Contradictory Trends in Global Income Inequality: A Tale of Two Biases," *Faculty of Economic and Commerce*. Australian National University.

Heston, Alan, and Robert Summers. 1991. "The Penn World Tables (Mark 5): An Expanded Set of International Comparisons, 1950–1988," *Quarterly Journal of Economics* (May), pp. 327–68.

Rodrik, Dani, 2001. "The Global Governance of Trade as If Development Really Mattered" (unpublished).

Sen, Amartya. 2001. "If It's Fair, It's Good: 10 Truths About Globalization," *International Herald Tribune,* July 14–15.

Wade, Robert Hunter. 1990. *Governing the Market: Economic Theory and the Role of Government in East Asia's Industrialization.* Princeton: Princeton University Press.

———. 2001a. "Winners and Losers," *Economist,* April 28.

———. 2001b. "Globalization and World Income Distribution: Trends, Causes, Consequences, and Public Policy" (unpublished, July).

4

Empirics of World Income Inequality

Glenn Firebaugh

In this chapter, Glenn Firebaugh disputes the findings of those who argue that the world continues to experience a widening of the gap between rich and poor countries. Firebaugh asserts that there are two ways of looking at world income distribution. The standard approach is to use the country as the unit of analysis, so that each country represents one unit in the comparisons. The second way, the one that Firebaugh argues is more persuasive, treats each person as the unit of analysis. He accomplishes this by weighting the country data by population size. When this is done, large countries, especially China, play a great role. Since China's income grew at breakneck speed in recent years, and China's total population size has also grown enormously, the trends found in other studies are reversed. Firebaugh also uses PPP (i.e., purchasing power–based income) data rather than the exchange rate–based income data. The reader needs to determine which method of measuring inequality is the more persuasive. Should we calculate the gap between nations as a function of their total population size or limit ourselves to comparing each nation against all others irrespective of population size? As you will see, good arguments can be made for each method, and Firebaugh is persuasive in arguing for the former. Yet, since we already know that income inequality is a major cause of insurgency (see Chapter 13), if two nations have widely different levels of income, it may not be too important what their respective population sizes are. Consider conflicts between Pakistan and India, or tensions between China and

Reprinted with permission of the University of Chicago Press and the author from the *American Journal of Sociology* 104, no. 6 (1999): 1597–1630.

North Korea. What seems to count in those cases is not the size of populations but many differences in culture, religion, income, and policy. In any event, even Firebaugh does not find evidence of convergence.

THE INDUSTRIAL REVOLUTION PRODUCED A STUNNING INCREASE IN THE income disparity between nations. At the beginning of the 19th century, average incomes in the richest nations were perhaps four times greater than those in the poorest nations. At the end of the 20th century, average incomes in the richest nations are 30 times larger—annual incomes of about $18,000 versus $600 (Summers, Heston, Aten, and Nuxoll 1994).

Is the income disparity between nations still increasing? The answer to that question is critical. Because of the great disparity in average income from nation to nation, it is intercountry inequality—not inequality within nations—that is the major component of total income inequality in the world today. A recent sociological study estimates that inequality across countries accounts for over 90% of current world income inequality as measured by the Gini index. Other studies give lower estimates, but all agree with Berry, Bourguignon, and Morrisson (1983b, p. 217) that "it is clear that the level of world inequality is . . . primarily due to differences in average incomes across countries rather than to intra-country inequality."

Although I begin with the question of whether intercountry inequality is still rising, the analysis does not end there. My aim is to provide the foundation for a general sociological literature on intercountry income inequality by getting the facts right about its key dimensions: Whether increasing or declining, is the trend in intercountry inequality due to differential economic growth across nations or to differential population growth across nations? Which countries contribute most to change in intercountry inequality? Are results robust over different inequality measures and income series? Although sociological studies of these important issues are rare, there is no good reason for sociologists to continue to shy away from studying intercountry inequality. Careful income estimates are available for over 100 nations, which constitutes a near-universe of the world's population (Summers et al. 1994), and convenient methods have been developed for analyzing income inequality for aggregates (Firebaugh 1998). The time is ripe for systematic sociological research on intercountry inequality. . . .

Cross-National Evidence

Cross-national studies of convergence appear at first glance to present a mishmash of conflicting results. In this section I show that consistent findings do emerge when the studies are sorted carefully. I will also show that sociologists should not be too hasty to use the findings from economics to reach conclusions about trends in world income inequality because economists and sociologists are asking different questions.

It is useful first to place the convergence studies in historical perspective. At the outset of the Industrial Revolution average income in the richest nations was perhaps four times the average income in the poorest nations (Maddison 1995, chap. 2). Average income in the richest nations and poorest nations now differs by a factor of about 30. Over the long haul, then—from the late 18th century through much of the 20th—national incomes diverged. No one disputes that.

The more vexing question is what has happened since about 1960. Some studies conclude that there has been little or no change in intercountry inequality in recent decades (Berry et al. 1983a; Peacock et al. 1988; Schultz 1998) whereas other studies conclude that national incomes have continued to diverge (Jackman 1982; Sheehey 1996; Jones 1997; Korzeniewicz and Moran 1997).

There are three keys to making sense of these findings. The first key is weighting. Studies that do not weight generally find divergence, whereas studies that weight generally find very little change in intercountry inequality over recent decades. The second key is whether or not the national income data have been adjusted for "purchasing power parity" (PPP—elaborated in a subsequent section). The use of unadjusted data results in spurious divergence (Schultz 1998). The third key is China. Weighted studies that exclude China are suspect.

Studies of Unweighted Convergence

Table 4.1 summarizes key convergence studies from economics, sociology, and political science. In each of these studies the dependent variable is per capita income. Note that the income measure of choice is based on purchasing power parity; among recent studies only Korzeniewicz and Moran (1997) rely exclusively on income estimates that are based on the foreign exchange method.

The top panel of Table 4.1 summarizes studies that do not weight nations by size and the bottom panel summarizes studies that do. I begin with the studies in the top panel. One of the earliest reliable studies of cross-national convergence is Jackman's (1982) study of the relative income growth rates of 98 nations from 1960 to 1978. Jackman found an inverted-U pattern for the relationship between income growth rate and initial income—a pattern that was subsequently replicated in studies using different income measures and longer time periods (e.g., Summers and Heston 1991, table 4; Sheehey 1996). Despite this faster growth in the middle of the distribution, there is overall divergence because growth rates tend to be higher for the richest nations than for the poorest nations. Subsequent research has replicated the divergence finding as well (Barro and Sala-i-Martin 1992, table 3 and fig. 4; Sheehey 1996, table 2; Jones 1997, tables 2 and 3).

Table 4.1 Summary of Major Studies of National Income Convergence*

Study	Data and Method	Conclusion
Unweighted by population:		
Jackman (1982; table 1, fig. 1)	Income growth rate,† 1960 (N=98); regression of rate on initial level	Divergence with inverted-U pattern
Abramovitz (1986)	1870–1979 income;‡ coefficient of variation; 16 industrial nations (from Maddison 1982)	Long-run convergence among rich nations
Baumol (1986).	Same historical data as Abramovitz (1986), but uses regression	Long-run convergence among rich nations
Barro and Sala-i-Martin (1992, table 3, fig. 4)	Income growth rate,‡ 1960–85 (N=98); regression of rate on initial level	Divergence
Sheehey (1996, table 2)	Income growth rate,‡ 1960–88 (N=107 non-OPEC nations)	Divergence with inverted-U pattern
Jones (1997, tables 2, 3)	1960 and 1990 income (N=74);‡ SD of logged income	Divergence for world but rich converge
Weighted by population:		
Berry et al. (1983a)	1950–77 income (N=124);‡ Gini; Theil, mean log deviation, Atkinson	No overall trend
Peacock, Hoover, and Killian (1988, figs. 1, 2)	1950–80 income (N=53);‡ Theil	No overall trend, with convergence within world system strata and divergence between strata
Ram (1989)		
Table 1	1960–80 income (N=115; excludes China);‡ Theil§	Divergence
Table 2	1960–80 inequality (N=21; regression of overall Theil on mean world income, 1960–80); excludes China in the Theil§	Inverted-U pattern
Korzeniewicz and Moran (1997)	1965–90 income (N=121);‡ Gini; Theil	Divergence, especially in 1980s
Schulz (1998)	1960–89 income (N=120);‖ Gini, variance of logged income, Theil	No trend for purchasing power parity income; divergence for foreign exchange (FX) rate income

Notes: *Because the object of this study is change in intercountry inequality, the table is restricted to studies of *unconditional* convergence, a term that refers to the absence of control variables. In regression analysis, unconditional convergence is examined by regressing growth rate of income per capita on initial level of income per capita. Conditional convergence is examined by adding control variables.
†Income estimates are based on foreign exchange rates.
‡Income estimates are based on purchasing power parity (PPP).
§The significance of excluding China in weighted analyses is addressed in the text. I do not note the unweighted analyses (top panel) that omit China because the omission of China hardly matters in those studies.
‖Income estimates are based both on foreign exchange rates and on purchasing power parity.

In short, when each national economy is given the same weight—the sort of convergence that interests economists because it bears on endogenous growth theory—there is an inverted-U pattern in which nations in the upper middle of the distribution tend to exhibit the fastest rates of income growth and those at the lower end of the distribution tend to exhibit the slowest rates of growth. The upshot is that national economies are diverging for the world as a whole even though there are convergence "clubs" (e.g., there is evidence of income convergence among Western European nations; see Abramovitz 1986; Baumol 1986; Jones 1997).

Studies of Weighted Convergence

Although it is weighted national convergence that bears most directly on sociologists' interest in world inequality, evidence on weighted national convergence is relatively scarce. In sharp contrast to the large and growing literature on unweighted convergence, the empirical literature on weighted convergence across nations consists of just a handful of studies.

The early study by Berry et al. (1983a) remains one of the best of these studies. Based on a large sample of nations containing most of the world's population, Berry et al. conclude, first, that economic growth in China was the most potent force equalizing world incomes from 1950 to 1977 and, second, that there was no clear-cut trend in intercountry income inequality from 1950 to 1977.

Remove China, then, and the data will show weighted divergence—precisely what Ram (1989) found for 1960–80 with China removed. Include China and the data will show no overall trend in intercountry income inequality in recent decades—precisely what Peacock et al. (1988) and Schultz (1998) found, replicating the main conclusion of Berry et al. (1983a). So the studies are quite consistent: Weighted by population, the data show no underlying trend in intercountry income inequality over recent decades; remove China, and the data show rising inequality.

Only one key finding remains to be explained: Korzeniewicz and Moran's (1997) anomalous finding of rising intercountry inequality despite their inclusion of China. Schultz (1998) provides the key to the puzzle. Schultz presents two sets of findings, one for income data based on purchasing power parity (PPP) and one for income data based on foreign exchange (FX) rates (the type of income data used by Korzeniewicz and Moran). Intercountry income inequality rises for the FX income series but not for the PPP income series.

The important lesson to be learned from Schultz's (1998) two sets of findings is that researchers should not rely on official exchange rates when studying trends in relative national incomes. Though early studies in economics used FX estimates because PPP estimates were unavailable, PPP-based income is now the industry standard (in addition to the studies listed in Table 4.1 above, see

Barro 1991; Mankiw et al. 1992; Levine and Renelt 1992; Quah 1996). The rationale for the switch to PPP income measures will be elaborated later.

To summarize: When each national economy is given the same weight, the data indicate national divergence. Yet weighted studies find stability (the weighted studies that find divergence do so because they exclude China or use dubious income data). So the issue turns on weighting: Do we want to give nations or individuals equal weight?

Weighted Versus Unweighted Convergence

Sociologists and economists are interested in intercountry convergence for different reasons. The stimulus for many economists is theoretical, to test theories of macroeconomic growth. Very often for economists, then, each nation represents one unit (one economy) and, in typical analyses, economic trends in Luxembourg count just as much as economic trends in China, even though China has nearly 3,000 times more people. By contrast, sociologists generally study intercountry income inequality because of what it can reveal about income inequality for the world as a whole (Korzeniewicz and Moran 1997), so sociologists are interested in whether there is intercountry convergence in the case where individuals, not nations, are given equal weight. Thus most sociologists are interested in weighted convergence. . . .

Weighting is likely to matter a lot in the case of intercountry inequality because nations vary so much in population size. Large nations such as China and India affect the weighted measure but have little effect on the unweighted measure, and the reverse is true for small, rich nations such as Luxembourg and Norway.

To verify the importance of weighting, Table 4.2 presents the weighted and unweighted trends in intercountry inequality from 1960 to 1989 (I use 1989 as the endpoint because the dissolution of the Soviet Union interrupts the income series at that point). I use variance of logged income (VarLog) because it is the inequality measure most often used in economic studies. Table 4.2 reports the results for five-year intervals.

The difference between the weighted and unweighted results is striking. The unweighted results confirm economists' findings of divergence. But when nations are weighted by size, intercountry inequality increases monotonically until 1975 and declines thereafter; as a result, there is little net change in inequality from 1960 to 1989. . . .

Trend in Intercountry Income Inequality

The Korzeniewicz-Moran (1997) study provides a convenient point of departure for studying the trend in intercountry income inequality. As noted earlier,

Table 4.2 The 1960–89 Trends in Intercountry Income Inequality: Weighted Versus Unweighted Results

	Average World Income*		Inequality (VarLog)	
Year	Weighted	Unweighted	Weighted	Unweighted (VarLog)
1960	2,277	2,294	.91	.74
1965	2,660	2,729	1.04	.84
1970	3,118	3,266	1.08	.90
1975	3,426	3,761	1.11	.96
1980	3,835	4,303	1.07	1.02
1985	4,059	4,421	.96	1.08
1989	4,367	4,826	.96	1.18
1960–89 change (%)	+92	+110	+5	+59

Source: Summers et al. (1994).

Note: Real gross domestic product per capita is given in constant U.S. dollars (variable RGDPPC in the Penn income series, ver. 5.6); N=120 nations containing 92%–93% of the world population.

*Average per capita income for the 120 nations, in constant U.S. dollars. "Weighted average" indicates that the national means are weighted by population size.

Korzeniewicz and Moran conclude that intercountry income inequality is rising. Because that conclusion fits nicely with a large body of sociological literature on world polarization, the study is likely to attract a good deal of attention among sociologists. Moreover, the finding seems plausible, given the growth spurt in world income in recent decades (Easterlin 1998): careful estimates (Summers et al. 1994) indicate that the world's per capita income, stated in constant U.S. dollars, almost doubled from 1960 to 1989 (from $2,277 in 1960 to $4,367 in 1989), and an increase of this magnitude certainly has enormous potential for destabilizing the distribution of income across nations. Have Korzeniewicz and Moran uncovered an important trend that other weighted studies have missed?

The answer is no. The Korzeniewicz-Moran findings are based on the FX rate method, which is an unreliable method for comparing national incomes (e.g., Summers and Heston 1991; Horioka 1994). It is well documented that the use of official exchange rates exaggerates intercountry inequality (Ram 1979) and produces spurious divergence in intercountry inequality (Summers and Heston 1991, table 4; Schultz 1998). When industry-standard income data are substituted for the data used by Korzeniewicz and Moran, the rise in intercountry inequality disappears. What Korzeniewicz and Moran have demonstrated is not world polarization but the "dangers of using market exchange rates when making international comparisons" (Horioka 1994, p. 298).

To demonstrate these points, it is necessary first to summarize central issues regarding the comparison of income across nations.

Income Data. International comparisons of economic activity traditionally were obtained by using the FX rate to convert each country's national account data to a common currency, usually the U.S. dollar. But FX rates are highly flawed calibrators of currencies for two reasons. First, many goods and services are not traded on the international market, so exchange rates are based on a restricted bundle of goods and services (Grosh and Nafziger 1986, p. 351). Because this failure to capture economic activity is especially acute for non-monetized exchange in nonindustrial nations, FX measures of national income tend to miss significant economic activity in poorer nations. Second, FX markets are not totally "free" but are routinely distorted by government policy and speculative capital movement. As a result, exchange rates fail to reflect accurately the actual purchasing power parities (PPPs) of currencies.

To alleviate the deficiencies of FX-based income measures, several economists at the University of Pennsylvania spearheaded an ambitious effort to estimate national incomes using PPP to calibrate local currencies. Cross-nation parity for goods and services was determined through detailed studies of national price structures. As a result of those efforts, there is now an income series—the Penn series (Summers, Kravis, and Heston 1980; Kravis, Heston, and Summers 1982; Summers and Heston 1991; Summers et al. 1994)—that does not rely on FX rate. Even critics of the PPP measure concede that it represents a big improvement over the old FX measure (Dowrick and Quiggin 1997).

To appreciate the severity of the problem with using foreign exchange rates to compare national incomes, consider the FX income estimates for China and Japan. The remarkable economic growth of China since 1978 (Nee 1991, fig. 1; Chow 1994; Mastel 1997) is reflected in the PPP income series, where China's income ratio jumps roughly 40% between 1975 and 1989. Incredibly, though, the FX-based World Bank income series used by Korzeniewicz and Moran fails to capture that growth; instead it indicates that China's growth rate lagged so far behind the rest of the world that the FX income ratio for China declined by a whopping one-third from 1970 to 1989 (from .139 to .090).

The FX estimates for Japan are just as misleading. Though Japan experienced brisk economic growth through the 1970s and 1980s (Tachi 1993; Argy and Stein 1997), per capita income in Japan at the end of the 1980s still fell well short of incomes in the richest nations in the West (Horioka 1994). Yet FX-based income estimates place Japan's 1989 per capita income above per capita incomes in many rich Western nations (12% higher than Sweden and 16% higher than the United States; see World Bank 1993).

How do FX income estimates become so distorted? The Japanese case is illustrative. The use of foreign exchange rates to compare incomes leads one to conclude that Japanese per capita income as a percentage of U.S. per capita income rose from 67% in 1985 to 121% in 1988 (Horioka 1994, table 1). Obviously an increase of this magnitude in just three years would have been nothing short of miraculous. In fact this stupendous increase is "nothing more than a statistical illusion" (Horioka 1994, p. 297) caused by the too-rapid appreciation of the yen from 238 yen to the dollar in 1985 to 128 yen to the dollar in 1988. As Horioka (1994, table 1) demonstrates, more realistic measurement indicates that the Japan/U.S. income ratio rose only marginally over those three years, from 0.74 in 1985 to 0.76 in 1988.

In addition to the evidence that official exchange rates yield implausible income estimates for specific nations such as Japan and China, there are critical theoretical reasons for using PPP-based estimates when comparing incomes across nations (Summers and Heston 1980, 1991; Grosh and Nafziger 1986). Though Korzeniewicz and Moran (1997, p. 1011) state that the FX rate method "provides a better relational indicator of *command over income*" (emphasis in original), to the extent that exchange rates bear on command over income, they do so in the *world marketplace*—a largely hypothetical concept in the workaday world of the vast majority of the world's population. For the vast majority of the world's population, foreign-exchange-rate income is largely moot, since most of what is produced is not traded internationally. People face local prices, not international prices. This is not to deny that foreign-exchange-rate price can affect local price, but it is to say that an ox does not become half-an-ox when a nation decides to devalue its currency by half relative to the U.S. dollar.

Trends for FX Versus PPP Income Estimates

Table 4.3 reports the 1965–89 trend in intercountry inequality based on both PPP and FX income. I try to replicate the Korzeniewicz and Moran (1997) study as closely as possible. First, I rely on the same source for FX income estimates—the World Bank (1993)—and I use the same population data. Second, I use 1965 as the starting point. Third, I use the inequality indexes they used, the Theil and the Gini (results for V^2 and VarLog are similar). Finally, to ensure that results do not vary because of sampling differences, both "samples" here represent a near-universe of the world's people.

The results vividly demonstrate the difference in the two income series. According to the PPP-based income estimates, intercountry inequality declined modestly from 1965 to 1989. Yet according to the FX-based estimates, intercountry income inequality shot up 32.2% based on the Theil and 10.9% based on the Gini. Korzeniewicz and Moran (1997, table 3) report similar results (increases of 38.2% based on the Theil and 12.5% based on the Gini). These results reinforce the warning of, among others, Summers and Heston (1991, p. 355) that "it really makes a difference if exchange rates are used rather than PPPs" so "the practice of using exchange rates as quick, easily obtained estimates of PPPs is invalidated" (p. 335).

To see if the misleading FX income estimates for China and Japan matter much, I estimated a second, adjusted set of FX-based trends in intercountry

Table 4.3   Results for PPP-Based Versus FX-Based Income Estimates

Year	PPP Theil	PPP Gini	FX Theil Nominal	FX Theil Adjusted	FX Gini Nominal	FX Gini Adjusted
1965	.552	.560	.816	.762	.661	.643
1970	.548	.558	.826	.771	.666	.647
1975	.540	.555	.847	.775	.674	.650
1980	.531	.550	.878	.782	.681	.650
1985	.512	.539	.963	.835	.706	.663
1989	.526	.543	1.079	.900	.733	.683
1965–89 Change (%)	–4.7	–3.0	+32.2	+18.1	+10.9	+6.2

Source: Summers et al. (1994) for the PPP income data and World Bank (1993) for the FX income data.

Note: There are 120 nations in the PPP data set and 112 nations in the FX data set. The data sets contain both capitalist and socialist nations and all populous nations and cover over 90% of the world's population. Theil and Gini results are reported to allow comparison with results offered by Korzeniewicz and Moran (1997). Results for V^2 and VarLog lead to the same conclusions. Under FX, "nominal" uses exchange-rate income estimates as given and "adjusted" uses more realistic estimates of income trends in China and Japan.

income inequality [table not included here]. These results are based on the same FX income data as before, except that I use better income ratio estimates for China and Japan. Using more defensible income ratios (based on PPP) for just those two nations reduces the observed increase in the Theil and the Gini by over 40%.

In short, Korzeniewicz and Moran found divergence because they used a dubious income measure. Lest there be any doubt that the FX data yield a specious increase in intercountry inequality, it should be noted that a recent technical analysis of the PPP data used here (Dowrick and Quiggen 1997) concludes that the PPP data are, if anything, biased in favor of polarization. If so, then my failure to replicate the Korzeniewicz-Moran polarization result using PPP income cannot be dismissed on the ground that the use of PPP income as the yardstick stacks the deck against the polarization thesis.

If the FX income estimates tell the wrong story about recent trends in intercountry inequality, what is the right story? I now use PPP income estimates to answer that question. . . .

The Intercountry Income Inequality Plateau of 1960–89

It is well documented that, since about the mid-1970s, income inequality within the United States has risen after a long period of decline (Fischer et al.

1996; Nielsen and Alderson 1997). This phenomenon has been dubbed "the great U-turn" (Harrison and Bluestone 1988). Less appreciated is the pause in the long-run trend of rising intercountry inequality. This pause spans at least the 1960s, 1970s, and 1980s.

The discovery of a "great plateau" in the historical trend has important implications for our understanding of trends in world income inequality. One implication is that if income inequality across individuals has been increasing sharply for the world as a whole, as Korzeniewicz and Moran (1997) conclude, then the increase must be due to increases within nations. To cause the sort of increase in total world inequality that Korzeniewicz and Moran describe, the within-nation increase would need to be of colossal proportions because most of the total world income inequality is between, not within, nations.

A second implication of the plateau is that intercountry income inequality does not inevitably rise (or fall) with rising world income. Intercountry inequality was about the same in 1989 as it was 30 years earlier, and an important challenge for future studies is to determine why intercountry inequality remained so stable in a period when the world's average income shot up so rapidly. During a period of such great potential for destabilizing the distribution of income across nations, why did the variance neither increase nor decline? This study provides one part of the answer: offsetting trends in the most populous nations. The inequality-enhancing effects of rapid economic growth in Japan and sluggish economic growth in India were blunted by the inequality-reducing effects of rapid economic growth in China and slower-than-world-average population and economic growth in the United States over this period.

Finally, the discovery of the great plateau in weighted intercountry income inequality adds to the clamor for new sociological theories of national development (Gereffi 1989; Firebaugh 1992; Firebaugh and Beck 1994). Stable variance in the distribution of logged income across nations in a period of active core-periphery exchange calls into question fundamental assumptions sociologists have made about the impact of international exchange on national development. If the benefits of core-periphery movement of goods and capital in fact accrue primarily to rich nations and if this differential benefit is in fact the principal cause of intercountry income divergence (as dependency theory appears to claim), then it is hard to explain why the long-standing trend toward intercountry divergence was interrupted during an era of active core-periphery exchange.

References

Abramovitz, Moses. 1986. "Catching Up, Forging Ahead, and Falling Behind." *Journal of Economic History* 46:385–406.
Argy, Victor, and Leslie Stein. 1997. *The Japanese Economy*. New York: New York University Press.

Barro, Robert J. 1991. "Economic Growth in a Cross-Section of Countries." *Quarterly Journal of Economics* 106:407–43.

Barro, Robert J., and Xavier Sala-i-Martin. 1992. "Convergence." *Journal of Political Economy* 100:223–51.

Baumol, William J. 1986. "Productivity Growth, Convergence, and Welfare: What the Long-Run Data Show." *American Economic Review* 76:1072–85.

Berry, Albert, Francois Bourguignon, and Christian Morrisson. 1983a. "Changes in the World Distribution of Income between 1950 and 1977." *Economic Journal* 93:331–50.

———. 1983b. "The Level of World Inequality: How Much Can One Say?" *Review of Income and Wealth* 29:217–41.

Chow, Gregory C. 1994. *Understanding China's Economy*. Singapore: World Scientific.

Dowrick, Steve, and John Quiggin. 1997. "True Measures of GDP and Convergence." *American Economic Review* 87:41–64.

Easterlin, Richard A. 1998. *Growth Triumphant*. Ann Arbor: University of Michigan.

Firebaugh, Glenn. 1998. "Measuring Inequality: A Convenient Unifying Framework." Paper presented at the annual meeting of the Population Association of America, Chicago.

———. 1992. "Growth Effects of Foreign and Domestic Investment." *American Journal of Sociology* 98:105–30.

Firebaugh, Glenn, and Frank D. Beck. 1994. "Does Economic Growth Benefit the Masses? Growth, Dependence, and Welfare in the Third World." *American Sociological Review* 59:631–53.

Fischer, Claude S., Michael Hout, Martin Sanchez Jankowski, Samuel R. Lucas, Ann Swidler, and Kim Voss. 1996. *Inequality by Design*. Princeton, N.J.: Princeton University Press.

Gereffi, Gary. 1989. "Rethinking Development Theory: Insights from East Asia and Latin America." *Sociological Forum* 4:505–33.

Grosh, Margaret E., and E. Wayne Nafziger. 1986. "The Computation of World Income Distribution." *Economic Development and Cultural Change* 34:347–59.

Harrison, Bennett, and Barry Bluestone. 1988. *The Great U-Turn: Corporate Restructuring and the Polarizing of America*. New York: Basic Books.

Horioka, Charles Yuji. 1994. "Japan's Consumption and Saving in International Perspective." *Economic Development and Cultural Change* 42:293–316.

Jackman, Robert W. 1982. "Dependence on Foreign Investment and Economic Growth in the Third World." *World Politics* 34:175–96.

Jones, Charles I. 1997. "Convergence Revisited." *Journal of Economic Growth* 2:131–53.

Korzeniewicz, Roberto P., and Timothy P. Moran. 1997. "World-Economic Trends in the Distribution of Income, 1965–1992." *American Journal of Sociology* 102:1000–39.

Kravis, Irving B., Alan Heston, and Robert Summers. 1982. *World Product and Income*. Baltimore: Johns Hopkins University Press.

Levine, Ross, and David Renelt. 1992. "A Sensitivity Analysis of Cross-Country Growth Regressions." *American Economic Review* 82:942–63.

Maddison, Angus. 1995. *Explaining the Economic Performance of Nations*. Brookfield, Vt.: Edward Elgar.

Mankiw, N. Gregory, David Romer, and David N. Weil. 1992. "A Contribution to the Empirics of Economic Growth." *Quarterly Journal of Economics* 107:407–37.

Mastel, Greg. 1997. *The Rise of the Chinese Economy*. London: M. E. Sharpe.

Nee, Victor. 1991. "Social Inequalities in Reforming State Socialism: Between Redistribution and Markets in China." *American Sociological Review* 56:267–82.

Nielsen, Francois, and Arthur S. Alderson. 1997. "The Kuznets Curve and the Great U-Turn: Income Inequality in U.S. Counties, 1970 to 1990." *American Sociological Review* 62:12–33.

Peacock, Walter Gillis, Greg A. Hoover, and Charles D. Killian. 1988. "Divergence and Convergence in International Development: A Decomposition Analysis of Inequality in the World System." *American Sociological Review* 53:838–52.

Quah, Danny T. 1996. "Convergence Empirics across Economies with (Some) Capital Mobility." *Journal of Economic Growth* 1:95–124.

Ram, Rati. 1979. "International Income Inequality: 1970 and 1978." *Economics Letters* 4:187–90.

Schultz, T. Paul. 1998. "Inequality in the Distribution of Personal Income in the World: How It Is Changing and Why." *Journal of Economics* 11:307–44.

Sheehey, Edmund J. 1996. "The Growing Gap between Rich and Poor Countries: A Proposed Explanation." *World Development* 24:1379–84.

Summers, Robert, and Alan Heston. 1991. "The Penn World Table (Mark 5): An Expanded Set of International Comparisons, 1950–1988." *Quarterly Journal of Economics* 106:327–68.

Summers, Robert, Alan Heston, Bettina Aten, and Daniel Nuxoll. 1994. *Penn World Table* (PWT) Mark 5.6a Data (MRDF). Center for International Comparisons, University of Pennsylvania.

Summers, Robert, Irving B. Kravis, and Alan Heston. 1980. "International Comparisons of Real Product and Its Composition, 1950–1977." *Review of Income and Wealth* 26:19–66.

Tachi, Ryuichiro. 1993. *The Contemporary Japanese Economy*, translated by Richard Walker. Tokyo: University of Tokyo Press.

World Bank. 1993. *World Tables of Economic and Social Indicators, 1950–1992* (MRDF). Washington, D.C.: World Bank, International Economics Department. Distributed by Inter-University Consortium for Political and Social Research, Ann Arbor, Michigan.

5

Assessing Contending Measures of the Gap, 1980–2010

John T Passé-Smith

*M*ost studies of the gap between rich and poor countries use
either exchange rate–converted or purchasing power parity (PPP)–
converted national account statistics. This chapter discusses the reason
many scholars have shifted to the PPP-converted measures. Three of
the major criticisms of exchange rate–converted data are explained:
the differential purchasing power of currencies from one country to
the next, the impact of potentially wild fluctuations in exchange rates,
and the unmeasured informal markets in developing countries.
John Passé-Smith concludes that the purchasing power in poorer
countries is captured by the PPP-converted data. However, the PPP-
converted data show no sign at all of smoothing fluctuations in exchange
rate–converted data. Finally, the PPP-converted data do behave as if they
are capturing informal markets. Then the gap between rich and poor
countries is examined using both measures to determine any major
differences. While the results are mixed, there is some evidence offered
by the coefficient of variation that the gap may have closed a bit
between 1980 and 2010.

AMARTYA SEN (2001), NOBEL LAUREATE IN ECONOMICS, WARNED THAT
debating the trends in global inequality was counterproductive because it di-
verted attention away from the sheer magnitude of the gap between rich and
poor countries and thus away from global poverty. Indeed, global poverty and
the extent of the gap between rich and poor countries are immensely important, and we should not be distracted from their impact on people. One

measure of this gap, the relative gap, shows that in 2010, poor countries' mean gross domestic product per capita (GDP/pc) was 1.63 percent of the GDP/pc of the rich (see Chapter 2). However, once one fills in the specifics of the degree of human suffering resulting from such conditions, the question arises: Is it getting better or worse? This question is really no less important than understanding the extent of the problem, because it allows policymakers and scholars to assess policy prescriptions. In other words, it is important to know if the liberal austerity policies required by the International Monetary Fund (IMF) when loaning money to developing countries improve their conditions or make them worse.

For many years the bulk of the evidence pointed to a widening gap. Most scholars seemed satisfied with the evidence and conclusion that the gap was expanding. Even staff writers at the IMF and studies commissioned by the World Bank concluded that the gap between rich and poor was growing (see Chapter 3). However, in the 1980s, economics journals began giving more column space to the proponents of convergence theory. In its purest form, convergence theory proposes that the poorer the country, the higher its economic growth potential. Theorists such as Moses Abramovitz (1986), Paul Romer (1994), and William Baumol (1986) argued that the productive technology invented and used in the very competitive markets of the first world relatively quickly lost its competitive advantage as innovation replaced innovation. This forced companies to adopt newer innovations and transfer antiquated productive technologies to the developing world, where they remained competitive. The poorer a country, the more generations of technology that had yet to be absorbed; thus they would have a higher potential to grow.

Although it may appear that most studies continue to find that the gap is growing (Korzeniewicz and Moran 2005, 1997; Babones 2002; Wade 2001; Pritchett 1996; Maddison 1995; Peacock et al. 1988; Breedlove and Nolan 1988; DeLong 1988; Morawetz 1977; Kirman and Tomasini 1969), a number of these studies began to challenge the conventional wisdom and suggest that the gap was either stable or shrinking (Firebaugh 2003, 1999, 1998; Goesling 2001; Williamson 1996; Mankiw, Romer, and Weil 1992; Ram 1989; Baumol 1986; Abramovitz 1986). While this listing of studies blurs the nuances in the methodologies and conclusions drawn, it does amply demonstrate that there is some degree of controversy concerning the behavior of the gap. Beyond the contradictory conclusions, the most striking factor differentiating the studies is that most of those that conclude that the gap is growing utilize exchange rate–converted (fx) national account statistics, and that those that find that the gap is stable or shrinking use purchasing power parity (PPP)–converted data. Since this choice of datasets appears to have such a profound impact on the conclusions drawn, it is important to pause and reexamine the reasons for choosing one dataset over the other.

The Problems with Exchange Rate–Converted Data

Over time, three major criticisms of *fx*-converted national account statistics have been raised. The first is sometimes referred to as the "traveler's dilemma." As a person travels from one country to the next, the money it takes to buy a common provision, such as bread (or its equivalent), can be drastically different. In other words, the currency it takes to purchase one bagel in Little Rock, Arkansas, when converted to Mexican pesos, may buy a bag full of tortillas in Guadalajara; yet that same currency, when converted to Japanese yen, may not be sufficient to purchase much of anything at all in Tokyo. Thus a straightforward conversion of currency using an exchange rate does not measure the difference in purchasing power from one country to the next. Therefore, a country that appears to be poor due to a low GDP/pc may not be so poor if its currency purchases a relatively high volume of goods in comparison to other currencies. According to proponents of PPP conversions, GDPs that are converted to a common currency that utilizes official exchange rates *overstate* the poverty of poor countries in a systematic way (Summers and Heston 1984; Morris 1979; Kravis et al. 1975; Heston 1973; Kuznets 1972). At the intuitive level, these proponents point out, humans simply could not survive at the apparent level of development as stated in *fx*-converted GDP/pc.

Second, even the most cursory examination of *fx* over time makes it manifestly clear that exchange rates fluctuate and, at times, do so rapidly and violently. A number of issues arise from these fluctuations that could inject significant error into the comparison of countries. For example, when attempting to compare a country's relative level of development, the simple act of selecting between the World Bank's beginning-of-year, midyear average, or end-of-year exchange rate for purposes of conversion can have a profound impact on a given country's apparent wealth. Indeed, M. D. Morris (1979: 10) illustrated this point when he highlighted the exchange rate behavior and its consequences for Brazil. During the first quarter of 1981, Brazil's official exchange rate was 70.8 cruzeiros per US dollar; by midyear the exchange rate had climbed to 91.8, and by year's end the official rate stood at 118.[1] A scholar's choice of which exchange rate to use to convert Brazil's national account statistics into a common currency would drastically change the apparent wealth of Brazil by up to 60 percent.

Further complicating the picture, economists suggest that when two countries enter into trade and neither government interferes in their respective economies in such a way as to distort prices, their exchange rate settles into "equilibrium." The equilibrium exchange rate is the perfect, or ideal, exchange rate for the countries at their current levels of development and interaction. Louka Katseli-Papaefstratiou (1979) asserted that if exchange rates were stable at the hypothesized equilibrium value, then exchange rate–converted GDPs per capita would be a more accurate reflection of a country's level of development; but, as pointed out earlier, exchange rates are not stable. As noted, exchange rates fluctuate rather quickly, and for a variety of reasons, including inflation, changes in production techniques, government intervention in exchange markets, import and export barriers, and price shocks originating domestically or internationally. The restoration of equilibrium, however, occurs very slowly (for further discussion, see Katseli-Papaefstratiou 1979: 4). The rapid fluctuations away from equilibrium and the ponderous return to it are not synchronized with the World Bank's reporting of exchange rate–converted national account statistics, thereby rendering any systematic decision (to always use midyear averages or end-of-year data) potentially flawed. Katseli-Papaefstratiou (1979: 4) further complicated the point by explaining that the equilibrium exchange rate itself is a hypothetical construct.

The third major criticism of *fx* data was described by Simon Kuznets (1972: 8), who asserted that because many low-income countries retain sizable elements of precapitalistic production and noncash trade that go unreported in national account statistics, their national accounts overstated poverty. For example, a farmer may have a number of pigs that can be traded for other foodstuffs, clothing, services, and the like, but none of this economic activity is captured by national account statistics because barter transactions never become part of the monied economy. Even monetary transactions in the informal sector are not included in national account statistics. For instance, a schoolteacher in Mexico City who earns extra cash by taping a "taxi" sign on his or her automobile without an official permit will probably not report those earnings and thus they will not be counted in the formal economy. As countries develop, Kuznets explained, these informal sectors gradually give way to the formal, monied economy that is measured with national account statistics.

Critics who adopt any or all of these three criticisms tend to support the same solution: the replacement of the exchange rate with a purchasing power parity conversion factor. There are three major datasets providing PPP-converted national account statistics. Angus Maddison produces one such dataset.[2] A second source would be the data produced by the International Comparisons Project (ICP). In 1984, Robert Summers and Alan Heston reported that the ICP had "develop[ed] a structural relationship between purchasing power parities and exchange rates . . . [that took] account of the variability of exchange rates" (1984: 207–208). The ICP conducts extensive research in thirty-four benchmark countries, and this information is used to extrapolate the data for the remaining nonbenchmark countries. This dataset has been regularly updated, and the current dataset, the Penn World Tables version 7.1, currently offers data for 190 countries between 1950 and 2010.[3] Both Maddison and the ICP begin with the data provided by the World Bank, the third source for PPP-converted data. Since both Maddison and the ICP use

World Bank data, I have chosen to present World Bank data in this chapter. While each of these three datasets are different, PPP proponents argue that they all correct for all three of the major problems of the *fx* conversion factor. They overcome the traveler's dilemma by producing a real GDP per capita (PPP-converted GDP/pc) that can be trusted to convey the ability of an individual to purchase a set basket of goods from one country to the next. They also overcome or adjust for the vicissitudinous nature of the exchange rate data. Finally, the PPP conversion factor is able to capture informal transactions by including variables measuring the structure of the economy.

Although economists have been quick to adopt PPP-converted national account statistics, sociologists and political scientists have only gradually migrated to PPP data. Although it has been slow, there does seem to be a trend toward the acceptance of the so-called real GDP/pc. In fact, two of the studies cited earlier used PPP data from the Penn World Tables (version 5.6a) to show that global inequality is either stable (Firebaugh 1999) or converging (Goesling 2001). While both of these studies were published in a prestigious sociological journal (the *American Journal of Sociology*), the *fx* versus PPP debate is far from settled. In 1997, Korzeniewicz and Moran (1997) specifically selected the more traditional World Bank *fx* data and concluded that divergence, not convergence, characterized international development. Salvatore Babones (2002) disputed the findings of Firebaugh, arguing that whether one uses PPP conversion factors or exchange rates, the gap is growing.

In the following section, I attempt to determine if the purchasing power parity conversion factor corrects for the problems identified here. In the final section, I examine the gap and its behavior across the two datasets.

GDP/pc and Real GDP/pc Compared

Turning to the data, this section compares exchange rate–converted with PPP-converted GDP/pc to determine if the real GDP per capita (rGDP/pc) corrects for the weaknesses of the *fx*-converted data. The exchange rate–converted and PPP-converted GDPs per capita were obtained from the World Bank's *World Development Indicators* online.[4] Only countries with data available for both the GDP/pc and the rGDP/pc for the entire thirty-one-year period between 1980 and 2010 were included. This reduced the number of countries to 124. Growth rates for both datasets were computed using the regression method described by the World Bank in the *World Development Report* (1988: 288–289).[5] The income groupings were borrowed from the World Bank's *World Development Indicators*.[6] The exchange rate–converted data are reported in constant US dollars with a base year of 2000. The PPP-converted data are reported in 2005 international dollars, which, according to the World Bank's technical notes, are equal to US dollars in terms of purchasing power in the United States. The

2005 constant was translated into 2000 dollars using the GDP deflator reported by the World Bank in the *World Bank Indicators* online.

1. *Criticism 1: The fx-converted data do not take into account purchasing power. Poverty in poor countries is overstated because any traveler can tell you that money seems to go much further in poor countries.* A comprehensive test of this criticism of exchange rate–converted data would have the researcher traveling from country to country purchasing a common basket of goods in order to see if the basket costs less in poorer countries, thus overstating the poverty of the poor. Since the money for that venture is unlikely to appear, a minimal test would be to see if the PPP dataset makes countries appear to be richer than does the *fx* dataset. Whether this increased wealth for the poor actually reflects increased purchasing power will be left for others to determine. It should be mentioned, however, that the PPP conversion factor is one factor for the entire country. This means that the United States has one conversion factor that is supposed to identify the price at which a common basket of goods can be purchased, whether that person happens to be in Conway, Arkansas; Nashville, Tennessee; or New York, New York.

To determine if the PPP data make poor countries appear richer, Table 5.1 offers a comparison of the PPP- and *fx*-converted GDP/pc for 2010. The first column in Table 5.1 lists all of the countries identified in the *fx* dataset as belonging to the lower-middle-income and low-income groups in 2010. The overwhelming conclusion to be drawn from the data presented in Table 5.1 is that the World Bank's PPP dataset does indeed make poor countries appear to be richer. The GDP/pc of lower-middle-income countries, when converted by PPP, is 166 percent higher than the exchange rate–converted data. As should occur if the purchasing power parity is working appropriately, the average GDP/pc for the low-income countries shows an even greater variation, with the poorest countries appearing 209 percent richer than when using the exchange rate–converted data. Without exception, the rGDP/pc of every single country in the lower-middle-income and low-income categories is higher than the GDP/pc.

The column on the far right side of the table reports the Human Development Index (HDI) for each country. The HDI is an attempt to measure countries' standard of living by creating a composite index of health, education, and income, with a minimum value of 0 and a high of 1. Countries that approach the 0 end of the scale are the less developed, more impoverished states, and countries that approach 1 have the highest standards of living. Even though the rGDP/pc calculation makes the poorest countries appear to be richer, the HDI scores still make intuitive sense. The average HDI score of the lower-middle-income countries is 0.645, while the poor countries average only 0.431, as one would expect. A bivariate correlation of the HDI, GDP/pc, and rGDP/pc for 2010 indicates that the HDI is slightly more in tune with the rGDP/pc ($r = 0.80$) than the GDP/pc ($r = 0.73$).

Table 5.1 GDP/pc and rGDP/pc for Lower-Middle-Income and Poor Countries, 2010

	GDP/pc (US$)	rGDP/pc (US$)	rGDP/pc – GDP/pc (difference) (US$)	rGDP/pc as Percentage of GDP/pc	HDI
Lower-middle-income countries					
Bulgaria	2,550	10,226	7,677	301.1	0.768
Romania	2,637	9,720	7,083	268.6	0.779
Albania	1,915	6,816	4,901	255.9	0.737
Ecuador	1,728	6,409	4,681	270.9	0.718
Algeria	2,232	6,732	4,500	201.6	0.696
Thailand	2,713	6,829	4,116	151.8	0.680
China	2,425	6,066	3,641	150.1	0.682
Egypt, Arab Republic	1,976	4,934	2,958	149.7	0.644
Swaziland	1,810	4,752	2,941	162.5	0.520
Georgia	1,259	4,051	2,792	221.8	0.729
El Salvador	2,557	5,323	2,766	108.1	0.672
Sri Lanka	1,296	4,054	2,758	212.9	0.686
Syria, Arab Republic	1,526	4,219	2,693	176.5	0.631
Bolivia	1,233	3,871	2,639	214.0	0.660
Paraguay	1,621	4,136	2,515	155.2	0.662
Namibia	2,667	5,169	2,502	93.8	0.622
Indonesia	1,144	3,453	2,309	201.9	0.613
Congo, Republic	1,253	3,389	2,136	170.4	0.282
Jordan	2,534	4,590	2,056	81.1	0.697
Vanuatu	1,544	3,547	2,003	129.8	0.615
Guatemala	1,861	3,820	1,959	105.3	0.573
Morocco	1,844	3,762	1,917	104.0	0.579
Philippines	1,383	3,169	1,785	129.1	0.641
Honduras	1,392	3,132	1,739	124.9	0.623
Guyana	1,201	2,740	1,539	128.2	0.629
Fiji	2,231	3,719	1,488	66.7	0.687
Nicaragua	948	2,326	1,377	145.2	0.587
Mean	1,833	4,850	3,018	166.0	0.645
Low-income countries					
India	787	2,735	1,948	247.6	0.542
Moldova	596	2,483	1,887	316.7	0.644
Pakistan	669	2,146	1,477	220.9	0.503
Nigeria	545	1,916	1,371	251.7	0.454
Mauritania	609	1,961	1,352	221.9	0.451
Sudan	524	1,801	1,277	243.7	0.406
Papua New Guinea	744	1,973	1,229	165.2	0.462
Kiribati	760	1,962	1,202	158.1	0.621
Cameroon	714	1,832	1,118	156.7	0.479
Senegal	562	1,545	983	175.0	0.457
Ghana	359	1,312	953	265.6	0.533
Côte d'Ivoire	591	1,516	925	156.5	0.401
Benin	377	1,267	890	236.1	0.425
Kenya	469	1,318	850	181.3	0.505
Chad	276	1,094	818	296.5	0.326

(continues)

Table 5.1   continued

	GDP/pc (US$)	rGDP/pc (US$)	rGDP/pc – GDP/pc (difference) (US$)	rGDP/pc as Percentage of GDP/pc	HDI
Zambia	432	1,247	815	188.5	0.425
Guinea-Bissau	161	947	786	487.2	0.351
Lesotho	496	1,278	783	157.9	0.446
Gambia	355	1,126	771	217.4	0.418
Bangladesh	558	1,325	767	137.4	0.496
Burkina Faso	276	1,003	726	263.0	0.329
Nepal	268	957	689	256.8	0.455
Rwanda	338	929	591	174.6	0.425
Mali	270	850	580	214.9	0.356
Comoros	336	875	539	160.2	0.431
Madagascar	243	773	531	218.7	0.481
Malawi	184	704	520	282.5	0.395
Togo	285	797	512	179.3	0.433
Niger	180	581	401	222.7	0.293
Sierra Leone	268	660	392	146.0	0.334
Central African Republic	240	630	390	162.9	0.339
Mozambique	390	752	362	93.0	0.317
Burundi	115	326	211	182.9	0.313
Liberia	155	334	179	115.7	0.325
Congo, Democratic Republic	104	277	173	166.9	0.528
Mean	407	1,235	828	209.2	0.431

Source: Computed from World Bank, *World Development Indicators* (Washington, DC, 2012).

2. *Criticism 2: Exchange rate–converted data are susceptible to fluctuations that are smoothed by the PPP conversion.* As mentioned, the criticism of *fx* data is that exchange rates are susceptible to wild and sometimes exaggerated fluctuations for a variety of reasons. One way to determine if the PPP converters are smoothing these fluctuations in exchange rates would be to examine correlation coefficients of GDP/pc and rGDP/pc for a select group of countries. Certainly this is not the most sophisticated test, but if one of two variables being correlated is fluctuating and the other corrects and smooths, then this should be detectable in a correlation coefficient. A relatively low correlation coefficient between a country's GDP/pc and rGDP/pc would likely indicate that the PPP conversion factor is smoothing the more active exchange rate, while a very robust coefficient would suggest that the measures are either both smoothing or both moving together.

The dataset was sorted by the GDP/pc in 1980, with the richest and poorest country in each income group selected and each country's GDP/pc and rGDP/pc from 1980 to 2010 correlated. The correlation coefficients are reported in Table 5.2. Admittedly, the correlation between GDP/pc and rGDP/pc

Table 5.2   Correlation Coefficients of GDP/pc and rGDP/pc for Selected
Countries, 1980–2010

Country	Income Group	Correlation Coefficient	Correlation Coefficient for ICP Data
United Arab Emirates	High income	1.000	—
Ireland	High income	1.000	—
Greece	Upper-middle income	1.000	0.999
Panama	Upper-middle income	1.000	0.980
Jamaica	Lower-middle income	1.000	—
Guyana	Lower-middle income	1.000	0.972
Thailand	Low income	1.000	—
Burundi	Low income	1.000	0.691

Sources: Computed from World Bank, *World Development Indicators* (Washington, DC, 2012); and Penn World Tables, version 6.2, http://pwt.econ.upenn.edu/icp.html.

should be high, but if the PPP conversion smooths fluctuations in exchange rate conversions, then it seems that the coefficient should be somewhat lower than r = 1.00. For every single case, the correlation coefficient was 1.00. Just as a check, I correlated the GDP/pc with the data from the ICP dataset. Here the correlations were rather high, except for the poorest country, Burundi, whose correlation coefficient was 0.691. This suggests that the ICP dataset does in fact smooth out some fluctuations, but that the World Bank's PPP conversion factor does not.

3. *Criticism 3: Low-income countries have active informal sectors that are not captured in the standard exchange rate conversion. This makes poor countries look poorer than they actually are.* According to proponents of PPP, *fx* conversions exaggerate the poverty of the poor because transactions in the informal sector are not measured by the *fx* conversion factor. Thus, a pig traded for clothes or some other good or service is not measured as a part of the formal economy, and therefore when the data are aggregated, the country looks poorer than it actually is. As a country develops, the bartering and informal-sector transactions disappear, so a much larger percentage of the actual economy is measured. Thus it is thought that the *fx* conversion produces a much more accurate measure of wealth for rich countries than for the poor. Table 5.3 shows the mean GDP/pc and rGDP/pc for each income group for the first year of each decade being analyzed. The column on the far right holds the GDP/pc as a percentage of the rGDP/pc. If PPP proponents are correct, the GDP/pc should be a relatively small percentage of the rGDP/pc when compared to the richer income groups. As countries grow richer, the GDP/pc as a

Table 5.3 GDP/pc as a Percentage of rGDP/pc, 1980–2010

	GDP/pc (US$)	rGDP/pc (US$)	GDP/pc as Percentage of rGDP/pc
1980			
High income	19,328	22,882	84.47
Upper-middle income	5,303	9,308	56.97
Lower-middle income	1,604	3,704	43.30
Low income	363	1,047	34.70
1990			
High income	21,598	24,462	88.29
Upper-middle income	5,373	9,635	55.77
Lower-middle income	1,736	4,132	42.02
Low income	354	1,025	34.54
2000			
High income	23,911	27,819	85.95
Upper-middle income	5,001	9,361	53.42
Lower-middle income	1,601	3,981	40.21
Low income	352	1,061	33.21
2010			
High income	25,143	29,266	85.91
Upper-middle income	5,422	10,601	51.15
Lower-middle income	1,833	4,850	37.78
Low income	407	1,235	32.93

Sources: Computed from World Bank, *World Development Indicators* (Washington, DC, 2012); and Penn World Tables, version 6.2, http://pwt.econ.upenn.edu/icp.html.

percentage of the rGDP/pc should become larger. Table 5.3 confirms this expectation. The GDP/pc for the poorest countries is only about 30 percent of the rGDP/pc. As countries grow richer, the GDP/pc as a percentage of the rGDP/pc grows larger.

In the cases of five high-income countries—Denmark, Iceland, Japan, Sweden, and Switzerland—the GDP/pc actually surpasses the rGDP/pc, thus making these five wealthy countries appear poorer. All five of these countries were rich throughout the entire thirty-one-year period. None of the countries that gained high-income status after 1980 ever had a higher GDP/pc than rGDP/pc. In all other cases, the rGDP/pc makes the rich look richer just as it does for the low-income countries.

Figures 5.1a through 5.1d graph both the GDP/pc and the rGDP/pc between 1980 and 2010 for Luxembourg, Singapore, Dominica, and Burundi. Luxembourg was selected because it is one of the few countries that has been in the high-income category for all thirty-one years and was the richest country in 2010. Burundi was selected because it remained in the poor category for the entire period under examination and is the poorest country for which I have data in 2010. Singapore was selected because it moved up from the upper-middle-income category into the high-income group. Dominica made the list because it moved up from the lower-middle-income category into the upper-middle-income group. With these four cases we should expect to see that the rGDP/pc should make countries appear richer than does the GDP/pc. This should be the most apparent with Burundi, because as the poorest country it should have the largest informal sector. The rGDP/pc should capture that activity and show Burundi to be richer than the GDP/pc indicates. The richer countries should show less of a gap between the GDP/pc and the rGDP/pc.

As shown in the figures, Luxembourg, Singapore, Dominica, and Burundi all behave as expected in terms of economic growth. The rGDP/pc makes all of the countries look slightly richer. However, as the countries grow richer, the gap between the GDP/pc and the rGDP/pc grows smaller.

The Gap Between Rich and Poor

A simple method of determining if the gap between rich and poor countries is opening or closing is to examine the standard deviation around the average GDP/pc of all countries over time. If the gap is closing, then the standard deviation should grow smaller, meaning that countries are moving closer to the world average GDP/pc. Figure 5.2 shows the mean rGDP/pc and GDP/pc for all countries (N = 124) in the dataset, and the standard deviations of both the rGDP/pc and the GDP/pc, between 1980 and 2010. It is clear that global economic growth has been rather consistent over the entire period. Around 1983 and 2008 there were dips, but other than that there has been rather consistent growth of the mean GDP/pc and rGDP/pc. As should not be surprising by this point, the rGDP/pc for the world is larger than the GDP/pc.

The two lines hovering above the vertical bars in the figure represent the standard deviations of the GDP/pc (the solid line) and the rGDP/pc (the dashed line). As one moves through time in the figure it is evident that the standard deviations drop between 1980 and about 1986 and then steadily rise until about 2007. The shrinking of the standard deviations in the initial period suggests that the gap between the richest and poorest countries may be shrinking, and then the steady growth of the standard deviations points to the potential of the expansion of the gap. It should also be noted that the standard deviation of the rGDP/pc is larger than the GDP/pc, which means that the gap between rich and poor as measured by the rGDP/pc may be larger than indicated by the GDP/pc. This is counterintuitive since, in theory, the rGDP/pc is supposed to increase the apparent wealth of the poor much more than that of the rich. If that were the case, then this pattern would be quite unexpected; however, the evidence also shows that the rGDP/pc is somewhat larger than the GDP/pc, so the larger standard deviation may simply reflect this size difference. Overall, the

Figure 5.1a GDP/pc and rGDP/pc for Luxembourg, 1980–2010

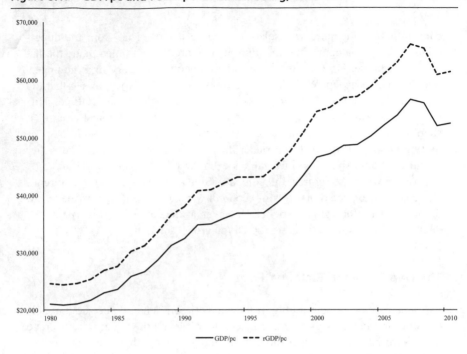

Figure 5.1b GDP/pc and rGDP/pc for Singapore, 1980–2010

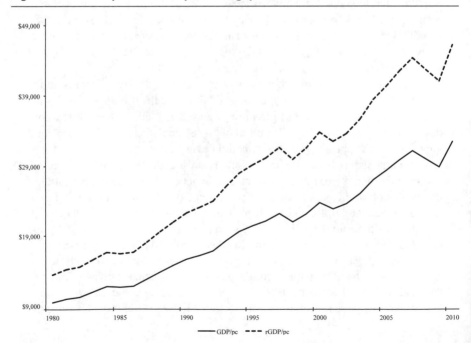

Figure 5.1c   GDP/pc and rGDP/pc for Dominica, 1980–2010

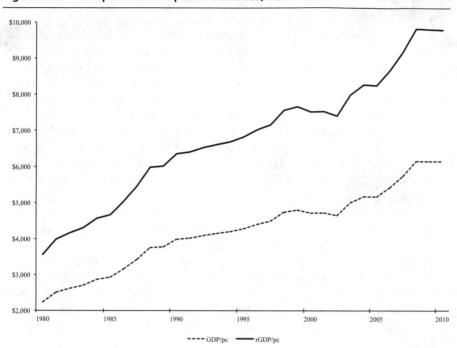

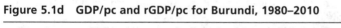

Figure 5.1d   GDP/pc and rGDP/pc for Burundi, 1980–2010

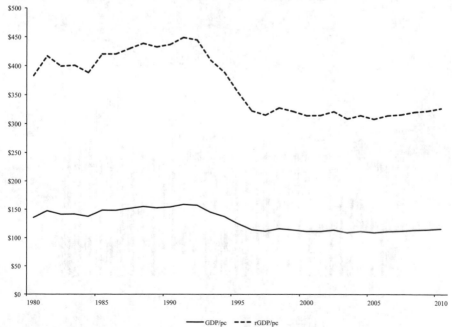

trend in both measures suggests that there was a very slight closing of the gap—or at least slowing of the expansion of the gap—between about 1986 and 2008.

The gap as illustrated in Figure 5.2, however, may be presenting a misleading picture. It would not be surprising that as the world grows richer, the increase in the standard deviation away from the mean would also grow larger as a reflection of that increase. The coefficient of variation, as shown in Figure 5.3, standardizes the deviation score for changing means so that one can be relatively sure that an increase in the coefficient of variation is not a relic of an increasing mean value.[7] As can be seen in the figure, the coefficient of variation for the rGDP/pc and the GDP/pc presents a slightly different picture of the world than appears in the previous figure.

The coefficient of variation grows larger as the gap grows wider, and shrinks as the gap closes. When the gap between rich and poor countries grows worse, the line representing the coefficient of variation in the figure will move upward, and when countries are becoming more equal, the line representing the coefficient of variation will move downward. Between 1980 and 1986, the coefficient of variation suggests that the gap between rich and poor countries is improving. Then around 1986, the gap remains rather constant, neither improving nor worsening, until around 2005, when it gradually improves. This

Figure 5.2   Mean World GDP/pc and rGDP/pc and Standard Deviations, 1980–2010

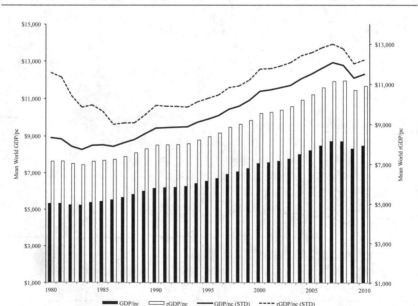

Figure 5.3   Coefficient of Variation, 1980–2010

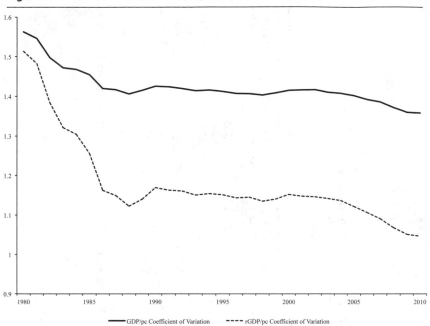

GDP/pc Coefficient of Variation   ---- rGDP/pc Coefficient of Variation

same pattern is apparent in the rGDP/pc as well, except it is a bit more exaggerated. It is quite remarkable that when looking at the entire thirty-one-year period, the general trend is toward a lessening of the gap.

Examining the standard deviations and the coefficient of variation thus yields some hopeful signs that the gap could be shrinking a bit. Another measure of the gap is the absolute gap, which is calculated by subtracting an income group's mean GDP/pc (or the rGDP/pc) from that of the high-income countries. This measure offers the dollar per capita difference between income groups. Table 5.4 displays the absolute gaps for the rGDP/pc and the GDP/pc to see if this too offers signs of hope. Here the signs are not as hopeful. The absolute gaps for the rGDP/pc and the GDP/pc are remarkably similar and they behave similarly. Again, since the rGDP/pc is a constant function of the GDP/pc, this should not be surprising. The absolute gap between the high-income countries and the upper-middle-income countries for the rGDP/pc is $14,642. On average, each year it expands $89. By 2010 the absolute gap (rGDP/pc) had grown to $17,409.

One thing to note is that the income groups used here are those offered by the World Bank. Given that the rGDP/pc makes poor countries look richer, it is not too surprising that fewer countries would be considered poor. Table 5.5 shows that in 1980 the rGDP/pc designated only fourteen countries as being

Table 5.4 Comparing Absolute Gap Measures for rGDP/pc and GDP/pc, 1980–2010 (US$)

	rGDP/pc			GDP/pc		
	Gap Between High-Income and Upper-Middle-Income Countries	Gap Between High-Income and Lower-Middle-Income Countries	Gap Between High-Income and Low-Income Countries	Gap Between High-Income and Upper-Middle-Income Countries	Gap Between High-Income and Lower-Middle-Income Countries	Gap Between High-Income and Low-Income Countries
1980	14,642	18,269	19,437	14,026	17,725	18,965
1985	14,655	18,546	19,627	14,459	18,246	19,581
1990	15,870	19,876	20,996	16,224	19,861	21,244
1995	16,419	20,463	21,663	16,826	20,652	22,075
2000	18,781	23,145	24,223	18,910	22,310	23,558
2005	18,836	23,286	24,492	20,401	24,214	25,566
2010	17,409	21,689	22,734	19,720	23,310	24,736
Mean annual change	89	110	106	184	180	186

Sources: Computed from *World Bank, World Development Indicators* (Washington, DC, 2012); and Penn World Tables, version 6.2, http://pwt.econ.upenn.edu/icp.html.

Table 5.5   Number of Countries in Each Income Group over Time, 1980–2010

	rGDP/pc				GDP/pc			
	High Income	Upper-Middle Income	Lower-Middle Income	Low Income	High Income	Upper-Middle Income	Lower-Middle Income	Low Income
1980	33	39	38	14	24	23	39	38
1985	32	42	35	15	24	22	41	37
1990	35	40	34	15	26	24	35	39
1995	37	38	33	16	27	24	34	39
2000	39	40	32	13	31	26	30	37
2005	44	36	32	12	31	27	32	34
2010	51	35	28	10	33	29	27	35

Sources: Computed from World Bank, *World Development Indicators* (Washington, DC, 2012); and Penn World Tables, version 6.2, http://pwt.econ.upenn.edu/icp.html.

poor. Included in this list of poor countries were India and China, making the percentage of the world that were poor top 50 percent. However, by 2010, according to the rGDP/pc, there were only ten countries that were poor: Burundi, the Central African Republic, the Democratic Republic of Congo, Liberia, Madagascar, Malawi, Mozambique, Niger, Sierra Leone, and Togo. Because India and China moved up to the lower-middle-income group, the population of the low-income group was only about 3 percent of the world's population. Most would probably assume that the poor constitute more than 3 percent of the world's population. It could be that the income groups that were originally devised by the World Bank for exchange rate–converted national account statistics do not provide adequate breakpoints for PPP-converted measures. It may be that new breakpoints need to be devised that would designate countries with higher rGDPs per capita as poor. The problem with this solution is that the *fx* currencies are said to overstate the poverty of the poor. If one moves to PPP conversion factors and then needs to move the PPP breakpoints for income groups upward, then it seems that the PPP is overstating the *wealth* of the poor. In comparison, Table 5.5 shows that the GDP/pc designated thirty-eight countries as poor at the beginning of the period, and that this number dropped to thirty-five by 2010. In terms of percentage of population, the GDP/pc data show that in 1980, 61 percent of the world's people lived in low-income countries, and that by 2010, this proportion had dropped to 37 percent.

Growth Rates

Between 1980 and 2010, the world economy grew at an annual average rate of 1.48 percent (see Table 5.6). For the period as a whole, the fastest-growing

Table 5.6   Annual Average Economic Growth Rates by Geographic Region, 1980–2010 (percentages)

	GDP/pc				rGDP/pc			
	1980–2010	1980–1989	1990–1999	2000–2010	1980–2010	1980–1989	1990–1999	2000–2010
High-income countries								
OECD (N = 26)	2.18	2.47	2.10	1.42	2.18	2.47	2.10	1.42
Non-OECD (N = 8)	1.68	0.05	1.81	1.40	1.68	0.05	1.81	1.40
Europe and Central Asia (N = 7)	0.38	2.01	–2.15	5.26	0.38	2.01	–2.15	5.26
East Asia and Pacific (N = 9)	2.67	1.92	3.21	2.98	2.67	1.92	3.21	2.98
Latin America and Caribbean (N = 27)	1.88	0.75	2.29	2.61	1.88	0.75	2.29	2.61
Middle East and North Africa (N = 6)	1.58	0.47	1.67	3.28	1.58	0.47	1.67	3.28
South Asia (N = 5)	2.89	2.32	2.88	4.05	2.89	2.32	2.88	4.05
Sub-Saharan Africa (N = 36)	0.33	–0.22	–0.12	1.93	0.33	–0.22	–0.12	1.93
World (N = 124)	1.48	0.99	1.33	2.35	1.48	0.99	1.33	2.35

Source: World Bank, *World Development Indicators* (Washington, DC, 2012).
Note: See Table 2.3 for definitions of region groupings.

geographic region was South Asia, whose economy grew at an annual average rate of 2.89 percent. Sub-Saharan Africa was the slowest grower, at 0.33 percent. Economic growth rates for the 1980s were noticeably lower than for the other decades, and the decade during which the most rapid growth took place was the first decade of the new century. From 2000 to 2010, the region of Europe and Central Asia experienced the most rapid economic growth (5.26 percent), while sub-Saharan Africa endured the slowest growth (1.93 percent).

This rate of economic growth for the world's regions is impressive, but the most remarkable thing about the table is that the growth rates for the GDP/pc and the rGDP/pc are identical. Recall in Table 5.2 that the GDP/pc and the rGDP/pc correlated at r = 1.00 for every country listed. That correlation holds for all countries in the dataset. If the correlation between the GDP/pc and the rGDP/pc is 1.0, then it makes sense that the growth rates should be the same as well. To emphasize this point, I have listed the GDP/pc and the rGDP/pc for the United Kingdom, from 1980 to 2010, in Table 5.7. For 1980, if we divide the rGDP/pc by the GDP/pc, we find that the rGDP/pc is 1.03099 times larger than the GDP/pc. This ratio, 1:1.031 (rounded), is maintained throughout the entire thirty-one-year period, such that the United Kingdom's rGDP/pc for any year can be calculated by finding its GDP/pc and multiplying that by 1.031. While the ratio differs for every country, this fact is true for the entire dataset. The ratio remains the same for every year. Thus, a

Table 5.7   Converting GDP/pc to rGDP/pc for the United Kingdom, 1980–2010

	GDP/pc (US$)	rGDP/pc (US$)	Ratio of rGDP/pc to GDP/pc
1980	15,005	15,470	1.031
1981	14,817	15,276	1.031
1982	15,149	15,618	1.031
1983	15,703	16,189	1.031
1984	16,100	16,599	1.031
1985	16,645	17,161	1.031
1986	17,274	17,809	1.031
1987	18,023	18,582	1.031
1988	18,888	19,473	1.031
1989	19,269	19,866	1.031
1990	19,361	19,961	1.031
1991	19,033	19,622	1.031
1992	19,009	19,598	1.031
1993	19,385	19,986	1.031
1994	20,163	20,788	1.031
1995	20,724	21,366	1.031
1996	21,267	21,926	1.031
1997	22,529	23,228	1.031
1998	23,326	24,049	1.031
1999	24,099	24,845	1.031
2000	25,083	25,860	1.031
2001	25,779	26,578	1.031
2002	26,367	27,184	1.031
2003	27,186	28,028	1.031
2004	27,848	28,711	1.031
2005	28,261	29,137	1.031
2006	28,820	29,713	1.031
2007	29,628	30,546	1.031
2008	29,107	30,009	1.031
2009	27,646	28,503	1.031
2010	28,033	28,902	1.031

Source: Computed from World Bank, *World Development Indicators* (Washington, DC, 2012).

correlation of the GDP/pc and the rGDP/pc will be r = 1.0, and the correlation between the growth rates will be the same.

Conclusions

This chapter has sought to explain the criticisms of the exchange rate–converted (*fx*) national account statistics that have led to the increased usage of the purchasing power parity–converted data offered by the World Bank and the International Comparisons Project, and to examine the World Bank's dataset to see if it has actually overcome the problems identified with the *fx* data. The chapter has also briefly examined the gap between rich and poor to compare the *fx* and PPP datasets to determine if they come to different conclusions about the gap.

The first criticism of the *fx* dataset is that it systematically overstates the poverty of the poor countries by not taking into account the fact that it takes less money to buy a common basket of goods in poor countries than in richer countries. Comparing the two datasets, I found that the purchasing power parity–converted data did in fact increase the apparent wealth of the poor countries. One issue noted was that the PPP-converted data provide one conversion factor for an entire country, so it assumes that the price of a basket of goods in Arkansas is the same price that would be paid for that same basket of goods in New York.

The second criticism of exchange rate–converted datasets is that exchange rates fluctuate and that this fluctuation could potentially inflate or deflate the apparent wealth of a country. A very simple examination of correlation coefficients showed that the rGDP/pc and the GDP/pc correlated perfectly; therefore the rGDP/pc could not be correcting for fluctuations, because there were no fluctuations.

The third criticism of the *fx*-converted data is that they do not measure the informal sector, meaning that, once again, the apparent poverty of the poor countries is overstated because the informal sector is so large and important in the developing world. The simple barter exchange of services for services or a pig for clothing is missed by the exchange rate conversion. PPP proponents argue that the poorest countries have the most vibrant informal sectors, and that as they develop, the informal sector fades and the exchange rate–converted data more accurately reflect the level of development. An examination of the data showed that the rGDP/pc did increase the apparent wealth of the poorest countries the most. The apparent increase in wealth grew smaller for middle-income countries and was at its smallest for the wealthiest countries. Assuming that the informal sector in the poorest countries is in fact larger, then the rGDP/pc is behaving just as it should.

The criticisms of exchange rate–converted data offered by the proponents of a purchasing power parity conversion factor are legitimate criticisms that should be taken seriously and addressed. However, effective criticism of the *fx*-converted GDP/pc does not mean that any alternative is better. Poverty may be overstated by the exchange rate–converted dataset, but any measure that makes the poor appear richer is not necessarily more accurate. That said, the rGDP/pc does boost the apparent wealth of the poorer countries.

Analysis of the coefficient of variation indicates that both PPP conversion factors and exchange rates lead to the conclusion that the gap between high-income and low-income countries has remained rather constant, with some sign that there may be a narrowing of the gap. While the time period is too brief to make too much of this, this is one positive sign. In terms of economic growth, the two measures are identical. The data show that the 1980s was a period of very slow growth and that the most recent decade, the first decade of the new century, has seen the most rapid growth. There are no distinctions to draw in terms comparing the growth rates arrived at through the two measures, because they are identical.

The absolute-gap measure shows that the gap between rich and poor is growing whether one selects the *fx*-converted data or the PPP-converted data. On average, the gap between the high-income countries and the low-income countries stood near $19,000 (both rGDP/pc and GDP/pc) in 1980, and grew to approximately $23,000 by 2010. However, in terms of percentage of population, the PPP-converted data show that only about 3 percent of the world's people were living in low-income countries as of 2010. This probably points to the need for the World Bank to reexamine the PPP measure and produce income breaks that accurately reflect the poverty level for the PPP-converted data. However, to do so suggests that the PPP is overstating the wealth of the poor.

Notes

1. The example follows the logic of that used by M. D. Morris in *Measuring the Condition of the World's Poor: The Physical Quality of Life Index* (New York: Pergamon, 1979), pp. 10–11.

2. See https://sites.google.com/site/econgeodata/maddison-data-on-population-gdp.

3. See https://pwt.sas.upenn.edu.

4. See http://data.worldbank.org/indicator.

5. The growth rates for both rGDP/pc and GDP/pc are calculated by the regression method described in the World Bank's 1988 *World Development Report* (Oxford: Oxford University Press, 1988), pp. 288–289. The least-squares method finds the growth rate by fitting a least-squares trend line to the log of the gross domestic product per capita. This takes the equation form of $X_t = a + bt + e_t$ where *x* equals the log of the GDP/pc, *a* is the intercept, *b* is the parameter to be estimated, *t* is time, and *e* is the error term. The growth rate, *r*, is the [antilog (*b*)] – 1. For a discussion of different methods of computing growth rates, see Robert Jackman, "A Note on the Measurement of Growth Rates in Cross-National Research," *American Journal of Sociology* 86 (1980): 604–610.

6. See the "Tables, Quick Reference" section at http://data.worldbank.org/about /country-classifications/country-and-lending-groups, where the technical notes offer "classification of economies by income and region." The cutoffs for the income groups were computed from those created by the World Bank. The online technical notes offered the following list: high-income countries are those with a GNI/pc of $12,276 and higher; upper-middle-income countries have a GNI/pc of between $3,976 and $12,275; lower-middle-income countries have a GNI/pc of between $1,006 and $3,975; and the poor countries are those with a GDP/pc of less than $1,006. Since these breaks were reported in GNI/pc, I first calculated each break's percentage of the GNI/pc of the United States. I then recalculated the income breaks for GDP/pc: high-income countries have a GNP/pc of $9,722 or higher; middle-income countries, between $3,149 and $9,721;

lower-middle-income countries, between $797 and $3,148; and low-income countries, less than $797.

7. The coefficient of variation is the standard deviation divided by the mean.

References

Abramovitz, Moses. 1986. "Catching Up, Forging Ahead, and Falling Behind." *Journal of Economic History* 46: 385–406.

Babones, Salvatore. 2002. "Population and Sample Selection Effects in Measuring International Income Inequality." *Journal of World-Systems Research* 8, no. 1 (Winter): 8–28.

Bairoch, P. 1981. "The Main Trends in National Economic Disparities Since the Industrial Revolution." In P. Bairoch and M. Lévy-Leboyer, eds., *Disparities in Economic Development Since the Industrial Revolution.* London: Macmillan.

Baumol, William J. 1986. "Productivity Growth, Convergence, and Welfare: What the Long-Run Data Show." *American Economic Review* 76 (December): 1072–1084.

Beckerman, W. 1966. *International Comparisons of Real Income.* Paris: OECD Development Center.

Berry, Albert, François Bourguignon, and Christian Morrisson. 1983a. "Changes in the World Distribution of Income Between 1950 and 1977." *Economic Journal* 93: 331–350.

———. 1983b. "The Level of World Inequality: How Much Can One Say?" *Review of Income and Wealth* 29: 217–241.

Breedlove, William L., and Patrick D. Nolan. 1988. "International Stratification and Inequality 1960-80." *International Journal of Contemporary Sociology* 25, nos. 3–4: 105–123.

Chou, Yuan K. 2002. "Convergence: Do Poor Countries Tend to Catch Up with the Rich?" *Australian Economic Review* 35, no. 2: 221–226.

De Long, J. Bradford. 1988. "Productivity Growth, Convergence, and Welfare: Comment." *American Economic Review* 78: 1138–1154.

Dowrick, Steve, and Muhammad Akmal. 2003. "Contradictory Trends in Global Income Inequality: A Tale of Two Biases." Unpublished paper presented at the UNU/WIDER Conference in Helsinki, Finland, May 2003.

Dube, S. C. 1988. *Modernization and Development: The Search for Alternative Paradigms.* London: Zed.

Durning, A. B. 1990. "Ending Poverty." In L. Starke, ed., *State of the World, 1990.* New York: Norton.

Firebaugh, Glenn. 1998. "Measuring Inequality: A Convenient Unifying Framework." Paper presented at the annual meeting of the Population Association of America, Chicago, April 2–4.

———. 1999. "Empirics of World Income Inequality." *American Journal of Sociology* 104, no. 6 (May): 1597–1630.

———. 2003. *The New Geography of Global Income Inequality* (Cambridge, MA: Harvard University Press).

Gilbert, M., and I. Kravis. 1954. *An International Comparison of National Products and the Purchasing Power of Currencies.* Paris: Organization for European Economic Cooperation.

———. 1958. *An International Comparison of Comparative National Products and Price Levels: A Study of Western Europe and the United States.* Paris: Organization for European Economic Cooperation.

Goesling, Brian. 2001. "Changing Income Inequalities Within and Between Nations: New Evidence." *American Sociological Review* 66, no. 5: 745–761.

Heston, A. 1973. "A Comparison of Some Short-Cut Methods of Estimating Real Product per Capita." *Review of Income and Wealth* (March): 79–104.

International Money Fund. 1980. *International Financial Statistics: Yearbook 1980.* Washington, DC.

———. 1984. *International Financial Statistics: Supplement on Output Statistics.* No. 8. Washington, DC.

Jackman, R. W. 1980. "A Note on the Measurement of Growth Rates in Cross-National Research." *American Journal of Sociology* 86: 604–610.

Katseli-Papaefstratiou, Louka T. 1979. *The Reemergence of the Purchasing Power Parity Doctrine in the 1970s.* Princeton: Princeton University Press.

Kirman, A., and L. Tomasini. 1969. "A New Look at International Income Inequalities." *Economia Internazionale* 22: 437–461.

Korzeniewicz, Roberto Patricio, and Timothy Patrich Moran. 1997. "World-Economic Trends in the Distribution of Income, 1965–1992." *American Journal of Sociology* 102: 1000–1039.

———. 2000. "Measuring World Income Inequalities." *American Journal of Sociology* 106: 209–214.

———. 2005. "Theorizing the Relationship Between Inequality and Economic Growth." *Theory and Society* 34: 277–316.

Kravis, I. B., Z. Kenessey, A. Heston, and R. Summers. 1975. *A System of International Comparisons of Gross Product and Purchasing Power.* Baltimore: Johns Hopkins University Press.

Kuznets, S. 1972. "The Gap: Concept, Measurement, Trends." In G. Ranis, ed., *The Gap Between Rich and Poor Nations.* London: Macmillan.

Loungani, Prakash. 2003. "Inequality: Now You See It, Now You Don't." *Finance and Development* (September): 22–23.

Lucas, Robert E. 1988. "On the Mechanics of Economic Development." *Journal of Monetary Economics* 22: 2–42.

Maddison, Angus. 1995. *Monitoring the World Economy.* Paris: Organization for Economic Cooperation and Development, Development Centre.

———. 2001. *The World Economy: A Millennial Perspective.* Paris: Organization for Economic Cooperation and Development.

Mankiw, N., David Romer Gregory, and David N. Weil. 1992. "A Contribution to the Empirics of Economic Growth." *Quarterly Journal of Economics* 107: 407–437.

Morawetz, D. 1977. *Twenty-Five Years of Economic Development: 1950–1975.* Washington, DC: World Bank.

Morris, M. D. 1979. *Measuring the Condition of the World's Poor: The Physical Quality of Life Index.* New York: Pergamon.

Peacock, Walter Gillis, Greg A. Hoover, and Charles D. Killian. 1988. "Divergence and Convergence in International Development: A Decomposition Analysis of Inequality in the World System." *American Sociological Review* 53: 838–852.

Pritchett, Lant. 1996. "Forget Convergence: Divergence Past, Present, and Future." *Finance and Development* 33, no. 2. http://www.imf.org/external/pubs/pubs/per.htm.

Ram, Rati. 1989. "Level of Development and Income Inequality: An Extension of Kuznets-Hypothesis to the World Economy." *Kyklos* 42: 73–88.

Reuveny, Rafael, and William Thompson. 2004. "World Economic Growth, Systemic Leadership, and Southern Debt Crisis." *Journal of Peace Research* 41, no. 1: 5–24.

Romer, Paul. 1994. "The Origins of Endogenous Growth." *Journal of Economic Perspectives* 8: 3–22.

Sen, Amartya. 2001. "If It's Fair, It's Good: 10 Truths About Globalization." *International Herald Tribune,* July 15.

Summers, R., and A. Heston. 1984. "Improved International Comparisons of Real Product and Its Composition: 1950–1980." *Review of Income and Wealth* 3 (September): 207–259.

———. 1988. "A New Set of International Comparisons of Real Product and Prices: Estimates for 130 Countries, 1950–1985." *Review of Income and Wealth* (March): 1–25.

Sutcliffe, Bob. 2002. "A More or Less Unequal World? World Income Inequality in the 20th Century." Unpublished manuscript.

Wade, Robert Hunter. 2001. "The Rising Inequality of World Income Distribution." *Finance and Development* 38, no. 4 (December). http://www.imf.org/external/pubs/ft/fandd/2013/09/index.htm.

Ward, M. 1985. *Purchasing Power Parities and Real Expenditures in the OECD.* Paris: Organization for Economic Cooperation and Development.

Whalley, John. 1979. "The Worldwide Income Distribution: Some Speculative Calculations." *Review of Income and Wealth* 25: 261–276.

Williamson, Jeffrey G. 1996. "Globalization, Convergence, and History." *Journal of Economic History* 56, no. 2: 277–306.

World Bank. 1988. *World Development Report.* Oxford: Oxford University Press.

———. 1992. *The World Tables of Economic and Social Indicators, 1960–86.* Washington, DC.

———. 2000. *World Development Indicators, 2000.* Washington, DC.

———. various years. *World Development Indicators Online.* http://data.worldbank.org/data-catalog/world-development-indicators.

6

The Economic Lives
of the Poor

Abhijit V. Banerjee and Esther Duflo

*W*hen discussing the gap between rich and poor countries, some
scholars have posed the question: How does one live on a dollar
a day? In this chapter, Abhijit Banerjee and Esther Duflo use the World
Bank's Living Standard Measurement Surveys and the Rand Corporation's
Family Life Surveys to answer that question. Surprisingly, the poor do not
put every available cent toward purchasing foodstuffs. The authors
examine the economic choices made by those living on $1 per day or less,
from spending on festivals, alcohol, and entertainment, to ownership of
assets such as land and houses. While this chapter does not answer what
causes the gap, it puts a human face on the numbers that represent the
gap. As the reader moves from one section of this book to the next, from
one explanation for the gap to the next, it may be useful to return to
this chapter and contemplate the complex lives of the poor.

IN WHAT TURNED OUT TO BE A RHETORICAL MASTER-MOVE, THE 1990
World Development Report from the World Bank defined the "extremely poor"
people of the world as those who are currently living on no more than $1 per
day per person, measured at the 1985 purchasing power parity (PPP) exchange
rate. In 1993, the poverty line was updated to $1.08 per person per day at the
1993 PPP exchange rate, which is the line we use in this paper. Poverty lines
have always existed—indeed $1 per day was chosen in part because of its

Reprinted with permission of the American Economic Association from the *Journal of Economic Perspectives* 21, no. 1 (2007): 141–143, 145–154, 161–165.

proximity to the poverty lines used by many poor countries. However the $1-a-day poverty line has come to dominate the conversations about poverty to a remarkable extent.

But how actually does one live on less than $1 per day? This essay is about the economic lives of the extremely poor: the choices they face, the constraints they grapple with, and the challenges they meet. The available evidence on the economic lives of the extremely poor is incomplete in many important ways. However, a number of recent data sets and a body of new research have added a lot to what we know about their lives, and taken together there is enough to start building an image of the way the extremely poor live their lives.

Our discussion of the economic lives of the extremely poor builds on household surveys conducted in 13 countries . . . : Cote d'Ivoire, Guatemala, India, Indonesia, Mexico, Nicaragua, Pakistan, Panama, Papua New Guinea, Peru, South Africa, Tanzania, and Timor Leste (East Timor). We mainly use the Living Standard Measurement Surveys (LSMS) conducted by the World Bank and the "Family Life Surveys" conducted by the Rand Corporation, all of which are publicly available. In addition, we also use two surveys that we conducted in India with our collaborators. The first was carried out in 2002 and 2003 in 100 hamlets of Udaipur District, Rajasthan (Banerjee, Deaton, and Duflo, 2004). Udaipur is one of the poorer districts of India, with a large tribal population and an unusually high level of female illiteracy. (At the time of the 1991 census, only 5 percent of women were literate in rural Udaipur.) Our second survey covered 2,000 households in "slums" (or informal neighborhoods) of Hyderabad, the capital of the state of Andhra Pradesh and one of the boomtowns of post-liberalization India (Banerjee, Duflo, and Glennerster, 2006). We chose these countries and surveys because they provide detailed information on extremely poor households around the world, from Asia to Africa to Latin America, including information on what they consume, where they work, and how they save and borrow. To flesh out our main themes further, we also draw freely on the existing research literature.

From each of these surveys we identified the extremely poor as those living in households where the consumption per capita is less than $1.08 per person per day, as well as the merely "poor" defined as those who live under $2.16 a day using 1993 purchasing power parity (PPP) as benchmark. In keeping with convention, we call these the $1 and $2 dollar poverty lines, respectively. The use of consumption, rather than income, is motivated by the better quality of the consumption data in these surveys (Deaton, 2004). . . .

How the Poor Spend Their Money

A common image of the extremely poor is that they have few real choices to make. Indeed, some people surely work as hard as they can—which may not be particularly hard, because they are underfed and weak and earn barely enough to cover their basic needs, which they always try to fulfill in the least expensive way. Historically, poverty lines in many countries were originally set to capture this definition of poverty—the budget needed to buy a certain amount of calories, plus some other indispensable purchases (such as housing). A "poor" person was essentially defined as someone without enough to eat.

Food and Other Consumption Purchases

Yet the average person living at under $1 per day does not seem to put every available penny into buying more calories. Among our 13 countries, food typically represents from 56 to 78 percent of consumption among rural households, and 56 to 74 percent in urban areas. For the rural poor in Mexico, slightly less than half the budget (49.6 percent) is allocated to food.

Of course, these people could be spending the rest of their money on other commodities they greatly need. Yet among the nonfood items that the poor spend significant amounts of money on, alcohol and tobacco show up prominently. The extremely poor in rural areas spent 4.1 percent of their budget on tobacco and alcohol in Papua New Guinea; 5.0 percent in Udaipur, India; 6.0 percent in Indonesia; and 8.1 percent in Mexico. However, in Guatemala, Nicaragua, and Peru, no more than 1 percent of the budget gets spent on these goods (possibly because the poor in these countries prefer other intoxicants).

Perhaps more surprisingly, spending on festivals is an important part of the budget for many extremely poor households. In Udaipur, over the course of the previous year, more than 99 percent of the extremely poor households spent money on a wedding, a funeral, or a religious festival. The median household spent 10 percent of its annual budget on festivals. In South Africa, 90 percent of the households living under $1 per day spent money on festivals. In Pakistan, Indonesia, and Cote d'Ivoire, more than 50 percent did likewise. Only in some Latin American countries in our sample—Panama, Guatemala, Nicaragua—are festivals not a notable part of the yearly expenditure for a significant fraction of the households. However, in the LSMS surveys, unlike the Udaipur survey, people are not asked to account separately for the food that they bought because of a festival. It is therefore probably no accident that the Udaipur spending on festivals is the highest across the surveys. The LSMS numbers would probably have been higher if data on food spending because of festivals had been directly collected in those surveys.

On the other hand, the under-$1-per-day households spend very little on forms of entertainment common in high-income countries such as movies, theater, or video shows. In all 13 countries in our sample, in the month preceding the survey the average extremely poor household spent less than 1 percent on any of these forms of entertainment. The comparable number for the United

States is 5 percent. We can only speculate about the roots of this difference. Has the importance given to festivals and other indigenous forms of entertainment crowded out movie going? Or is the answer as simple as a lack of access to movie theaters?

The propensity to own a radio or a television, a widespread form of entertainment for American households, varies considerably across low-income countries. For example, among rural households living under $1 per day, ownership of a radio is 11 percent in the Udaipur survey, almost 60 percent in Nicaragua and Guatemala, and above 70 percent in South Africa and Peru. Similarly, no one owns a television in Udaipur, but in Guatemala nearly a quarter of households do, and in Nicaragua, the percentage is closer to a half.

These phenomena of spending on festivals and ownership of radios or televisions appear to be related. In Udaipur, where the share spent on festivals is the highest, radio and television ownership is very low. In Pakistan, the fraction spent on festivals is 3.3 percent and only 30 percent have a radio. By contrast, in Nicaragua where among respectively the rural and the urban poor 57 and 38 percent have a radio and 21 percent and 19 percent own a television, very few households report spending anything on festivals. One wrinkle on this explanation is that the urban poor who are much more likely to own a television than the rural poor (60 versus 33 percent in Indonesia, 61 versus 10 percent in Peru, 38 versus 17 percent in South Africa), do not spend less on festivals than their rural counterparts. While this observation is based on only a few data points, it hints at the possibility of an unmet demand for entertainment among the rural poor—they might like to buy a television, but perhaps the television signal does not reach their neighborhoods.

In either case, the poor do see themselves as having a significant amount of choice, but they choose not to exercise that choice in the direction of spending more on food. The typical poor household in Udaipur could spend up to 30 percent more on food than it actually does, just based on what it spends on alcohol, tobacco, and festivals. Indeed, in most of the surveys the share spent on food is about the same for the poor and the extremely poor, suggesting that the extremely poor feel no extra compulsion to purchase more calories.

This conclusion echoes an old finding in the literature on nutrition: even the extremely poor do not seem to be as hungry for additional calories as one might expect. Deaton and Subramanian (1996), using 1983 data from the Indian state of Maharashtra, found that even for the poorest, a 1 percent increase on overall expenditure translates into about a two-thirds of a percent increase in the total food expenditure of a poor family. Remarkably, the elasticity is not very different for the poorest individuals in the sample and the richest (although nobody is particularly rich in this sample). The Deaton and Subramanian estimate is one of the higher estimates. Thomas and Strauss (1997) found an elasticity of demand for food with respect to expenditure per capita of about a quarter for the poorest Brazilians.

Another way to make the same point is to look at what edibles the extremely poor are buying. Deaton and Subramanian (1996) note that among grains, in terms of calories per rupee, the millets (jowar and bajra) are clearly the best buy. Yet in their data, only about two-thirds of the total spending on grains is on these grains, while another 20 percent is on rice, which costs more than twice as much per calorie, and a further 10 percent or so is spent on wheat, which is a 70 percent more expensive way to get calories. In addition, the poor spend almost 7 percent of their total budget on sugar, which is both more expensive than grains as a source of calories and bereft of other nutritional value. The same affinity for sugar also shows up in our Udaipur data, in which the poor spend almost 10 percent of their food budget on the category "sugar, salt, and other processed foods" (this does not include cooking oil, which makes up another 6 percent of the expenditures on food). Even for the extremely poor, for every 1 percent increase in the food expenditure, about half goes into purchasing more calories, and half goes into purchasing more expensive (and presumably better tasting) calories.

Finally, the trend seems to be to spend even less money on food. In India, for example, spending on food went from 70 percent in 1983 to 62 percent in 1999–2000, and the share of millet in the food budget dropped to virtually zero (Deaton, 2006). Not surprisingly, the poor are also consuming fewer calories over time (Meenakshi and Vishwanathan, 2003), though this change may also reflect that their work involves less physical effort (Jha, 2004).

The Ownership of Assets

While all the surveys have some information about assets, the list of assets varies. To obtain a relatively coherent list across countries, we focus on radios, televisions, and bicycles. The share of people who own these particular assets varies significantly across countries.

As we already discussed, ownership of radio and television varies from country to country, but is low in some countries. One reason may be the lack of signal. Another reason may be that a television is an expensive and lumpy transaction for which one has to save if one is born poor. We do see a fairly steep income gradient in the ownership of radio and television: In all countries, the share of rural households owning a television is substantially larger for those who live on less than $2 a day than those living on less than $1 a day. For example, the share owning a television increases from 14 percent for those living on $1 a day to 45 percent for those living on less than $2 a day in Cote d'Ivoire; from 7 to 17 percent in South Africa; and from 10 to 21 percent in Peru. This pattern has been observed in other contexts (Filmer and Pritchett, 2001) and has been the basis for using the lack of durable goods as a marker for poverty. Our data suggest that this proxy can be appropriate within a country, but it could easily be misleading in a cross-country comparison.

Among productive assets, land is the one that many people in the rural surveys seem to own, although enormous country-to-country variation exists. Only 4 percent of those living under $1 a day own land in Mexico, 1.4 percent in South Africa, 30 percent in Pakistan, 37 percent in Guatemala, 50 percent in Nicaragua and Indonesia, 63 percent in Cote d'Ivoire, 65 percent in Peru, and 85 percent in Panama. In the Udaipur sample, 99 percent of the households below $1 a day own some land in addition to the land on which their house is built, although much of it is dry scrubland that cannot be cultivated for most of the year. However, when the extremely poor do own land, the plots tend to be quite small. The median landholding among the poor who own land is one hectare or less in Udaipur, Indonesia, Guatemala, and Timor; between one and two hectares in Peru, Tanzania, Pakistan; and between two and three hectares in Nicaragua, Cote d'Ivoire, and Panama.

Apart from land, extremely poor households in rural areas tend to own very few durable goods, including productive assets: 34 percent own a bicycle in Cote d'Ivoire, but less than 14 percent in Udaipur, Nicaragua, Panama, Papua New Guinea, Peru, and East Timor. In Udaipur, where we have detailed asset data, most extremely poor households have a bed or a cot, but only about 10 percent have a chair or a stool and 5 percent have a table. About half have a clock or a watch. Fewer than 1 percent have an electric fan, a sewing machine, a bullock cart, a motorized cycle of any kind, or a tractor. No one has a phone. As we will see below, this situation does not mean that most of these households are employees and have little use for such assets. On the contrary, many extremely poor households operate their own businesses, but do so with almost no productive assets.

The Pursuit of Health and Well-being

Should we worry about the fact that the poor are buying less food than they could? According to Deaton and Subramanian (1996), the poorest people—the ones in the bottom decile in terms of per capita expenditure—consume on average slightly less than 1400 calories a day. This level is about half of what the Indian government recommends for a man with moderate activity, or a woman with heavy physical activity (see http://www.fao.org/documents/show_cdr.asp ?url_file=/ DOCREP/x0172e/x0172e02.htm). The shortfall seems enormous. The Udaipur data, which include other health indicators, suggest that health is definitely reason for concern.

Among the extremely poor in Udaipur, only 57 percent report that the members of their household had enough to eat throughout the year. Among the poor adults in Udaipur, the average "body mass index" (that is, weight in kilograms divided by the square of the height in meters) is 17.8. Sixty-five percent of adult men and 40 percent of adult women have a body mass index below

18.5, the standard cutoff for being underweight (WHO expert consultation, 2004). Moreover, 55 percent of the poor adults in Udaipur are anemic, which means they have an insufficient number of red blood cells. The poor are frequently sick or weak. In Udaipur, 72 percent report at least one symptom of disease and 46 percent report an illness which has left them bedridden or necessitated a visit to the doctor over the last month. Forty-three percent of the adults and 34 percent of the adults aged under 50 report difficulty carrying out at least one of their "activities of daily living," such as working in the field, walking, or drawing water from a well. Diarrhea is extremely frequent among children. About one-seventh of the poor have vision problems, which may be caused by either poor nutrition, or the diseases that afflict them, or a combination of the two.

Detailed information on health is not available in all the surveys, but most report the incidence over the last month of health episodes that left a household member bedridden for a day or more, or that required a household member to see a doctor. The general pattern is a remarkably high level of morbidity. Among the rural poor living under $1 a day in Peru, South Africa, East Timor, Panama, and Tanzania, between 11 and 15 percent of households report having a member either being bedridden for at least a day or requiring a doctor. The number is between 21 and 28 percent in Pakistan, Indonesia, and Cote d'Ivoire, and between 35 and 46 percent in Nicaragua, Udaipur, and Mexico.

Even these high numbers may be an understatement if the poor are less prone to recall and report such sicknesses than those with higher incomes. The poor generally do not complain about their health—but then they also do not complain about life in general, either. While the poor certainly feel poor, their levels of self-reported happiness or self-reported health levels are not particularly low (Banerjee, Duflo, and Deaton, 2004). On the other hand, the poor do report being under a great deal of stress, both financial and psychological. In Udaipur, about 12 percent say that there has been a period of one month or more in the last year in which they were so "worried, tense, or anxious" that it interfered with normal activities like sleeping, working, and eating. Case and Deaton (2005) compare data from South Africa to the data from Udaipur and data from the United States. They find that the answers of poor South Africans and poor Indians about stress look very similar, while reported levels of stress are very much lower in the United States. The most frequently cited reason for such tensions is health problems (cited by 29 percent of respondents), with lack of food and death coming next (13 percent each). Over the last year, in 45 percent of the extremely poor households in Udaipur (and 35 percent of those living under $2 a day) adults had to cut the size of their meal at some point during the year and in 12 percent of them, children had to cut the size of their meals. In the extremely poor households under $1 per day, 37 percent report that, at some point in the past year, the adults in the household went without a meal for an entire day. Cutting meals is also strongly correlated with unhappiness.

Even poor households should be able to save enough to make sure that they never have to cut meals, because as discussed above they do have substantial slack in their budgets and cutting meals is not that common. Additional savings would also make it easier to deal with healthcare emergencies. For these households, saving a bit more would seem like a relatively inexpensive way to reduce stress.

Investment in Education

The extremely poor spend very little on education. The expenditure on education generally hovers around 2 percent of household budgets: higher in Pakistan (3 percent), Indonesia (6 percent), and Cote d'Ivoire (6 percent), but much lower in Guatemala (0.1 percent), and South Africa (0.8 percent). The fraction does not really change very much when we compare the poor to the extremely poor, or rural areas to urban areas, though in a few countries like Pakistan, urban families spend substantially more than rural families. This low level of expenditure on education is not because the children are out of school. In 12 of the 13 countries in our sample, with the exception of Cote d'Ivoire, at least 50 percent of both boys and girls aged 7 to 12 in extremely poor households are in school. In about half the countries, the proportion enrolled is greater than 75 percent among girls, and more than 80 percent among boys.

The reason education spending is low is that children in poor households typically attend public schools or other schools that do not charge a fee. In countries where poor households spend more on education, it is typically because government schools have fees, as in Indonesia and Cote d'Ivoire. However, mounting evidence, reported below, suggests that public schools in these countries are often dysfunctional, which could explain why even very poor parents in Pakistan are pulling their children out.

How the Poor Earn Their Money

Walking down the main street of the biggest slum in the medium-sized southern Indian city of Guntur at nine in the morning, the first thing one notices are the eateries. In front of every sixth house that directly faced the road, by our count, a woman was sitting behind a little kerosene stove with a round cast-iron griddle roasting on it. Every few minutes someone would walk up to her and order a *dosa,* the rice and beans pancakes that almost everyone eats for breakfast in south India. She would throw a cupful of the batter on the griddle, swirl it around to cover almost the entire surface, and drizzle some oil around the edges. A minute or two later, she would slide an off-white pock-marked pancake off the griddle, douse it in some sauce, fold it in a newspaper or a banana leaf and hand it to her client, in return for a rupee (roughly 15 cents).

When we walked back down that same street an hour later, the women were gone. We found one inside her house, filling her daughter's plate with lunch that she had cooked while making the dosas. She told us that later that day, she was going out to vend her saris, the long piece of decorative cloth that Indian women drape around themselves. She gets plain nylon saris from the shop and stitches beads and small shiny pieces on them. Once a week, she takes them from house to house, hoping that women would buy them to wear on special occasions. And they do buy them, she said confidently. All the other *dosa* women we met that day had a similar story: once they are done frying *dosas*, they do something else. Some collect trash; others make pickles to sell; others work as laborers.

Entrepreneurship and Multiple Occupations among the Poor

All over the world, a substantial fraction of the poor act as entrepreneurs in the sense of raising capital, carrying out investment, and being the full residual claimants for the resulting earnings. In Peru, 69 percent of the households who live under $2 a day in urban areas operate a nonagricultural business. In Indonesia, Pakistan, and Nicaragua, the numbers are between 47 and 52 percent. A large fraction of the rural poor operate a farm: 25 to 98 percent of the households who earn less than a dollar a day report being self-employed in agriculture, except in Mexico and South Africa where self-employment in agriculture is very rare. Moreover, many of the rural poor—from 7 percent in Udaipur up to 36 percent in Panama—also operate a nonagricultural business.

Many poor households have multiple occupations. Like the *dosa* women of Guntur, 21 percent of the households living under $2 a day in Hyderabad who have a business actually have more than one, while another 13 percent have both a business and a laborer's job. This multiplicity of occupations in urban areas is found in many other countries as well, though not everywhere. Among those earning less than $2 a day, 47 percent of the urban households in Cote d'Ivoire and Indonesia get their income from more than one source; 36 percent in Pakistan; 20.5 percent in Peru; and 24 percent in Mexico. However, in urban South Africa and Panama, almost no one has more than one occupation and only 9 percent do so in Nicaragua and Timor Leste.

This pattern of multiple occupations is stronger in rural areas. In Udaipur district, as we discussed earlier, almost everybody owns some land and almost everybody does at least some agriculture. Yet only 19 percent of the households describe self-employment in agriculture as the main source of their income. Working on someone else's land is even rarer, with only 1 percent reporting this as their main source of income. In other words, the poor cultivate the land they own, no less and usually, no more. Yet, agriculture is not the mainstay of most of these households. The most common occupation for the poor in Udaipur is working as a daily laborer: 98 percent of households living under $1 per day in rural areas report doing this, and 74 percent claim it is their main source of earnings.

This pattern is confirmed by data from a smaller survey of 27 villages randomly sampled from eight districts in West Bengal (Banerjee, 2006). In this survey, even households that claim to be the operators for a plot of land spend only 40 percent of their time in agricultural activities on their own land. The fraction is not very different for men and women—women do less direct agricultural work but more animal rearing, along with growing fruits and vegetables. Their other activities include teaching, sewing and embroidery, unpaid household work, and gathering fuel. Strikingly, almost 10 percent of the time of the average household is spent on gathering fuel, either for use at home or for sale. The median family in this survey has three working members and seven occupations.

In most of the Living Standard Measurement Surveys, households are not asked their main source of earnings, but the pattern of diversification among rural households is apparent nevertheless. In Guatemala, 65 percent of the rural extremely poor say they get some income from self-employment in agriculture, 86 percent work as laborers outside agriculture, and 24 percent are self-employed outside agriculture. In Indonesia, 34 percent of the rural, extremely poor households work as laborers outside of agriculture, and 37 percent earn income from self-employment outside of agriculture. In Pakistan, 51 percent of the rural, extremely poor earn income from labor outside of agriculture and 35 percent from a business outside of agriculture. Overall, the fraction of the rural extremely poor households who report that they conduct more than one type of activity to earn a living is 50 percent in Indonesia, 72 percent in Cote d'Ivoire, 84 percent in Guatemala, and 94 percent in Udaipur. It is smaller, but not negligible—between 10 and 20 percent—in Nicaragua, Panama, Timor Leste, and Mexico. Once again, an exception to this general pattern is South Africa, where less than 1 percent of the rural poor or extremely poor report multiple occupations.

Temporary Migration to Work

Where do rural households, which are often a walk of a half-hour or more from the nearest road, find all this nonagricultural work? They migrate.

Temporary migration is rarely documented in surveys, but in the Udaipur survey, which had questions about this activity, 60 percent of the poorest households report that someone from their family had lived outside for a part of the year to obtain work. For 58 percent of the families, the head of the household had migrated. The migrants typically complete multiple trips in a year. However, people do not leave for very long. The median length of a completed migration is one month, and only 10 percent of migration episodes exceed three months. Nor do most of the migrants travel very far: 28 percent stay in the district of Udaipur and only 42 percent leave the state of Rajasthan.

Permanent migration for work reasons is rare, although many women move when they marry. Even if we look at households currently living in urban areas, where the inflow of immigrants is presumably higher than in rural areas, the share of extremely poor households who had one member that was born elsewhere and had migrated for work reasons was just 4 percent in Pakistan, 6 percent in Cote d'Ivoire, 6 percent in Nicaragua, and almost 10 percent in Peru. The 1991 Census of India reports that only 14.7 percent of the male population lives somewhere other than where they were born. Indonesia is the only country in our data where the proportion is higher: 41 percent of the urban households came from elsewhere. Indonesia is also the only country in this sample where migration was explicitly subsidized.

Lack of Specialization

A pattern seems to emerge. Poor families do seek out economic opportunities, but they tend not to become too specialized. They do some agriculture, but not to the point where it would afford them a full living (for example, by buying/renting/sharecropping more land). They also work outside, but only in short bursts, and they do not move permanently to their place of occupation.

This lack of specialization has its costs. Many of these poor households receive most of their earnings from these outside jobs, despite only being away for 18 weeks of the year on average (in the case of Udaipur). As short-term migrants, they have little chance of learning their jobs better, or ending up in a job that suits their specific talents, or being promoted.

Even the nonagricultural businesses that the poor operate typically require relatively few specific skills. For example, the businesses in Hyderabad include 11 percent tailors, 8 percent fruit and vegetable sellers, 17 percent small general stores, 6.6 percent telephone booths, 4.3 percent auto owners, and 6.3 percent milk sellers. Except for tailoring, none of these jobs require the high levels of specialized competence that take a long time to acquire, and therefore are associated with higher earnings. In several ways, the poor are trading off opportunities to have higher incomes.

The Problem of Scale

The businesses of the poor typically operate at a remarkably small scale. As we saw, the average landholding for those who own land is usually quite tiny, and renting land is infrequent. Furthermore, most of this land is not irrigated and cannot be used all year.

The scale of nonagricultural businesses run by the poor also tends to be small. In the 13 countries in our sample, the median business operated by people living under $2 dollars a day either in a rural or an urban location has no paid staff, and the average number of paid employees range between 0.14 in rural Nicaragua to 0.53 in urban Panama. Businesses are operated on average by 1.38 (in Peru) to 2.59 (in Cote d'Ivoire) people—most of them being family members. Most of these businesses have very few assets as well. In Hyderabad, only 20 percent of the businesses operate out of a separate room. In Pakistan, about 40 percent of the businesses of those living under $1 or $2 dollars a day have a vehicle, but only 4 percent have a motorized vehicle and none have any machinery. In other countries, even nonmotorized vehicles are rare. In Hyderabad, where we have an exhaustive list of business assets, the most common assets are tables, scales, and pushcarts.

Many of these businesses are probably operating at too small a scale for efficiency. The women making dosas spend a lot of time waiting: having fewer dosa-makers who do less waiting would be more efficient. In fact, it might make sense in efficiency terms for the dosa-makers to work in pairs: one to make the dosas and one to wrap them and make change.

References

Banerjee, Nirmala. 2006. "A Survey of Occupations and Livelihoods of Households in West Bengal," Sachetana. Unpublished paper.

Banerjee, Abhijit, Angus Deaton, and Esther Duflo. 2004. "Wealth, Health, and Health Services in Rural Rajasthan." *American Economic Review,* 94(2): 326–30.

Banerjee, Abhijit, Esther Duflo, and Rachel Glennerster. 2006. "A Snapshot of Micro Enterprises in Hyderabad," Unpublished paper, MIT.

Case, Anne, and Deaton, Angus. 2005. "Health and Wealth among the Poor: India and South Africa Compared." *American Economic Review Papers and Proceedings,* 95(2): 229–33.

Deaton, Angus. 2004. "Measuring Poverty." In *Understanding Poverty,* ed. Abhijit Banerjee, Roland Benabou, and Dilip Mookherjee. Oxford University Press.

Deaton, Angus. 2006. "Purchasing Power Parity Exchange Rates for the Poor: Using Household Surveys to Construct PPPs." http://www.princeton.edu/~rpds/down loads/Deaton_PPPP_version_aug_06.pdf.

Deaton, Angus, David Cutler, and Adriana Lleras-Muney. 2006. "The Determinants of Mortality." *Journal of Economic Perspectives,* Summer, 20(3): 97–120.

Deaton, Angus, and Shankar Subramanian. 1996. "The Demand for Food and Calories." *Journal of Political Economy,* 104(1): 133–62.

Duflo, Esther, Michael Kremer, and Jonathan Robinson. 2006. "Why Don't Farmers use Fertilizer: Evidence from Field Experiments." Unpublished paper, MIT.

Duflo, Esther, Rachel Glennerster, Daniel Keniston, Stuti Khemani, and Marc Shotland. 2006. "Can Information Campaigns Raise Awareness and Local Participation in Primary Education? A Study of Jaipur District in Uttar Pradesh." http://econ-www.mit.edu/faculty/download_pdf.php?id=1425.

Fafchamps, Marcel, and Forhad Shilpi. 2006 "Subjective Welfare, Isolation, and Relative Consumption." http://www.economics.ox.ac.uk/members/marcel.fafchamps/homepage/nepwel.pdf.

Filmer, Deon, and Lant Pritchett. 2001. "Estimating Wealth Effects without Expenditure Data—or Tears: An Application to Educational Enrollments in States of India." *Demography,* 38(1): 115–32.

Jha, Raghavendra. 2004. "Calories Deficiency in Rural India in the Last Three Quinquennial Rounds of the NSS." http://eprints.anu.edu.au/archive/00001701/.

Meenakshi, J.V., and Brinda Vishwanathan. 2003. "Calorie Deprivation in Rural India, 1983–1999/2000." *Economic and Political Weekly,* January 25, pp. 369–75.

Munshi, K., and M. Rosenzweig. 2005. "Why is Social Mobility in India so Low? Social Insurance, Inequality, and Growth." BREAD [Bureau for Research and Economic Analysis of Development] Working Paper 097.

Thomas, D., and J. Strauss. 1997. "Health and Wages: Evidence on Men and Women in Urban Brazil." *Journal of Econometrics,* 77(1): 159–85.

Thomas, Duncan, et al. 2004. "Causal Effect of Health on Labor Market Outcomes: Evidence from a Random Assignment Iron Supplementation Intervention," Mimeo, UCLA, http://www.ccpr.ucla.edu/ccprwpseries/ccpr_022_04.

World Health Organization Expert Consultation. 2004. "Appropriate Body-Mass Index for Asian Populations and Its Implications for Policy and Intervention Strategies." *Lancet,* 363(9403): 157–63.

Part 2

Historical Origins
of the Gap

7

The World Economy: A Millennial Perspective

Angus Maddison

*A*ngus Maddison has long been one of the most prominent economic historians, providing development scholars with some of the most reliable historical data with which to judge long-term economic growth patterns. In this chapter, Maddison discusses world economic growth since 1000 C.E. Maddison provides evidence that after reaching a low point around 1000, Western Europe began to grow such that it surpassed the production per capita of the rest of the world by the year 1500. After this point the gap between Western Europe and the rest of the world widened. By 1820 Western Europe produced about twice that produced by the rest of the world and from that point on, the gap grew very rapidly. In Part 4 of this book, we turn to convergence theory, which proposes that over the long run, per capita incomes will converge. Maddison's conclusions suggest that the long-term pattern is one marked by divergence rather than convergence.

GDP Per Capita

Long-term estimates of world GDP are very recent. Research on real income growth by quantitative economic historians has been heavily concentrated on Europe, and generally confined to the past two centuries. Until recently what was known about earlier centuries was in large degree conjectural.

Reprinted with permission of the OECD from *The World Economy: A Millennial Perspective*, pp. 44–48. Copyright © 2001 by the OECD.

Maddison (1995) contained detailed estimates for different parts of the world economy for 1820 onwards, with a very crude provisional assessment for 1500 to 1820. Here I have made a much more careful scrutiny of the evidence for centuries before 1820 and incorporated the results of Maddison (1998) on Chinese economic performance over two millennia.

The level and movement of per capita GDP is the primary general purpose indicator of changes in well-being and production potential, but one should keep in mind that per capita consumption has increased less over the long run because of the increased share of product allocated to investment and government. Labour productivity does not always move parallel to per capita income. The advances achieved in Sung China (960–1279) and in Japan in the seventeenth and eighteenth centuries required substantial increases in per capita labour effort. In the twentieth century we find the opposite phenomenon. Labour input per person fell substantially in Western Europe and Western Offshoots.

Table 7.1 summarises my findings for the past millennium. It shows clearly the exceptionalism of Western Europe's very lengthy ascension, and origins of the great divergence between the West (Group A) and the rest of the world (Group B).

The major conclusions I draw from the long-term quantitative evidence are as follows:

(a) West European income was at a nadir around the year 1000. Its level was significantly lower than it had been in the first century. It was below that in China, India and other parts of East and West Asia;

(b) There was a turning point in the eleventh century when the economic ascension of Western Europe began. It proceeded at a slow pace, but by 1820 real income had tripled. The locus and characteristics of economic leadership changed. The North Italian city states and, in particular, Venice initiated the growth process and reopened Mediterranean trade. Portugal and Spain opened trade routes to the Americas and Asia, but were less dynamic than the Netherlands which became the economic leader around 1600, followed by the United Kingdom in the nineteenth century;

(c) Western Europe overtook China (the leading Asian economy) in per capita performance in the fourteenth century. Thereafter China and most of the rest of Asia were more or less stagnant in per capita terms until the second half of the twentieth century. The stagnation was initially due to indigenous institutions and policy, reinforced by colonial exploitation which derived from Western hegemony and was most marked from the eighteenth century onwards;

(d) West European appropriation of the natural resources of North America, introduction of European settlers, technology and organisation added a substantial new dimension to Western economic ascension from the eighteenth century onwards. Towards the end of the nineteenth century, the United States became the world economic leader;

Table 7.1a   Growth of Per Capita GDP by Major Region, 1000–1998 (annual average compound growth rate)

	1000–1500	1500–1600	1600–1700	1700–1820	1820–1998
Western Europe	0.13	0.14	0.15	0.15	1.51
Western Offshoots	0.00	0.00	0.17	0.78	1.75
Japan	0.03	0.03	0.09	0.13	1.93
Average Group A	0.11	0.13	0.12	0.18	1.67
Latin America	0.01	0.09	0.19	0.19	1.22
Eastern Europe & Former USSR	0.04	0.10	0.10	0.10	1.06
Asia (excluding Japan)	0.05	0.01	–0.01	0.01	0.92
Africa	–0.01	0.00	0.00	0.04	0.67
Average Group B	0.04	0.02	0.00	0.03	0.95

Table 7.1b   Level of Per Capita GDP, Groups A and B, 1000–1998 (1990 international dollars)

	1000	1500	1600	1700	1820	1998
Average Group A	405	704	805	907	1,130	21,470
Average Group B	440	535	548	551	573	3,102

Table 7.1c   Population of Groups A and B, 1000–1998 (millions)

	1000	1500	1600	1700	1820	1998
Total Group A	35	76	95	110	175	838
Total Group B	233	362	461	493	866	5,069

Table 7.1d   GDP of Groups A and B, 1000–1998 (billions of 1990 international dollars)

	1000	1500	1600	1700	1820	1998
Total Group A	14.1	53.2	76.1	100.0	198.0	17,998
Total Group B	102.7	194.0	252.9	271.8	496.5	15,727

Source: Appendix B [of original text; not included here].

(e) Japan was an exception to the Asian norm. In the course of the seventeenth, eighteenth and the first half of the nineteenth century, it caught up with and overtook China in per capita income. The Meiji takeover in 1868 involved massive institutional change aimed at catching up with the West. This was achieved in income terms in the 1980s, but not yet in productivity;

(f) The colonial takeover in Latin America had some analogy to that in North America, but Iberian institutions were less propitious to capitalist development than those in North America. Latin America included a much larger indigenous population which was treated as an underclass without access to land or education. The social order was not greatly changed after independence.

Over the long run the rise in per capita income was much smaller than in North America, but faster than in Asia or Africa;

(g) African per capita income was lower in 1820 than in the first century. Since then there has been slower advance than in all other regions. The income level in 1998 was little better than that of Western Europe in 1820. Population growth is now faster than in any other region—eight times as fast as in Western Europe;

(h) The most dynamic growth performance has been concentrated on the past two centuries. Since 1820 per capita income has risen 19-fold in Group A, and more than 5-fold in the rest of the world—dwarfing any earlier advance and compressing it into a very short time span.

One may ask what is new in these findings. In the first place there is the quantification which clarifies issues that qualitative analysis leaves fuzzy. It helps to separate stylised facts from the stylised fantasies which are sometimes perceived to be reality. It is more readily contestable and likely to be contested. It sharpens scholarly discussion, and contributes to the dynamics of the research process. It is also useful to have a world picture because it helps to identify what is normal and what is exceptional.

My findings differ in some respects from earlier interpretations of the length and pace of Western Europe's economic ascension. There has been a general tendency to date it from 1500 when Europeans encountered America and first made a direct entry into the trading world of Asia. Max Weber attributed Europe's advance to the rise of Protestantism, and this thesis attracted attention because it was congruent with the conventional wisdom about the beginning of the European ascension. I no longer believe that there was a sharp break in the pace of advance of per capita income around 1500.

Kuznets (1966, Chapter 1) suggested that "modern economic growth" is a distinctive economic epoch preceded by merchant capitalism in Western Europe "from the end of the fifteenth to the second half of the eighteenth century," and an "antecedent epoch of feudal organisation." In Kuznets (1973, pp. 139–41), he advanced what seemed to be a reasonable view about the rate of per capita GDP growth in Western Europe in the merchant capitalist period. In Maddison (1995), I accepted Kuznets' hypothesis for his merchant capitalist period, but I now believe that growth was slower then than Kuznets suggested, and that the pace of advance between the eleventh and the fifteenth centuries was not much different. For this reason, it does not seem valid to distinguish between epochs of "feudal organisation" and "merchant capitalism." Instead I would characterise the whole period 1000–1820 as "proto-capitalist."

I also differ from Kuznets on the timing of the transition to what he called "modern economic growth" (which I call "capitalist development"). The evidence now available suggests that the transition took place around 1820 rather than in 1760. The revisionist work of Crafts (1983 and 1992) and others has helped to break the old notion of a sudden take-off in the second half of the eighteenth century in England. Recent research on the Netherlands shows income to have been higher there than in the United Kingdom at the end of the eighteenth century. Work in the past twenty years on the quantitative history of other West European countries provides further reason for postdating the transition and modifying the old emphasis on British exceptionalism.

My analysis of US economic performance shows a rapid advance in the eighteenth century in contrast to the findings of Gallman (1972) and Mancall and Weiss (1999). The essential reason for the difference is that I include rough estimates of the indigenous population and its GDP as well as the activity of European settlers (I also did this for Australia, Canada and New Zealand).

My assessment of Japanese development differs from the conventional wisdom. I have quantified its economic performance in the Tokugawa period and compared it with China. Most analysts concentrate on comparisons between Japan and Western Europe in the Meiji period, and ignore the Asian context.

Gerschenkron (1965) and Rostow (1960 and 1963) both emphasised the idea that "take-offs" were staggered throughout the nineteenth century in West European countries. Kuznets (1979, p. 131) endorsed this view. In fact growth acceleration was more synchronous in Western Europe than they believed.

There are two schools of thought about the relative performance of Europe and Asia. The mainstream view was clearly expressed by Adam Smith in 1776. He was not a practitioner of political arithmetic but on the basis of the "price of labour" and other evidence, his ordinal ranking from the top downwards was as follows for the 1770s: Netherlands, England, France, British North American colonies, Scotland, Spain, Spanish colonies in America, China, Bengal (depressed by the East India Company's plundering).

This mainstream view is reflected in Landes (1969, pp. 13–14) whose overall assessment, like that of Smith, was similar to mine. "Western Europe was already rich before the Industrial Revolution—rich by comparison with other parts of the world of that day. This wealth was the product of centuries of slow accumulation, based in turn on investment, the appropriation of extra-European resources and labour, and substantial technological progress, not only in the production of material goods, but in the organisation and financing of their exchange and distribution . . . it seems clear that over the near-millennium from the year 1000 to the eighteenth century, income per head rose appreciably—perhaps tripled."

In Maddison (1983), I contrasted the Landes view with Bairoch's (1981) assessment of relative income per head. He suggested that China was well ahead of Western Europe in 1800, Japan and the rest of Asia only 5 per cent lower than Europe, Latin America well ahead of North America, and Africa about two thirds of the West European level. This highly improbable scenario was never documented in the case of Asia, Latin America or Africa. His figures for these areas were essentially guesstimates. Bairoch consistently took the position that the third world had been impoverished by the rich countries (see Bairoch, 1967), and he was, in fact, fabricating ammunition for this hypothesis (see the critique of Chesnais, 1987).

In spite of its shaky foundations, Bairoch's assessment has been influential. Braudel (1985, vol. 3, pp. 533–34) acknowledged "the great service Paul Bairoch has rendered to historians" and believed "it is virtually beyond question that Europe was less rich than the worlds it was exploiting, even after the fall of Napoleon." Andre Gunder Frank (1998, pp. 171 and 284) cites Bairoch and suggests that "around 1800 Europe and the United States, after long lagging behind, suddenly caught up and then overtook Asia economically and politically. Pomeranz (2000) cites Bairoch more cautiously (p. 16) but his sinophilia drives him to the same conclusion. He suggests (p. 111), there is "little reason to think that West Europeans were more productive than their contemporaries in various other densely populated regions of the Old World prior to 1750 or even 1800."

Maddison (1983) contrasted the assessments of Landes and Bairoch and commented: "These remarkably different quantitative conclusions have very different analytical implications. If Bairoch is right, then much of the backwardness of the third world presumably has to be explained by colonial exploitation, and much less of Europe's advantage can be due to scientific precocity, centuries of slow accumulation, and organisational and financial prosperity."

In view of the laborious efforts I have since made to accumulate quantitative evidence on this topic, I now conclude that Bairoch and his epigoni are quite wrong. To reject them is not to deny the role of colonial exploitation, but this can be better understood by taking a more realistic view of Western strength and Asian weakness around 1800.

The major problem in growth analysis is to explain why such a large divergence developed between the advanced capitalist group and the rest of the world. There are, of course, some examples of past convergence, e.g., Europe's rise from its nadir to overtake China, the Japanese catch-up with China in Tokugawa times, and subsequently with the advanced capitalist group. Western Europe achieved a very substantial degree of catch-up on the United States in the golden age after the second world war; resurgent Asia (China, India, the so-called tigers and others) have narrowed their degree of backwardness substantially over the past quarter century.

In attempting to understand the causes of divergence and the possibilities for catch-up in different parts of the world economy, there is no universal schema which covers the whole millennium. The operative forces have varied between place and period.

References

Bairoch, P. 1981. "The Main Trends in National Economic Disparities since the Industrial Revolution." Pp. 3–17 in *Disparities in Economic Development since the Industrial Revolution,* edited by P. Bairoch and M. Levy-Leboyer. Macmillan, London.

Bairoch, P. 1967. *Diagnostic de l'évolution économique du tiers-monde 1900–1966,* Gauthiers-Villars, Paris.

Braudel. F. 1985. *Civilisation and Capitalism, 15th–18th Century,* 3 vols., Fontana, London.

Chesnais, J.-C. 1987. *La Revanche du Tiers-Monde,* Laffont, Paris.

Crafts, N.F.R. 1983. "British Economic Growth, 1700–1831: A Review of the Evidence," *Economic History Review,* May, pp. 177–199.

Crafts, N.F.R., and C. K. Harley. 1992. "Output Growth and the British Industrial Revolution: A Restatement of the Crafts-Harley View," *Economic History Review,* November, pp. 703–730.

Frank. A.G. 1998. *Reorient: Global Economy in the Asian Age,* University of California Press, Berkeley.

Gallman, R.E. 1972. "The Pace and Pattern of American Economic Growth," in Davis and Associates.

Gerschenkron, A. 1965. *Economic Backwardness in Historical Perspective,* Praeger, New York.

Kuznets, S. 1979, *Growth, Population and Income Distribution,* Norton, New York.

Kuznets, S. 1973. *Population, Capital and Growth: Selected Essays,* Norton, New York.

Kuznets, S. 1966. *Modern Economic Growth,* Yale.

Landes, D.S. 1969. *The Unbound Prometheus,* Cambridge University Press, Cambridge.

Maddison, A. 1998. *Chinese Economic Performance in the Long Run,* OECD Development Centre, Paris.

Maddison, A. 1995. *Monitoring the World Economy 1820–1992,* OECD Development Centre, Paris.

Maddison, A. 1983. "A Comparison of Levels of GDP Per Capita in Developed and Developing Countries, 1700–1980," *Journal of Economic History,* March, pp. 27–41.

Mancall, Peter C., and Thomas Weiss. 1999. "Was Economic Growth Likely in Colonial British North America?" *Journal of Economic History,* Vol. 59, Issue 1, pp. 17–40.

Pomeranz, K. 2000. *The Great Divergence,* Princeton University Press, Princeton.

Rostow, W.W. 1963. *The Economics of Takeoff into Sustained Growth,* Macmillan, London.

Rostow, W.W. 1960. *The Stages of Economic Growth,* Cambridge University Press, Cambridge.

8

Why Did Human History Unfold Differently on Different Continents?

Jared Diamond

This chapter reflects a new debate over how the gap came into existence and why certain countries are the ones that are now rich. In other words, why did development occur and wealth amass in Europe and not in sub-Saharan Africa? This is the question addressed by Jared Diamond in his tremendously influential book, Guns, Germs, and Steel. *Diamond's appeal went well beyond the academic world, landing the book on the* New York Times *bestseller list and winning him a Pulitzer Prize. The book opens with Diamond being asked by a villager in a developing country, why had Europeans developed so much material wealth while people in his region had developed so little? Diamond then begins to weave his geographic explanation for why development first began to occur in the West. The following excerpt is from a lecture by Diamond in which he offers a brief overview of the arguments offered in* Guns, Germs, and Steel.

I'VE SET MYSELF THE MODEST TASK OF TRYING TO EXPLAIN THE BROAD pattern of human history, on all the continents, for the last 13,000 years. Why did history take such different evolutionary courses for peoples of different continents? This problem has fascinated me for a long time, but it's now ripe for a new synthesis because of recent advances in many fields seemingly remote from history, including molecular biology, plant and animal genetics and biogeography, archaeology, and linguistics.

As we all know, Eurasians, especially peoples of Europe and eastern Asia, have spread around the globe, to dominate the modern world in wealth and power. Other peoples, including most Africans, survived, and have thrown off European domination but remain behind in wealth and power. Still other peoples, including the original inhabitants of Australia, the Americas, and southern Africa, are no longer even masters of their own lands but have been decimated, subjugated, or exterminated by European colonialists. Why did history turn out that way, instead of the opposite way? Why weren't Native Americans, Africans, and Aboriginal Australians the ones who conquered or exterminated Europeans and Asians?

This big question can easily be pushed back one step further. By the year A.D. 1500, the approximate year when Europe's overseas expansion was just beginning, peoples of the different continents already differed greatly in technology and political organization. Much of Eurasia and North Africa was occupied then by Iron Age states and empires, some of them on the verge of industrialization. Two Native American peoples, the Incas and Aztecs, ruled over empires with stone tools and were just starting to experiment with bronze. Parts of sub-Saharan Africa were divided among small indigenous Iron Age states or chiefdoms. But all peoples of Australia, New Guinea, and the Pacific islands, and many peoples of the Americas and sub-Saharan Africa, were still living as farmers or even still as hunter/gatherers with stone tools.

Obviously, those differences as of A.D. 1500 were the immediate cause of the modern world's inequalities. Empires with iron tools conquered or exterminated tribes with stone tools. But how did the world evolve to be the way that it was in the year A.D. 1500?

This question too can be easily pushed back a further step, with the help of written histories and archaeological discoveries. Until the end of the last Ice Age around 11,000 B.C., all humans on all continents were still living as Stone Age hunter/gatherers. Different rates of development on different continents, from 11,000 B.C. to A.D. 1500, were what produced the inequalities of A.D. 1500. While Aboriginal Australians and many Native American peoples remained Stone Age hunter/gatherers, most Eurasian peoples, and many peoples of the Americas and sub-Saharan Africa, gradually developed agriculture, herding, metallurgy, and complex political organization. Parts of Eurasia, and one small area of the Americas, developed indigenous writing as well. But each of these new developments appeared earlier in Eurasia than elsewhere.

So, we can finally rephrase our question about the evolution of the modern world's inequalities as follows. Why did human development proceed at such different rates on different continents for the last 13,000 years? Those differing rates constitute the broadest pattern of history, the biggest unsolved problem of history, and my subject today.

Historians tend to avoid this subject like the plague, because of its apparently racist overtones. Many people, or even most people, assume that the answer involves biological differences in average IQ among the world's populations, despite the fact that there is no evidence for the existence of such IQ differences. Even to ask the question why different peoples had different histories strikes some of us as evil, because it appears to be justifying what happened in history. In fact, we study the injustices of history for the same reason that we study genocide, and for the same reason that psychologists study the minds of murderers and rapists: not in order to justify history, genocide, murder, and rape, but instead to understand how those evil things came about, and then to use that understanding so as to prevent their happening again. In case the stink of racism still makes you feel uncomfortable about exploring this subject, just reflect on the underlying reason why so many people accept racist explanations of history's broad pattern: we don't have a convincing alternative explanation. Until we do, people will continue to gravitate by default to racist theories. That leaves us with a huge moral gap, which constitutes the strongest reason for tackling this uncomfortable subject.

Let's proceed continent-by-continent. As our first continental comparison, let's consider the collision of the Old World and the New World that began with Christopher Columbus's voyage in A.D. 1492, because the proximate factors involved in that outcome are well understood. I'll now give you a summary and interpretation of the histories of North America, South America, Europe, and Asia from my perspective as a biogeographer and evolutionary biologist—all that in ten minutes; two minutes per continent. . . .

Most of us are familiar with the stories of how a few hundred Spaniards under Cortés and Pizarro overthrew the Aztec and Inca Empires. The populations of each of those empires numbered tens of millions. We're also familiar with the gruesome details of how other Europeans conquered other parts of the New World. The result is that Europeans came to settle and dominate most of the New World, while the Native American population declined drastically from its level as of A.D. 1492. Why did it happen that way? Why didn't it instead happen that the Emperor Montezuma or Atahuallpa led the Aztecs or Incas to conquer Europe?

The proximate reasons are obvious. Invading Europeans had steel swords, guns, and horses, while Native Americans had only stone and wooden weapons and no animals that could be ridden. Those military advantages repeatedly enabled troops of a few dozen mounted Spaniards to defeat Indian armies numbering in the thousands.

Nevertheless, steel swords, guns, and horses weren't the sole proximate factors behind the European conquest of the New World. Infectious diseases introduced with Europeans, like smallpox and measles, spread from one Indian tribe to another, far in advance of Europeans themselves, and killed an estimated 95% of the New World's Indian population. Those diseases were endemic in Europe, and Europeans had had time to develop both genetic and immune resistance to them, but Indians initially had no such resistance. That role played by infectious diseases in the European conquest of the New World was duplicated in many other parts of the world, including Aboriginal Australia, southern Africa, and many Pacific islands.

Finally, there is still another set of proximate factors to consider. How is it that Pizarro and Cortés reached the New World at all, before Aztec and Inca conquistadors could reach Europe? That outcome depended partly on technology in the form of oceangoing ships. Europeans had such ships, while the Aztecs and Incas did not. Also, those European ships were backed by the centralized political organization that enabled Spain and other European countries to build and staff the ships. Equally crucial was the role of European writing in permitting the quick spread of accurate detailed information, including maps, sailing directions, and accounts by earlier explorers, back to Europe, to motivate later explorers.

So far, we've identified a series of proximate factors behind European colonization of the New World: namely, ships, political organization, and writing that brought Europeans to the New World; European germs that killed most Indians before they could reach the battlefield; and guns, steel swords, and horses that gave Europeans a big advantage on the battlefield. Now, let's try to push the chain of causation back further. Why did these proximate advantages go to the Old World rather than to the New World? Theoretically, Native Americans might have been the ones to develop steel swords and guns first, to develop oceangoing ships and empires and writing first, to be mounted on domestic animals more terrifying than horses, and to bear germs worse than smallpox.

The part of that question that's easiest to answer concerns the reasons why Eurasia evolved the nastiest germs. It's striking that Native Americans evolved no devastating epidemic diseases to give to Europeans, in return for the many devastating epidemic diseases that Indians received from the Old World. There are two straightforward reasons for this gross imbalance. First, most of our familiar epidemic diseases can sustain themselves only in large dense human populations concentrated into villages and cities, which arose much earlier in the Old World than in the New World. Second, recent studies of microbes, by molecular biologists, have shown that most human epidemic diseases evolved from similar epidemic diseases of the dense populations of Old World domestic animals with which we came into close contact. For example, measles and TB evolved from diseases of our cattle, influenza from a disease of pigs, and smallpox possibly from a disease of camels. The Americas had very few native domesticated animal species from which humans could acquire such diseases.

Let's now push the chain of reasoning back one step further. Why were there far more species of domesticated animals in Eurasia than in the Americas? The Americas harbor over a thousand native wild mammal species, so you might initially suppose that the Americas offered plenty of starting material for domestication.

In fact, only a tiny fraction of wild mammal species has been successfully domesticated, because domestication requires that a wild animal fulfill many prerequisites: the animal has to have a diet that humans can supply; a rapid growth rate; a willingness to breed in captivity; a tractable disposition; a social structure involving submissive behavior towards dominant animals and humans; and lack of a tendency to panic when fenced in. Thousands of years ago, humans domesticated every possible large wild mammal species fulfilling all those criteria and worth domesticating, with the result that there have been no valuable additions of domestic animals in recent times, despite the efforts of modern science.

Eurasia ended up with the most domesticated animal species in part because it's the world's largest land mass and offered the most wild species to begin with. That preexisting difference was magnified 13,000 years ago at the end of the last Ice Age, when most of the large mammal species of North and South America became extinct, perhaps exterminated by the first arriving Indians. As a result, Native Americans inherited far fewer species of big wild mammals than did Eurasians, leaving them only with the llama and alpaca as a domesticate. Differences between the Old and New Worlds in domesticated plants, especially in large-seeded cereals, are qualitatively similar to these differences in domesticated mammals, though the difference is not so extreme.

Another reason for the higher local diversity of domesticated plants and animals in Eurasia than in the Americas is that Eurasia's main axis is east/west, whereas the main axis of the Americas is north/south. Eurasia's east/west axis meant that species domesticated in one part of Eurasia could easily spread thousands of miles at the same latitude, encountering the same day length and climate to which they were already adapted. As a result, chickens and citrus fruit domesticated in Southeast Asia quickly spread westward to Europe; horses domesticated in the Ukraine quickly spread eastward to China; and the sheep, goats, cattle, wheat, and barley of the Fertile Crescent quickly spread both west and east.

In contrast, the north/south axis of the Americas meant that species domesticated in one area couldn't spread far without encountering day lengths and climates to which they were not adapted. As a result, the turkey never spread from its site of domestication in Mexico to the Andes; llamas and alpacas never spread from the Andes to Mexico, so that the Indian civilizations of Central and North America remained entirely without pack animals; and it took thousands of years for the corn that evolved in Mexico's climate to become modified into a corn adapted to the short growing season and seasonally changing day length of North America.

Eurasia's domesticated plants and animals were important for several other reasons besides letting Europeans develop nasty germs. Domesticated plants and animals yield far more calories per acre than do wild habitats, in which most species are inedible to humans. As a result, population densities of farmers and herders are typically ten to a hundred times greater than those of hunter/gatherers. That fact alone explains why farmers and herders everywhere in the world have been able to push hunter/gatherers out of land suitable for farming and herding. Domestic animals revolutionized land transport. They also revolutionized agriculture, by letting one farmer plough and manure much more land than the farmer could till or manure by the farmer's own efforts. Also, hunter/gatherer societies tend to be egalitarian and to have no political organization beyond the level of the band or tribe, whereas the food surpluses and storage made possible by agriculture permitted the development of stratified, politically centralized societies with governing elites. Those food surpluses also accelerated the development of technology, by supporting craftspeople who didn't raise their own food and who could instead devote themselves to developing metallurgy, writing, swords, and guns.

Thus, we began by identifying a series of proximate explanations—guns, germs, and so on—for the conquest of the Americas by Europeans. Those proximate factors seem to me ultimately traceable in large part to the Old World's greater number of domesticated plants, much greater number of domesticated animals, and east/west axis. The chain of causation is most direct in explaining the Old World's advantages of horses and nasty germs. But domesticated plants and animals also led more indirectly to Eurasia's advantage in guns, swords, oceangoing ships, political organization, and writing, all of which were products of the large, dense, sedentary, stratified societies made possible by agriculture.

Let's next examine whether this scheme, derived from the collision of Europeans with Native Americans, helps us understand the broadest pattern of African history, which I'll summarize in five minutes. I'll concentrate on the history of sub-Saharan Africa, because it was much more isolated from Eurasia by distance and climate than was North Africa, whose history is closely linked to Eurasia's history. Here we go again:

Just as we asked why Cortés invaded Mexico before Montezuma could invade Europe, we can similarly ask why Europeans colonized sub-Saharan Africa before sub-Saharans could colonize Europe. The proximate factors were the same familiar ones of guns, steel, oceangoing ships, political organization, and writing. But again, we can ask why guns and ships and so on ended up being developed in Europe rather than in sub-Saharan Africa. To the student of human evolution, that question is particularly puzzling, because humans have been evolving for millions of years longer in Africa than in Europe, and even anatomically modern *Homo sapiens* may have reached Europe from Africa only within the last 50,000 years. If time were a critical factor in the development of human societies, Africa should have enjoyed an enormous head start and advantage over Europe.

Again, that outcome largely reflects biogeographic differences in the availability of domesticable wild animal and plant species. Taking first domestic animals, it's striking that the sole animal domesticated within sub-Saharan Africa was (you guessed) a bird, the Guinea fowl. All of Africa's mammalian domesticates—cattle, sheep, goats, horses, even dogs—entered sub-Saharan Africa from the north, from Eurasia or North Africa. At first that sounds astonishing, since we now think of Africa as the continent of big wild mammals. In fact, none of those famous big wild mammal species of Africa proved domesticable. They were all disqualified by one or another problem such as: unsuitable social organization, intractable behavior, slow growth rate, and so on. Just think what the course of world history might have been like if Africa's rhinos and hippos had lent themselves to domestication! If that had been possible, African cavalry mounted on rhinos or hippos would have made mincemeat of European cavalry mounted on horses. But it couldn't happen.

Instead, as I mentioned, the livestock adopted in Africa were Eurasian species that came in from the north. Africa's long axis, like that of the Americas, is north/south rather than east/west. Those Eurasian domestic mammals spread southward very slowly in Africa, because they had to adapt to different climate zones and different animal diseases.

The difficulties posed by a north/south axis to the spread of domesticated species are even more striking for African crops than they are for livestock. Remember that the food staples of ancient Egypt were Fertile Crescent and Mediterranean crops like wheat and barley, which require winter rains and seasonal variation in day length for their germination. Those crops couldn't spread south in Africa beyond Ethiopia, beyond which the rains come in the summer and there's little or no seasonal variation in day length. Instead, the development of agriculture in the sub-Sahara had to await the domestication of native African plant species like sorghum and millet, adapted to Central Africa's summer rains and relatively constant day length.

Ironically, those crops of Central Africa were for the same reason then unable to spread south to the Mediterranean zone of South Africa, where once again winter rains and big seasonal variations in day length prevailed. The southward advance of native African farmers with Central African crops halted in Natal, beyond which Central African crops couldn't grow—with enormous consequences for the recent history of South Africa.

In short, a north/south axis and a paucity of wild plant and animal species suitable for domestication were decisive in African history, just as they were in Native American history. Although native Africans domesticated some plants in the Sahel and in Ethiopia and in tropical West Africa, they acquired valuable domestic animals only later, from the north. The resulting advantages of Europeans in guns, ships, political organization, and writing permitted Europeans to colonize Africa, rather than Africans to colonize Europe.

9

Institutions Rule: The Primacy of Institutions over Geography and Integration in Economic Development

Dani Rodrik, Arvind Subramarian, and Francesco Trebbi

In the previous chapter Jared Diamond proposed a geographic explanation for the origins of the gap. In this chapter the authors identify three contending explanations for the origins of the gap: (1) the geographic explanation, as represented by Diamond's work; (2) expansion of and participation in international trade; and (3) the establishment of effective government and the respect of private property. The authors conclude that "geography is not destiny." They then cautiously describe the varied policies and institutions that promote economic success.

AVERAGE INCOME LEVELS IN THE WORLD'S RICHEST AND POOREST NA-tions differ by a factor of more than 100. Sierra Leone, the poorest economy for which we have national income statistics, has a per-capita GDP of $490, compared to Luxembourg's $50,061. What accounts for these differences, and what (if anything) can we do to reduce them? It is hard to think of any question in economics that is of greater intellectual significance, or of greater relevance to the vast majority of the world's population.

Excerpted from Dani Rodrik, Arvind Subramarian, and Francesco Trebbi, "Institutions Rule: The Primacy of Institutions over Geography and Integration in Economic Development," *Journal of Economic Growth* 9 (November 2004): 131–165. Reprinted by permission.

In the voluminous literature on this subject, three strands of thought stand out. First, there is a long and distinguished line of theorizing that places *geography* at the center of the story. Geography is a key determinant of climate, endowment of natural resources, disease burden, transport costs, and diffusion of knowledge and technology from more advanced areas. It exerts therefore a strong influence on agricultural productivity and the quality of human resources. Recent writings by Jared Diamond and Jeffrey Sachs are among the more notable works in this tradition. . . .

A second camp emphasizes the role of international trade as a driver of productivity change. We call this the *integration* view, as it gives market integration, and impediments thereof, a starring role in fostering economic convergence between rich and poor regions of the world.

Finally, a third group of explanations centers on *institutions,* and in particular the role of property rights and the rule of law. In this view, what matters are the rules of the game in a society and their conduciveness to desirable economic behavior.

Growth theory has traditionally focused on physical and human capital accumulation, and, in its endogenous growth variant, on technological change. But accumulation and technological change are at best proximate causes of economic growth. No sooner have we ascertained the impact of these two on growth—and with some luck their respective roles also—that we want to ask: But why did some societies manage to accumulate and innovate more rapidly than others? The three-fold classification offered above—geography, integration, and institutions—allows us to organize our thoughts on the "deeper" determinants of economic growth. These three are the factors that determine which societies will innovate and accumulate, and therefore develop, and which will not.

Since long-term economic development is a complex phenomenon, the idea that any one (or even all) of the above deep determinants can provide an adequate accounting of centuries of economic history is, on the face of it, preposterous. Historians and many social scientists prefer nuanced, layered explanations where these factors interact with human choices and many other not-so-simple twists and turns of fate. But economists like parsimony. We want to know how well these simple stories do, not only on their own or collectively, but more importantly, vis-à-vis each other. How much of the astounding variation in cross-national incomes around the world can geography, integration, and institutions explain? . . .

Trade fundamentalists and institutionalists have a considerably more difficult job to do, since they have to demonstrate causality for their preferred determinant, as well as identify the effective channel(s) through which it works. For the former, the task consists of capturing the direct impact of integration on income and the indirect impact through institutions, respectively, are the relevant ones, while feedbacks from incomes and institutions, respectively, are relatively insignificant. Reverse causality cannot be ruled out easily, since expanded trade and integration can be mainly the result of increased productivity in the economy and/or improved domestic institutions, rather than a cause thereof.

Institutionalists, meanwhile, have to worry about different kinds of reverse causality. They need to show that improvements in property rights, the rule of law, and other aspects of the institutional environment are an independent determinant of incomes . . . and are not simply the consequence of higher incomes . . . or of greater integration. . . .

Acemoglu, Johnson, and Robinson (AJR, 2001) use mortality rates of colonial settlers as an instrument for institutional quality. They argue that settler mortality had an important effect on the type of institutions that were built in lands that were colonized by the main European powers. Where the colonizers encountered relatively few health hazards to European settlement, they erected solid institutions that protected property rights and established the rule of law. In other areas, their interests were limited to extracting as much resources as quickly as possible, and they showed little interest in building high-quality institutions. Under the added assumption that institutions change only gradually over time, AJR argue that settler mortality rates are therefore a good instrument for institutional quality.

Our approach in this paper consists of using the Frankel and Romer and Acemoglu instruments simultaneously. . . .

This exercise yields some sharp and striking results. Most importantly, we find that the quality of institutions trumps everything else. Once institutions are controlled for, integration has no direct effect on incomes, while geography has at best weak direct effects. Trade often enters the income regression with the "wrong" (i.e., negative) sign, as do many of the geographical indicators. By contrast, our measure of property rights and the rule of law always enters with the correct sign, and is statistically significant, often with t-statistics that are very large. . . .

Our estimates indicate that an increase in institutional quality of one standard deviation, corresponding roughly to the difference between measured institutional quality in Bolivia and South Korea, produces a 2 log-points rise in per-capita incomes, or a 6.4-fold difference—which, not coincidentally, is also roughly the income difference between the two countries. . . .

We also use a large number of alternative indicators of geography, integration, and institutions. To get a sense of the magnitude of the potential impacts, we can compare two countries, say Nigeria and Mauritius, both in Africa. If the OLS [ordinary least squares] relationship is indeed causal, the coefficients . . . would suggest that Mauritius's per capita GDP should be 5.2 times that of Nigeria, of which 21 percent would be due to better institutions, 65 percent due to greater openness, and 14 percent due to better location. In practice, Mauritius's income ($11,400) is 14.8 times that of Nigeria ($770).

What Does It All Mean?

A. An instrument does not a theory make. One reading of the AJR paper, and the one strongly suggested by their title—"The Colonial Origins of Comparative Development"—is that they regard experience under the early period of colonization as a fundamental determinant of current income levels. While the AJR paper is certainly suggestive on this score, in our view this interpretation of the paper's central message would not be entirely correct. One problem is that AJR do not carry out a direct test of the impact of colonial policies and institutions. Furthermore, if colonial experience were the key determinant of income levels, how would we account for the variation in incomes among countries that had never been colonized by the Europeans? . . .

B. The primacy of institutional quality does not imply policy ineffectiveness. Easterly and Levine (2002) assert that (macroeconomic) policies do not have an effect on incomes, once institutions are controlled for. Our view on the effectiveness of policy is similar to that expressed in AJR (2001, 1395): there are "substantial economic gains from improving institutions, for example as in the case of Japan during the Meiji Restoration or South Korea during the 1960s" or, one may add, China since the late 1970s. The distinction between institutions and policies is murky, as these examples illustrate. The reforms that Japan, South Korea, and China undertook were policy innovations that eventually resulted in a fundamental change in the institutional underpinning of their economies. . . .

This suggests that it is inappropriate to regress income levels on institutional quality *and* policies, as Easterly and Levine (2002) do. The problem is not just that incomes move slowly while policies can take sudden turns. In principle this could be addressed by taking long-term averages of policies. (Easterly and Levine average their policy measures over a number of decades.) It is that measures of institutional quality already contain all the relevant information about the impact of policies. . . .

Moreover, a geography theory of institutions can understate the impact that policies can play in changing them over time. As an empirical matter, institutions have changed remarkably in the last three decades. . . .

A purely geographical theory of institutions would have difficulty in accounting for these changes. Indeed, if the first-stage regressions reported in Panel C of Table 2 [of the original work] are run over the last three decades, the coefficient on settler mortality declines from 0.94 in the 1970s to 0.87 in the 1980s and 0.71 in the 1990s, illustrating the mutability of institutions, and the declining importance of history (on the AJR interpretation of settler mortality) or geography (on the EL interpretation of settler mortality) in explaining the cross-national variation in institutions.

C. The hard work is still ahead. How much guidance do our results provide to policymakers who want to improve the performance of their economies? Not much at all. Sure, it is helpful to know that geography is not destiny,

Table 9.1 Determinants of Development: Core Specifications, Ordinary Least Squares Estimates

| | | | | | Log GDP per Capita | | | | |
| | Acemoglu et al. Sample | | | Extended Acemoglu et al. Sample | | | Large Sample | | |
Dependent variable	(1)	(2)	(3)	(4)	(5)	(6)	(7)	(8)	(9)
Geography (DISTEQ)	0.74 (4.48)*	0.20 (1.34)	0.32 (1.85)**	0.80 (5.22)*	0.22 (1.63)	0.33 (2.11)**	0.76 (10.62)*	0.20 (2.48)**	0.23 (2.63)*
Institutions (RULE)		0.78 (7.56)*	0.69 (6.07)*		0.81 (9.35)*	0.72 (6.98)*		0.81 (12.12)*	0.78 (10.49)*
Integration (LCOPEN)			0.16 (1.48)			0.15 (1.53)			0.08 (1.24)
Observations	64	64	64	79	79	79	137	137	137
R-square	0.25	0.57	0.59	0.26	0.61	0.62	0.42	0.71	0.71

Notes: The dependent variable is per capita GDP in 1995, PPP basis. There are three samples for which the core regressions are run: (i) the first three columns correspond to the sample of 64 countries in Acemoglu et al. (2001); (ii) columns (4)–(6) use a sample of 79 countries for which data on settler mortality (LOGEM4) have been compiled by Acemoglu et al.; and (iii) columns (7)–(9) use a larger sample of 137 countries. The regressors are: (i) DISTEQ, the variable for geography, which is measured as the absolute value of latitude of a country; (ii) Rule of Law (RULE), which is the measure for institutions; and (iii) LCOPEN, the variable for integration, which is measured as the ratio of nominal trade to nominal GDP. All regressors, except DISTEQ and RULE, in the three panels are in logs. See the Appendix [in the original text] for more detailed variable definitions and sources. *T-statistics* are reported under coefficient estimates. Significance at the 1, 5, and 10 percent levels is denoted respectively by *, **, and ***.

or that focusing on increasing the economy's links with world markets is unlikely to yield convergence. But the operational guidance that our central result on the primacy of institutional quality yields is extremely meager.

We illustrate the difficulty of extracting policy-relevant information from our findings using the example of property rights. Obviously, the presence of clear property rights for investors is a key, if not the key, element in the institutional environment that shapes economic performance. Our findings indicate that when investors believe their property rights are protected, the economy ends up richer. But nothing is implied about the actual form that property rights should take. We cannot even necessarily deduce that enacting a *private* property-rights regime would produce superior results compared to alternative forms of property rights.

If this seems stretching things too far, consider the experiences of China and Russia. China still retains a socialist legal system, while Russia has a regime of private property rights in place. Despite the absence of formal private property rights, Chinese entrepreneurs have felt sufficiently secure to make large investments, making that country the world's fastest growing economy over the last two decades. In Russia, by contrast, investors have felt insecure, and private investment has remained low. . . . Credibly signaling that property rights will be protected is apparently more important than enacting them into law as a formal private property rights regime.

So our findings do not map into a determinate set of policy desiderata. Indeed, there is growing evidence that desirable institutional arrangements have a large element of context specificity, arising from differences in historical trajectories, geography, political economy, or other initial conditions. . . . [T]his could help explain why successful developing countries—China, South Korea, and Taiwan among others—have almost always combined unorthodox elements with orthodox policies. It could also account for why important institutional differences persist among the advanced countries of North America, Western Europe, and Japan—in the role of the public sector, the nature of the legal systems, corporate governance, financial markets, labor markets, and social insurance mechanisms, among others.

Consequently, there is much to be learned still about what improving institutional quality means on the ground. This, we would like to suggest, is a wide open area of research. Cross-national studies of the present type are just a beginning that point us in the right direction.

References

Acemoglu, Daron, Simon Johnson, and James A. Robinson. 2001. "The Colonial Origins of Comparative Development: An Empirical Investigation," *American Economic Review*, 91, 5, December, 1369–1401.

Diamond, Jared. 1997. *Guns, Germs, and Steel*. New York: W. W. Norton & Co.

Easterly, W., and R. Levine. 2002. "Tropics, Germs, and Crops: How Endowments Influence Economic Development," mimeo, Center for Global Development and Institute for International Economics.

Rodrik, Dani. 2003. "Institutions, Integration, and Geography: In Search of the Deep Determinants of Economic Growth," in Rodrik, ed., *In Search of Prosperity: Analytic Country Studies on Growth*. Princeton, NJ: Princeton University Press.

10

The Colonial Origins of Comparative Development

Daron Acemoglu, Simon Johnson, and James Robinson

This chapter provides strong evidence that the contemporary gap between rich and poor nations has its origins in the colonial period. According to the authors, two very different kinds of colonies were established by the European powers. One of these was the "extractive state," in which the main goal of the colonizing power was to transfer as much wealth as possible back home to the imperial power. In those states, the institutions that emerged did not protect private property or provide for checks on authority. In contrast, "neo-European" colonies emerged with an emphasis on local development, protection of private property, and strong checks on the power of authorities. According to the authors, the kind of state that formed determined its long-run development success. If this argument is supported by subsequent research, then it suggests that the gap between rich and poor nations was actually predetermined centuries ago.

WHAT ARE THE FUNDAMENTAL CAUSES OF THE LARGE DIFFERENCES IN INcome per capita across countries? Although there is still little consensus on the answer to this question, differences in institutions and property rights have received considerable attention in recent years. Countries with better "institutions,"

Excerpted from Daron Acemoglu, Simon Johnson, and James A. Robinson, "The Colonial Origins of Comparative Development: An Empirical Investigation," *American Economic Review* 91, no. 5 (2001): 1369–1401. Reprinted with permission. The authors' notes have been deleted.

more secure property rights, and less distortionary policies will invest more in physical and human capital, and will use these factors more efficiently to achieve a greater level of income. . . .

At some level it is obvious that institutions matter. Witness, for example, the divergent paths of North and South Korea, or East and West Germany, where one part of the country stagnated under central planning and collective ownership, while the other prospered with private property and a market economy. Nevertheless, we lack reliable estimates of the effect of institutions on economic performance. It is quite likely that rich economies choose or can afford better institutions. Perhaps more important, economies that are different for a variety of reasons will differ both in their institutions and in their income per capita. To estimate the impact of institutions on economic performance, we need a source of exogenous variation in institutions. In this paper, we propose a theory of institutional differences among countries colonized by Europeans, and exploit this theory to derive a possible source of exogenous variation. Our theory rests on three premises:

1. There were different types of colonization policies which created different sets of institutions. At one extreme, European powers set up "extractive states," exemplified by the Belgian colonization of the Congo. These institutions did not introduce much protection for private property, nor did they provide checks and balances against government expropriation. In fact, the main purpose of the extractive state was to transfer as much of the resources of the colony to the colonizer. At the other extreme, many Europeans migrated and settled in a number of colonies, creating what the historian Alfred Crosby (1986) calls "Neo-Europes." The settlers tried to replicate European institutions, with strong emphasis on private property and checks against government power. Primary examples of this include Australia, New Zealand, Canada, and the United States.

2. The colonization strategy was influenced by the feasibility of settlements. In places where the disease environment was not favorable to European settlement, the cards were stacked against the creation of Neo-Europes, and the formation of the extractive state was more likely.

3. The colonial state and institutions persisted even after independence. Colonies where Europeans faced higher mortality rates are today substantially poorer than colonies that were healthy for Europeans. Our theory is that this relationship reflects the effect of settler mortality working through the institutions brought by Europeans. . . .

The Hypothesis and Historical Background

We hypothesize that settler mortality affected settlements; settlements affected early institutions; and early institutions persisted and formed the basis of current institutions. In this section, we discuss and substantiate this hypothesis. The next subsection discusses the link between mortality rates of settlers and settlement decisions, then we discuss differences in colonization policies, and finally, we turn to the causes of institutional persistence.

Mortality and Settlements

There is little doubt that mortality rates were a key determinant of European settlements. Curtin (1964, 1998) documents how both the British and French press informed the public of mortality rates in the colonies. Curtin (1964) also documents how early British expectations for settlement in West Africa were dashed by very high mortality among early settlers, about half of whom could be expected to die in the first year. In the "Province of Freedom" (Sierra Leone), European mortality in the first year was 46 percent, in Bulama (April 1792–April 1793) there was 61 percent mortality among Europeans. In the first year of the Sierra Leone Company (1792–1793), 72 percent of the European settlers died. On Mungo Park's Second Expedition (May–November 1805), 87 percent of Europeans died during the overland trip from Gambia to the Niger, and all the Europeans died before completing the expedition.

An interesting example of the awareness of the disease environment comes from the Pilgrim fathers. They decided to migrate to the United States rather than Guyana because of the high mortality rates in Guyana (see Crosby 1986, pp. 143–44). Another example comes from the Beauchamp Committee in 1795, set up to decide where to send British convicts who had previously been sent to the United States. One of the leading proposals was the island of Lemane, up the Gambia River. The committee rejected this possibility because they decided mortality rates would be too high even for the convicts. Southwest Africa was also rejected for health reasons. The final decision was to send convicts to Australia.

The eventual expansion of many of the colonies was also related to the living conditions there. In places where the early settlers faced high mortality rates, there would be less incentive for new settlers to come.

Types of Colonization and Settlements

The historical evidence supports both the notion that there was a wide range of different types of colonization and that the presence or absence of European settlers was a key determinant of the form colonialism took. Historians, including Robinson and Gallagher (1961), Gann and Duignan (1962), Denoon (1983), and Cain and Hopkins (1993), have documented the development of "settler colonies," where Europeans settled in large numbers, and life was modeled after the home country. Denoon (1983) emphasizes that settler colonies had representative institutions which promoted what the settlers wanted and that what they wanted was freedom and the ability to get rich by engaging in trade. He argues that "there was undeniably something capitalist in the structure of these colonies. Private ownership of land and livestock was well established very early . . ." (p. 35).

When the establishment of European-like institutions did not arise naturally, the settlers were ready to fight for them against the wishes of the home country. Australia is an interesting example here. Most of the early settlers in Australia were ex-convicts, but the land was owned largely by ex-jailors, and there was no legal protection against the arbitrary power of landowners. The settlers wanted institutions and political rights like those prevailing in England at the time. They demanded jury trials, freedom from arbitrary arrest, and electoral representation. Although the British government resisted at first, the settlers argued that they were British and deserved the same rights as in the home country (see Robert Hughes 1987). Cain and Hopkins write (1993, p. 237): "from the late 1840s the British bowed to local pressures and, in line with observed constitutional changes taking place in Britain herself, accepted the idea that, in mature colonies, governors should in future form ministries from the majority elements in elected legislatures." They also suggest that "the enormous boom in public investment after 1870 [in New Zealand] . . . was an attempt to build up an infrastructure . . . to maintain high living standards in a country where voters expected politicians actively to promote their economic welfare" (p. 225).

This is in sharp contrast to the colonial experience in Latin America during the seventeenth and eighteenth centuries, and in Asia and Africa during the nineteenth and early twentieth centuries. The main objective of the Spanish and the Portuguese colonization was to obtain gold and other valuables from America. Soon after the conquest, the Spanish crown granted rights to land and labor (the encomienda) and set up a complex mercantilist system of monopolies and trade regulations to extract resources from the colonies.

Europeans developed the slave trade in Africa for similar reasons. Before the mid-nineteenth century, colonial powers were mostly restricted to the African coast and concentrated on monopolizing trade in slaves, gold, and other valuable commodities—witness the names used to describe West African countries: the Gold Coast, the Ivory Coast. Thereafter, colonial policy was driven in part by an element of superpower rivalry, but mostly by economic motives. Michael Crowder (1968, p. 50), for example, notes: "it is significant that Britain's largest colony on the West Coast [Nigeria] should have been the one where her traders were most active and bears out the contention that, for Britain . . . flag followed trade." Lance E. Davis and Robert A. Huttenback (1987, p. 307) conclude that "the colonial Empire provides strong evidence for the belief that government was attuned to the interests of business and willing to divert resources to ends that the business community would have found profitable." They find that before 1885 investment in the British empire had a return 25 percent higher than that on domestic investment, though afterwards the two converged. Andrew

Roberts (1976, p. 193) writes: "[from] . . . 1930 to 1940 Britain had kept for itself 2,400,000 pounds in taxes from the Copperbelt, while Northern Rhodesia received from Britain only 136,000 pounds in grants for development." Similarly, Patrick Manning (1982) estimates that between 1905 and 1914, 50 percent of GDP in Dahomey was extracted by the French, and Crawford Young (1994, p. 125) notes that tax rates in Tunisia were four times as high as in France.

Probably the most extreme case of extraction was that of King Leopold of Belgium in the Congo. Gann and Duignan (1979, p. 30) argue that following the example of the Dutch in Indonesia, Leopold's philosophy was that "the colonies should be exploited, not by the operation of a market economy, but by state intervention and compulsory cultivation of cash crops to be sold to and distributed by the state at controlled prices." Jean-Philippe Peemans (1975) calculates that tax rates on Africans in the Congo approached 60 percent of their income during the 1920s and 1930s. Bogumil Jewsiewicki (1983) writes that during the period when Leopold was directly in charge, policy was "based on the violent exploitation of natural and human resources," with a consequent "destruction of economic and social life . . . [and] . . . dismemberment of political structures."

Overall, there were few constraints on state power in the nonsettler colonies. The colonial powers set up authoritarian and absolutist states with the purpose of solidifying their control and facilitating the extraction of resources. Young (1994, p. 101) quotes a French official in Africa: "the European commandant is not posted to observe nature. . . . He has a mission . . . to impose regulations, to limit individual liberties . . . , to collect taxes." Manning (1988, p. 84) summarizes this as: "In Europe the theories of representative democracy won out over the theorists of absolutism. . . . But in Africa, the European conquerors set up absolutist governments, based on reasoning similar to that of Louis XIV."

Institutional Persistence

There is a variety of historical evidence, as well as our regressions, suggesting that the control structures set up in the nonsettler colonies during the colonial era persisted, while there is little doubt that the institutions of law and order and private property established during the early phases of colonialism in Australia, Canada, New Zealand, the United States, Hong Kong, and Singapore have formed the basis of the current-day institutions of these countries.

Young emphasizes that the extractive institutions set up by the colonialists persisted long after the colonial regime ended. He writes: "although we commonly described the independent polities as 'new states,' in reality they were successors to the colonial regime, inheriting its structures, its quotidian routines and practices, and its more hidden normative theories of governance" (1994, p. 283). An example of the persistence of extractive state institutions into the independence era is provided by the persistence of the most prominent extractive policies. In Latin America, the full panoply of monopolies and regulations, which had been created by Spain, remained intact after independence, for most of the nineteenth century. Forced labor policies persisted and were even intensified or reintroduced with the expansion of export agriculture in the latter part of the nineteenth century. Slavery persisted in Brazil until 1886, and during the sisal boom in Mexico, forced labor was reintroduced and persisted up to the start of the revolution in 1910. Forced labor was also reintroduced in Guatemala and El Salvador to provide labor for coffee growing. In the Guatemalan case, forced labor lasted until the creation of democracy in 1945. Similarly, forced labor was reinstated in many independent African countries, for example, by Mobutu in Zaire.

There are a number of economic mechanisms that will lead to institutional persistence of this type. Here, we discuss three possibilities.

1. Setting up institutions that place restrictions on government power and enforce property rights is costly (see, e.g., Acemoglu and Thierry Verdier 1998). If the costs of creating these institutions have been sunk by the colonial powers, then it may not pay the elites at independence to switch to extractive institutions. In contrast, when the new elites inherit extractive institutions, they may not want to incur the costs of introducing better institutions, and may instead prefer to exploit the existing extractive institutions for their own benefits.

2. The gains to an extractive strategy may depend on the size of the ruling elite. When this elite is small, each member would have a larger share of the revenues, so the elite may have a greater incentive to be extractive. In many cases where European powers set up authoritarian institutions, they delegated the day-to-day running of the state to a small domestic elite. This narrow group often was the one to control the state after independence and favored extractive institutions.

3. If agents make irreversible investments that are complementary to a particular set of institutions, they will be more willing to support them, making these institutions persist (see, e.g., Acemoglu, 1995). For example, agents who have invested in human and physical capital will be in favor of spending money to enforce property rights, while those who have less to lose may not be. . . .

Mortality of Early Settlers

Sources of European Mortality in the Colonies

In this subsection, we give a brief overview of the sources of mortality facing potential settlers. Malaria (particularly *Plasmodium falciporum*) and yellow fever were the major sources of European mortality in the colonies. In the tropics, these two diseases accounted for 80 percent of European deaths, while gastrointestinal diseases accounted for another 15 percent (Curtin 1989, p. 30). Throughout the nineteenth century, areas without malaria and yellow fever, such as New Zealand, were more healthy than Europe because the major causes of death in Europe—tuberculosis, pneumonia, and smallpox—were rare in these places (Curtin 1989, p. 13).

Both malaria and yellow fever are transmitted by mosquito vectors. In the case of malaria, the main transmitter is the *Anopheles gambiae* complex and the mosquito *Anopheles funestus,* while the main carrier of yellow fever is *Aedes aegypti.* Both malaria and yellow fever vectors tend to live close to human habitation.

In places where the malaria vector is present, such as the West African savanna or forest, an individual can get as many as several hundred infectious mosquito bites a year. For a person without immunity, malaria (particularly *Plasmodium falciporum*) is often fatal, so Europeans in Africa, India, or the Caribbean faced very high death rates. In contrast, death rates for the adult local population were much lower (see Curtin [1964] . . . .). Curtin (1998, pp. 7–8) describes this as follows:

> Children in West Africa . . . would be infected with malaria parasites shortly after birth and were frequently reinfected afterwards; if they lived beyond the age of about five, they acquired an apparent immunity. The parasite remained with them, normally in the liver, but clinical symptoms were rare so long as they continued to be infected with the same species of *P. falciporum.*

The more recent books on malariology confirm this conclusion. For example, "In stable endemic areas a heavy toll of morbidity and mortality falls on young children but malaria is a relatively mild condition in adults" (Herbert M. Gilles and David A. Warren 1993, p. 64; see also the classic reference on this topic, Leonard J. Bruce-Chwatt 1980, Chapter 4; Roy Porter, 1996). Similarly, the World Health Organization (WHO) points out that in endemic malaria areas of Africa and the Western Pacific today ". . . the risk of malaria severity and death is almost exclusively limited to non-immunes, being most serious for young children over six months of age . . . surviving children develop their own immunity between the age of 3–5 years" (Jose A. Najera and Joahim Hempel 1996).

People in areas where malaria is endemic are also more likely to have genetic immunity against malaria. For example, they tend to have the sickle-cell trait, which discourages the multiplication of parasites in the blood, or deficiencies in glucose-6-phosphate dehydrogenase and thalassaemia traits, which also protect against malaria. Porter (1996, p. 34) writes: "In such a process, . . . close to 100 percent of Africans acquired a genetic trait that protects them against vivax malaria and probably against falciporum malaria as well." Overall, the WHO estimates that malaria kills about 1 million people per year, most of them

children. It does not, however, generally kill adults who grew up in malaria endemic areas (see Najera and Hempel 1996).

Although yellow fever's epidemiology is quite different from malaria, it
was also much more fatal to Europeans than to non-Europeans who grew up
in areas where yellow fever commonly occurred. Yellow fever leaves its surviving victims with a lifelong immunity, which also explains its epidemic pattern, relying on a concentrated nonimmune population. Curtin (1998, p. 10)
writes: "Because most Africans had passed through a light case early in life,
yellow fever in West Africa was a strangers' disease, attacking those who grew
up elsewhere." Similarly, Michael B.A. Oldstone (1998, p. 49) writes:

> Most Black Africans and their descendants respond to yellow fever infection
> with mild to moderate symptoms such as headache, fever, nausea, and vom-
> iting, and then recover in a few days. This outcome reflects the long relation-
> ship between the virus and its indigenous hosts, who through generations of
> exposure to the virus have evolved resistance.

In contrast, fatality rates among nonimmune adults, such as Europeans, could
be as high as 90 percent.

Advances in medical science have reduced the danger posed by malaria
and yellow fever. Yellow fever is mostly eradicated (Oldstone 1998, Chapter
5), and malaria has been eradicated in many areas. Europeans developed methods of dealing with these diseases that gradually became more effective in the
second half of the nineteenth century. For example, they came to understand
that high doses of quinine, derived from the cinchona bark, acted as a prophy-
lactic and prevented infection or reduced the severity of malaria. They also
started to undertake serious mosquito eradication efforts and protect themselves against mosquito bites. Further, Europeans also learned that an often effective method of reducing mortality from yellow fever is flight from the area,
since the transmitter mosquito, *Aedes aegypti,* has only a short range. Nevertheless, during much of the nineteenth century, there was almost a complete
misunderstanding of the nature of both diseases. For example, the leading theory for malaria was that it was caused by "miasma" from swamps, and quinine
was not used widely. The role of small collections of water to breed mosquitoes and transmit these diseases was not understood. It was only in the late
nineteenth century that Europeans started to control these diseases.

These considerations, together with the data we have on the mortality of
local people and population densities before the arrival of Europeans, make us
believe that settler mortality is a plausible instrument for institutional development: these diseases affected European settlement patterns and the type of institutions they set up, but had little effect on the health and economy of indigenous people.

A final noteworthy feature, helpful in interpreting our results, is that
malaria prevalence depends as much on the microclimate of an area as on its

temperature and humidity, or on whether it is in the tropics; high altitudes reduce the risk of infection, so in areas of high altitude, where "hill stations" could be set up, such as Bogota in Colombia, mortality rates were typically lower than in wet coastal areas. However, malaria could sometimes be more serious in high-altitude areas. For example, Curtin (1989, p. 47) points out that in Ceylon mortality was lower in the coast than the highlands because rains in the coast washed away the larvae of the transmitter mosquitoes. Similarly, in Madras many coastal regions were free of malaria, while northern India had high rates of infection. Curtin (1998, Chapter 7) also illustrates how there were marked differences in the prevalence of malaria within small regions of Madagascar. This suggests that mortality rates faced by Europeans are unlikely to be a proxy for some simple geographic or climatic feature of the country.

Data on Potential Settler Mortality

Our data on the mortality of European settlers come largely from the work of Philip Curtin. Systematic military medical record keeping began only after 1815, as an attempt to understand why so many soldiers were dying in some places. The first detailed studies were retrospective and dealt with British forces between 1817 and 1836. The United States and French governments quickly adopted similar methods (Curtin 1989, pp. 3, 5). Some early data are also available for the Dutch East Indies. By the 1870s, most European countries published regular reports on the health of their soldiers.

The standard measure is annualized deaths per thousand mean strength. This measure reports the death rate among 1,000 soldiers where each death is replaced with a new soldier. Curtin (1989, 1998) reviews in detail the construction of these estimates for particular places and campaigns, and assesses which data should be considered reliable.

Curtin (1989), *Death by Migration,* deals primarily with the mortality of European troops from 1817 to 1848. At this time modern medicine was still in its infancy, and the European militaries did not yet understand how to control malaria and yellow fever. These mortality rates can therefore be interpreted as reasonable estimates of settler mortality. They are consistent with substantial evidence from other sources (see, for example, Curtin [1964, 1968]). Curtin (1998), *Disease and Empire,* adds similar data on the mortality of soldiers in the second half of the nineteenth century. In all cases, we use the earliest available number for each country, reasoning that this is the best estimate of the mortality rates that settlers would have faced, at least until the twentieth century.

The main gap in the Curtin data is for South America since the Spanish and Portuguese militaries did not keep good records of mortality. Hector Gutierrez (1986) used Vatican records to construct estimates for the mortality rates of bishops in Latin America from 1604 to 1876. Because these data overlap with the Curtin estimates for several countries, we are able to construct a data series for South America. Curtin (1964) also provides estimates of mortality in naval squadrons for different regions which we can use to generate alternative estimates of mortality in South America. . . .

Concluding Remarks

Many economists and social scientists believe that differences in institutions and state policies are at the root of large differences in income per capita across countries. There is little agreement, however, about what determines institutions' and government attitudes towards economic progress, making it difficult to isolate exogenous sources of variation in institutions to estimate their effect on performance. In this paper we argued that differences in colonial experience could be a source of exogenous differences in institutions.

Our argument rests on the following premises: (1) Europeans adopted very different colonization strategies, with different associated institutions. In one extreme, as in the case of the United States, Australia, and New Zealand, they went and settled in the colonies and set up institutions that enforced the rule of law and encouraged investment. In the other extreme, as in the Congo or the Gold Coast, they set up extractive states with the intention of transferring resources rapidly to the metropole. These institutions were detrimental to investment and economic progress. (2) The colonization strategy was in part determined by the feasibility of European settlement. In places where Europeans faced very high mortality rates, they could not go and settle, and they were more likely to set up extractive states. (3) Finally, we argue that these early institutions persisted to the present. Determinants of whether Europeans could go and settle in the colonies, therefore, have an important effect on institutions today. We exploit these differences as a source of exogenous variation to estimate the impact of institutions on economic performance.

There is a high correlation between mortality rates faced by soldiers, bishops, and sailors in the colonies and European settlements; between European settlements and early measures of institutions; and between early institutions and institutions today. We estimate large effects of institutions on income per capita using this source of variation. We also document that this relationship is not driven by outliers, and is robust to controlling for latitude, climate, current disease environment, religion, natural resources, soil quality, ethnolinguistic fragmentation, and current racial composition.

It is useful to point out that our findings do not imply that institutions today are predetermined by colonial policies and cannot be changed. We emphasize colonial experience as one of the many factors affecting institutions. Since mortality rates faced by settlers are arguably exogenous, they are useful as an instrument to isolate the effect of institutions on performance. In fact, our reading is that these results suggest substantial economic gains from improving institutions, for example as in the case of Japan during the Meiji Restoration or South Korea during the 1960s.

There are many questions that our analysis does not address. Institutions are treated largely as a "black box": The results indicate that reducing expropriation risk (or improving other aspects of the "cluster of institutions") would result in significant gains in income per capita, but do not point out what concrete steps would lead to an improvement in these institutions. Institutional features, such as expropriation risk, property rights enforcement, or rule of law, should probably be interpreted as an equilibrium outcome, related to some more fundamental "institutions," e.g., a presidential versus parliamentary system, which can be changed directly. A more detailed analysis of the effect of more fundamental institutions on property rights and expropriation risk is an important area for future study.

References

Acemoglu, Daron. "Reward Structures and the Allocation of Talent." *European Economic Review,* January 1995, 39(1), pp. 17–33.

Acemoglu, Daron and Verdier, Thierry. "Property Rights, Corruption and the Allocation of Talent: A General Equilibrium Approach." *Economic Journal,* September 1998, 108(450), pp. 1381–403.

Bruce-Chwatt, Leonard J. *Essential malariology.* London: Wiley Medical Publications, 1980.

Cain, Philip J. and Hopkins, Antony G. *British imperialism: Innovation and expansion 1688–1914.* New York: Longman, 1993.

Crosby, Alfred. *Ecological imperialism: The biological expansion of Europe 900–1900.* New York: Cambridge University Press, 1986.

Crowder, Michael. *West Africa under colonial rule.* Chicago: Northwestern University Press, 1968.

Curtin, Philip D. *The image of Africa.* Madison, WI: University of Wisconsin Press, 1964.

———. "Epidemiology and the Slave Trade." *Political Science Quarterly,* June 1968, 83(2), pp. 181–216.

———. *Death by migration: Europe's encounter with the tropical world in the 19th century.* New York: Cambridge University Press, 1989.

———. *Disease and empire: The health of European troops in the conquest of Africa.* New York: Cambridge University Press, 1998.

Davis, Lance E. and Huttenback, Robert A. *Mammon and the pursuit of empire: The political economy of British imperialism, 1860–1912.* Cambridge: Cambridge University Press, 1987.

Denoon, Donald. *Settler capitalism: The dynamics of dependent development in the southern hemisphere.* Oxford: Clarendon Press, 1983.

Gann, Lewis H. and Duignan, Peter. *White settlers in tropical Africa.* Baltimore, MD: Penguin, 1962.

———. *The rulers of Belgian Africa.* Princeton, NJ: Princeton University Press, 1979.

Gilles, Herbert M. and Warren, David A. Bruce-Chwatt's *Essential malariology,* 3rd ed. London: Arnold, 1993.

Gutierrez, Hector. "La Mortalité des Eveques Latino-Americains aux XVIIe et XVIII Siècles." *Annales de Demographie Historique,* 1986, pp. 29–39.

Hughes, Robert. *The fatal shore.* London: Collins Harvill, 1987.

Jewsiewicki, Bogumil. "Rural Society and the Belgian Colonial Economy," in D. Birmingham and P. M. Martin, eds., *The history of Central Africa,* volume II. New York: Longman, 1983, pp. 95–125.

Manning, Patrick. *Slavery, colonialism, and economic growth in Dahomey, 1640–1980.* New York: Cambridge University Press, 1982.

———. *Francophone sub-Saharan Africa, 1880–1995.* New York: Cambridge University Press, 1988.

Najera, Jose A. and Hempel, Joahim. "The Burden of Malaria." 1996, downloaded from the World Health Organization's Roll Back Malaria website, http://mosquito.who.int/docs/b.

Oldstone, Michael B. A. *Viruses, plagues, and history.* New York: Oxford University Press, 1998.

Peemans, Jean-Philippe. "Capital Accumulation in the Congo under Colonialism: The Role of the State," in Lewis H. Gann and Peter Duignan, eds., *Colonialism in Africa 1870–1960,* volume 4, *The economics of colonialism.* Stanford, CA: Hoover Institution Press, 1975, 165–212.

Porter, Roy, ed. *The Cambridge illustrated history of medicine.* Cambridge: Cambridge University Press, 1996.

Roberts, Andrew. *A history of Zambia.* London: Heinemann, 1976.

Robinson, Ronald E. and Gallagher, John. *Africa and the Victorians: The official mind of imperialism.* London: Macmillan, 1961.

Young, Crawford. *The African colonial state in comparative perspective.* New Haven, CT: Yale University Press, 1994.

11

Macroeconomic Narratives from Africa and the Diaspora: Institutions Versus Policies: A Tale of Two Islands

Peter Blair Henry and Conrad Miller

In contrast to Diamond (Chapter 8), who argues that geography is an important determinant of economic growth, and Acemoglu, Johnson, and Robinson (Chapter 10), who provide evidence of economic growth resulting from the type of state created after colonialism, Peter Blair Henry and Conrad Miller here insist that government policies, not institutions, are what determine economic success or failure. Henry and Miller argue that Jamaica and Barbados offer ideal cases because their historical experiences and institutions are extraordinarily similar. They briefly trace the roots of these countries' Westminster parliamentary system and common-law legal structures and then turn to their divergent economic experiences. They make the case that while the two countries' institutions are similar, their divergent economic experiences came about due to Jamaica's decision to implement democratic socialist policies while Barbados decided upon tight monetary policies and an outward-looking growth policy. Thus, Jamaica's economic struggles and Barbados's relative success are due to policy choices rather than the long-term effects of institutions.

A LONG LINE OF WORK EMPHASIZES THE CORRELATION BETWEEN INSTITU-tions and economic performance (Adam Smith 1776; W. Arthur Lewis 1955; Douglass C. North 1990). Rich countries have laws that provide incentives to

Reprinted with permission of the American Economic Association from *American Economic Review: Papers and Proceedings 2009* 99, no. 2 (2009): 261–267.

engage in productive economic activity. Investors rely on secure property rights, facilitating investment in human and physical capital; government power is balanced and restricted by an independent judiciary; contracts are enforced effectively, supporting private economic transactions.

Recent research moves from correlation to causation by observing that countries whose colonizers established strong property rights hundreds of years ago have, on average, much higher levels of income today than countries whose colonizers did not (Daron Acemoglu, Simon Johnson, and James A. Robinson 2001). Since a country's colonial origin—literally determined centuries ago—can in no meaningful way be said to be caused by its present-day level of income, the nature of countries' colonial origins enables researchers to estimate the causal impact of property rights on long-run economic outcomes. Differences in the legal tradition that countries inherited from their colonial masters also have a long-run impact on economic outcomes. Countries with English common law origins provide investors with stronger protection and are less prone to government ownership and regulation than countries with civil law origins (Rafael La Porta, Florencio Lopez-de-Silanes, and Andrei Shleifer 2008). In turn, common law countries have greater financial development, less corruption, smaller informal economies, and lower unemployment.

Case studies seem to suggest that institutions also exert a causal influence on economic outcomes over periods of time somewhat shorter than the centuries-long span emphasized by the colonial and legal origins literature. For instance, following the Armistice of 1953, Korea broke into two separate nations with similar levels of income, almost identical ethnic and cultural makeup, but starkly different institutional arrangements of the economy. North Korea resorted to central planning while South Korea relied on property rights and markets (with a healthy dose of state intervention). More than 50 years later South Korea's income per capita is more than ten times as large as North Korea's. The divergence of the East and West German economies following the partition of Germany after World War II ostensibly provides another piece of evidence in favor of the view that institutions play the dominant role.

While institutions undoubtedly affect economic outcomes, the macroeconomic policies that governments choose to implement may exert just as much influence on the trajectory of their economies as the broader institutional framework within which those policy decisions take place. As a matter of arithmetic, long-run income levels are the sum of a series of short- and medium-run growth rates that are heavily influenced by fiscal, monetary, and exchange rate policy (to name a few). This article demonstrates the relevance of the point by examining a very different kind of policy experiment from the ones in the existing literature on institutions and growth.

In contrast to the examples of North and South Korea and East and West Germany, we examine a pair of countries—Barbados and Jamaica—whose income levels diverge over a 40-year stretch in spite of no obvious differences in the institutional arrangements of their economies at the beginning of the observation period.

Standards of Living in Barbados and Jamaica

Barbados and Jamaica are both former British colonies, small island economies, and predominantly inhabited by the descendants of Africans who were brought to the Caribbean to cultivate sugar. As former British colonies, Barbados and Jamaica inherited almost identical political, economic, and legal institutions: Westminster Parliamentary democracy, constitutional protection of property rights, and legal systems rooted in English common law. The standard of living in the two countries diverged in the roughly 40-year period following their independence from Great Britain.

Figure 11.1 plots the natural logarithm of an index of real GDP per capita (measured in US dollars) in Barbados and Jamaica from 1960 through 2002. By construction, the value of the index is one in 1960 so that the natural log of the index is zero in 1960. While Barbados has not exactly experienced a growth miracle, its economy performed reasonably well over the 42-year period and substantially better than Jamaica's. To be exact, by 2002, the natural log of the index is 0.917 for Barbados and 0.356 for Jamaica, so that the average growth rate of real GDP per capita for Barbados over the entire sample is 2.2 percent per year (0.917 divided by 42) versus 0.8 percent per year for Jamaica (0.356 divided by 42).

One particularly striking feature of Figure 1 is the sharp decline in Jamaica's standard of living that sets in after 1972. Of course, the first oil price

Figure 11.1 Standards of Living in Barbados and Jamaica Diverge After Independence

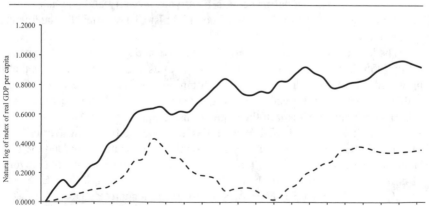

shock in 1973 precipitated a general slowdown in world economic growth, but the central point (laid out in more detail later in the paper) is that growth in Jamaica slowed more dramatically than it did in Barbados. While Jamaica's economy contracted at a rate of 2.3 percent per year from 1972 to 1987, Barbados, whose economy has a similar structure . . . and was subject to the same external shocks, grew by 1.2 percent per year. In other words, for a 15-year period income per head in Barbados grew by 3.5 percentage points faster than it did in Jamaica.

Turning from growth rates to levels gives a tangible sense of the impact of these growth-rate differentials on long-run standards of living. In 1960 real GDP per capita was $3,395 in Barbados and $2,208 in Jamaica. In 2002 Barbados's GDP per capita was $8,434 while Jamaica's was $3,165. The $1,187 income gap that existed between Barbados and Jamaica around the time of independence now stands at $5,269 dollars. Put another way, the income gap between the two countries now exceeds Jamaica's level of GDP per capita.

Since their initial conditions were similar at the time of independence, it stretches credulity to argue that Barbados and Jamaica diverged because of differences in colonial origins, legal origins, geography, or some other exogenous feature of their economies. We argue below that the explanation for the divergence lies not with differences in institutions but differences in macroeconomic policy.

Institutions

Jamaica won its independence from Britain in 1962, Barbados in 1966. At the time they became sovereign nations, both countries possessed the two institutional characteristics that the literature identifies as critical to long-run prosperity: strong constitutional protection of private property and English common law. A brief review of the islands' colonial histories verifies the statement in the preceding sentence.

The English settled Barbados in 1627 and wrested Jamaica from the Spanish in 1655. Both islands entered the modern era as plantation economies that produced sugar and other agricultural commodities using slave labor (Eric Williams 1970). By the end of the eighteenth century, African slaves comprised more than 85 percent of the populations of Barbados and Jamaica. Slavery was abolished in the British West Indies in 1834, and following World War I the region began a process of "constitutional decolonization" that led the islands down a gradual, if difficult, path toward greater self-government (Trevor Munroe 1972). Reporting on his visit to the region in 1922, Major E. F. L. Wood, Britain's Under Secretary of State for Colonies wrote:

> The whole history of the African population of the West Indies inevitably drives them towards representational institutions fashioned after the British

Model. Transplanted by the slave trade or other circumstances to foreign soil, losing in the process their social system, language and traditions. . . . Small wonder if they look for political growth to be the only course and pattern that they know, and aspire to share in what has been the particularly British gift of representational institutions. (Wood 1921)

Three subsequent empirical observations demonstrate the accuracy of Wood's prediction that the British West Indies (Barbados and Jamaica in particular) were destined to establish institutions that mirrored the mother country.

First, as sovereign nations, both Barbados and Jamaica organized their governments as parliamentary democracies in the Westminster- Whitehall tradition (Anthony Payne 1993). Since independence, Barbados and Jamaica have maintained two-party political systems and consistently held free and fair elections with no unconstitutional transfers of power. While sporadic violence often accompanies elections in Jamaica, neither Barbados nor Jamaica has suffered a coup or civil war, and both countries have a free and vocal press. Four postindependence elections in Jamaica resulted in the ruling party peacefully turning over power to the opposition. Three such transitions occurred in Barbados.

Second, the constitutions of Barbados and Jamaica explicitly protect private property. The joint parliamentary committee that drafted Jamaica's constitution was chaired by Norman Manley—a lawyer, Rhodes Scholar, and father of the nation's future prime minister. Discussing the constitution in front of Jamaica's House of Parliament on 23 January 1962, Manley says:

We have put into this constitution a clause which provides that property may not be, in effect, arbitrarily acquired. Property is protected in that it can only be taken under a law which has been passed. And when so taken, it must be taken in accordance with the terms of that law. What the law provides for compensation, you must get. . . . [I]t is of the highest importance for a country like Jamaica to let the world know that . . . people can come here to invest . . . fully protected by the laws of the land. . . . (Manley 1962, 306)

Barbados, which attained full independence four years after Jamaica, adopted a constitution with an effectively identical coverage of private property. Both constitutions assert that property cannot be compulsorily acquired except under written law that describes a procedure for determining and providing compensation and grants claimants the right of appeal to a court (Chapter 3, Section 16, of Barbadian Constitution; Chapter 3, Section 18, of Jamaican Constitution). The constitutions also delineate similar sets of exceptions to this clause, such as cases where property is acquired in satisfaction of a tax, property is in a condition dangerous to the health of others, or property is acquired to pay debt of the insolvent.

Third, Barbados and Jamaica adopted legal systems based on English common law (Rose-Marie Antoine 1999). Describing the essence of this adoption to the Philadelphia Bar Association in 1967, Manley says: "As to the law, we took over the English common law holus bolus. But what was more important we took over the structure and machinery which England built up for the administration of justice" (Manley 1967, 340). For most of their histories, both countries shared the Judicial Committee of the Privy Council in England as their highest court of appeals.

Because Barbados and Jamaica possess similar economic institutions and legal systems, neither the property-rights nor legal-origins theory of long-run income determination can explain their postindependence divergence. Although the institutional structures of Barbados and Jamaica are very close, the same cannot be said of their approaches to macroeconomic policy.

Macroeconomic Policies

When Jamaica gained independence in 1962 the Jamaican Labor Party (JLP) held a parliamentary majority. For the next ten years the JLP remained in power and GDP per capita grew at a rate of 5.4 percent per year, with the lion's share of growth stemming from two principal sources: strong US growth in the 1960s created a robust export market for Jamaican bauxite; and rising incomes in North America boosted growth in Jamaica's tourism industry.

But all was not well. In classic Dutch Disease fashion, growth in the bauxite sector drove up the relative price of nontradeables, reducing the competitiveness of Jamaica's agricultural sector and precipitating an exodus of workers from the countryside to the cities (Carl Stone and Stanislaw Wellisz 1993). Because of strong unions, wages in other sectors did not adjust downward to absorb the excess labor released from agriculture (Caribbean Policy Research Institute 2005). Consequently, during its first decade of independence Jamaica experienced the odd combination of strong growth coupled with an unemployment rate that rose from 13 percent in 1962 to 23.2 percent in 1972.

Rising unemployment, income inequality, and the attendant societal tensions proved too much for the JLP at the ballot box. In 1972 the People's National Party (PNP) rose to power under the leadership of Prime Minister Michael Manley (son of Norman) and the promise of "democratic socialism." The two cornerstones of democratic socialism and the PNP's economic policies were "self-reliance" and "social justice." Self-reliance translated as extensive state intervention in the economy. The PNP nationalized companies, erected import barriers, and imposed strict exchange controls (R. DeLisle Worrell 1987). Social justice meant income redistribution through job creation programs, housing development schemes, and subsidies on basic food items.

Whatever merits the PNP's economic program may have had, it was expensive. Government spending rose from 23 percent of GDP in 1972 to 45 percent in 1978. Revenue did not keep pace with the rise in expenditure. From 1962 through 1972 Jamaica's average fiscal deficit was 2.3 percent of GDP.

. . . In contrast, from 1973 to 1980 the average fiscal deficit was 15.5 percent of GDP! The PNP financed much of the deficit by borrowing directly from the Bank of Jamaica. Predictably, inflation rose. From 1962 to 1972 inflation averaged 4.4 percent per year. By 1980 inflation was 27 percent per year, investment had collapsed (to 14 percent of GDP, down from 26 percent in 1972), and the PNP was voted out of power.

Because Jamaica's reversal of fortune coincided with the oil price shock of 1973 and the onset of worldwide stagflation, it is tempting to blame the country's downward spiral on external events. While many have done so (see Manley 1987), even a cursory comparison with Barbados makes it difficult for an objective observer to embrace that conclusion.

The inflation rate in Barbados also spiked in the early 1970s, hitting a peak of 39 percent in 1975, but Barbados's policy response to the external shocks that precipitated the spike could not have been more different from Jamaica's. First of all, Barbados avoided nationalization, kept state ownership to a minimum, and adopted an outward-looking growth strategy (Courtney Blackman 2006, 390). Second, instead of taking an accommodative stance that delayed the inevitable retrenchment needed to adjust to higher energy prices, policymakers in Barbados kept government spending under control. While the fiscal deficit in Barbados did climb to 7.7 percent of GDP in 1973, by 1978 that number was down to 2.9 percent. Since much of deficit financing comes from the central bank, by extension, Barbados also ran a tighter monetary ship than Jamaica.

Exchange Rate Policies

In 1975 Barbados pegged its currency to the US dollar at a parity of B$2: US$1. The parity came under threat when Barbados suffered a deep recession in the early 1990s and real GDP per capita contracted by 5.1 percent per year from 1989 to 1992. In the midst of the crisis in 1991, Barbados entered formal negotiations with the International Monetary Fund (IMF) to request financial assistance. Among other things, the IMF recommended devaluation to stimulate production and return the economy to full employment. Deeply attached to the stability of their currency, the Barbadians resisted the recommendation. Instead of devaluing, the government began a set of negotiations with employers, unions, and workers that culminated with a tripartite protocol on wages and prices in 1993.

Under the 1993 Wage and Price Protocol, workers and unions assented to a one-time cut in real wages of about 9 percent and agreed to keep their demands for future pay raises in line with increases in productivity. Firms promised to moderate their price increases, the government maintained the parity of the currency, and all parties agreed to the creation of a national productivity board to provide better data on which to base future negotiations.

To be sure, the protocol involved costly bargaining. When negotiations began, public demonstrations broke out and the government's wage-cut proposal was challenged in court, all the way up to the Privy Council (Alvin Wint 2004, ch. 3). Nevertheless, the center held. The fall in real wages helped restore external competitiveness and profitability, thereby achieving the same result as a devaluation but without the risk of triggering an inflationary spiral. The economy recovered quickly. From 1993 to 2000 GDP per capita grew by 2.7 percent per year.

Unlike Barbados, Jamaica devalued its currency several times between 1975 and 2002. From this fact, many observers draw the specious conclusion that the difference in exchange rate policy accounts for Barbados's superior economic performance. But Barbados's fixed exchange rate did not cause its economy to outperform Jamaica's. Rather, the proximate source of Barbados' superior performance was a set of growth-facilitating policies—monetary restraint, fiscal discipline, openness to trade, and ultimately wage cuts to restore competitive unit labor costs—that had the side effect of enabling the monetary authority to maintain the exchange-rate parity without losing external competitiveness. In contrast, Jamaica's policies were never consistent with maintaining commitment to any parity the government might have wanted to adopt.

The differences in exchange rate policy do, however, raise an important issue. Faced with a scenario like that of Barbados in 1991, would Jamaica be able to achieve the social consensus needed to adopt the measures required to avoid a competitive devaluation? As stated in the previous paragraph, we think the Jamaican record speaks for itself. Answering the deeper question—why do some democratic societies (of which Barbados is just one example) manage to reach constructive policy compromises while others (such as Jamaica) do not?—remains an important research challenge.

Conclusion

It may be tempting for readers to regard this paper as a quaint tale of two exotic islands better known for their beaches, music, and Olympic sprinters than their significance in the global economy. On the contrary, we think that important general lessons lie at the heart of this Caribbean parable. Recent work focuses on the very long-run effects of institutions to the point of exclusion of almost all other factors. But the macroeconomic decisions of governments can exert just as much influence on the trajectory of the economy as the institutional framework within which those decisions take place. Countries have no control over their geographic location, colonial heritage, or legal origin, but they do have agency over the policies that they implement. Of particular importance for small open economies (i.e., most countries in the world) is the response of policy to macroeconomic shocks such as a fall in the terms of trade. Pedestrian as it may seem, changes in policy, even those that do not have a permanent effect on growth rates of GDP per capita, can have a significant impact on a country's standard of living within a single generation.

References

Acemoglu, Daron, Simon Johnson, and James A. Robinson. 2001. "The Colonial Origins of Comparative Development: An Empirical Investigation." *American Economic Review,* 91(5): 1369–1401.

Antoine, Rose-Marie. 1999. *Commonwealth Caribbean Law and Legal Systems.* London: Cavendish Publishers.

Blackman, Courtney. 2006. *The Practice of Economic Management: A Caribbean Perspective.* Kingston: Ian Randle Publishers.

Caribbean Policy Research Institute. 2005. *Taking Responsibility: The Jamaican Economy Since Independence.* http://www.takingresponsibility.org.

La Porta, Rafael, Florencio Lopez-de-Silanes, and Andrei Shleifer. 2008. "The Economic Consequences of Legal Origins." *Journal of Economic Literature,* 46(2): 285–332.

Lewis, W. Arthur. 1955. *The Theory of Economic Growth.* Homewood, Illinois: Unwyn Hyman.

Manley, Michael. 1987. *Up the Down Escalator: Development and the International Economy: A Jamaican Case Study.* London: Andre Deutsch.

Manley, Norman Washington. 1962. "The Independence Constitution." In *Norman Washington Manley and the New Jamaica: Selected Speeches and Writings 1938–68,* ed. Rex Nettleford, 1971. London: Longman Caribbean.

Munroe, Trevor. 1972. *The Politics of Decolonization: Jamaica, 1944–1962.* Jamaica: University of the West Indies Institute of Social and Economic Research.

North, Douglass C. 1990. *Institutions, Institutional Change, and Economic Performance.* Cambridge: Cambridge University Press.

Payne, Anthony. 1993. "Westminster Adapted: The Political Order of the Commonwealth Caribbean." In *Democracy in the Caribbean: Political Economic, and Social Perspectives,* ed. Jorgé I. Dominguez, Robert A. Pastor, and R. DeLisle Worrell. Baltimore: Johns Hopkins University Press.

Robotham, Donald. 1998. "Transnationalism in the Caribbean: Formal and Informal." *American Ethnologist,* 25(2): 307–21.

Smith, Adam. 1776. *An Inquiry into the Nature and Causes of the Wealth of Nations.* In Mortimer Adler (ed.), 2005, *Great Books of the Western World,* Encyclopedia Brittanica.

Stone, Carl, and Stanislaw Wellisz. 1993. "Jamaica." In *The Political Economy of Poverty, Equity, and Growth: Five Small Open Economies,* ed. Ronald Findlay and Stanislaw Wellisz, 140–218. New York: Oxford University Press.

Williams, Eric. 1970. *From Columbus to Castor: The History of the Caribbean 1492–1969.* New York: Random House.

Wint, Alvin. 2003. *Competitiveness in Small Developing Economies: Insights from the Caribbean.* Kingston: University of the West Indies Press.

Wood, Hon. E. F. L., M.P. 1921. "Report of a Visit to Certain West Indian Colonies and to British Guiana," as cited in Anthony Payne (op. cit.) 1993, 58–59.

Worrell, R. DeLisle. 1987. *Small Island Economies: Structure and Performance in the English Speaking Caribbean Since 1970.* New York: Praeger.

Part 3
The Other Gap: Domestic Income Inequality

12

Economic Growth and Income Inequality

Simon Kuznets

*M*ost debate on the internal gap between rich and poor people in
developing nations begins with this seminal presidential address
delivered by Simon Kuznets to the American Economic Association in
1954. The address, portions of which are reprinted here, uses limited data
from Germany, the United Kingdom, and the United States to show that
since the 1920s, and perhaps even earlier, there has been a trend toward
equalization in the distribution of income. Kuznets discusses in some
detail the possible causes for this trend, examining those factors in the
process of industrialization that tend to counteract the concentration of
savings in the hands of the wealthy. That particular discussion is not
included here, but the interested reader can consult the original piece.
Our interest lies in Kuznets's conclusion that the central factor in
equalizing income must have been the rising incomes of the poorer
sectors outside of the traditional agricultural economy. Kuznets
introduces the critically important notion of the "Inverted U-curve"
(although he does not label it as such in the address), arguing that there
seems to be increasing inequality in the early phases of industrialization,
followed by declines in the later phases only. Finally, Kuznets opens the
debate over the relevance of these findings for the developing nations
by examining data from India, Ceylon (Sri Lanka), and Puerto Rico. The
findings that income inequality in the developing countries is greater
than that in the advanced countries and that such inequality may be
growing form the basis of virtually all subsequent research and debate
on this subject.

Reprinted with permission of the *American Economic Review* 45 (March 1955): 1, 3–6,
17–26.

THE CENTRAL THEME OF THIS CHAPTER IS THE CHARACTER AND CAUSES of long-term changes in the personal distribution of income. Does inequality in the distribution of income increase or decrease in the course of a country's economic growth? What factors determine the secular level and trends of income inequalities?

These are broad questions in a field of study that has been plagued by looseness in definitions, unusual scarcity of data, and pressures of strongly held opinions. . . .

Trends in Income Inequality

Forewarned of the difficulties, we turn now to the available data. These data, even when relating to complete populations, invariably classify units by income for a given year. From our standpoint, this is their major limitation. Because the data often do not permit many size groupings, and because the difference between annual income incidence and longer-term income status has less effect if the number of classes is small and the limits of each class are wide, we use a few wide classes. This does not resolve the difficulty; and there are others due to the scantiness of data for long periods, inadequacy of the unit used—which is, at best, a family and very often a reporting unit—errors in the data, and so on through a long list. Consequently, the trends in the income structure can be discerned but dimly, and the results considered as preliminary informed guesses.

The data are for the United States, England, and Germany—a scant sample, but at least a starting point for some inferences concerning long-term changes in the presently developed countries. The general conclusion suggested is that the relative distribution of income, as measured by annual income incidence in rather broad classes, has been moving toward equality—with these trends particularly noticeable since the 1920s but beginning perhaps in the period before the first world war.

Let me cite some figures, all for income before direct taxes, in support of this impression. In the United States, in the distribution of income among families (excluding single individuals), the shares of the two lowest quintiles rise from 13.5 percent in 1929 to 18 percent in the years after the second world war (average of 1944, 1946, 1947, and 1950); whereas the share of the top quintile declines from 55 to 44 percent, and that of the top 5 percent from 31 to 20 percent. In the United Kingdom, the share of the top 5 percent of units declines from 46 percent in 1880 to 43 percent in 1910 or 1913, to 33 percent in 1929, to 31 percent in 1938, and to 24 percent in 1947; the share of the lower 85 percent remains fairly constant between 1880 and 1913, between 41 and 43 percent, but then rises to 46 percent in 1929 and 55 percent in 1947. In Prussia, income inequality increases slightly between 1875 and 1913—the shares of the top quintile rising from 48 to 50 percent, of the top 5 percent from 26 to 30 percent; the share of the lower 60 percent, however, remains about the same. In Saxony, the change between 1880 and 1913 is minor: the share of the two lowest quintiles declines from 15 to 14.5 percent; that of the third quintile rises from 12 to 13 percent, of the fourth quintile from 16.5 to about 18 percent; that of the top quintile declines from 56.5 to 54.5 percent, and of the top 5 percent from 34 to 33 percent. In Germany as a whole, relative income inequality drops fairly sharply from 1913 to the 1920s, apparently due to decimation of large fortunes and property incomes during the war and inflation, but then begins to return to prewar levels during the depression of the 1930s.[1]

Even for what they are assumed to represent, let alone as approximations to shares in distribution by secular income levels, the data are such that differences of two or three percentage points cannot be assigned significance. One must judge by the general weight and consensus of the evidence—which unfortunately is limited to a few countries. It justifies a tentative impression of constancy in the relative distribution of income before taxes, followed by some narrowing of relative income inequality after the first world war—or earlier.

Three aspects of this finding should be stressed. First, the data are for income before direct taxes and exclude contributions by government (e.g., relief and free assistance). It is fair to argue that both the proportion and progressivity of direct taxes and the proportion of total income of individuals accounted for by government assistance to the less privileged economic groups have grown during recent decades. This is certainly true of the United States and the United Kingdom, but in the case of Germany is subject to further examination. It follows that the distribution of income after direct taxes and including free contributions by government would show an even greater narrowing of inequality in developed countries with size distributions of pre-tax, ex-government-benefits income similar to those for the United States and the United Kingdom.

Second, such stability or reduction in the inequality of the percentage shares was accompanied by significant rises in real income per capita. The countries now classified as developed have enjoyed rising per capita incomes except during catastrophic periods such as years of active world conflict. Hence, if the shares of groups classified by their annual income position can be viewed as approximations to shares of groups classified by their secular income levels, a constant percentage share of a given group means that its per capita real income is rising at the same rate as the average for all units in the country; and a reduction in inequality of the shares means that the per capita income of the lower-income groups is rising at a more rapid rate than the per capita income of the upper-income groups.

The third point can be put in the form of a question. Do the distributions by annual incomes properly reflect trends in distribution by secular incomes? As technology and economic performance rise to higher levels, incomes are less subject to transient disturbances, not necessarily of the cyclical order that can be recognized and allowed for by reference to business cycle chronology, but of a more irregular type. If in the earlier years the economic fortunes of units were subject to greater vicissitudes—poor crops for some farmers, natural calamity losses for some nonfarm business units—if the over-all proportion of individual entrepreneurs whose incomes were subject to such calamities, more yesterday but some even today, was larger in earlier decades, these earlier distributions of income would be more affected by transient disturbances. In these earlier distributions the temporarily unfortunate might crowd the lower quintiles and depress their shares unduly, and the temporarily fortunate might dominate the top quintile and raise its share unduly—proportionately more than in the distributions for later years. If so, distributions by longer-term average incomes might show less reduction in inequality than do the distributions by annual incomes; they might even show an opposite trend.

One may doubt whether this qualification would upset a narrowing of inequality as marked as that for the United States, and in as short a period as twenty-five years. Nor is it likely to affect the persistent downward drift in the spread of the distributions in the United Kingdom. But I must admit a strong element of judgment in deciding how far this qualification modifies the finding of long-term stability followed by reduction in income inequality in the few developed countries for which it is observed or is likely to be revealed by existing data. The important point is that the qualification is relevant; it suggests need for further study if we are to learn much from the available data concerning the secular income structure; and such study is likely to yield results of interest in themselves in their bearing upon the problem of trends in temporal instability of income flows to individual units or to economically significant groups of units in different sectors of the national economy. . . .

Hence we may conclude that the major offset to the widening of income inequality associated with the shift from agriculture and the countryside to industry and the city must have been a rise in the income share of the lower groups within the nonagricultural sector of the population. This provides a lead for exploration in what seems to me a most promising direction: consideration of the pace and character of the economic growth of the urban population, with particular reference to the relative position of lower-income groups. Much is to be said for the notion that once the early turbulent phases of industrialization and urbanization had passed, a variety of forces converged to bolster the economic position of the lower-income groups within the urban population. The very fact that, after a while, an increasing proportion of the urban population was "native," i.e., born in cities rather than in the rural areas, and hence more able to take advantage of the possibilities of city life in preparation for the economic struggle, meant a better chance for organization and adaptation, a better basis for securing greater income shares than was possible for the newly "immigrant" population coming from the countryside or from abroad.

The increasing efficiency of the older, established urban population should also be taken into account. Furthermore, in democratic societies the growing political power of the urban lower-income groups led to a variety of protective and supporting legislation, much of it aimed to counteract the worst effects of rapid industrialization and urbanization and to support the claims of the broad masses for more adequate shares of the growing income of the country. Space does not permit the discussion of demographic, political, and social considerations that could be brought to bear to explain the offsets to any declines in the shares of the lower groups, declines otherwise deducible from the trends suggested in the numerical illustration.

Other Trends Related to Those in Income Inequality

One aspect of the conjectural conclusion just reached deserves emphasis because of its possible interrelation with other important elements in the process and theory of economic growth. The scanty empirical evidence suggests that the narrowing of income inequality in the developed countries is relatively recent and probably did not characterize the earlier stages of their growth. Likewise, the various factors that have been suggested above would explain stability and narrowing in income inequality in the later rather than in the earlier phases of industrialization and urbanization. Indeed, they would suggest widening inequality in these early phases of economic growth, especially in the older countries where the emergence of the new industrial system had shattering effects on long-established pre-industrial economic and social institutions. This timing characteristic is particularly applicable to factors bearing upon the lower-income groups: the dislocating effects of the agricultural and industrial revolutions, combined with the "swarming" of population incident upon a rapid decline in death rates and the maintenance or even rise of birth rates, would be unfavorable to the relative economic position of lower-income groups. Furthermore, there may also have been a preponderance in the earlier periods of factors favoring maintenance or increase in the shares of top-income groups: in so far as their position was bolstered by gains arising out of new industries, by an unusually rapid rate of creation of new fortunes, we would expect these forces to be relatively stronger in the early phases of industrialization than in the later when the pace of industrial growth slackens.

One might thus assume a long swing in the inequality characterizing the secular income structure: widening in the early phases of economic growth when the transition from the pre-industrial to the industrial civilization was most rapid; becoming stabilized for a while; and then narrowing in the later phases. This long secular swing would be most pronounced for older countries where the dislocation effects of the earlier phases of modern economic growth were most conspicuous; but it might be found also in the "younger" countries like the United States if the period preceding marked industrialization could be compared with the early phases of industrialization, and if the latter could be compared with the subsequent phases of greater maturity.

If there is some evidence for assuming this long swing in relative inequality in the distribution of income before direct taxes and excluding free benefits from government, there is surely a stronger case for assuming a long swing in inequality of income net of direct taxes and including government benefits. Progressivity of income taxes and, indeed, their very importance characterize only the more recent phases of development of the presently developed countries; in narrowing income inequality they must have accentuated the downward phase of the long swing, contributing to the reversal of trend in the secular widening and narrowing of income inequality.

No adequate empirical evidence is available for checking this conjecture of a long secular swing in income inequality;[2] nor can the phases be dated precisely. However, to make it more specific, I would place the early phase in which income inequality might have been widening from about 1780 to 1850 in England; from about 1840 to 1890, and particularly from 1870 on in the United States; and from the 1840s to the 1890s in Germany. I would put the phase of narrowing income inequality somewhat later in the United States and Germany than in England—perhaps beginning with the first world war in the former and the last quarter of the nineteenth century in the latter.

Is there a possible relation between this secular swing in income inequality and the long swing in other important components of the growth process? For the older countries a long swing is observed in the rate of growth of population—the upward phase represented by acceleration in the rate of growth reflecting the early reduction in the death rate which was not offset by a decline in the birth rate (and in some cases was accompanied by a rise in the birth rate); and the downward phase represented by a shrinking in the rate of growth reflecting the more pronounced downward trend in the birth rate. Again, in the older countries, and also perhaps in the younger, there may have been a secular swing in the rate of urbanization, in the sense that the proportional additions to urban population and the measures of internal migration that produced this shift of population probably increased for a while—from the earlier much lower levels; but then tended to diminish as urban population came to dominate the country and as the rural reservoirs of migration became proportionally much smaller. For old, and perhaps for young countries also, there must have been a secular swing in the proportions of savings or capital formation to total economic product. Per capita product in pre-industrial times was not large enough to permit as high a nationwide rate of saving or capital formation as was attained in the course of industrial development: this is suggested by present comparisons between net capital formation rates of 3 to 5 percent of national product in underdeveloped countries and rates of 10 to 15 percent in developed countries. If then, at least in the older countries, and perhaps even in the younger ones—prior to initiation of the process of modern development—we begin with low secular levels in the savings proportions, there would be a rise in the early phases to appreciably higher levels. We also know that during recent periods the net capital formation proportion, and even the gross, failed to rise and perhaps even declined.

Other trends might be suggested that would possibly trace long swings similar to those for inequality in income structure, rate of growth of population, rate of urbanization and internal migration, and the proportion of savings or capital formation to national product. For example, such swings might be found in the ratio of foreign trade to domestic activities; in the aspects, if we could only measure them properly, of government activity that bear upon market forces (there must have been a phase of increasing freedom of market forces, giving way to greater intervention by government). But the suggestions already made suffice to indicate that the long swing in income inequality must be viewed as part of a wider process of economic growth, and interrelated with similar movements in other elements. The long alternation in the rate of growth of population can be seen partly as a cause, partly as an effect of the long swing in income inequality which was associated with a secular rise in real per capital income levels. The long swing in income inequality is also probably closely associated with the swing in capital formation proportions— in so far as wider inequality makes for higher, and narrower inequality for lower, countrywide savings proportions.

Comparison of Developed and Underdeveloped Countries

What is the bearing of the experience of the developed countries upon the economic growth of underdeveloped countries? Let us examine briefly the data on income distribution in the latter, and speculate upon some of the implications.

As might have been expected, such data for underdeveloped countries are scanty. For the present purpose, distributions of family income for India in 1949–50, for Ceylon in 1950, and for Puerto Rico in 1948 were used. While the coverage is narrow and the margin of error wide, the data show that income distribution in these underdeveloped countries is somewhat *more* unequal than in the developed countries during the period after the second world war. Thus the shares of the lower 3 quintiles are 28 percent in India, 30 percent in Ceylon, and 24 percent in Puerto Rico—compared with 34 percent in the United States and 36 percent in the United Kingdom. The shares of the top quintile are 55 percent in India, 50 percent in Ceylon, and 56 percent in Puerto Rico, compared with 44 percent in the United States and 45 percent in the United Kingdom.[3]

This comparison is for income before direct taxes and excluding free benefits from governments. Since the burden and progressivity of direct taxes are much greater in developed countries, and since it is in the latter that substantial volumes of free economic assistance are extended to the lower-income groups, a comparison in terms of income net of direct taxes and including government benefits would only accentuate the wider inequality of income distributions in the underdeveloped countries. Is this difference a reliable reflection of wider inequality also in the distribution of *secular* income levels in underdeveloped countries? Even disregarding the margins of error in the data, the possibility raised earlier in this chapter that transient disturbances in income levels may be more conspicuous under conditions of primitive material and economic technology would affect the comparison just made. Since the distributions cited reflect the annual income levels, a greater allowance should perhaps be made for transient disturbances in the distributions for the underdeveloped than in those for the developed countries. Whether such a correction would obliterate the difference is a matter on which I have no relevant evidence.

Another consideration might tend to support this qualification. Underdeveloped countries are characterized by low average levels of income per capita, low enough to raise the question of how the populations manage to survive. Let us assume that these countries represent fairly unified population groups, and exclude, for the moment, areas that combine large native populations with small enclaves of nonnative, privileged minorities, e.g., Kenya and Rhodesia, where income inequality, because of the excessively high income shares of the privileged minority, is appreciably wider than even in the underdeveloped countries cited above.[4] On this assumption, one may infer that in countries with low average income, the secular level of income in the lower brackets could not be below a fairly sizable proportion of average income— otherwise, the groups could not survive. This means, to use a purely hypothetical figure, that the secular level of the share of the lowest decile could not fall far short of 6 or 7 percent, i.e., the lowest decile could not have a per capita income less than six- or seven-tenths of the countrywide average. In more advanced countries, with higher average per capita incomes, even the *secular* share of the lowest bracket could easily be a smaller fraction of the countrywide average, say as small as 2 or 3 percent for the lowest decile, i.e., from a fifth to a third of the countrywide average—without implying a materially impossible economic position for that group. To be sure, there is in all countries continuous pressure to raise the relative position of the bottom-income groups; but the fact remains that the lower limit of the proportional share in the secular income structure is higher when the real countrywide per capita income is low than when it is high.

If the long-term share of the lower-income groups is larger in the underdeveloped than in the average countries, income inequality in the former should be narrower, not wider as we have found. However, if the lower brackets receive larger shares, and at the same time the very top brackets also receive larger shares—which would mean that the intermediate income classes would not show as great a progression from the bottom—the net effect may well be wider inequality. To illustrate, let us compare the distributions for India and the United States. The first quintile in India receives 8 percent of total income, more than the 6 percent share of the first quintile in the United States. But the second quintile in India receives only 9 percent, the third 11, and the fourth 16; whereas in the United States, the shares of these quintiles are 12, 16, and 22 respectively. This is a rough statistical reflection of a fairly common observation relating to income distributions in underdeveloped compared with developed countries. The former have no "middle" classes: there is a sharp contrast between the preponderant proportion of population whose average income is well below the generally low countrywide average, and a small top group with a very large relative income excess. The developed countries, on the other hand, are characterized by a much more gradual rise from low to high shares, with substantial groups receiving more than the high countrywide income average, and the top groups securing smaller shares than the comparable ordinal groups in underdeveloped countries.

It is, therefore, possible that even the distributions of secular income levels would be more unequal in underdeveloped than in developed countries—not in the sense that the shares of the lower brackets would be lower in the former than in the latter, but in the sense that the shares of the very top groups would be higher and that those of the groups below the top would all be significantly lower than a low countrywide income average. This is even more likely to be true of the distribution of income net of direct taxes and inclusive of free government benefits. But whether a high probability weight can be attached to this conjecture is a matter for further study.

In the absence of evidence to the contrary, I assume that it is true: that the secular income structure is somewhat more unequal in underdeveloped countries than in the more advanced—particularly in those of Western and Northern Europe and their economically developed descendants in the New World (the United States, Canada, Australia, and New Zealand). This conclusion has a variety of important implications and leads to some pregnant questions, of which only a few can be stated here.

In the first place, the wider inequality in the secular income structure of underdeveloped countries is associated with a much lower level of average income per capita. Two corollaries follow—and they would follow even if the income inequalities were of the same relative range in the two groups of countries. First, the impact is far sharper in the underdeveloped countries, where the failure to reach an already low countrywide average spells much greater material and psychological misery than similar proportional deviations from the average in the richer, more advanced countries. Second, positive savings are obviously possible only at much higher relative income levels in the underdeveloped countries: if in the more advanced countries some savings are possible in the fourth quintile, in the underdeveloped countries savings could be realized only at the very peak of the income pyramid, say by the top 5 or 3 percent. If so, the concentration of savings and of assets is even more pronounced than in the developed countries; and the effects of such concentration in the past may serve to explain the peculiar characteristics of the secular income structure in underdeveloped countries today.

The second implication is that this unequal income structure presumably coexisted with a low rate of growth of income per capita. The underdeveloped countries today have not always lagged behind the presently developed areas in level of economic performance; indeed, some of the former may have been the economic leaders of the world in the centuries preceding the last two. The countries of Latin America, Africa, and particularly those of Asia, are underdeveloped today because in the last two centuries, and even in recent decades, their rate of economic growth has been far lower than that in the Western world—and low indeed, if any growth there was, on a per capita basis. The underlying shifts in industrial structure, the opportunities for internal mobility and for economic improvement, were far more limited than in the more rapidly growing countries now in the developed category. There was no hope, within the lifetime of a generation, of a significantly perceptible rise in the level of real income, or even that the next generation might fare much better. It was this hope that served as an important and realistic compensation for the wide inequality in income distribution that characterized the presently developed countries during the earlier phases of their growth.

The third implication follows from the preceding two. It is quite possible that income inequality has not narrowed in the underdeveloped countries within recent decades. There is no empirical evidence to check this conjectural implication, but it is suggested by the absence, in these areas, of the dynamic forces associated with rapid growth that in the developed countries checked the upward trend of the upper-income shares that was due to the cumulative effect of continuous concentration of past savings; and it is also indicated by the failure of the political and social systems of underdeveloped countries to initiate the governmental or political practices that effectively bolster the weak positions of the lower-income classes. Indeed, there is a possibility that inequality in the secular income structure of underdeveloped countries may have widened in recent decades—the only qualification being that where there has been a recent shift from colonial to independent status, a privileged, *nonnative* minority may have been eliminated. But the implication, in terms of the income distribution among the *native* population proper, still remains plausible.

The somber picture just presented may be an oversimplified one. But I believe that it is sufficiently realistic to lend weight to the questions it poses— questions as to the bearing of the recent levels and trends in income inequality, and the factors that determine them, upon the future prospect of underdeveloped countries within the orbit of the free world.

The questions are difficult, but they must be faced unless we are willing completely to disregard past experience or to extrapolate mechanically over-simplified impressions of past development. The first question is: Is the pattern of the older developed countries likely to be repeated in the sense that in the early phases of industrialization in the underdeveloped countries income inequalities will tend to widen before the leveling forces become strong enough first to stabilize and then reduce income inequalities? While the future cannot be an exact repetition of the past, there are already certain elements in the present conditions of underdeveloped societies, e.g., "swarming" of population due to sharp cuts in death rates unaccompanied by declines in birth rates, that threaten to widen inequality by depressing the relative position of lower-income groups even further. Furthermore, if and when industrialization begins, the dislocating effects on these societies, in which there is often an old hardened crust of economic and social institutions, are likely to be quite sharp—so sharp as to destroy the positions of some of the lower groups more rapidly than opportunities elsewhere in the economy may be created for them.

The next question follows from an affirmative answer to the first. Can the political framework of the underdeveloped societies withstand the strain which further widening of income inequality is likely to generate? This query is pertinent if it is realized that the real per capita income level of many underdeveloped societies today is lower than the per capita income level of the presently developed societies before *their* initial phases of industrialization. And yet the stresses of the dislocations incident to early phases of industrialization in the developed countries were sufficiently acute to strain the political and social fabric of society, force major political reforms, and sometimes result in civil war.

The answer to the second question may be negative, even granted that industrialization may be accompanied by a rise in real per capita product. If, for many groups in society, the rise is even partly offset by a decline in their proportional share in total product; if, consequently, it is accompanied by widening of income inequality, the resulting pressures and conflicts may necessitate drastic changes in social and political organization. This gives rise to the next and crucial question: How can either the institutional and political framework of the underdeveloped societies or the processes of economic growth and industrialization be modified to favor a sustained rise to higher levels of economic performance and yet avoid the fatally simple remedy of an authoritarian regime that would use the population as cannon-fodder in the fight for economic achievement? How to minimize the cost of transition and avoid paying the heavy price—in internal tensions, in long-run inefficiency in providing means for satisfying wants of human beings as individuals—which the inflation of political power represented by authoritarian regimes requires?

Facing these acute problems, one is cognizant of the dangers of taking an extreme position. One extreme—particularly tempting to us—is to favor repetition of past patterns of the now developed countries, patterns that, under the markedly different conditions of the presently underdeveloped countries, are almost bound to put a strain on the existing social and economic institutions and eventuate in revolutionary explosions and authoritarian regimes. There is danger in simple analogies; in arguing that because an unequal income distribution in Western Europe in the past led to accumulation of savings and financing of basic capital formation, the preservation or accentuation of present income inequalities in the underdeveloped countries is necessary to secure the same result. Even disregarding the implications for the lower-income groups, we may find that in at least some of these countries today the consumption propensities of upper-income groups are far higher and savings propensities far lower than were those of the more puritanical upper-income groups of the presently developed countries. Because they may have proved favorable in the past, it is dangerous to argue that completely free markets, lack of penalties implicit in progressive taxation, and the like are indispensable for the economic growth of the now underdeveloped countries. Under present conditions the results may be quite the opposite—withdrawal of accumulated assets to relatively "safe" channels, either by flight abroad or into real estate; and the inability of governments to serve as basic agents in the kind of capital formation that is indispensable to economic growth. It is dangerous to argue that, because in the past foreign investment provided capital resources to spark satisfactory economic growth in some of the smaller European countries or in Europe's descendants across the seas, similar effects can be expected today if only the underdeveloped countries can be convinced of the need of a "favorable climate." Yet, it is equally dangerous to take the opposite position and claim that the present problems are entirely new and that we must devise solutions that are the product of imagination unrestrained by knowledge of the past, and therefore full of romantic violence. What we need, and I am afraid it is but a truism, is a clear perception of past trends and of conditions under which they occurred, as well as knowledge of the conditions that characterize the underdeveloped countries today. With this as a beginning, we can then attempt to translate the elements of a properly understood past into the conditions of an adequately understood present.

Notes

1. The following sources were used in calculating the figures cited: *United States.* For recent years we used *Income Distribution by Size, 1944–1950* (Washington, 1953) and Selma Goldsmith and others, "Size Distribution of Income Since the Mid-Thirties," *Rev. Econ. Stat.,* Feb. 1954, XXXVI, 1–32; for 1929, the Brookings Institution data as adjusted in Simon Kuznets, *Shares of Upper Groups in Income and Savings* (New York, 1953), p. 220.

United Kingdom. For 1938 and 1947, Dudley Seers, *The Levelling of Income Since 1938* (Oxford, 1951), p. 39; for 1929, Colin Clark, *National Income and Outlay*

(London, 1937) Table 47, p. 109; for 1880, 1910, and 1913, A. Bowley, *The Change in the Distribution of the National Income, 1880–1913* (Oxford, 1920).

Germany. For the constituent areas (Prussia, Saxony and others) for years before the first world war, based on S. Prokopovich, *National Income of Western European Countries* (published in Moscow in the 1920s). Some summary results are given in Prokopovich, "The Distribution of National Income," *Econ. Jour.,* March 1926, XXXVI, 69–82. See also, "Das Deutsche Volkseinkommen vor und nach dem Kriege," *Einzelschrift zur Stat. des Deutschen Reichs,* no. 24 (Berlin, 1932), and W. S. and E. S. Woytinsky, *World Population and Production* (New York, 1953) Table 192, p. 709.

2. Prokopovich's data on Prussia, from the source cited in footnote 1, indicate a substantial widening in income inequality in the early period. The share of the lower 90 percent of the population declines from 73 percent in 1854 to 65 percent in 1875; the share of the top 5 percent rises from 21 to 25 percent. But I do not know enough about the data for the early years to evaluate the reliability of the finding.

3. For sources of these data see "Regional Economic Trends and Levels of Living," submitted at the Norman Waite Harris Foundation Institute of the University of Chicago in November 1954 (in press in the volume of proceedings). This paper, and an earlier one, "Underdeveloped Countries and the Pre-industrial Phases in the Advanced Countries: An Attempt at Comparison," prepared for the World Population Meetings in Rome held in September 1954 (in press) discuss issues raised in this section.

4. In one year since the second world war, the non-African group in Southern Rhodesia, which accounted for only 5 percent of total population, received 57 percent of total income; in Kenya, the minority of only 2.9 percent of total population, received 51 percent of total income; in Northern Rhodesia, the minority of only 1.4 percent of total population, received 45 percent of total income. See United Nations, *National Income and Its Distribution in Underdeveloped Countries,* Statistical Paper, Ser. E, no. 3, 1951, Table 12, p. 19.

13

Inequality and Insurgency

Edward N. Muller and Mitchell A. Seligson

What are the consequences of the widespread domestic income inequality that has been noted in Part 3 of this volume? In this chapter Edward Muller and Mitchell Seligson conduct a cross-national test using a large database. They find that when income inequality is high, the probability of domestic political violence increases substantially. This finding suggests that income inequality can lead to uprisings, guerrilla movements, and civil wars, as have occurred in Vietnam, Central America, and elsewhere. Since the violence invariably causes considerable destruction of property, not to speak of the lives lost, economic growth is adversely affected. Thus, in addition to creating normative problems, income inequality seems to be responsible for violence and, in turn, slowed economic growth. The inescapable conclusion is that income inequality matters a great deal, for when it is high, a vicious circle of violence and slowed growth is the result.

MANY STUDENTS OF DOMESTIC POLITICAL CONFLICT CONSIDER INEQUALITY in the distribution of land and/or lack of land ownership (landlessness) to be among the more fundamental economic preconditions of insurgency and revolution (e.g., Huntington 1968; Midlarsky 1981, 1982; Midlarsky and Roberts 1985; Paige 1975; Prosterman 1976; Prosterman and Riedinger 1982; Russett 1964; Tanter and Midlarsky 1967). Huntington (1968, 375), whose writing on the

Reprinted with permission of the American Political Science Association from *American Political Science Review* 81, no. 2 (1987): 425–450.

subject has been particularly influential, advanced a strong version of the land maldistribution hypothesis as follows: "Where the conditions of land-ownership are equitable and provide a viable living for the peasant, revolution is unlikely. Where they are inequitable and where the peasant lives in poverty and suffering, revolution is likely, if not inevitable, unless the government takes prompt measures to remedy these conditions." However, because mass revolutions are rare events, it is more plausible to relax the postulate that revolution is an inevitable consequence of land maldistribution and to restate the hypothesis: the greater the maldistribution of land, the greater the probability of mass-based political insurgency and, consequently, the greater the *vulnerability* of a country to revolution from below. This weaker, necessary-but-not-sufficient version of the land-maldistribution-leads-to-revolution hypothesis directs attention to the relationship between land distribution and mass political violence.

The land maldistribution hypothesis is based on the assumption that discontent resulting from a highly concentrated distribution of land and/or lack of land ownership (landlessness) in agrarian societies is an important direct cause of mass political violence. Advocates of what has come to be called the "resource mobilization" approach to the explanation of collective protest and violence (e.g., Gamson 1975; Oberschall 1973; Tilly 1978) reject such discontent hypotheses for the reason that inequality and discontent are more or less always present in virtually all societies and that consequently the most direct and influential explanatory factor must not be discontent per se but rather the *organization* of discontent. Thus Skocpol (1979, 112–57), who is skeptical of discontent theories of revolution, argues that the peasant revolts that were a crucial insurrectionary ingredient in the French, Russian, and Chinese revolutions occurred not because of the maldistribution of landholdings but rather because communities of French, Russian, and Chinese peasants had sufficient autonomy from local landlords to enable them to mobilize collectively. By contrast, Midlarsky (1982, 15–20), a proponent of discontent theory, explains the peasant revolts in each of these cases by the fact that rapid population growth severely exacerbated land inequality until a level of deprivation was reached that no longer could be tolerated.

Two contemporary cases cited by Midlarsky and Roberts (1985) in support of the land maldistribution hypothesis are El Salvador and Nicaragua.[1] Compared with other middle-income developing countries, population growth in El Salvador and Nicaragua was above average during the 1960s and 1970s (see World Bank 1981, tbl. 17). Maldistribution of land also was a serious problem, as the Gini coefficient of land concentration was .80 for Nicaragua and .81 for El Salvador (values well above the global mean of .60) and agricultural households without land (i.e., tenants, sharecroppers, and agricultural laborers) amounted to 40% of the total labor force in El Salvador circa 1970, which was the highest level of landlessness in the world at that time (data are not available for Nicaragua).[2] Each country subsequently experienced a relatively high rate of mass political violence, which in the Nicaraguan case culminated in revolution.

But the seemingly obvious conclusion that land maldistribution must have been a primary cause of political violence in El Salvador and Nicaragua ignores the fact that, during the same period of time, two other Central American states, Costa Rica and Panama, remained quite peaceful despite the presence of exactly the same preconditions supposed to have caused the insurgency in El Salvador and Nicaragua. Costa Rica and Panama experienced above-average population growth (in fact, Costa Rica's 3.4% annual population-growth rate during 1960–70 not only exceeded the 2.9% rate registered by El Salvador and Nicaragua but was also among the highest in the entire world); land was concentrated in the hands of the few to about the same degree in Costa Rica (the Gini coefficient was .82) and Panama (Gini coefficient of .78) as in El Salvador and Nicaragua; and the amount of landlessness in Costa Rica (24%) and in Panama (36.2%) ranked ninth and third highest in the world, respectively. Nevertheless, during 1970–77 Panama registered only a single death from political violence, and there were no instances of deadly political violence in Costa Rica (see Taylor and Jodice 1983, vol. 2, tbl. 2.7).

Comparison of Costa Rica and Panama with El Salvador and Nicaragua thus raises the issue of the general validity of the land maldistribution hypothesis: Are Costa Rica and Panama merely exceptions to the rule, or is maldistribution of land in reality a minor or even irrelevant factor in the process that generates insurgency and revolution? That question is significant not only because inequality is frequently assumed in academic writing to be an important determinant of political instability; it also has profound policy implications because land reform has traditionally been a cornerstone of U.S. efforts to promote political stability in developing countries.

Inequality, Resource Mobilization, and the Structure of the State

We argue that theories emphasizing land maldistribution as a fundamental precondition of insurgency and revolution are misspecified. They attribute direct causal significance to an inequality variable that plays only a relatively small, indirect part in the generation of mass political violence. We hypothesize that the more important direct cause of variation in rates of political violence cross-nationally is inequality in the distribution of income rather than maldistribution of land. This hypothesis is predicated on the following assumptions:

1. Inequality in the contemporary world generates discontent;
2. Although inequality is present to some degree in all societies, some societies are significantly more inegalitarian than others;
3. Inequality in the distribution of land and inequality in the distribution of income are not necessarily tightly connected; in particular, they are sufficiently independent of each other that an effect of one on a response

variable such as the rate of political violence does not necessarily imply that the other will have a similar effect;

4. Given the existence of inequality-based discontent, it is more difficult to mobilize peasant communities than urban populations for political protest; peasants normally become the foot soldiers of insurgent movements only if they are effectively organized by a "vanguard" of urban professional revolutionaries.

From these assumptions we derive the following postulates:

1. A high level of income inequality nationwide significantly raises the probability that at least some dissident groups will be able to organize for aggressive collective action. This is because, first, the pool of discontented persons from which members can be drawn will include the more easily mobilized urban areas; and, second, it may be possible for urban revolutionaries to establish cross-cutting alliances with groups in the countryside.

2. A high level of agrarian inequality does not necessarily raise the probability that dissident groups will be able to organize for aggressive collective action; this is because the pool of discontented persons from which members can be drawn may be restricted to the countryside, which is difficult to mobilize; consequently, we predict that if income inequality is relatively low, the rate of political violence will tend to be relatively low, even if agrarian inequality is relatively high; whereas if income inequality is relatively high, the rate of political violence will tend to be relatively high, even if agrarian inequality is relatively low.

Our inequality hypothesis, which is based on an integration of discontent (or relative deprivation) arguments (e.g., Gurr 1970) with the resource mobilization approach, can be illustrated by the cases of Costa Rica and Venezuela, where egalitarian redistribution of income occurred despite persisting high agrarian inequality; and the case of Iran, where income inequality worsened, especially in urban areas, despite an egalitarian land reform.

Costa Rica circa 1960 had a relatively inegalitarian distribution of land (the 1963 Gini coefficient was .78) and an extremely inegalitarian distribution of income (the richest 20% of families received 61% of total personal income in 1961). During the decade of the 1960s the distribution of land in Costa Rica became slightly more concentrated (the 1973 Gini coefficient was .82). The distribution of income, however, was substantially altered in an egalitarian direction by democratically elected reformist administrations who pursued welfare-state policies similar to those of European social democratic governments. By 1970 the share of national income accruing to the richest quintile of Costa Rican households had been reduced to 50%.[3] As mentioned above, violent conflict was absent from Costa Rican politics during the 1970s.

Venezuela was a similarly inegalitarian society circa 1960, when a democratic regime was inaugurated. The 1956 Gini index of land concentration was .91—the second highest in the world next to Peru—and the richest quintile of Venezuelan households received 59% of total personal income in 1962. During the 1960s the distribution of land in Venezuela remained highly concentrated (the 1971 Gini coefficient was .91), but the distribution of income became more egalitarian—although not as dramatically so as in Costa Rica—due to a combination of reformist administrations and an expanding petroleum-based economic pie (by 1970 the income share of the richest quintile of households had been reduced to 54%). Deaths from political violence in Venezuela registered a sharp decline over this period (according to Taylor and Jodice 1983, vol. 2, tbl. 2.7, they amounted to 1,392 during the years 1958–62; 155 during 1963–67; 53 during 1968–72; and 9 during 1973–77). . . .

Of course, income inequality is not the only cause of mass political violence. In Panama, for example, income was distributed very unequally circa 1970, as the richest 20% of households earned 62% of total national income. But by the early 1970s, General Omar Torrijos Herrera, who had led a successful coup d'etat by officers of the national guard in 1968, had crushed all opposition, established firm censorship of the media, and taken control of the judiciary. Ratings of political rights and civil liberties in Panama during the mid-1970s on a scale of one to seven (most free to least free) averaged 6.5.[4] During this period (1973–77) the Torrijos regime in Panama was the most repressive in the Western Hemisphere next to Cuba, where the rating of political rights and civil liberties averaged 6.9. Inequality-induced discontent presumably existed in Panama, and it probably was relatively widespread, but there was little or no opportunity to organize it.

By contrast, Panama's next-door neighbor to the northwest, Costa Rica, enjoyed the distinction in the mid-1970s of being the oldest democracy in Latin America. Since 1949 Costa Rica had held regularly scheduled free and fair elections, the media were uncensored, unions were free to organize, the judiciary was independent of the executive and legislative branches of government, and citizens were not subject to arbitrary arrest. Costa Rica's political and civil rights ratings averaged a maximum score of 1.0 during 1973–77.

The "open" and "closed" political systems of Costa Rica and Panama exemplify polar extremes of regime repressiveness. Differences in regime structure are relevant to the explanation of cross-national variation in mass political violence because they can be assumed to affect three important variables emphasized in some versions of resource mobilization theory (e.g., McAdam 1982): (1) the extent to which dissident groups are able to develop strong organizations, (2) their belief in the likelihood of success of collective action, and (3) the range of political opportunities available to them for achieving their goals.

In the context of an extremely repressive regime, dissident groups are severely restricted in their ability to organize; their belief in the likelihood of success of collective action will probably be low; and opportunities to engage in collective action of any kind will be quite limited. Consequently, under the condition of a high level of regime repressiveness, rational actors most likely will attach a relatively low utility to violent collective action, and the rate of mass political violence therefore should be relatively low.

In the context of a nonrepressive or "democratic" regime, dissident groups will not face significant restrictions on their ability to organize for collective action, and their belief in the likelihood of achieving at least some success from collective action will probably be relatively high. Moreover, a democratic regime structure will afford a variety of opportunities for dissident groups to participate legally and peacefully in the political process. Because the costs of peaceful collective action will be lower than those of violent collective action and because the likelihood of success of peaceful collective action will be reasonably high, rational actors under the condition of a nonrepressive regime structure presumably will usually attach a much higher utility to peaceful as opposed to violent collective action, and, therefore, the rate of mass political violence here too should be relatively low.

In the context of a semirepressive regime, it is possible for dissident groups to develop relatively strong organizations. However, opportunities to engage in nonviolent forms of collective action that effectively exert influence on the political process are limited. Semirepressive regimes allow only for, in Green's (1984, 154) apt terminology, "pseudoparticipation . . . an elaborate charade of the participatory process." Polities with pseudoparticipation typically have elections that are not free and fair, legislatures that are little more than debating societies, and a judiciary that is not independent of the will of the executive; the media are subject to censorship at the whim of the executive; and citizens are subject to arbitrary arrest and detention by security forces, which are under the exclusive control of the executive. In short, semirepressive regimes erect a facade of participatory institutions but do not permit popular input to significantly influence governmental output. Because opportunities for genuine participation are restricted, many politically activated citizens may come to perceive civil disobedience and violence as being more efficacious than legal means of pseudoparticipation; and since the expected costs of insurgency may not be perceived to be prohibitive, rational actors may well attach a relatively high utility to aggressive political behavior. Therefore, it is plausible to expect that the rate of mass political violence cross-nationally will be highest under semirepressive authoritarian regimes.

The analysis of the causes of the Iranian revolution by Green (1982, 1984) documents in detail how the Shah vacillated between fully restricting mass participation and allowing pseudoparticipation and concludes that "the effects of such tactics served to increase popular hostility among those socially mobilized Iranians eager to have a measure of influence over the manner in which their society was ruled" (Green, 1984, 155). Green's case study description is corroborated by global comparative measures of regime repressiveness, which show that Iran in the late 1950s was classified as having a "semi-competitive" regime (Coleman 1960); was scored for 1960 and 1965 as intermediate (34.9 and 45.0, respectively) on a 0–100 scale of extent of political democracy (Bollen 1980); was ranked circa 1969 at an intermediate level on a scale of opportunity for political opposition (Dahl 1971); received a mean rating of 5.7 on political and civil rights for 1973–77; and had shifted in 1978 to a mean rating of 5.0 on political and civil rights. Thus, while pursuing a strategy of economic development that had the short-term consequence of increasing inequality in the distribution of income, the Pahlavi government would appear to have added fuel to the fire by following a semirepressive political development strategy that allowed opposition groups to organize but did not enable them to participate effectively.

If one takes income inequality and the repressiveness of the regime into account simultaneously, it might be argued that each variable could have an independent causal impact on the likelihood of mass political violence. An equally plausible specification of the joint relationship is that discontent resulting from income inequality will affect political violence only (or most strongly) in countries with semirepressive regime structures; whereas in countries with nonrepressive regime structures, inequality-induced discontent will tend to be channeled into peaceful participation; and in countries with repressive regime structures, it will be borne apathetically or else perhaps lead to various kinds of nonpolitical deviant behavior. . . .

A Cross-National Test of the Causal Model

There have been no studies reported to date that compare the causal importance of land maldistribution versus income inequality as determinants of mass political violence cross-nationally.[5] Until the 1970s, reasonably reliable information on the distribution of land and income was available for only a limited number of countries. Thus in Hibbs's (1973) comprehensive cross-national study of determinants of mass political violence during the 1948–67 period, inequality variables had to be excluded because of insufficient data. We now have been able to compile a relatively comprehensive data set on inequality circa 1970 [appendix in original—Eds.]. Information on land inequality is available for approximately three-quarters of the population of independent political units in 1970, while information on landlessness and income inequality is available for approximately one-half of the population. Regionally, these data are quite comprehensive for Europe and the Americas. In regard to landlessness and, especially, income distribution, coverage is poor for states in the Middle East and North Africa, and it is somewhat limited for the states of sub-Saharan Africa. Since it is unlikely that much new data on inequality circa

1970 will emerge in the future, results using the current data set can probably be regarded as being about as definitive as possible for this time period.

Measurement of the Dependent Variable

Political violence is measured by the natural logarithm of the death rate from domestic conflict per one million population.[6] Annual death counts are from Table 2.7 of Taylor and Jodice (1983, vol. 2). Current political violence is the logged sum of annual deaths from domestic political conflict during 1973–77 divided by midinterval population; lagged political violence is the logged sum of annual deaths from domestic political conflict during 1968–72 divided by midinterval population. Countries where domestic political conflict overlaps with major interstate wars are excluded: Kampuchea, Laos, and South Vietnam for the 1968–77 period; and Pakistan for the 1968–72 period (where an extremely high death rate reflects the conflict between India and Pakistan in 1971 over the secession of Bangladesh). Ireland also is excluded for the 1973–77 period because the relatively high death rate there reflects a spillover from the Northern Ireland conflict.

In the vast majority of countries, the death rate from political violence per one million population is less than 50. A few countries register very extreme scores, however; for example, Zimbabwe's 1973–77 death rate from political violence was 544 per million and Argentina's death rate was 177 per million. Even after logging, countries with political violence death rates of 50 or more almost always show up as outliers in regression equations (i.e., they usually have extremely high standardized residuals). Consequently, in order to reduce the problem of extreme scores on the dependent variable, it is desirable to set a ceiling on the death rate. The upper limit that we have selected is 50 deaths per million. The adjusted death rate variables thus range from a minimum value of 0 to a maximum value of 50 or more; and the range of the logged death rate variables is from 0 to 3.93.

Measurement of the Independent Variables

The data on land inequality circa 1970 encompass 85 states in which agriculture was not collectivized. Land inequality is measured by the Gini coefficient of land concentration. A weighted index of land inequality is the geometric mean of the Gini coefficient (expressed as a percentage) and the percentage of the labor force employed in agriculture in 1970 (see Taylor and Jodice 1983, vol. 1). Apart from measurement of the extent to which land is concentrated in the hands of the few, we also take into account a second aspect of land maldistribution, landlessness, as measured by agricultural households without land as a proportion of the total labor force. These data are derived from estimates by Prosterman and Riedinger (1982) of the proportion in 64 countries of agricultural households without land.

Income inequality is measured by the size of the share of personal income accruing to the richest quintile of recipients, based on information about the nationwide distribution of income in 63 countries compiled principally from publications of the World Bank. Although some previous studies have used Gini coefficients of income concentration, this measure tends to be unduly sensitive to inequality in the middle of the distribution, whereas inequality in reference to the top of the distribution probably is more relevant to political violence. In any event, income shares also have a more direct meaning than Gini coefficients and are currently more frequently used in research on income inequality.

Regime repressiveness is measured by a country's 1973–77 average annual combined rating on 7-point rank-order scales of political rights and civil liberties that have been reported by Raymond D. Gastil since 1973 (the data are from Taylor and Jodice 1983). A semirepressive regime structure is defined operationally as a mean political rights and civil liberties rank in the range of 2.6–5.5. These cutpoints are identical to those used by Gastil for classifying political systems as "free" (1.0–2.5), "partly free" (2.6–5.5), and "not free" (5.6–7.0).

The indicator of governmental acts of coercion is the negative sanctions variable (imposition of sanctions) from Taylor and Jodice 1983 (vol. 2, tbl. 3.1). Current negative sanctions is the frequency of negative sanctions summed over the years 1973–77 and divided by midinterval total population in millions; lagged negative sanctions are the 1968–72 frequency per one million midinterval population. The negative sanctions variables are expressed as natural logarithms (after adding an increment of one).

The indicator of intensity of separatism is an ordinal scale developed by Ted and Erika Gurr. The data for circa 1975 are from Taylor and Jodice 1983, 55–57 and tbl. 2.5. We express intensity of separatism as a dummy variable, scored 1 (i.e., high intensity) if groups or regions actively advocating greater autonomy were forcibly incorporated into the state (codes 3 and 4) and 0 (i.e., low intensity) otherwise (codes 0, 1, and 2).[7]

Level of economic development is measured by energy consumption per capita in 1970 (from Taylor and Jodice 1983, vol. 1). Values of this variable are expressed as natural logarithms.

Land Maldistribution, Income Inequality, and Political Violence

According to what is generally considered to be the most appropriate specification of the land inequality hypothesis (e.g., Huntington 1968; Nagel 1976; Prosterman 1976), the strongest effect on political violence should be observed when inequality in the distribution of land is weighted by the proportion of the labor force employed in the agricultural sector of the economy. This specification implies a multiplicative interaction between land inequality and the size of the agricultural labor force, which we call *agrarian inequality,* defined operationally as the geometric mean of Gini land concentration and the percentage of the labor force employed in agriculture (i.e., the square root of the product of these variables). . . .

Results

The results of testing the inequality hypotheses in the context of a multivariate model of determinants of political violence are summarized in Figure 13.1. All of the evidence that we have considered points to the presence of a robust, positive monotonic (positively accelerated) relationship between income inequality and political violence that is independent of the other variables in the model. The effect of income inequality on political violence may be enhanced by the presence of a semirepressive regime, but the evidence is not conclusive in that regard, so we represent the possibility of an interaction between income inequality and semirepressiveness by arrows. The other solid arrows linking explanatory variables to political violence also denote relationships that hold for change as well as level of violence and seem to be robust. We have tested the regime-repressiveness hypothesis with a dummy variable in this study (in order to take into account the possibility of an interaction with income inequality). It should be noted, however, that the same kind of effect appears if regime repressiveness is expressed as a continuous quantitative variable—that is, if the semirepressive-regime dummy variable is replaced by regime repressiveness and its square, a statistically significant nonmonotonic-inverted-U-curve relationship between regime repressiveness and political violence is consistently observed in multivariate equations that include income inequality and the other explanatory variables. We have not tested for the possibility of an instantaneous reciprocal relationship between political violence and governmental acts of coercion (see Hibbs 1973) because that is a complex topic requiring

Figure 13.1   Observed Causal Paths in the Multivariate Causal Model

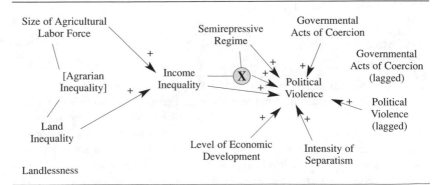

a separate paper. From preliminary work, however, we are confident that it is valid to infer the presence of a positive effect of current governmental acts of coercion on current political violence. . . .

The only completely irrelevant variable in the model is landlessness, a finding that runs counter to the strong claim of causal importance for this variable made by Prosterman (1976). Moreover, at least as a general determinant of mass political violence, the condition of high agrarian inequality also fails to warrant the strong causal claims made for it by many scholars. The components of agrarian inequality, land inequality and size of the agricultural labor force, affect income inequality and, therefore, are indirectly relevant to political violence, but neither the weighted index of agrarian inequality nor land inequality per se has any direct effect on political violence.

Discussion

The finding that agrarian inequality is relevant only to the extent that it is associated with inequality in the nationwide distribution of income has important policy implications. Land reform in third world countries all too often is considered to be a panacea for problems of inequality. However, as Huntington (1968, 385) points out, redistribution of land is the most difficult of reforms for modernizing governments because it almost always entails some degree of outright confiscation. And our study indicates that land redistribution is also not necessarily the most meaningful of reforms. If land redistribution is carried through to the point of actually effecting an egalitarian redistribution of income, as seems to have been the case in countries as diverse as Taiwan and Egypt, and/or if other economic development policies do not exacerbate income inequality, then land reform can make a contribution to the promotion of political stability. However, there are cases such as Bolivia and Mexico in which land reform has not been associated with egalitarian income redistribution. Land reform without income redistribution is probably at best merely a temporary palliative; and at worst, as the case of Iran demonstrates, it can be quite counterproductive by alienating powerful conservative groups such as the nobility and the clergy. Indeed, by simultaneously encouraging both land reform and a policy of rapid economic growth that ignored inegalitarian distributional consequences, U.S. advisors to the Shah would appear unwittingly to have exacerbated the economic preconditions of revolution in Iran.

If the effect of income inequality on change in political violence and its level, observed for 60 and 62 cases, is reliable and more or less generalizable across time in the contemporary world (at least for nontraditional societies where modern values like equality can be assumed to have become salient), it follows that redistribution of income must be ranked as one of the more meaningful reforms that a modernizing government can undertake in the interest of achieving political stability. Unfortunately, redistribution of income may conflict not only with the class interests of many third world governments but also with their predilection for rapid industrialization. The Shah's great dream of surpassing Sweden by the year 2000 was dashed in part by his single-minded concern with economic growth and the raising of per capita income. As Green (1982, 70–71) points out, "the premise of the Pahlavi development ethos rested on the assumption that economic development was more important than political rights or justice." Iran in the years immediately preceding the revolution indeed registered an extraordinary growth of per capita gross national product, which averaged an increase of 13.3% annually during 1970–78, the highest rate of growth of GNP per capita in the world (see Taylor and Jodice 1983, vol. 1, tbl. 3.6); but at the same time that per capita income was increasing phenomenally, the distribution of that income was apparently becoming more concentrated at the top, presumably heightening perceptions of economic injustice. It is important to emphasize, however, that there is no necessary trade-off between rapid economic growth and income inequality. Taiwan's average annual growth of GNP per capita during 1960–78 was 6.6% (see World Bank 1980, tbl. 1), a rate that, although surpassed by Iran (the world leader excluding Romania), was nevertheless almost twice as high as the average rate (3.7%) for all middle-income countries. At the same time (1964–78), the income share of the richest 20% of households in Taiwan declined from 41.1% to 37.2% (see Tsiang 1984, tbl. 9). Thus, by following a different set of economic policies than the Shah, the government of Taiwan achieved growth with equity. And the death rate from political violence in Taiwan during 1973–77 was .06, as compared with Iran's rate of .91. . . .

Notes

A version of this paper was presented at the 1985 Midwest Political Science Association meeting in Chicago, April 18–21. Support for this research was provided by National Science Foundation Grant SES83-2021.

1. Midlarsky and Roberts distinguish between these cases in regard to the dynamics of coalition formation leading to different kinds of revolutionary movements. Although both countries had inegalitarian distributions of land, creating a potential for insurgency in each case, the revolutionary movement in El Salvador was more narrowly class-based than in Nicaragua, due to differences in population density that produced greater land scarcity in El Salvador than in Nicaragua. This difference is thought to have enhanced the likelihood of a successful revolution in Nicaragua.

2. Unless otherwise noted, data on land and income distribution referred to in the text are either from Table A-1 [see original work] or, for years other than those in Table A-1, from the sources cited therein.

3. Based on a study reported by Céspedes (1979). Trejos (1983) reports the income share of the richest 20% of households in Costa Rica as 51.1% in 1971, 52.1% in 1974, and 53% in 1977.

4. These and all subsequent data on civil and political liberties referred to in the text are calculated from the data file of the *World Handbook of Political and Social Indicators*. For a description of the ratings, see Taylor and Jodice 1983 (1:58–65).

5. The only previous research on this topic is reported in Midlarsky 1981, where income distribution is measured by an index of intersectoral inequality. As Sigelman and Simpson (1977, 111) have pointed out, however, this index "is at best a second-rate measurement proxy for personal income, lacking theoretical interest of its own."

6. Deaths from political violence are an attribute of political-protest events like riots, armed attacks, and assassinations. Deaths are thus a summary measure of the intensity of political-protest events. Deaths are used in preference to a composite index for the following reasons: (1) a single-variable indicator is more easily interpretable than a composite measure; (2) deaths will necessarily correlate very strongly with a composite measure such as that constructed by Hibbs (1973), which includes deaths, armed attacks, and assassinations; and (3) there is probably less reporting bias for deaths than for indicators such as armed attacks (see Weede 1981). Death *rate* is preferred over raw counts because the former is an indicator of the extent to which the regime is threatened by insurgency, which depends not on the absolute frequency of political violence but rather on its frequency relative to size of population (for further discussion of this issue see Linehan 1976; Muller 1985; and Weede 1981). The logarithmic transformation is theoretically appropriate because death rate from political violence is expected to vary as a positively accelerated function of inequality; it is also necessary because of the presence of extreme values—although the problem of extreme values still exists after logging. An increment of one is added to each death score before logging because the log of zero is undefined.

7. In testing the multivariate model across 62 cases, the following countries are missing data on intensity of separatism: Barbados, Gabon, Honduras, Ivory Coast, Malawi, Nepal, Sierra Leone, and Trinidad and Tobago. Based on country descriptions from Banks 1976, these countries were scored zero on intensity of separatism.

References

Ahluwalia, Montak S. 1976. Inequality, Poverty, and Development. *Journal of Development Economics* 3:307–42.

Bandura, Albert. 1973. *Aggression: A Social Learning Analysis*. Englewood Cliffs, NJ: Prentice-Hall.

Banks, Arthur S., ed. 1976. *Political Handbook of the World: 1976*. New York: Mc-Graw-Hill.

Bharier, Julian. 1971. *Economic Development in Iran 1900–1970*. New York: Oxford University Press.

Bollen, Kenneth A. 1980. Issues in the Comparative Measurement of Political Democracy. *American Sociological Review* 45:370–90.

Bornschier, Volker, and Peter Heintz, eds. 1979. *Compendium of Data for World System Analysis*. Zurich: Soziologisches Institut der Universität.

Buss, Arnold H. 1961. *A Psychology of Aggression*. New York: Wiley.

Céspedes, Victor H. 1979. *Evolución de la distribución del ingreso en Costa Rica*. Serie divulgación económica, No. 18. Costa Rica: Ciudad Universitaria Rodrigo Facio.

Coleman, James S. 1960. Conclusion: The Political Systems of the Developing Areas. In *The Politics of the Developing Areas,* ed. Gabriel A. Almond and James S. Coleman. Princeton: Princeton University Press.

Dahl, Robert A. 1971. *Polyarchy.* New Haven: Yale University Press.

Fei, John C. H., Gustav Ranis, and Shirley W. Y. Kuo. 1979. *Growth with Equity: The Taiwan Case.* New York: Oxford University Press.

Food and Agriculture Organization of the United States. 1981. *Nineteen Seventy World Census of Agriculture: Analysis and International Comparison of the Results.* Rome: author.

Gamson, William A. 1975. *The Strategy of Social Protest.* Homewood, IL: Dorsey.

Green, Jerrold D. 1982. *Revolution in Iran.* New York: Praeger.

Green, Jerrold D. 1984. Countermobilization as a Revolutionary Form. *Comparative Politics* 16:153–69.

Gurr, Ted Robert. 1970. *Why Men Rebel.* Princeton: Princeton University Press.

Hardy, Melissa A. 1979. Economic Growth, Distributional Inequality, and Political Conflict in Industrial Societies. *Journal of Political and Military Sociology* 5:209–27.

Hibbs, Douglas A. 1973. *Mass Political Violence.* New York: Wiley.

Huntington, Samuel P. 1968. *Political Order in Changing Societies.* New Haven: Yale University Press.

Jabbari, Ahmad. 1981. Economic Factors in Iran's Revolution: Poverty, Inequality, and Inflation. In *Iran: Essays on a Revolution in the Making,* ed. Ahmad Jabbari and Robert Olson. Lexington, KY: Mazda.

Jain, Shail. 1975. *Size Distribution of Income.* Washington, DC: World Bank.

Keddie, Nikki R. 1968. The Iranian Village before and after Land Reform. *Journal of Contemporary History* 3:69–91.

Leal, Maria Angela. 1983. Heritage of Hunger: Population, Land, and Survival. In *Revolution in Central America,* ed. Stanford Central America Action Network. Boulder, CO: Westview.

Linehan, William J. 1976. Models for the Measurement of Political Instability. *Political Methodology* 3:441–86.

McAdam, Doug. 1982. *Political Process and the Development of Black Insurgency.* Chicago: University of Chicago Press.

Midlarsky, Manus I. 1981. The Revolutionary Transformation of Foreign Policy: Agrarianism and Its International Impact. In *The Political Economy of Foreign Policy Behavior,* ed. Charles W. Kegley and Patrick J. McGowan. Beverly Hills, CA: Sage.

Midlarsky, Manus I. 1982. Scarcity and Inequality. *Journal of Conflict Resolution* 26:3–38.

Midlarsky, Manus I., and Kenneth Roberts. 1985. Class, State, and Revolution in Central America: Nicaragua and El Salvador Compared. *Journal of Conflict Resolution* 29:163–93.

Muller, Edward N. 1985. Income Inequality, Regime Repressiveness, and Political Violence. *American Sociological Review* 50:47–61.

Muller, Edward N. 1986. Income Inequality and Political Violence: The Effect of Influential Cases. *American Sociological Review* 51:441–45.

Nagel, Jack. 1976. Erratum. *World Politics* 28:315.

Norusis, Marija J. 1986. *SPSS/PC+.* Chicago: SPSS.

Oberschall, Anthony. 1973. *Social Conflict and Social Movements.* Englewood Cliffs, NJ: Prentice-Hall.

Paige, Jeffery M. 1975. *Agrarian Revolution.* New York: Free Press.

Paukert, Felix. 1973. Income Distribution at Different Levels of Development: A Survey of Evidence. *International Labour Review* 108:97–125.

Prosterman, Roy L. 1976. IRI: A Simplified Predictive Index of Rural Instability. *Comparative Politics* 8:339–54.

Prosterman, Roy L., and Jeffrey M. Riedinger. 1982. Toward an Index of Democratic Development. In *Freedom in the World: Political Rights and Civil Liberties 1982,* ed. Raymond D. Gastil. Westport, CT: Greenwood Press.

Roberti, Paolo. 1974. Income Distribution: A Time-Series and a Cross-Section Survey. *Economic Journal* 84:629–38.

Russett, Bruce M. 1964. Inequality and Instability: The Relation of Land Tenure to Politics. *World Politics* 16:442–54.

Sawyer, Malcolm. 1976. Income Distribution in OECD Countries. *OECD Economic Outlook,* Occasional Studies, July, 3–36.

Seligson, Mitchell A., Richard Hough, John Kelley, Stephen Miller, Russell Derossier, and Fred L. Mann. 1983. *Land and Labor in Guatemala: An Assessment.* Washington, DC: Agency for International Development and Development Associates.

Sigelman, Lee, and Miles Simpson. 1977. A Cross-National Test of the Linkage between Economic Inequality and Political Violence. *Journal of Conflict Resolution* 21:105–28.

Skocpol, Theda. 1979. *States and Social Revolutions.* New York: Cambridge University Press.

Tanter, Raymond, and Manus I. Midlarsky. 1967. A Theory of Revolution. *Journal of Conflict Resolution* 11:264–80.

Taylor, Charles L., and Michael C. Hudson. 1972. *World Handbook of Political and Social Indicators.* 2d ed. New Haven: Yale University Press.

Taylor, Charles L., and David A. Jodice. 1983. *World Handbook of Political and Social Indicators.* 3d ed. Vols. 1 and 2. New Haven: Yale University Press.

Tilly, Charles. 1969. Collective Violence in European Perspective. In *Violence in America: Historical and Comparative Perspectives,* ed. Hugh Davis Graham and Ted Robert Gurr. New York: Signet Books.

Tilly, Charles. 1978. *From Mobilization to Revolution.* Reading, MA: Addison-Wesley.

Trejos, Juan Diego. 1983. *La distribución del ingreso de las familes Costarricenses: Algunas caracteristicas en 1977.* San Jose: Instituto investigaciones en ciencias económicas, Universidad de Costa Rica, No. 50.

Tsiang, S. C. 1984. Taiwan's Economic Miracle: Lessons in Economic Development. In *World Economic Growth,* ed. Arnold C. Harberger. San Francisco: Institute for Contemporary Studies.

United States Agency for International Development. 1983. *Country Development Strategy Statement: Jamaica, FY 1985.* Washington, DC: Government Printing Office.

Webb, Richard C. 1976. The Distribution of Income in Peru. In *Income Distribution in Latin America,* ed. Alejandro Foxley. New York: Cambridge University Press.

Weede, Erich. 1981. Income Inequality, Average Income, and Domestic Violence. *Journal of Conflict Resolution* 25:639–53.

Weede, Erich. 1986. Income Inequality and Political Violence Reconsidered. *American Sociological Review* 51:438–41.

World Bank. 1979, 1980, 1981, 1982, 1983, 1984, 1985. *World Development Report.* New York: Oxford University Press.

14

Global Inequality: Beyond the Bottom Billion

Isabel Ortiz and Matthew Cummins

In this chapter, Isabel Ortiz and Matthew Cummins provide an overview of income inequality between 1990 and 2007. They also compare levels of income inequality found when examining exchange rate–converted data with levels found when using market exchange rates. Using market exchange rate data, they find that the richest quintile receive 83 percent of global income while the poorest 20 percent earn only 1 percent. At the current rate of change, the authors argue, it would take 800 years for the bottom billion to earn 10 percent of the world's income. In terms of children, the authors point out that almost half of the world's young are in the bottom two income quintiles.

VIEWED AS AN "UNWELCOMED" AND "POLITICALLY SENSITIVE" TOPIC, world income inequality received little attention in international fora for decades. In 2004, however, the International Labour Organization (ILO) published its pioneering report on the social dimension of globalization, *A Fair Globalization*. Soon after, major development institutions began to focus flagship publications on inequality, including the United Nations 2005 Report on the World Social Situation, *The Inequality Predicament*, the United Nations Development Programme's (UNDP) 2005 Human Development Report, *Aid,*

Reprinted from I. Ortiz and M. Cummins, "Global Inequality: Beyond the Bottom Billion—A Rapid Review of Income Distribution in 141 Countries," Social and Economic Policy Working Paper, UNICEF, 2011.

Trade and Security in an Unequal World, the World Bank's 2006 World Development Report, *Equity and Development*, and the International Monetary Fund's (IMF) 2007 World Economic Outlook, *Globalization and Inequality*. UNICEF also initiated its Global Study on Child Poverty and Disparities in 2007, and the United Nations University's World Institute for Development Economics Research (UNU-WIDER) released a comprehensive study, The World Distribution of Household Wealth, in 2008 based on its World Income Inequality Database. More recently, the World Bank opened a research line fully devoted to global inequality: Poverty and Inequality. The unanimous drive of international institutions to understand and focus attention on income disparities shows that inequality can no longer be avoided in development policy discussions. . . .

This working paper focuses exclusively on income inequality. While income is just one measure of inequality, it is often closely associated with social inequalities in terms of coverage and outcomes. . . .

Market Exchange Rates

We first look at global income distribution using market exchange rates, where all national income estimates are compared in constant 2000 U.S. dollars. Figure 14.1 and Table 14.1 show the distribution of world income from 1990 to 2007 according to the *global* accounting model, which decomposes national income by population quintiles and compares those across countries. This includes all individuals for which data are available, from the poorest quintile in the Democratic Republic of Congo to the richest quintile in Luxembourg. . . . The distribution data reveal an incredibly unequal planet. As of 2007, the wealthiest 20 percent of mankind enjoyed nearly 83 percent of total global income compared to the poorest 20 percent, which had exactly a single percentage point under the global accounting model. Perhaps more shocking, the poorest 40 percent of the global population increased its share of total income by less than one percent between 1990 and 2007. . . .

However, not all countries have distribution data. As Table 14.1 shows, we have data for 100 countries in 1990, 126 countries in 2000 and 135 countries in 2007. Still under market exchange rates, we now turn to a second approach to measuring global income distribution, which is known as the *inter-country* accounting model. This method looks at the average income differences between large groupings of countries by treating all members of a country as if they have the same income and then dividing the world into population quintiles. This method is less precise, but allows us to estimate global income distribution for most of the world, a total of 182 countries in 2007. Figure 14.2 and Table 14.2 present the income distribution results from 1990 to

Figure 14.1 Global Income Distribution by Population Quintile, 1990–2007 (or latest available) in Constant 2000 U.S. dollars

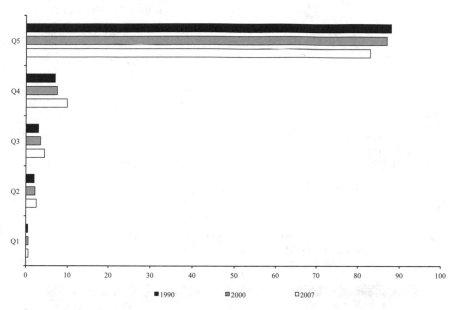

Source: Authors' calculations using World Bank (2011), UNU-WIDER (2008) and Eurostat (2011).

Table 14.1 Summary Results of Global Income Distribution by Population Quintiles, 1990-2007

	Global Distribution (%)		
	1990	2000	2007
Q5	87	86.8	82.8
Q4	8.1	7.5	9.9
Q3	2.8	3.2	4.2
Q2	1.4	1.6	2.1
Q1	0.8	0.8	1
# of observations	100	126	135
% of global population	86.3	91.1	92.4
% of global GDP	79	81.4	82.6

Source: Authors' calculations using World Bank (2011), UNU-WIDER (2008) and Eurostat (2011).

Table 14.2   Summary Results of Global Income Distribution by Countries, 1990–2007

	Inter-country Distribution (%)		
	1990	2000	2007
Q5	85.7	85.2	81.2
Q4	9.6	7.9	9.4
Q3	2.0	3.5	5.6
Q2	1.6	2.1	2.4
Q1	1.2	1.3	1.4
# of observations	173	180	182
% of global population	97.0	97.6	97.6
% of global GDP	98.3	98.3	98.1

Source: Authors' calculations using World Bank (2011).

Figure 14.2   Global Income Distribution, 1990–2007 (or latest available) in Constant 2000 U.S. dollars

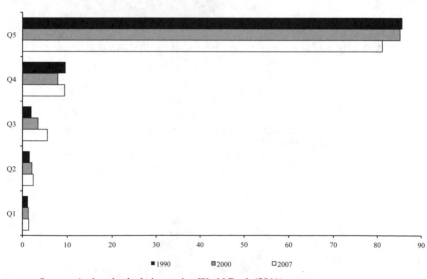

Source: Authors' calculations using World Bank (2011).

2007. Here, the wealthiest 20 percent of the population enjoyed more than 81 percent of the world's income as of 2007, with the poorest 20 percent holding on to just over one percent. Similar to the global accounting model, the rate of change for the poorest 40 percent of the world population remains dismal at one percent between 1990 and 2007. . . .

PPP Exchange Rates

The earlier set of findings for the global accounting model was based on market exchange rates. But what happens if we compare national income estimates using PPP-adjusted exchange rates?

While the overall picture of global inequality improves under the PPP measure, the data still confirm grave income disparities. As of 2007, the top 20 percent of the world controlled about 70 percent of total income compared to just two percent for the bottom 20 percent. Regarding change, the poorest 40 percent of the global population increased its share of total income by a meager 1.7 percent between 1990 and 2007. . . .

We also present the inter-country accounting model using PPP estimates in order to allow us to see the picture for almost the entire world countries instead of a smaller set of countries. As in the PPP-adjusted global accounting model, inequality marginally improves under this method, but world income disparities are still severe. Whereas the top 20 percent of the global population controlled about 64 percent of total income as of 2007, the bottom 20 percent had just over three percent. Similarly, in terms of change, the poorest 40 percent of the global population increased its share of total income by only three percentage points over nearly two decades. . . .

The Takeaway

Both income distribution accounting models offer strikingly similar results. Under market exchange rates, we inhabit a planet in which the top quintile controls more than 80 percent of global income contrasted by a paltry percentage point for those at the bottom. While the disparity improves under PPP exchange rates (67 to 2.6 percent), both models reveal a world that is deeply corroded by income disparities. Each of the accounting methods and exchange rate scenarios also suggest that some progress is taking place for the poorest; however, the sluggish pace of change is clearly unacceptable. Using the rate of change under the global accounting model with market exchange rates, it took 17 years for the bottom billion to improve their share of world income by 0.18 percentage points, from 0.77 percent in 1990 to 0.95 percent in 2007 (see Q1 in Table 14.1). At this speed, it would take more than eight centuries (855 years to be exact) for the bottom billion to have ten percent of global income.

Global Income Inequality Trends
and the Poor, Children and Women

While the previous section showed the vast income inequalities that characterize our world, this section sets out to answer some of the more pressing questions regarding the overlying trends and impacts of this reality. In particular, what do we know about global inequality trends over a longer-term horizon? What do the extreme distortions in income distribution at the global level mean for different groups, such as the poor, children, women or the middle classes? And are there alternative measures of wealth that could shed further light on the overall state of global inequality at present?

Income Inequality in Historical Perspective

What do we know about world income inequalities over the past centuries? Studies using longer time series conclude that income inequality has been constantly increasing since the early 19th century. Milanovic (2009), for example, calculates Gini indices over time and finds that global income inequality rose steadily from 1820 to 2002, with a significant increase from 1980 onwards. To further inform the more recent trajectory, Cornia (2003) concludes that inequality increased globally between the early 1980s and 1990s following a review of different studies. While our analysis shows some reversal of this trend, there is a significant likelihood that income inequality is being exacerbated in the ongoing global economic crisis.

The Poor

What does global inequality mean for the poor? . . . [A]pproximately 1.2 billion were living on less than $1.25 per day in 2007 (22 percent of the world population) and about 2.2 billion on less than $2 per day (or about 40 percent of the world population). An alternative way of viewing the "champagne glass" is to compare the top percent of world income earners versus the bottom. In doing so, we find that the wealthiest 61 million individuals (or one percent of the global population) had the same amount of income as the poorest 3.5 billion (or 56 percent) as of 2007.

Children and Youth

What does global inequality mean for children and youth? At the global level, most children live in the poorest income quintiles (Figure 14.3). When comparing the concentration of youth populations across global income distribution quintiles, we find that about half (48.5 percent) of the world's young persons are confined to the bottom two income quintiles. This means that out of the three billion persons under the age of 24 in the world as of 2007, approximately 1.5 billion were living in situations in which they and their families had access to just nine percent of global income. Moving up the distribution pyramid, children and youth do not fare much better: more than two-thirds of the world's youth have access to less than 20 percent of global wealth, with 86 percent of all young people living on about one-third of world income. For the

Figure 14.3   Global Income Distribution and Children/Youth in 2007 in PPP Constant 2005 International Dollars*

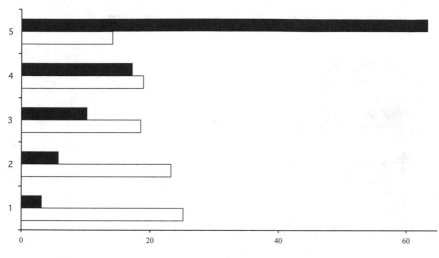

■ Income distribution (% of global GDP)   □ Children/Youth Population (% of global total, ages 0-24)

Source: Author's calculations using World Bank (2011), UNU-WIDER (2008), and United Nations (2009).
Note: *According to the Inter-country accounting model.

just over 400 million youth who are fortunate enough to rank among families or situations atop the distribution pyramid, however, opportunities abound with more than 60 percent of global income within their reach.

Women

Unlike youth, income disparities do not appear to have a disproportionate, negative impact on women (Figure 14.4). When examining the percentage of females across global income distribution quintiles, we find that the dispersion is, in fact, nearly equal, with each income quintile containing about 20 percent of the global female population. This means that female populations, on the aggregate, face the same levels of income inequality as the population at large. Given that the female-to-male ratio was about 1:1 as of 2007, this comes as little surprise. Even if further restricting the global female population to girls and young women, gender disparities are not evident: about half of women 24 years old or younger are situated in the bottom two income quintiles, which mirrors the proportion of children and youth as presented in Figure 14.4. In sum, income inequality has a much stronger impact on age than gender, which is largely due to higher fertility rates among poorer women.

Figure 14.4   Global Income Distribution and Gender in 2007 in PPP Constant 2005 International Dollars*

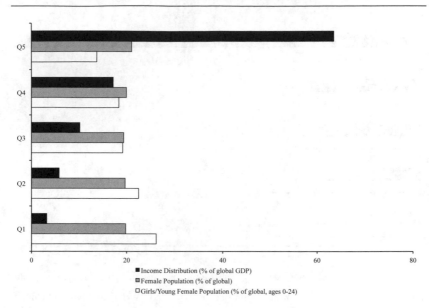

■ Income Distribution (% of global GDP)
▨ Female Population (% of global)
☐ Girls/Young Female Population (% of global, ages 0-24)

Source: Authors' calculations using World Bank (2011), UNU-WIDER (2008) and United Nations (2009).

Note: *According to the Inter-country accounting model.

Still, the numbers of adult women and girls living in poverty are alarming. As of 2007, roughly 20 percent of women were below the $1.25/day international poverty line, and 40 percent below the $2/day mark. Girls and younger women also suffer disproportionately from poverty, as more than one-quarter of females under the age of 25 were below the $1.25/day international poverty line, and about half on less than $2/day.

15

Equality and Efficiency: Is There a Trade-off Between the Two or Do They Go Hand in Hand?

Andrew G. Berg and Jonathan D. Ostry

Highly regarded economists have long argued that there is a trade-off between equality and economic growth, such that the more equal the distribution, the slower the growth. If that were true, then development agencies and national governments should not make any effort to reduce inequality, since doing so would only impoverish the nation. Moreover, it would suggest that the gap between rich and poor, the central focus of this volume, is a good thing, since greater inequality would produce more wealth. In this chapter, Andrew Berg and Jonathan Ostry argue that equality does not slow growth, but actually speeds it up. The key to the difference between the two analyses is short-term versus long-term growth. Berg and Ostry show that while high inequality may produce a growth spurt, such advances are not sustainable over the long run. They concur with Muller and Seligson (Chapter 13), pointing to the Middle East, that high inequality leads to unrest. In addition, high inequality can cause unsustainable booms (or bubbles), in which the poor borrow more than they are able to repay, leading to financial crises like the Great Depression of the 1930s and the meltdown of 2008. Based on an empirical analysis, Berg and Ostry conclude that for each 10-percentile decline in inequality, the length of a growth spell increases by 50 percent. Thus the key challenge is achieving sustained growth, and only when inequality is low is this possible for most countries.

Reprinted with permission of the Initiative for Policy Dialogue from the *Journal of Globalization and Development* 1, no. 2 (2010).

IN HIS INFLUENTIAL 1975 BOOK *EQUALITY AND EFFICIENCY: "THE BIG Tradeoff,"* Arthur Okun argued that pursuing equality can reduce efficiency (the total output produced with given resources). The late Yale University and Brookings Institution economist said that not only can more equal distribution of incomes reduce incentives to work and invest, but the efforts to redistribute—through such mechanisms as the tax code and minimum wages—can themselves be costly. Okun likened these mechanisms to a "leaky bucket." Some of the resources transferred from rich to poor "will simply disappear in transit, so the poor will not receive all the money that is taken from the rich"— the result of administrative costs and disincentives to work for both those who pay taxes and those who receive transfers.

Do societies inevitably face an invidious choice between efficient production and equitable wealth and income distribution? Are social justice and social product at war with one another?

In a word, no.

In recent work (Berg, Ostry, and Zettelmeyer, 2011; and Berg and Ostry, 2011), we discovered that when growth is looked at over the long term, the trade-off between efficiency and equality may not exist. In fact equality appears to be an important ingredient in promoting and sustaining growth. The difference between countries that can sustain rapid growth for many years or even decades and the many others that see growth spurts fade quickly may be the level of inequality. Countries may find that improving equality may also improve efficiency, understood as more sustainable long-run growth.

Inequality matters for growth and other macroeconomic outcomes, in all corners of the globe. One need look no further than the role inequality is thought to have played in creating the disaffection that underlies much of the recent unrest in the Middle East. And, taking a historical perspective, the increase in U.S. income inequality in recent decades is strikingly similar to the increase that occurred in the 1920s. In both cases there was a boom in the financial sector, poor people borrowed a lot, and a huge financial crisis ensued (see "Leveraging Inequality," F&D, December 2010 and "Inequality = Indebtedness" in this issue of F&D). The recent global economic crisis, with its roots in U.S. financial markets, may have resulted, in part at least, from the increase in inequality. With inequality growing in the United States and other important economies, the relationship between inequality and growth takes on more significance.

How Do Economies Grow?

Most thinking about long-run growth assumes implicitly that development is something akin to climbing a hill, that it entails more or less steady increases in real income, punctuated by business cycle fluctuations. The pattern in Figure 15.1—which shows the level of real (after-inflation) per capita income in two

Figure 15.1   Climbing the Hill

For advanced economies like the United Kingdom and the United States, income grows at a more or less steady pace over the long run.

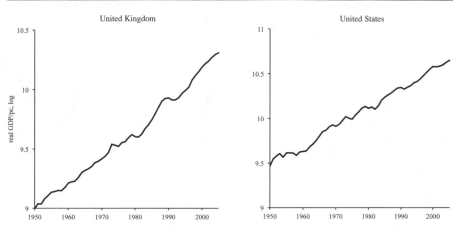

Source: Penn World Tables Version 6.2.

Note: Real GDP per capita is measured in logarithms, which means that the straighter the line, the more constant the growth rate.

advanced economies, the United Kingdom and the United States—is consistent with this idea.

The experiences in developing and emerging economies, however, are far more varied (see Figure 15.2). In some cases, the experience is like climbing a hill. But in others, the experience is more like a roller coaster. Looking at such cases, Pritchett (2000) and other authors have concluded that an understanding of growth must involve looking more closely at the turning points—ignoring the ups and downs of growth over the horizon of the business cycle, and concentrating on why some countries are able to keep growing for long periods whereas others see growth break down after just a few years, followed by stagnation or decay.

A systematic look at this experience suggests that igniting growth is much less difficult than sustaining it (Hausmann, Pritchett, and Rodrik, 2005). Even the poorest of countries have managed to get growth going for several years, only to see it peter out. Where growth laggards differ from their more successful peers is in the degree to which they have been able to sustain growth for long periods of time.

Income Distribution and Growth Sustainability

In our research we looked at the extent to which the duration of a growth episode is related to differences in country characteristics and policies. The

Figure 15.2   Roller Coaster

In developing and emerging markets, long-run growth paths can be steady—or not so steady.

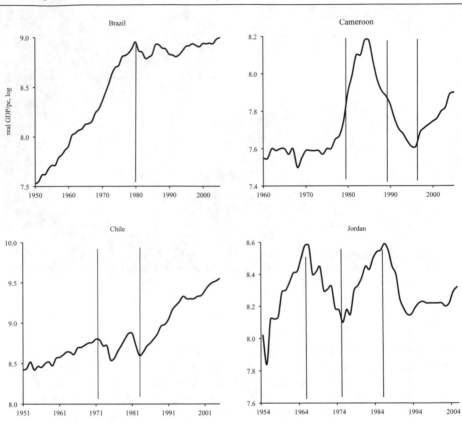

Source: Penn World Tables Version 6.2.

Note: Real GDP per capita is measured in logarithms, which means that the straighter the line, the more constant the growth rate. The vertical lines represent periods when the growth rate makes a significant and persistent change up or down.

quality of economic and political institutions, an outward orientation of an economy, macroeconomic stability, and human capital accumulation have long been recognized as important determinants of economic growth. And we found that they matter for the duration of growth episodes too.

We argue that income distribution may also—and independently—belong in this pantheon of critical determinants of growth duration. At the level of simple correlation, more inequality seems associated with less sustained growth. Figure 15.3 shows the length of growth spells and the average income distribution during the spell for a sample of countries. We define a growth spell as a period of at least five years that begins with an unusual increase in the

Figure 15.3 Lasting Effects
More inequality seems to spell less sustained growth.

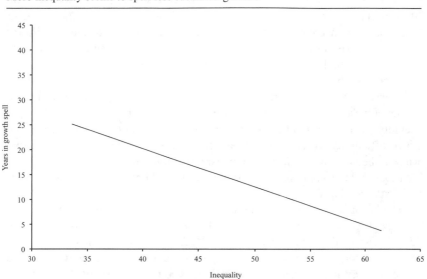

Sources: Penn World Tables; and Wide World Inequality Database.
Note: Inequality is measured by the Gini coefficient, which ranges from zero, where all households have the same income, to 100, where one household has all the income. All spells lasted a minimum of five years. No incomplete spells are included. The data cover the period from 1950 to 2006. Countries in the sample include Belgium, Brazil, Cameroon, Colombia, Ecuador, El Salvador, Greece, Guatemala, Jamaica, Jordan, Pakistan, Panama, Singapore, Thailand, and Zambia.

growth rate and ends with an unusual drop in growth. The measure of inequality is the Gini coefficient, which varies from zero (all households having the same income) to 100 (all income received by one household).

It may seem counterintuitive that inequality is strongly associated with less sustained growth. After all, some inequality is essential to the effective functioning of a market economy and the incentives needed for investment and growth (Chaudhuri and Ravallion, 2007). But too much inequality might be destructive to growth. Beyond the risk that inequality may amplify the potential for financial crisis, it may also bring political instability, which can discourage investment. Inequality may make it harder for governments to make difficult but necessary choices in the face of shocks, such as raising taxes or cutting public spending to avoid a debt crisis. Or inequality may reflect poor people's lack of access to financial services, which gives them fewer opportunities to invest in education and entrepreneurial activity.

Against this background, the question is whether a systematic look at the data supports the notion that societies with more equal income distributions have more durable growth.

We study growth spells as medical researchers might examine life expectancy. They study the effects of age, weight, gender, and smoking habits on life expectancy; we look at whether factors such as political institutions, health and education, macroeconomic instability, debt, and trade openness might influence the likelihood that a growth spell will end. The result is a statistical model of growth duration that relates the expected length of a growth episode (or, equivalently, the risk that it will end in a given year) to several of these variables. We compare the risk that the spell will end in a given year with the values of these variables in previous years—at the beginning of the spell or the previous year—to minimize the risk of reverse causality. In the face of the usual difficulties involved in disentangling cause and effect, and the risk that we have been unable to find good measures of important variables, the results we report below should nonetheless be interpreted only as empirical regularities ("stylized facts").

The analysis suggests that a number of variables found to be important in other contexts also tend to be associated with longer growth spells (see Figure 15.4). To show the importance of each variable, the chart (which covers 1950 to 2006) reports the increase in the expected duration of a growth spell for a given increase in the variable in question, keeping other factors constant. To compare the effects of the different variables on growth duration, we calculate expected duration when all the variables are at their median values (the value greater than that observed in 50 percent of the observations in the sample). Then we increase each variable, one variable at a time, and look at what happens to expected duration. We want the size of each of these increases to be readily comparable. To achieve this, we increase each variable by an amount such that it moves from the median value to a value greater than that observed in 60 percent of the sample (a 10 percentile increase).

Hazard to Sustained Growth

Somewhat surprisingly, income inequality stood out for the strength and robustness of its relationship with the duration of growth spells: a 10 percentile decrease in inequality (represented by a change in the Gini coefficient from 40 to 37) increases the expected length of a growth spell by 50 percent. The effect is large, but is the sort of improvement that a number of countries have experienced during growth spells. We estimate that closing, say, half the inequality gap between Latin America and emerging Asia would more than double the expected duration of a growth spell in Latin America.

Remarkably, inequality retains its statistical and economic significance even when we include many potential determinants at the same time, a claim that we cannot make for many of the conventional determinants of good growth performance, such as the quality of institutions and trade openness.

Figure 15.4   Growth Spells

Factors have differing impacts on how long growth periods last. Income distribution appears quite important, whereas other factors are less so.

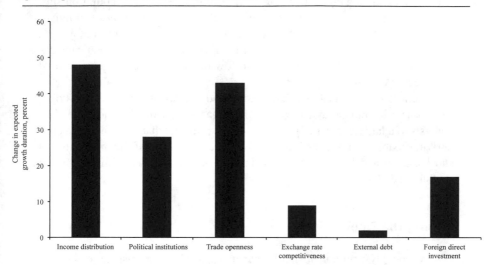

Note: The height of each factor represents the percentage change in a growth spell between 1950 and 2006 when the factor moves from the 50th percentile to the 60th percentile and all other factors are held constant. Income distribution uses the Gini coefficient. The political institutions factor is based on an index from the Polity IV Project database that ranges from +10 for the most open and democratic societies to −10 for the most closed and autocratic. Trade openness measures the effect of changes in trade liberalization on year-to-year growth. Exchange rate competitiveness is calculated as the deviation of an exchange rate from purchasing power parity, adjusted for per capita income.

Inequality still matters when we allow for regional differences in expected growth duration (such as between emerging Asia and Africa). This all suggests that inequality seems to matter in itself and is not just proxying for other factors. Inequality also preserves its significance more systematically across different samples and definitions of growth spells than the other variables do. Of course, inequality is not the only thing that matters but, from our analysis, it clearly belongs on the list of well-established growth factors such as the quality of political institutions or trade openness.

Do these statistical results find a voice in the political and economic narratives of the actual country growth episodes? It appears to be the case in, for example, Cameroon. Growth averaged 7 percent from 1978 through 1985. Then the economy fell apart and declined by 6 percent a year over the subsequent decade. Oil wealth in the 1970s initially financed large increases in the public sector, particularly in public employee wages, which proved very difficult to cut when oil prices fell. "Although these measures [to cut government spending] were necessary to rescue the country from further economic crisis, they were very unpopular because they least affected the political elite and those in the upper echelon of government, whose privileges remained intact" (Mbaku and Takougang, 2003). Our statistical model of growth duration suggests that the risk that the growth spell would end in 1985 was very high—more than 100 times higher than would be typical for a country enjoying a growth spell. The model attributes this high risk mostly to Cameroon's unusually high inequality as well as its low inflow of foreign direct investment and high degree of autocracy.

Cameroon is typical. We have examined six historical cases, including Colombia, Guatemala, and Nigeria. These cases, and our broader statistical analysis of a large number of growth episodes, suggest that inequality is an underlying feature that makes it more likely that a number of factors—external shocks, external debt, ethnic fractionalization—come together to bring a growth spell to an end.

Raising the Tide

One reasonably firm conclusion is that it would be a big mistake to separate analyses of growth and income distribution. To borrow a marine analogy: a rising tide lifts all boats, and our analysis indicates that helping raise the smallest boats may help keep the tide rising for all craft, big and small. The immediate role for policy, however, is less clear. More inequality may shorten the duration of growth, but poorly designed efforts to reduce inequality could be counterproductive. If these efforts distort incentives and undermine growth, they can do more harm than good for the poor. For example, the initial reforms that ignited growth in China involved giving stronger incentives to farmers. This increased the income of the poor and reduced overall inequality as it gave a tremendous spur to growth. However, it probably led to some increased inequality among farmers, and efforts to resist this component of inequality would likely have been counterproductive (Chaudhuri and Ravallion, 2007).

Still, there may be some win-win policies, such as better targeted subsidies, better access to education for the poor that improves equality of economic opportunity, and active labor market measures that promote employment.

When there are short-run trade-offs between the effects of policies on growth and income distribution, the evidence we have does not in itself say what to do. But our analysis should tilt the balance toward the long-run benefits—including for growth—of reducing inequality. Over longer horizons, reduced inequality and sustained growth may be two sides of the same coin.

The analysis calls to mind the developing country debt crises of the 1980s and the resulting "lost decade" of slow growth and painful adjustment. That experience brought home the fact that sustainable economic reform is possible only when its benefits are widely shared. In the face of the current global economic turmoil and the need for difficult economic adjustment and reform in many countries, it would be better if these lessons were remembered rather than relearned.

References

Barro, Robert J., 2000, "Inequality and Growth in a Panel of Countries," *Journal of Economic Growth,* Vol. 5, No. 1, pp. 5–32.

Berg, Andrew, and Jonathan D. Ostry, 2011, "Inequality and Unsustainable Growth: Two Sides of the Same Coin?" IMF Staff Discussion Note 11/08 (Washington: International Monetary Fund).

———, and Jeromin Zettelmeyer, 2011, "What Makes Growth Sustained?" forthcoming in *Journal of Development Economics.*

Chaudhuri, Shubham, and Martin Ravallion, 2007, "Partially Awakened Giants: Uneven Growth in China and India," in *Dancing with Giants: China, India and the Global Economy,* ed. by L. Alan Winters and Shahid Yusuf (Washington: World Bank).

Hausmann, Ricardo, Lant Pritchett, and Dani Rodrik, 2005, "Growth Accelerations," *Journal of Economic Growth,* Vol. 10, No. 4, pp. 303–29.

Mbaku, John M., and Joseph Takougang, eds., 2003, *The Leadership Challenge in Africa: Cameroon under Paul Biya* (Trenton, New Jersey: Africa World Press).

Okun, Arthur, 1975, *Equality and Efficiency: The Big Tradeoff* (Washington: Brookings Institution Press).

Polity IV Project. www.systemicpeace.org/polity/polity4.htm

Pritchett, Lant, 2000, "Understanding Patterns of Economic Growth: Searching for Hills among Plateaus, Mountains, and Plains," *World Bank Economic Review,* Vol. 14, No. 2, pp. 221–50.

Wacziarg, Romain, and Karen Horn Welch, 2008, "Trade Liberalization and Growth: New Evidence," *World Bank Economic Review,* Vol. 22, No. 2, pp. 187–231.

16

Do Poorer Countries Have Less Capacity for Redistribution?

Martin Ravallion

Inequality in the distribution of wealth within countries has been shown by Muller and Seligson (Chapter 13) to lead to social unrest and possibly even insurgency. Yet according to Kuznets (Chapter 12), developing countries inevitably face growing inequality. In this chapter, Martin Ravallion takes on the important question of the ability of poor countries to redistribute wealth. He argues that it has long been assumed that poor countries can improve their distribution of income only by becoming richer (and thus follow the Kuznets curve). For one thing, poor countries rarely rely heavily on income taxes, and thus an important tool of redistribution (progressive income taxation) is not available in those countries. This chapter questions that assumption, with Ravallion arguing that the implementation of strong redistribution policies can be a matter of political will. He then carries out a data analysis and finds that redistribution is possible, but only among the middle-income countries—those with GNP per capita above $4,000. Among most poor countries, reducing poverty by taking from the rich would require tax rates of 100 percent or higher, meaning that in those countries, the only solution is rapid growth accompanied with external development assistance for the poor.

SOME PEOPLE IN EVEN THE POOREST COUNTRIES WOULD NOT BE CONSIDered poor in the US, say. And all developing countries have access to redistributive policy instruments. These facts have not gone unnoticed by aid donors.

The government of a rich country hoping to reduce poverty in poor countries will (understandably) be disinclined to give its aid to a country that has ample internal capacity to address its poverty problem through redistribution from people at a similar standard of living to taxpayers in that rich country. Yet, while the idea that different countries have different capacities for redistribution comes up often in aid discussions, it is invariably assumed that it can be adequately proxied by a measure of average income. I do not know of any past effort to formalize and test that assumption.

The issue of country capacity for redistribution also arises (at least implicitly) in discussions of development policy within developing countries. It is often argued that "sustained poverty reduction is impossible without sustained growth." To accept this claim one must essentially reject its corollary: "sustained poverty reduction is impossible through income redistribution." Yet I can find no demonstration of that point in the literature.

The governments of all developing countries have access to tax and spending instruments with distributional impacts, and significant impacts on poverty and inequality by such means appear to be feasible. Progressive income tax systems are not yet as important in developing countries as in most developed ones, though this is changing and there appear to be feasible options in developing-country settings. Indirect taxes with distributional impacts are widespread. On the spending side, there are many actual or potential instruments available even in poor countries including workfare programs and targeted transfers.

Whether the available policy instruments are actually used and how effective they are— how well they are designed and implemented—depend on the redistributive efforts of countries, stemming in no small measure from their political will for redistribution. That is a different concept from their capacity for redistribution, which is what matters to development aid and policy choices. At any one time, the scope for redistribution as an anti-poverty strategy is naturally constrained by both the extent of poverty in a country and the affluence of the country's rich, which determines the potential tax base. However, the literature does not contain a systematic assessment across countries of how much the existing distribution of income constrains redistribution prospects. There are also deficiencies in past measures for assessing the capacity for redistribution, as reviewed in section 2 of this paper.

The paper tries to fill this gap in knowledge by quantifying how much the distribution of income constrains the scope for redistribution as a means of reducing poverty in developing countries. It is assumed that an external aid donor wants to know: Which countries have distributions that yield little or no potential for internal redistribution as a means of addressing the problem of poverty? Are these necessarily the poorest countries by standard measures? Is the capacity to redistribute to the poor stable over time? And how does it respond to economic growth?

To address these questions, the paper provides a simple but intuitively appealing (inverse) measure of the capacity for redistribution, namely the marginal tax rate (MTR) on the "rich"—those living in a developing country who would not be considered poor by rich country standards—that is needed to provide the revenue for a specific redistribution. At a sufficiently high MTR, the redistribution can be considered "prohibitive," although it is a judgment call just how high is "too high." It is at least suggestive that MTRs rarely exceed 60% in rich countries. Two types of redistributions are considered: a progressive tax on the rich sufficient to cover a given proportion of the aggregate poverty gap and various "basic income" schemes financed the same way. . . .

The Proposed Measure and Its Antecedents in the Literature

The simplest way one might measure the capacity for redistribution is by normalizing the aggregate poverty gap—the sum of all income shortfalls from the poverty line per capita—by the overall mean income. This has long been interpreted as a measure of a "country's *potential* ability to meet the challenge of poverty" (Sen, 1981, p. 190). A variation on this measure is instead to normalize the poverty gap by the aggregate income of the non-poor defined as those living above that poverty line; the aggregate income can be either gross income or income net of the poverty line. This can be interpreted as the tax that would be needed on the non-poor to cover the poverty gap. The earliest examples I know of are Anand (1977) and Kawkani (1977) both using survey data for Malaysia in 1970. Anand (1977, p. 11) reported that " . . . if poverty were to be eliminated by a transfer from the non-poor to the poor, the non-poor would need to sacrifice 8.3 percent of their income (or 12.7 percent of their income in excess of poverty line income)."

However, when we confront the problem of how an aid donor might assess a developing county's capacity for redistribution, one can question whether these past measures use an appropriate normalization. Aid donors will surely not be indifferent to how incomes are distributed above the poverty line when assessing the capacity for redistribution to the poor. It is clearly not acceptable to say that a country has a high capacity if (given its income distribution) redistribution would require putting almost all the tax burden on people living just above the poverty line. Some countries have a greater affluence—with more people living well above the poverty line—than others, and this must be brought into the picture.

The desirability of financing assistance for the poorest by taxing the middle class is questionable on both intrinsic and instrumental grounds. In assessing a poor country's capacity for redistribution it can be argued that citizens of a rich country would find it intrinsically (ethically or politically) unacceptable to expect a poor country to address its poverty problem by taxing people who would be considered poor in the rich country. Popular judgments about "inequality" appear to give greater weight to redistributions from the rich to the poor than redistributions amongst the middle class or from the middle class to the poor. The instrumental arguments point to the expected role of the middle class as agents of progress and also the likely incentive effects on those near the poverty line. Aid donors might also question the political feasibility within a developing country of asking middle-income groups to shoulder the burden of poverty relief.

This paper's main proposed measure of country capacity for redistribution focuses instead on the implied tax burden on the "rich" that would be needed to generate sufficient revenue to cover the aggregate poverty gap, or some proportion. In other words, a "middle class" is identified that is not subject to redistribution—essentially building "middle-class exemptions" into past measures of the tax burden of eliminating poverty.

But what level of income defines the "rich"? Various *ad hoc* definitions have been used in the literature (see, for example, Danziger et al., 1989) but, in the context of the problem studied in this paper, there is a natural approach. The paper argues that only those who are not poor by Western standards should be considered eligible for bearing the required tax. This is motivated by the presumption that aid donors would not ask—and it would surely be morally objectionable if they did—developing countries to deal with their poverty problem by redistribution from those who are poor by the standards prevailing in the donor countries. Progressivity can be built into the hypothetical redistributive tax, to better reflect country differences in the capacity to pay of those living in developing countries that are not poor by rich-country standards.

There are other ways that the poverty gap has been used in the literature, related to the concerns of this paper. Instead of asking what tax rate on the "rich" is needed to cover the poverty gap, one can set the tax rate at 100% and ask who would need to pay it. This gives [*sic*] Medeiros's (2006) "affluence line"—defined as the income level above which the total income in excess of that level is sufficient to cover the poverty gap with a 100% MTR. People living above this line are identified as the "rich" by Medeiros and on calculating the line for Brazil he finds that the rich represent 1% of the population in 1999. As will be shown later, Medeiros's line need not exist in poor countries, and (indeed) does not exist in a non-negligible number of countries in the data used for this study. When it exists, it has the seemingly odd feature that an increase in the extent of poverty, leading to a higher poverty gap, automatically implies that there are more "rich" people. Aside from these concerns, Medeiros's "affluence line" does not help in addressing the question posed by this paper, since the capacity to pay relative to the poverty gap is fixed by construction (at unity).

There are also measures of country performance against poverty that penalize higher incomes of the non-poor. Kanbur and Mukherjee (2007) have proposed a measure of "poverty reduction failure." This says that country A has done worse than B if A's resources—again defined by the incomes above the poverty line—are greater, even if the extent of poverty is the same in A and B. Instead of deflating the poverty gap by the income of the non-poor this measure essentially inflates the poverty gap by those incomes. Kanbur and Mukherjee characterize a class of indices of poverty-reduction failure satisfying a set of seemingly desirable axioms and present calculations for 90 developing countries. However, while it is an interesting measure in its own right, this does not capture in any intuitively obvious way the "capacity for redistribution." In particular, a higher income share held by the non-poor should presumably increase that capacity even though it signals greater poverty reduction failure.

All of the measures discussed above are anchored to the poverty gap. A strand of the literature has also discussed various proposals for a "basic-income" (also called a "guaranteed income" or "citizenship income") which provides a uniform (un-targeted) transfer to everyone, whether poor or not. This has been proposed for both developed and developing countries (Standing, 2008). Advocates typically propose that it should be financed by a progressive income tax, with an exemption for the poor (Raventós, 2007). I will also consider some stylized basic income schemes as anti-poverty policies.

Building on these ideas, the following section provides a more formal treatment of the paper's proposed measures. . . .

Estimates for Developing Countries

Two "poor-country" poverty lines are considered. The first is $1.25 (converted using 2005 PPPs for consumption); this is the average national poverty line found in the poorest 15 countries (Ravallion et al., 2009). The second is $2.00 a day at 2005 PPP, which is the median poverty line for all developing countries with the available data. In setting the "rich-country" poverty line I shall use $13 a day at 2005 PPP, which is the poverty line per person for a family of four in the US; see US Department of Health and Human Services.

So the hypothetical redistribution is from those living in each developing country who are not poor by US standards to those who are poor by the standards of either the poorest countries (giving the $1.25 line) or developing countries as a whole (giving the $2 line). . . . For notational brevity, the MTR required to reduce the poverty gap for the $1.25 line when $z_r = \$13$ is denoted $\tau_k(1) = \tau_k (1.25,13)$, while $\tau_k (2)$ is the corresponding value for the $2 line.

The data are from *PovcalNet,* which facilitates estimation of τ_k in the form of equation (3). The estimates were possible for 89 countries with at least some poverty assessed by the $1.25 a day line and at least two surveys over time (to allow inter-temporal comparisons). The underlying surveys provide distributions of household consumption expenditure or income per person. (The difference between consumption and income is ignored for the present purpose.)

Before discussing the implications for the question posed in the title, it is instructive to first consider a few country examples, and I will focus on Brazil, China and India for this purpose. For Brazil in 2005, covering the poverty gap for $1.25 a day would only require a MTR of 1% on those who are not poor by US standards. Even for the $2 a day line, the necessary marginal rate would only be 4%. The required tax rates would also have been higher for Brazil in 1981 (say) than 2005, but still quite low; for example, $\tau_i(2)$ would have been about 11% in 1981, as compared to 4% in 2005. Recall that these are international lines, and they are lower than the poverty line commonly used in discussing poverty in Brazil, which is about $3 a day at 2005 PPP; filling the poverty gap for this line would call for a MTR of about 12% on those living over $13 a day.

Next consider China, which actually has an anti-poverty program quite similar in spirit at least to the stylized program modeled here; I refer to China's *Dibao* program, which aims to fill the poverty gaps relative to (municipality-specific) poverty lines. The marginal tax on Chinese living above the US poverty line that would be needed to cover the poverty gap for $1.25 a day is 37% in 2005, i.e., all those living above $13 a day would need to pay a tax of roughly one-third of the difference between their income and $13 to bring everyone in China up to the $1.25 a day line. China's national poverty line is closer to $1 a day, which would only require a MTR of 30%. However, the tax rate needed to cover the $2 a day poverty gap would require a prohibitive rate of 100%. Also, if one repeats these calculations in 1981 (the earliest available national surveys for China), covering the poverty gap through redistribution would have been impossible: the required MTR would have been far greater than 100%. The poverty gap was so large then, and the country so poor, that redistribution was not a realistic option.

The capacity for redistribution in India is far more limited than in China or (especially) Brazil. Indeed, it would be impossible to raise enough revenue from a tax on Indian incomes above the US poverty line to fill India's poverty gap relative to the $1.25 a day line; the required MTR would exceed 100%. Indeed, even at a 100% MTR, the revenue generated could fill only 20% of India's aggregate poverty gap.

Turning to the 90 countries as a whole, one finds that the (unweighted) mean $\tau_1(1)$ is 41.6% while for $\tau_1(2)$ it is 52.4%. Looking at the distributions around the mean it can be seen that these averages for $\tau_1(1)$ and $\tau_1(2)$ are deceptive given that the distribution of the implied MTRs is strikingly bi-modal, as is evident in Figure 16.1, panel (a). Almost half (45) of the countries have $\tau_1(1) < 20\%$, while $\tau_1(1) = 100\%$ for 29 countries. For the $2 line, one finds that 36 of the countries have $\tau_1(1) < 20\%$ and 37 have $\tau_1(1) = 100\%$. The reason for this bi-modality will soon become clear when we look at the relationship with the mean.

Figure 16.1 Density Functions for Marginal Tax Rate Needed to Cover the Poverty Gap for $1.25 a Day and $2.00

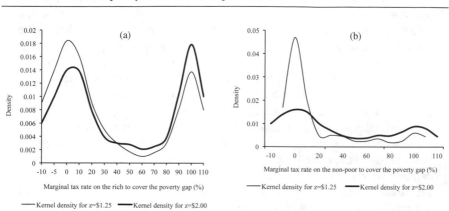

Notes: (a) This paper's measure, excluding the middle class from the tax base for redistribution. (b) Including the middle class in the tax base.

It is instructive to compare the proposed measure with the past approaches to assessing the capacity for redistribution that include everyone that is not poor by developing-country standards in the tax base (setting z_p, z_r in equation 1). The corresponding mean marginal tax rates are 18.4% and 37.4% for $1.25 and $2 respectively—appreciably lower than when the middle class is exempted. Nonetheless, despite the tax progressivity, the large middle-class population shares mean that the bulk of the tax burden is borne by the middle class. Across the full sample, the mean share borne by those living between $1.25 and $13 a day is 78.1% while the mean share borne by those between $2 and $13 is 62.0%. In half the countries the share borne by those between $1.25 and $13 a day exceeds 86.5% while it exceeds 73.2% for the $2 and $3 interval. Also note that the measures obtained when one includes the middle class in the tax base for redistribution do not exhibit the same degree of separation as when it is excluded; indeed, there is no sign of bi-modality for the $1.25 poverty line (panel (b) of Figure 16.1). Note, however, that $\tau_1(z_p, z_p)$ is 100% or higher for seven countries using z_p =$1.25 and 24 countries using $2. Thus $\tau_1(z_p, z_r)>1$ for all $z_r>z_p$ (noting that $\tau_1(z_p, z_r)$ is strictly increasing in z_r), implying that Medeiros's (2006) "affluence line" does not exist for these countries. . . .

Conclusions

In assessing a developing country's capacity for attacking poverty with its own resources, a potential aid donor will presumably prefer the richest citizens of that country to carry the largest burden and (in particular) the donor will not want people to contribute if they are poor by rich-country standards (whether they live in a rich country or a poor one). Yet the results reported here indicate that past measures of the capacity for redistribution (implicitly) impose the bulk of the cost on people who would be considered poor in rich countries. The proposed alternative measures makes a more appealing assumption about how the burden is to be allocated amongst those living above the poverty line: the burden is set to zero until one reaches a standard of living that would not constitute poverty in a representative rich country, and then rises as a share of income in excess of the rich-country poverty line.

On implementing this measure using data for 90 developing countries, the paper finds that developing countries fall into two distinct groups. The first appears to have little or no scope for making a serious impact on the problem of extreme poverty through internal redistribution from those who are not poor by Western standards. The second group appears to have far more scope for such redistribution. Most of the poorest countries in terms of mean consumption fall into the first group. The marginal tax rates needed to fill the poverty gap for the international poverty line of $1.25 a day are clearly prohibitive (marginal tax rates of 100% or more) for the majority of countries with consumption per capita under $2,000 per year at 2005 PPP. Even covering half the poverty gap would require prohibitive MTRs in the majority of poor countries. Yet amongst better-off developing countries—over $4,000 per year (say)—the marginal tax rates needed for substantial pro-poor redistribution are very small—less than 1% on average, and under 6% in all cases.

Of course the capacity for redistribution varies amongst countries at any given level of mean consumption. And the variance is highest amongst the poorest countries; there are even a few poor countries where the poverty gap could be covered by seemingly light taxation of the rich. (Similarly, there is a sizeable variance in the impact of a given rate of growth on the capacity for redistribution.) These differences bear little relationship to a standard measure of inequality, but reflect the deeper parameters of the distribution of income in each country that have generated lower poverty to start with.

Basic-income schemes financed by progressive income taxes also require prohibitive marginal tax rates in the poorest half of developing countries. Indeed, if the tax burden is confined to those who are not poor by developed-country standards, then providing a basic income of $1.25 a day would call for marginal tax rates of 100% or more for three-quarters of countries. Even for middle-income developing countries, this type of redistribution only starts to look feasible if one allows for a basic income appreciably less than $1.25 a day and/or significant tax burdens on the middle class.

This inquiry offers support for focusing development aid on poorer countries—on the grounds that they have less scope for addressing poverty internally. The emphasis often given to the role of economic growth for poverty reduction in poor countries can also claim support from these findings, given that they cast doubt on the feasibility of redistribution from the rich to the poor as a poverty-reduction strategy in poor countries. While the poorest countries appear to have weak capacity for attacking poverty through income redistribution—given the sheer weight of poverty and thinness of the rich strata in their starting distribution—with sufficient economic growth the tax rates on the rich required for covering the poverty gap start to fall rapidly. So it makes sense for the relative emphasis on growth versus redistribution, and the reliance on external aid, to change with the level of economic development. This paper's various measures of the capacity for redistribution clearly leave out things that would be relevant to a complete assessment at country level. The paper has focused on what can be thought of as the "first-order" constraint on redistribution from the rich to the poor, stemming from the properties of the initial distribution of income. There are other country-specific constraints that could be important in practice (though they are also ignored by past measures of the potential for redistribution and poverty reduction failure). There will of course be country-specific administrative costs in implementing both the taxes and the transfers needed. There will also be efficiency costs that one would want to bring into a complete assessment of the capacity for redistribution. There may well be benefits too, such as when redistribution relieves credit constraints facing poor investors (including in human capital). To some extent these costs and benefits are endogenous to policy choices, and should not then be considered constraints. But it can still be acknowledged that the measure used here is missing some country-specific constraints on the scope for redistribution. Arguably, taking account of the administrative costs and incentive effects would expand the size of the first group of countries (for which there is less scope for redistribution). However, there may well be efficiency gains (notably through the relaxation of credit constraints facing the poor) with the opposite effect.

Some of these other factors will no doubt also vary with the overall level of economic development. It does not seem plausible that these costs would tend to be lower in poor countries; indeed, if anything, one would expect the opposite, to the extent that economic development brings greater governmental capacity for effective intervention in most areas of the economy. I would conjecture that a broader accounting of the factors relevant to the capacity for redistribution would strengthen this paper's main finding that poorer countries tend to have less scope for domestically financing a redistribution strategy for fighting extreme poverty.

References

Anand, Sudhir, 1977, "Aspects of Poverty in Malaysia," *Review of Income and Wealth* 23(1): 1–16.

Danziger, S., P. Gottschalk and E. Smolensky, 1989, "How the Rich Have Fared, 1973–87." *American Economic Review* 79 (2): 310–314.

Kakwani, Nanak, 1977, "Measurement of Poverty and Negative-Income Tax," *Australian Economic Papers* 16: 237–248.

———, 1993, "Poverty and Economic Growth with Application to Côte D'Ivoire," *Review of Income and Wealth* 39: 121–139.

Kanbur, Ravi, 1987, "Measurement and Alleviation of Poverty," *IMF Staff Papers* 34: 60–85.

Kanbur, Ravi and Diganta Mukherjee, 2007, "Poverty, Relative to the Ability to Eradicate It: An Index of Poverty Reduction Failure," *Economics Letters* 97(1): 52–57.

Medeiros, Marcelo, 2006, "The Rich and the Poor: The Construction of an Affluence Line from the Poverty Line," *Social Indicators Research* 78(1): 1–18.

Ravallion, Martin, 2009, "The Developing World's Bulging (But Vulnerable) Middle Class," Policy Research Working Paper 4816, World Bank.

Ravallion, Martin, Shaohua Chen and Prem Sangraula, 2009, "Dollar a Day Revisited," *World Bank Economic Review* 23(2): 163–184.

Raventós, Daniel, 2007, *Basic Income: The Material Conditions of Freedom*, London: Pluto Press.

Sen, Amartya, 1981, *Poverty and Famines: An Essay on Entitlement and Deprivation.* Oxford: Oxford University Press.

Standing, Guy, 2008, "How Cash Transfers Promote the Case for Basic Income," *Basic Income Studies* 3(1): 1–30.

Part 4

The Classical Thesis: Convergence or Divergence?

17

The Five Stages of Growth

W. W. Rostow

*E*arly research on economic underdevelopment suggested that the problem was only short-term and that in the end all countries would become rich. In this excerpt from W. W. Rostow's classic work, The Stages of Economic Growth, Rostow outlines this optimistic scenario by positing five stages of economic development all societies eventually experience as they mature into industrialized developed countries: tradition, the preconditions for takeoff, the takeoff, the drive to maturity, and the age of high mass consumption. Although this tremendously influential publication did not focus specifically on the causes of the gaps, the author suggests the reason they arise and their potential resolution. As a country moves out of the traditional stage and prepares for economic takeoff, its economy begins to grow much faster than the economies of countries that remain in the first stage. The gap between rich and poor would then be explained by the fact that not all countries enter the development process at the same time. Thus the gap between rich and poor countries would be expected to disappear as the countries progress into the later stages of growth. As a country progresses through the stages of development, those who adopt the new economic rules and succeed accumulate the profits of their success, and internal inequality arises. As more people join the monied economy and play by the new rules, the extent of the inequality should diminish.*

Reprinted with permission from *American Economic Review* 45 (March 1955): 1, 3–6, 17–26.

IT IS POSSIBLE TO IDENTIFY ALL SOCIETIES, IN THEIR ECONOMIC DIMEN-
sions, as lying within one of five categories: the traditional society, the preconditions for take-off, the take-off, the drive to maturity, and the age of high
mass-consumption.

The Traditional Society

First, the traditional society. A traditional society is one whose structure is developed within limited production functions, based on pre-Newtonian science
and technology, and on pre-Newtonian attitudes towards the physical world.
Newton is here used as a symbol for that watershed in history when men came
widely to believe that the external world was subject to a few knowable laws,
and was systematically capable of productive manipulation.

The conception of the traditional society is, however, in no sense static;
and it would not exclude increases in output. Acreage could be expanded;
some *ad hoc* technical innovations, often highly productive innovations, could
be introduced in trade, industry and agriculture; productivity could rise with,
for example, the improvement of irrigation works or the discovery and diffusion of a new crop. But the central fact about the traditional society was that a
ceiling existed on the level of attainable output per head. This ceiling resulted
from the fact that the potentialities which flow from modern science and technology were either not available or not regularly and systematically applied.

Both in the longer past and in recent times the story of traditional societies
was thus a story of endless change. The area and volume of trade within them
and between them fluctuated, for example, with the degree of political and social
turbulence, the efficiency of central rule, the upkeep of the roads. Population—
and, within limits, the level of life—rose and fell not only with the sequence of
the harvests, but with the incidence of war and of plague. Varying degrees of
manufacture developed; but, as in agriculture, the level of productivity was limited by the inaccessibility of modern science, its applications, and its frame of
mind.

Generally speaking, these societies, because of the limitation on productivity, had to devote a very high proportion of their resources to agriculture; and
flowing from the agricultural system there was an hierarchical social structure,
with relatively narrow scope—but some scope—for vertical mobility. Family
and clan connexions played a large role in social organization. The value system of these societies was generally geared to what might be called a long-run
fatalism; that is, the assumption that the range of possibilities open to one's
grandchildren would be just about what it had been for one's grandparents. But
this long-run fatalism by no means excluded the short-run option that, within a
considerable range, it was possible and legitimate for the individual to strive to
improve his lot, within his lifetime. In Chinese villages, for example, there was

an endless struggle to acquire or to avoid losing land, yielding a situation where land rarely remained within the same family for a century.

Although central political rule—in one form or another—often existed in traditional societies, transcending the relatively self-sufficient regions, the centre of gravity of political power generally lay in the regions, in the hands of those who owned or controlled the land. The landowner maintained fluctuating but usually profound influence over such central political power as existed, backed by its entourage of civil servants and soldiers, imbued with attitudes and controlled by interests transcending the regions.

In terms of history then, with the phrase "traditional society" we are grouping the whole pre-Newtonian world: the dynasties in China; the civilization of the Middle East and the Mediterranean; the world of medieval Europe. And to them we add the post-Newtonian societies which, for a time, remained untouched or unmoved by man's new capability for regularly manipulating his environment to his economic advantage.

To place these infinitely various, changing societies in a single category, on the ground that they all shared a ceiling on the productivity of their economic techniques, is to say very little indeed. But we are, after all, merely clearing the way in order to get at the subject of this book; that is, the post-traditional societies, in which each of the major characteristics of the traditional society was altered in such ways as to permit regular growth: its politics, social structure, and (to a degree) its values, as well as its economy.

The Preconditions for Take-off

The second stage of growth embraces societies in the process of transition; that is, the period when the preconditions for take-off are developed; for it takes time to transform a traditional society in the ways necessary for it to exploit the fruits of modern science, to fend off diminishing returns, and thus to enjoy the blessings and choices opened up by the march of compound interest.

The preconditions for take-off were initially developed, in a clearly marked way, in Western Europe of the late seventeenth and early eighteenth centuries as the insights of modern science began to be translated into new production functions in both agriculture and industry, in a setting given dynamism by the lateral expansion of world markets and the international competition for them. But all that lies behind the break-up of the Middle Ages is relevant to the creation of the preconditions for take-off in Western Europe. Among the Western European states, Britain, favoured by geography, natural resources, trading possibilities, social and political structure, was the first to develop fully the preconditions for take-off.

The more general case in modern history, however, saw the stage of preconditions arise not endogenously but from some external intrusion by more advanced societies. These invasions—literal or figurative—shocked the traditional society and began or hastened its undoing; but they also set in motion ideas and sentiments which initiated the process by which a modern alternative to the traditional society was constructed out of the old culture.

The idea spreads not merely that economic progress is possible, but that economic progress is a necessary condition for some other purpose, judged to be good: be it national dignity, private profit, the general welfare, or a better life for the children. Education, for some at least, broadens and changes to suit the needs of modern economic activity. New types of enterprising men come forward—in the private economy, in government, or both—willing to mobilize savings and to take risks in pursuit of profit or modernization. Banks and other institutions for mobilizing capital appear. Investment increases, notably in transport, communications, and in raw materials in which other nations may have an economic interest. The scope of commerce, internal and external, widens. And, here and there, modern manufacturing enterprise appears, using the new methods. But all this activity proceeds at a limited pace within an economy and a society still mainly characterized by traditional low-productivity methods, by the old social structure and values, and by the regionally based political institutions that developed in conjunction with them.

In many recent cases, for example, the traditional society persisted side by side with modern economic activities, conducted for limited economic purposes by a colonial or quasi-colonial power.

Although the period of transition—between the traditional society and the take-off—saw major changes in both the economy itself and in the balance of social values, a decisive feature was often political. Politically, the building of an effective centralized national state—on the basis of coalitions touched with a new nationalism, in opposition to the traditional landed regional interests, the colonial power, or both, was a decisive aspect of the preconditions period; and it was, almost universally, a necessary condition for take-off. . . .

The Take-off

We come now to the great watershed in the life of modern societies: the third stage in this sequence, the take-off. The take-off is the interval when the old blocks and resistances to steady growth are finally overcome. The forces making for economic progress, which yielded limited bursts and enclaves of modern activity, expand and come to dominate the society. Growth becomes its normal condition. Compound interest becomes built, as it were, into its habits and institutional structure.

In Britain and the well-endowed parts of the world populated substantially from Britain (the United States, Canada, etc.) the proximate stimulus for take-off was mainly (but not wholly) technological. In the more general case, the take-off awaited not only the build-up of social overhead capital and a surge of technological development in industry and agriculture, but also the emergence to political power of a group prepared to regard the modernization of the economy as serious, high-order political business.

During the take-off, the rate of effective investment and savings may rise from say, 5 percent of the national income to 10 percent or more; although where heavy social overhead capital investment was required to create the technical preconditions for take-off the investment rate in the preconditions period could be higher than 5 percent, as, for example, in Canada before the 1890s and Argentina before 1914. In such cases capital imports usually formed a high proportion of total investment in the preconditions period and some-times even during the take-off itself, as in Russia and Canada during their pre-1914 railway booms.

During the take-off new industries expand rapidly, yielding profits a large proportion of which are reinvested in new plants; and these new industries, in turn, stimulate, through their rapidly expanding requirement for factory work-ers, the services to support them, and for other manufactured goods, a further expansion in urban areas and in other modern industrial plants. The whole process of expansion in the modern sector yields an increase of income in the hands of those who not only save at high rates but place their savings at the disposal of those engaged in modern sector activities. The new class of entre-preneurs expands; and it directs the enlarging flows of investment in the pri-vate sector. The economy exploits hitherto unused natural resources and meth-ods of production.

New techniques spread in agriculture as well as industry, as agriculture is commercialized, and increasing numbers of farmers are prepared to accept the new methods and the deep changes they bring to ways of life. The revolution-ary changes in agricultural productivity are an essential condition for success-ful take-off; for modernization of a society increases radically its bill for agri-cultural products. In a decade or two both the basic structure of the economy and the social and political structure of the society are transformed in such a way that a steady rate of growth can be, thereafter, regularly sustained.

. . . One can approximately allocate the take-off of Britain to the two decades after 1783; France and the United States to the several decades pre-ceding 1860; Germany, the third quarter of the nineteenth century; Japan, the fourth quarter of the nineteenth century; Russia and China the quarter-century or so preceding 1914; while during the 1950s India and China have, in quite different ways, launched their respective take-offs.

The Drive to Maturity

After take-off there follows a long interval of sustained if fluctuating progress, as the now regularly growing economy drives to extend modern technology over the whole front of its economic activity. Some 10–20 percent of the national income is steadily invested, permitting output regularly to outstrip the increase in population. The make-up of the economy changes unceasingly as technique improves, new industries accelerate, older industries level off. The economy finds its place in the international economy: goods formerly imported are produced at home; new import requirements develop, and new export commodities to match them. The society makes such terms as it will with the requirements of modern efficient production, balancing off the new against the older values and institutions, or revising the latter in such ways as to support rather than to retard the growth process.

Some sixty years after take-off begins (say, forty years after the end of take-off) what may be called maturity is generally attained. The economy, focused during the take-off around a relatively narrow complex of industry and technology, has extended its range into more refined and technologically often more complex processes; for example, there may be a shift in focus from the coal, iron, and heavy engineering industries of the railway phase to machine-tools, chemicals, and electrical equipment. This, for example, was the transition through which Germany, Britain, France, and the United States had passed by the end of the nineteenth century or shortly thereafter. But there are other sectoral patterns which have been followed in the sequence from take-off to maturity. . . .

Formally, we can define maturity as the stage in which an economy demonstrates the capacity to move beyond the original industries which powered its take-off and to absorb and to apply efficiently over a very wide range of its resources—if not the whole range—the most advanced fruits of (then) modern technology. This is the stage in which an economy demonstrates that it has the technological and entrepreneurial skills to produce not everything, but anything that it chooses to produce. It may lack (like contemporary Sweden and Switzerland, for example) the raw materials or other supply conditions required to produce a given type of output economically; but its dependence is a matter of economic choice or political priority rather than a technological or institutional necessity.

Historically, it would appear that something like sixty years was required to move a society from the beginning of take-off to maturity. Analytically the explanation for some such interval may lie in the powerful arithmetic of compound interest applied to the capital stock, combined with the broader consequences for a society's ability to absorb modern technology of three successive generations living under a regime where growth is the normal condition. But, clearly, no dogmatism is justified about the exact length of the interval from take-off to maturity.

The Age of High Mass-Consumption

We come now to the age of high mass-consumption, where, in time, the leading sectors shift towards durable consumers' goods and services: a phase from which Americans are beginning to emerge; whose not unequivocal joys Western Europe and Japan are beginning energetically to probe; and with which Soviet society is engaged in an uneasy flirtation.

As societies achieved maturity in the twentieth century two things happened: real income per head rose to a point where a large number of persons gained a command over consumption which transcended basic food, shelter, and clothing; and the structure of the working force changed in ways which increased not only the proportion of urban to total population, but also the proportion of the population working in offices or in skilled factory jobs—aware of and anxious to acquire the consumption fruits of a mature economy.

In addition to these economic changes, the society ceased to accept the further extension of modern technology as an overriding objective. It is in this post-maturity stage, for example, that, through the political process, Western societies have chosen to allocate increased resources to social welfare and security. The emergence of the welfare state is one manifestation of a society's moving beyond technical maturity; but it is also at this stage that resources tend increasingly to be directed to the production of consumers' durables and to the diffusion of services on a mass basis, if consumers' sovereignty reigns. The sewing-machine, the bicycle, and then the various electric-powered household gadgets were gradually diffused. Historically, however, the decisive element has been the cheap mass automobile with its quite revolutionary effects—social as well as economic—on the life and expectations of society.

For the United States, the turning point was, perhaps, Henry Ford's moving assembly line of 1913–14; but it was in the 1920s, and again in the postwar decade, 1946–56, that this stage of growth was pressed to, virtually, its logical conclusion. In the 1950s Western Europe and Japan appeared to have fully entered this phase, accounting substantially for a momentum in their economies quite unexpected in the immediate post-war years. The Soviet Union is technically ready for this stage, and, by every sign, its citizens hunger for it; but Communist leaders face difficult political and social problems of adjustment if this stage is launched.

Beyond Consumption

Beyond, it is impossible to predict, except perhaps to observe that Americans, at least, have behaved in the past decade as if diminishing relative marginal utility sets in, after a point, for durable consumers' goods; and they have chosen, at the margin, larger families—behavior in the pattern of Buddenbrooks dynamics.[1] Americans have behaved as if, having been born into a system that provided economic security and high mass-consumption, they placed a lower valuation on acquiring additional increments of real income in the conventional form as opposed to the advantages and values of an enlarged family. But even in this adventure in generalization it is a shade too soon to create—on the basis of one case—a new stage-of-growth, based on babies, in succession to the age of consumers' durables: as economists might say, the income-elasticity of demand for babies may well vary from society to society. But it is true that the implications of the baby boom along with the not wholly unrelated deficit in social overhead capital are likely to dominate the American economy over the next decade rather than the further diffusion of consumers' durables.

Here then, in an impressionistic rather than an analytic way, are the stages-of-growth which can be distinguished once a traditional society begins its modernization: the transitional period when the preconditions for take-off are created generally in response to the forces making for modernization; the take-off itself; the sweep into maturity generally taking up the life of about two further generations; and then, finally, if the rise of income has matched the spread of technological virtuosity (which, as we shall see, it need not immediately do) the diversion of the fully mature economy to the provision of durable consumers' goods and services (as well as the welfare state) for its increasingly urban—and then suburban—populations. Beyond lies the question of whether or not secular spiritual stagnation will arise, and, if it does, how man might fend it off. . . .

Note

1. In Thomas Mann's novel of three generations, the first sought money; the second, born to money, sought social and civic position; the third, born to comfort and family prestige, looked to the life of music. The phrase is designed to suggest, then, the changing aspirations of generations, as they place a low value on what they take for granted and seek new forms of satisfaction.

18

Productivity Growth, Convergence, and Welfare: What the Long-Run Data Show

William J. Baumol

In this chapter William Baumol provides empirical analysis of convergence theory and finds that for a sample of sixteen countries between 1870 and 1979, labor productivity and its growth are inversely related. Convergence theorists have long argued that not all countries will experience convergence because they lack the social capacity to utilize technology to achieve rapid growth. Baumol turns to the post–World War II era (1950–1980) to see if this relationship can be found for all countries. Using real GDP/pc and growth rates as proxies for labor productivity, Baumol finds that the poorest countries have the slowest rGDP/pc growth, thus failing to converge with the rich. The rest of the countries belong to what Baumol calls a "convergence club." Hence, if Baumol is correct, convergence will take place, but will exclude the poorest countries from the process, meaning that the gap will widen between them and the rest of the world.

> No matter how refined and how elaborate the analysis, if it rests solely on the short view it will still be . . . a structure built on shifting sands.
> —Jacob Viner (1958, pp. 112–131)

Recent years have witnessed a reemergence of interest on the part of economists and the general public in issues relating to long-run economic growth. There has

Reprinted with permission of the *American Economic Review* 76 (December 1986): 1072–1084.

been a recurrence of doubts and fears for the future—aroused in this case by the protracted slowdown in productivity growth since the late 1960s, the seeming erosion of the competitiveness of U.S. industries in world markets, and the spectre of "deindustrialization" and massive structural unemployment. These anxieties have succeeded in redirecting attention to long-run supply-side phenomena that formerly were a central preoccupation of economists in the industrializing West, before being pushed aside in the crisis of the Great Depression and the ensuing triumph of Keynesian ideas.

Anxiety may compel attention, but it is not necessarily an aid to clear thinking. For all the interest now expressed in the subject of long-run economic growth and policies ostensibly directed to its stimulation, it does not seem to be widely recognized that adequate economic analysis of such issues calls for the careful study of economic history—if only because it is there that the pertinent evidence is to be found. Economic historians have provided the necessary materials, in the form of brilliant insights, powerful analysis as well as a surprising profusion of long-period data. Yet none of these has received the full measure of attention they deserve from members of the economics profession at large.

To dramatize the sort of reorientation long-term information can suggest, imagine a convincing prediction that over the next century, U.S. productivity growth will permit a trebling of per capita GNP while cutting nearly by half the number of hours in the average work year, and that this will be accompanied by a sevenfold increase in exports. One might well consider this a very rosy forecast. But none of these figures is fictitious. For these developments in fact lay before the United Kingdom in 1870, just as its economic leadership began to erode.

This chapter outlines some implications of the available long-period data on productivity and related variables—some tentative, some previously noted by economic historians, and some throwing a somewhat surprising light on developments among industrialized nations since World War II. Among the main observations that will emerge here is the remarkable convergence of output per labor hour among industrialized nations. Almost all of the leading free enterprise economies have moved closer to the leader, and there is a strong inverse correlation between a country's productivity standing in 1870 and its average rate of productivity growth since then. Postwar data suggest that the convergence phenomenon also extends to both "intermediate" and centrally planned economies. Only the poorer, less developed countries show no such trend.

It will also emerge that over the century, the U.S. productivity growth rate has been surprisingly steady, and despite frequently expressed fears, there is no sign recently of any *long-term* slowdown in growth of either total factor productivity or labor productivity in the United States. And while, except in wartime, *for the better part of a century,* U.S. productivity growth rates have been low relative to those of Germany, Japan, and a number of other countries, this may be no more than a manifestation of the convergence phenomenon which requires countries that were previously behind to grow more rapidly. Thus, the chapter will seek to dispel these and a number of other misapprehensions apparently widespread among those who have not studied economic history.

Nonspecialists may well be surprised at the remarkably long periods spanned in time-series contributed by Beveridge, Deane, Kuznets, Gallman, Kendrick, Abramovitz, David, and others. The Phelps Brown-Hopkins indices of prices and real wages extend over seven centuries. Maddison, Feinstein (and his colleagues), and Kendrick cover productivity, investment, and a number of other crucial variables for more than 100 years. Obviously, the magnitudes of the earlier figures are more than a little questionable, as their compilers never cease to warn us. Yet the general qualitative character of the time paths is persuasive, given the broad consistency of the statistics, their apparent internal logic and the care exercised in collecting them. In this chapter, the period used will vary with topic and data availability. In most cases, something near a century will be examined, using primarily data provided by Angus Maddison (1982) and R.C.O. Matthews, C. H. Feinstein, and J. C. Odling-Smee (1982—henceforth, M-F-O).

Magnitude of the Accomplishment

The magnitude of the productivity achievement of the past 150 years resists intuitive grasp, and contrasts sharply with the preceding centuries. As the *Communist Manifesto* put the matter in 1848, with remarkable foresight, "The bourgeoisie, during its rule of scarce one hundred years, has created more massive and more colossal productive forces than have all preceding generations together." There obviously are no reliable measures of productivity in antiquity, but available descriptions of living standards in Ancient Rome suggest that they were in many respects higher than in eighteenth-century England (see Colin Clark, 1957, p. 677). This is probably true even for the lower classes—certainly for the free urban proletariat, and perhaps even with the inclusion of slaves. An upper-class household was served by sophisticated devices for heating and bathing not found in eighteenth-century homes of the rich. A wealthy Roman magically transported into an eighteenth-century English home would probably have been puzzled by the technology of only a few products—clocks, window panes, printed books and newspapers, and the musket over the fireplace.

It is true that even during the Middle Ages (see, for example, Carlo Cipolla, 1976), there was substantial technological change in the workplace and elsewhere. Ship design improved greatly. Lenses and, with them, the telescope and microscope appeared in the sixteenth century, and the eighteenth century brought the ship's chronometer which revolutionized water transport by permitting calculation of longitude. Yet, none of this led to rates of productivity growth anywhere near those of the nineteenth and twentieth centuries.

Nonhistorians do not usually recognize that initially the Industrial Revolution was a fairly minor affair for the economy as a whole. At first, much of the new equipment was confined to textile production (though some progress in fields such as iron making had also occurred). And, as David Landes (1969) indicates, an entrepreneur could undertake the new types of textile operations with little capital, perhaps only a few hundred pounds, which (using the Phelps Brown-Hopkins data) translates into some 100,000 1980 dollars. Jeffrey Williamson (1983) tells us that in England during the first half-century of the Industrial Revolution, real per capita income grew only about 0.3 percent per annum,[1] in contrast with the nearly 3 percent achieved in the Third World in the 1970s (despite the decade's economic crises).

Table 18.1 shows the remarkable contrast of developments since 1870 for Maddison's 16 countries. We see (col. 1) that growth in output per work-hour ranged for the next 110 years from approximately 400 percent for Australia all the way to 2500 percent (in the case of Japan). The 1100 percent increase of labor productivity in the United States placed it somewhat below the middle of the group, and even the United Kingdom managed a 600 percent rise. Thus, after not manifesting any substantial long-period increase for at least 15 centuries, in the course of 11 decades the median increase in productivity among the 16 industrialized leaders in Maddison's sample was about 1150 percent. The rise in productivity was sufficient to permit output per capita (col. 2) to

Table 18.1   Total Growth from 1870 to 1979:[a] Productivity, GDP per Capita, and Exports, Sixteen Industrialized Countries[b]

	Real GDP per Work-Hour	Real GDP per Capita	Volume of Exports
Australia	398	221	—
United Kingdom	585	310	930
Switzerland	830	471	4,400
Belgium	887	439	6,250
Netherlands	910	429	8,040
Canada	1,050	766	9,860
United States	1,080	693	9,240
Denmark	1,098	684	6,750
Italy	1,225	503	6,210
Austria	1,270	643	4,740
Germany	1,510	824	3,730
Norway	1,560	873	7,740
France	1,590	694	4,140
Finland	1,710	1,016	6,240
Sweden	2,060	1,083	5,070
Japan	2,480	1,661	293,060

Source: Angus Maddison (1982, pp. 8, 212, 248–53).
Notes: a. In 1970 U.S. dollars.
b. Shown in percent.

increase more than 300 percent in the United Kingdom, 800 percent in West Germany, 1700 percent in Japan, and nearly 700 percent in France and the United States. Using Robert Summers and Alan Heston's sophisticated international comparison data (1984), this implies that in 1870, U.S. output per capita was comparable to 1980 output per capita in Honduras and the Philippines, and slightly below that of China, Bolivia, and Egypt!

The growth rates of other pertinent variables were also remarkable. One more example will suffice to show this. Table 18.1, which also shows the rise in volume of exports from 1870 to 1979 (col. 3), indicates that the median increase was over 6,000 percent.

The Convergence of National Productivity Levels

There is a long and reasonably illustrious tradition among economic historians centered on the phenomenon of convergence. While the literature devoted to the subject is complex and multifaceted, as revealed by the recent reconsideration of these ideas by Moses Abramovitz (1985), one central theme is that forces accelerating the growth of nations who were latecomers to industrialization and economic development give rise to a long-run tendency towards convergence of levels of per capita product or, alternatively, of per worker product. Such ideas found expression in the works of Alexander Gerschenkron (see, for example, 1952), who saw his own views on the advantages of "relative backwardness" as having been anticipated in important respects by Thorstein Veblen's writings on the penalties of being the industrial leader (1915). Although such propositions also have been challenged and qualified (for example, Edward Ames and Nathan Rosenberg, 1963), it is difficult to dismiss the idea of convergence on the basis of the historical experience of the industrialized world. (For more recent discussions, see also the paper by Robin Marris, with comments by Feinstein and Matthews in Matthews, 1982, pp. 12–13, 128–147, as well as Dennis Mueller, 1983.)

Using 1870–1973 data on gross domestic product (GDP) per work-year for 7 industrialized countries, M-F-O have shown graphically that those nations' productivity levels have tended to approach ever closer to one another. . . .[2]

The convergence toward the vanguard (led in the first decades by Australia—see Richard Caves and Laurence Krause, 1984—and the United Kingdom and, approximately since World War I, by the United States) is sharper than it may appear to the naked eye. In 1870, the ratio of output per work-hour in Australia, then the leader in Maddison's sample, was about eight times as great as Japan's (the laggard). By 1979, that ratio for the leader (the United States) to the laggard (still Japan) had fallen to about 2. The ratio of the standard deviation from the mean of GDP per work-hour for the 16 countries has also fallen quite steadily, except for a brief but sharp rise during World War II.

The convergence phenomenon and its pervasiveness are confirmed by Figure 18.1, on which my discussion will focus. The horizontal axis indicates each Maddison country's absolute level of GDP per work-hour in 1870. The vertical axis represents the growth rate of GDP per work-hour in the 110 years since 1870. The high inverse correlation between the two is evident. Indeed, we obtain an equation (subject to all sorts of statistical reservations)[3]

$$Growth\ Rate\ (1870\text{--}1979) = 5.25 - 0.75ln\ (GDP\ per\ WorkHr,\ 1870),$$
$$R^2 = 0.88.$$

That is, with a very high correlation coefficient, the higher a country's productivity level in 1870 the more slowly that level grew in the following century.

Implications of the Inverse Correlation: Public Goods Property of Productivity Policy

The strong inverse correlation between the 1870 productivity levels of the 16 nations and their subsequent productivity growth record seems to have a startling implication. Of course, hindsight always permits "forecasts" of great accuracy—that itself is not surprising. Rather, what is striking is the apparent implication that *only one variable,* a country's 1870 GDP per work-hour, or its relation to that of the productivity leader matters to any substantial degree, and that other variables have only a peripheral influence. It seems not to have mattered much whether or not a particular country had free markets, a high propensity to invest, or used policy to stimulate growth. Whatever its behavior, that nation was apparently fated to land close to its predestined position in Figure 18.1.

However, a plausible alternative interpretation is that while national policies and behavior patterns do substantially affect productivity growth, the spillovers from leader economies to followers are large—at least among the group of industrial nations. If country A's extraordinary investment level and superior record of innovation enhance its own productivity, they will almost automatically do the same in the long run for industrialized country B, though perhaps to a somewhat more limited extent. In other words, for such nations a successful productivity-enhancing measure has the nature of a public good. And because the fruits of each industrialized country's productivity-enhancement efforts are ultimately shared by others, each country remains in what appears to be its predestined *relative* place along the growth curve of Figure 18.1. I will note later some considerations which might lead one to doubt that the less developed countries will benefit comparably from this sharing process.

This sharing of productivity growth benefits by industrialized countries involves both innovation and investment. The innovation-sharing process is

Figure 18.1 Productivity Growth Rate, 1870–1979 vs. 1870 Level (in percent)

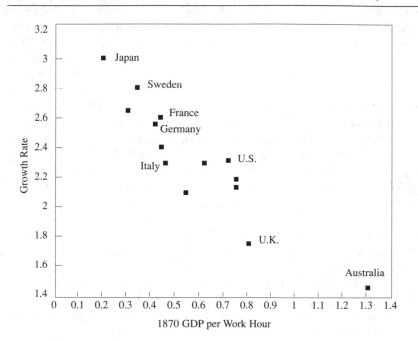

Source: Maddison (p. 212).

straightforward. If industry in country A benefits from a significant innovation, those industries in other countries which produce competing products will find themselves under pressure to obtain access to the innovation, or to an imitation or to some other substitute. Industrialized countries, whose product lines overlap substantially and which sell a good deal in markets where foreign producers of similar items are also present, will find themselves constantly running in this Schumpeterian race, while those less developed countries which supply few products competing with those of the industrialized economies will not participate to the same degree.

There is reason to suspect that the pressures for rapidity in imitation of innovation in industrial countries have been growing. The explosion in exports reported in Table 18.1 has given them a considerably larger share of gross national product than they had in 1870. This suggests that more of each nation's output faces the direct competition of foreign rivals. Thus, the penalties for failure to keep abreast of innovations *in other countries* and to imitate them where appropriate have grown.

Second, the means required for successful imitations have improved and expanded enormously. World communications are now practically instantaneous, but required weeks and even months at the birth of the Industrial Revolution.

While today meetings of scientists and technicians are widely encouraged, earlier mercantilist practices entailed measures by each country to prevent other nations from learning its industrial techniques, and the emigration of specialized workers was often forbidden. Though figures in this arena are difficult to interpret, much less substantiate, one estimate claims that employment in "information activities" in the United States has grown from less than 1 percent of the labor force in 1830 to some 45 percent today (James Beniger, forthcoming, p. 364, leaning heavily on Marc Porat, 1977). Presumably, growth of the information sector in other industrialized nations has been similar. This must surely facilitate and speed the innovative, counterinnovative, and imitative tasks of the entrepreneur. The combination of direct U.S. manufacturing investment in Europe, and the technology transfer activities of multinational corporations in the postwar era were also of great significance (see, for example, David Teece, 1976). All of this, incidentally, suggests that as the forces making for convergence were stronger in the postwar era than previously, the rate of convergence should have been higher. The evidence assembled by Abramovitz (1985) on the basis of Maddison's data indicates that this is in fact what has happened.

The process that has just been described, then, provides mutual benefits, but it inherently helps productivity laggards more than leaders. For the laggards have more to learn from the leaders, and that is why the process makes for convergence.

Like innovation, investment, generally considered the second main source of growth in labor productivity, may also exhibit international public good properties. Suppose two industrialized countries, A and B, each produce two traded products: say automobiles and shoes, with the former more capital intensive. If A's investment rate is greater than B's then, with time, A's output mix will shift toward the cars while B's will move toward shoes. The increased demand for auto workers in A will raise their real wages, while A's increased demand for imports of B's shoes will raise real wages in B, and will raise the *value* of gross domestic product per labor hour in that country. Thus, even investment in country A automatically tends to have a spillover effect on value productivity and real wages *in those other countries that produce and trade in a similar array of goods.*

While, strictly speaking, the factor-price equalization theorem is not applicable to my discussion because it assumes, among other things, that technology is identical in all the countries involved, it does suggest why (for the reasons just discussed) a high investment rate may fail to bring a relative wage advantage to the investing country. In practice, the conditions of the theorem are not satisfied precisely, so countries in which investment rates are relatively high do seem to obtain increased relative real wages. Yet the analysis suggests that the absolute benefits are contagious—that one country's successful investment policy will also raise productivity and living standards in other industrialized countries.[4]

Thus, effective growth policy does contribute to a nation's living standards, but it may also help other industrialized countries and to almost the same degree; meaning that relative deviations from the patterns indicated in Figure 18.1 will be fairly small, just as the diagram shows. (However, see Abramovitz, 1985, for a discussion of the counterhypothesis, that growth of a leader creates "backwash" effects inhibiting growth of the followers.)

All this raises an obvious policy issue. If productivity growth does indeed have such public good properties, what will induce each country to invest the socially optimal effort and other resources in productivity growth, when it can instead hope to be a free rider? In part, the answer is that in Western capitalistic economies, investment is decentralized and individual firms can gain little by free riding on the actions of investors in other economies, so that the problem does not appear to be a serious one at the national policy level.

Is Convergence Ubiquitous?

Does convergence of productivity levels extend beyond the free-market industrialized countries? Or is the convergence "club" a very exclusive organization? While century-long data are not available for any large number of countries, Summers and Heston provide pertinent figures for the 30-year period 1950–80 (data for more countries are available for briefer periods).[5] Instead of labor productivity figures, they give output per capita, whose trends can with considerable reservations be used as a rough proxy for those in productivity, as Maddison's figures confirm.

Figure 18.2 tells the story. Constructed just like Figure 18.1, it plots the 1950–80 real growth rate of GDP per capita for all 72 Summers-Heston countries against the initial (1950) level of this variable. The points form no tight relationship, and unlike those for the industrial countries, the dots show no negatively sloping pattern. Indeed, a regression yields a slightly positive slope. Thus, rather than sharing in convergence, some of the poorest countries have also been growing most slowly.

Figure 18.2 brings out the patterns more clearly by surrounding the set of points representing Maddison's 16 countries with a thin boundary and the centrally planned economy points[6] with a heavier boundary. We see that the Maddison country points lie near a sort of upper-right-hand boundary, meaning that most of them had the high incomes in 1950 (as was to be expected) and, for any given per capita income, the highest growth rates between 1950 and 1980. This region is very long, narrow, and negatively sloped, with the absolute slope declining toward the right. As in Figure 18.1, productivity data for a 110-year

Figure 18.2   Growth Rate, 1950–80, GDP/pc vs. 1950 Level, 72 Countries

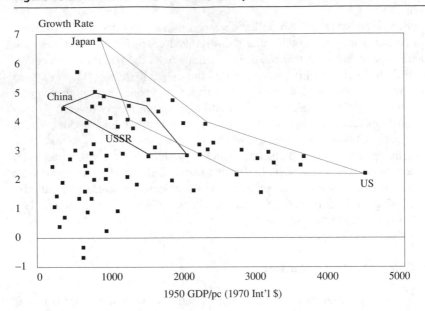

Source: Summers and Heston, 1984.

period, this is exactly the shape one expects with convergence. Second, we see that the centrally planned economies are members of a convergence club of their own, forming a negatively sloping region lying below and to the left of the Maddison countries. The relationship is less tight, so convergence within the group is less pronounced, but it is clearly there.

Finally, there is the region of remaining points (aside from the rightmost non-Maddison points in the graph) which lies close to the origin of the graph and occupies something like a distorted circle without any apparent slope. The points closest to the origin are less developed countries which were poor in 1950, and have grown relatively slowly since. They show no convergence among themselves, much less with other groups.

A few numbers suggest the difference in performance of various subgroups of the 72 countries. Using a four-set classification Summers, I. B. Kravis and Heston (1984, p. 254) provide Gini coefficients by decade from 1950 to 1980. For their set of industrialized countries, this coefficient falls precipitously from 0.302 in 1950 to 0.129 in 1980—a sharp drop in inequality. For the centrally planned economies the drop is much smaller—from 0.381 to 0.301. The middle-income group exhibits an even smaller decline, from 0.269 to 0.258. But the low-income countries underwent a small *rise* over the period, from 0.103 to 0.112, and the world as a whole experienced a tiny rise from 0.493 to 0.498.

There has also been little convergence among the groups. For the entire period, Summers et al. report (p. 245) an average annual growth rate in per capita real GDP of 3.1 percent for industrialized countries, 3.6 percent for centrally planned economies, 3.0 percent for middle-income market economies, and only 1.5 percent for the low-income group, with a world average group rate of 2.7 percent.

This suggests that there is more than one convergence club. Rather, there are perhaps three, with the centrally planned and the intermediate groups somewhat inferior in performance to that of the free-market industrialized countries. It is also clear that the poorer, less developed countries are still largely barred from the homogenization processes. Since any search for "the causes" of a complex economic phenomenon of reality is likely to prove fruitless, no attempt will be made here to explain systematically why poorer, less developed countries have benefited to a relatively small degree from the public good properties of the innovations and investments of other nations. But part of the explanation may well be related to product mix and education. A less developed country that produces no cars cannot benefit from the invention and adoption of a better car-producing robot in Japan (though it does benefit to a lesser degree from new textile and rice-growing technology), nor can it benefit from the factor-price equalization effect of the accompanying Japanese investments, since it cannot shift labor force out of its (nonexistent) auto industry as the theorem's logic requires. Lack of education and the associated skills prevent both the presence of high-tech industries and the effective imitation (adoption) of the Japanese innovation. Obviously, there is much more to any reasonably fuller explanation of the exclusion of many less developed countries from the convergence process, but that is not my purpose here. . . .

Notes

1. This observation does not quite seem to square with Charles Feinstein's estimates (1972, pp. 82–94) which indicate that while output per worker in the United Kingdom increased 0.2 percent per year between 1761 and 1800, between 1801 and 1830 the growth rate leaped up to 1.4 percent per annum. He estimates that total factor productivity behaved similarly. However, between 1801 and 1810, total annual investment fell to 10 percent of gross domestic product, in comparison with its 14 percent rate in the immediately preceding and succeeding periods.

2. Space prevents extensive consideration of Paul Romer's (1985) objection to the evidence offered for the convergence hypothesis provided here and elsewhere, i.e., that the sample of countries studied is an *ex post* selection of successful economies. Successes, by definition, are those which have done best relative to the leader. However, the Summers-Heston 1950–80 data for 72 countries represented in Figure 18.2 do permit an *ex ante* selection. Tests ranking countries both by 1950 and by 1960 GDP levels confirm that even an *ex ante* sample of the wealthiest countries yields a pattern of convergence which, while less pronounced than that calculated from an *ex post* group, is still unambiguous.

3. The high correlation should not be taken too seriously. Aside from the reasons why its explanation may be misunderstood that are presently discussed in the text, the

tight fit of the data points is undoubtedly ascribable in good part to several biassing features of the underlying calculation. First, the 1870 figures were calculated by Maddison using backward extrapolation of growth rates, and hence their correlation is hardly surprising. Second, since growth rate, r, is calculated by solving $y_t = e^{rt}y^0$ for r, to obtain $r = (\ln y_t - \ln y_0)/t$, where $y_t = GDP$ per capita in period t, a regression equation $r = f(y_0)$ contains the same variable, y_0 on both sides of the equation, thus tending to produce a spurious appearance of close relationship. Indeed, if the convergence process were perfect, so that we would have $y_t = k$ with k the same for every country in the sample, every dot in the diagram would necessarily perfectly fit the curve $r = lnk/t - lny_0/t$, and the r^2 would be unity, identically. The 72-country data depicted in Figure 18.2 hardly constitute a close fit (the R^2 is virtually zero), and do not even yield a negatively sloping regression line. Thus, a relationship such as that in Figure 18.1 is no tautology, nor even a foregone conclusion.

In addition, if the 1870 productivity levels are measured with considerable error, this must result in some significant downward bias in the regression coefficient on $ln(GDP$ per $WorkHr$, 1870). This is a point distinct from the one concerning the size of the correlation coefficient, although the latter is affected by the fact that relatively large measurement errors in the 1870 productivity levels enter as inversely correlated measurement errors in the 1870–1979 growth rate. The argument that this bias is not sufficient to induce a negative correlation in the 72-country sample may not be wholly germane, as the relative seriousness of the measurement errors in the initial and terminal observations may be much the same for observations confined to the period 1950–80.

4. It must be conceded that the longer-run data do not seem to offer impressive support for the hypothesis that the forces of factor-price equalization have, albeit imperfectly, extended the benefits of exceptional rates of investment from those economies that carried out the successful investment programs to other industrialized economies. Since we have estimates of relative real wages, capital stock, and other pertinent variables for the United Kingdom and Germany, these have been compared below:

	Period	Ratio: German Increase to U.K. Increase[b]
Real Wages	1860–1980	4.25
GDP per Labor Hour	1870–1979	2.35
Capital Stock[a]	1870–1979	6.26
Capital Stock per Worker	1870–1979	3.8
Capital Stock per Capita	1870–1979	5.4

Sources: Real wages, same as in Note 6 [of original text; not included here]; all other data from Maddison.

Notes: a. Net nonresidential fixed tangible capital stock.

b. (German 1979 figure/German 1870 figure)/(U.K. 1979 figure/U.K. 1987 figure) with appropriate modification of the dates for the wage figures.

If the public goods attribute hypothesis about the effects of investment in one country were valid and if factor-price equalization were an effective force, we would expect the relative rise in German real wages and in productivity to be small (on some criterion) in comparison with the relative increase in its capital stock. However, the figures do not seem to exhibit such a pattern.

5. There are at least two sources of such data: the World Bank and the University of Pennsylvania group. Here I report only data drawn from the latter, since their international comparisons have been carried out with unique sophistication and insight. Instead of translating the different currencies into one another using inadequate exchange rate comparisons, they use carefully constructed indices of relative purchasing power. I have also replicated my calculations using World Bank data and obtained exactly the same qualitative results.

6. The centrally planned economies are Bulgaria, China, Czechoslovakia, East Germany, Hungary, Poland, Romania, USSR, and Yugoslavia. The 5 countries with relatively high 1950 incomes included neither in Maddison's sample nor in the planned group are, in descending order of GDP per capita, Luxembourg, New Zealand, Iceland, Venezuela, and Argentina. The countries with negative growth rates are Uganda and Nigeria.

References

Abramovitz, Moses. 1979. "Rapid Growth Potential and Its Realization: The Experience of the Capitalist Economies in the Postwar Period," in Edmond Malinvaud, ed., *Economic Growth and Resources, Proceedings of the Fifth World Congress of the International Economic Association,* Vol. 1, London: Macmillan.
———. 1985. "Catching Up and Falling Behind," delivered at the Economic History Association, September 20, 1985.
Ames, Edward and Rosenberg, Nathan. 1963. "Changing Technological Leadership and Industrial Growth," *Economic Journal* 73 (March): 13–31.
Beniger, James R. Forthcoming. *The Control Revolution: Technological and Economic Origins of the Information Society.* Cambridge: Harvard University Press.
Caves, Richard E. and Krause, Lawrence B. 1984. *The Australian Economy: A View from the North.* Washington: The Brookings Institution.
Cipolla, Carlo M. 1976. *Before the Industrial Revolution: European Society and Economy, 1000–1700.* New York: W. W. Norton.
Clark, Colin. 1957. *The Conditions of Economic Progress,* 3rd ed. London: Macmillan.
Darby, Michael. 1984. "The U.S. Productivity Slowdown: A Case of Statistical Myopia," *American Economic Review,* 74 (June): 301–322.
David, Paul A. 1977. "Invention and Accumulation in America's Economic Growth: A Nineteenth-Century Parable," in K. Brunner and A. H. Meltzer, eds., *International Organization, National Policies and Economic Development,* pp. 179–228. Amsterdam: North-Holland.
Deane, Phyllis and Cole, W. A. 1962. *British Economic Growth 1688–1959.* Cambridge: Cambridge University Press.
Feinstein, Charles. 1972. *National Income, Expenditure and Output of the United Kingdom, 1855–1965.* Cambridge: Cambridge University Press.
Gerschenkron, Alexander. 1952. "Economic Backwardness in Historical Perspective," in Bert F. Hoselitz, ed., *The Progress of Underdeveloped Areas.* Chicago: University of Chicago Press.
Landes, David S. 1969. *The Unbound Prometheus.* Cambridge: Cambridge University Press.
Lawrence, Robert Z. 1984. *Can America Compete?* Washington: The Brookings Institution.
Maddison, Angus. 1982. *Phases of Capitalist Development.* New York: Oxford University Press.

Marx, Karl and Engels, Friedrich. 1946. *Manifesto of the Communist Party* (1848). London: Lawrence and Wishart.

Matthews, R.C.O. 1982. *Slower Growth in the Western World.* London: Heinemann.

———, Feinstein, C. H. and Odling-Smee, J. C. 1982. *British Economic Growth, 1856–1973.* Stanford: Stanford University Press.

McCloskey, D. N. 1981. *Enterprise and Trade in Victorian Britain.* London: Allen & Unwin.

Mueller, Dennis C. 1983. *The Political Economy of Growth.* New Haven: Yale University Press.

Phelps Brown, E. H. and Hopkins, S. V. 1955. "Seven Centuries of Building Wages," *Economica,* 22 (August): 195–206.

———. 1956. "Seven Centuries of the Prices of Consumables," *Economica,* 23 (November): 296–314.

Porat, Marc Uri. 1977. "The Information Economy, Definitions and Measurement," Office of Telecommunications, Special Publication, 77-12(1), U.S. Department of Commerce, Washington.

Romer, Paul M. 1985. "Increasing Returns and Long Run Growth," Working Paper No. 27. University of Rochester, October.

Summers, Robert and Heston, Alan. 1984. "Improved International Comparisons of Real Product and Its Composition, 1950–1980," *Review of Income and Wealth,* 30 (June): 207–262.

Summers, Robert, Kravis, I. B., and Heston, Alan. 1986. "Changes in World Income Distribution," *Journal of Policy Modeling,* 6 (May): 237–269.

Teece, David J. 1976. *The Multinational Corporation and the Resources Cost of International Technology Transfer.* Cambridge: Ballinger.

U.S. Bureau of Census. 1973. *Long Term Economic Growth 1860–1970.* Washington, D.C., June.

Veblen, Thorstein. 1915. *Imperial Germany and the Industrial Revolution.* New York: Macmillan.

Viner, Jacob. 1958. *The Long View and the Short.* Glencoe: Free Press.

Williamson, Jeffrey G. 1983. "Why Was British Growth So Slow During the Industrial Revolution?" Unpublished, Harvard Institute of Economic Research.

19

Productivity Growth, Convergence, and Welfare: Comment

J. Bradford DeLong

In the previous chapter, William Baumol confirmed the expectations of convergence theory by finding that between 1870 and 1979, productivity rates of poorer countries grew more rapidly than those of richer countries. In this chapter, J. Bradford DeLong argues that because only countries that converged by 1979 were included in the dataset used by Baumol, convergence was ensured. When DeLong corrects for this sample-selection bias, convergence disappears. DeLong then analyzes other variables to determine if the pattern of growth that he found can be explained. He does not find an association between democracy in 1870 and subsequent growth. DeLong did find a significant relationship between religion and growth: Protestant cultures grew faster. But the author notes that the correlations will not hold for long given the growth rates of countries such as Japan and Italy. The optimistic view that there is a process of economic homogenization, a closing of the gap between rich and poor, is not sustained by the data. As the author concludes, "It pushes us away from the belief that even the nations of the now industrial West will have roughly equal standards of living in 2090 or 2190."

ECONOMISTS HAVE ALWAYS EXPECTED THE "CONVERGENCE" OF NATIONAL productivity levels. The theoretical logic behind this belief is powerful. The per capita income edge of the West is based on its application of the storehouse of industrial and administrative technology of the Industrial Revolution. This

Reprinted with permission of the *American Economic Review* 78, no. 5 (1986): 1038–1048.

storehouse is open: modern technology is a public good. The benefits of tapping this storehouse are great, and so nations will strain every nerve to assimilate modern technology and their incomes will converge to those of industrial nations.

William Baumol (1986) argues that convergence has shown itself strongly in the growth of industrial nations since 1870.[1] According to Baumol, those nations positioned to industrialize are much closer together in productivity now than a century ago. He bases this conclusion on a regression of growth since 1870 on 1870 productivity for sixteen countries covered by Angus Maddison (1982).[2]

Baumol's finding of convergence might—even though Baumol himself does not believe that it should—naturally be read to support two further conclusions. First, slow relative growth in the United States since World War II was inevitable: convergence implies that in the long run divergent national cultures, institutions, or policies cannot sustain significant productivity edges over the rest of the developed world. Second, one can be optimistic about future development. Maddison's sixteen all assimilated modern technology and converged; perhaps all developing nations will converge to Western living standards once they acquire a foundation of technological literacy.

But when properly interpreted Baumol's finding is less informative than one might think. For Baumol's regression uses an *ex post* sample of countries that are now rich and have successfully developed. By Maddison's choice, those nations that have not converged are excluded from his sample because of their resulting present relative poverty. Convergence is thus all but guaranteed in Baumol's regression, which tells us little about the strength of the forces making for convergence among nations that in 1870 belonged to what Baumol calls the "convergence club."

Only a regression run on an *ex ante* sample, a sample not of nations that have converged but of nations that seemed in 1870 likely to converge, can tell us whether growth since 1870 exhibits "convergence." The answer to this *ex ante* question—have those nations that a century ago appeared well placed to appropriate and utilize industrial technology converged?—is no. . . .

Maddison (1982) compiles long-run national income and aggregate productivity data for sixteen successful capitalist nations.[3] Because he focuses on nations which (a) have a rich data base for the construction of historical national accounts and (b) have successfully developed, the nations in Maddison's sixteen are among the richest nations in the world today. Baumol regresses the average rate of annual labor productivity growth over 1870–1979 on a constant and on the log of labor productivity in 1870 for this sample. He finds the inverse relationship of the first line of Table 19.1. The slope is large enough to erase by 1979 almost all initial income gaps, and the residual variance is small.

Regressing the log difference in per capita income between 1870 and 1979 on a constant and the log of per capita income in 1870 provides a slightly stronger case for convergence, as detailed in the second line of Table 19.1. The

Table 19.1   Regressions Using Maddison's Sixteen

Independent Variable	Dependent Variable	Constant	Slope Coefficient	Standard Error of Estimate	R^2
Natural Log of 1870 Productivity	Annual Percent Productivity Growth	5.251	−0.749 .075	.14	.87
Natural Log of 1870 Income	Log Difference of 1979 and 1870 Income	8.457	−0.995 .094	.15	.88

Source: Data from Maddison (1982).

logarithmic income specification offers two advantages. The slope has the intuitive interpretation that a value of minus one means that 1979 and 1870 relative incomes are uncorrelated, and extension of the sample to include additional nations becomes easier.

Baumol's regression line tells us little about the strength of forces making for convergence since 1870 among industrial nations. The sample suffers from selection bias, and the independent variable is unavoidably measured with error. Both of these create the appearance of convergence whether or not it exists in reality. Sample selection bias arises because any nations relatively rich in 1870 that have not converged fail to make it into Maddison's sixteen. Maddison's sixteen thus include Norway but not Spain, Canada but not Argentina, and Italy but not Ireland. . . .

The unbiased sample used here meets three criteria. First, it is made up of nations that had high potential for economic growth as of 1870, in which modern economic growth had begun to take hold by the middle of the nineteenth century. Second, inclusion in the sample is not conditional on subsequent rapid growth. Third, the sample matches Baumol's as closely as possible, both because the best data exist for Maddison's sixteen and because analyzing an unbiased sample close to Baumol's shows that different conclusions arise not from different estimates but from removing sample selection and errors in variables' biases.

Per capita income in 1870 is an obvious measure of whether a nation was sufficiently technologically literate and integrated into world trade in 1870 to be counted among the potential convergers. . . .

. . . The choice of cutoff level itself requires balancing three goals: including only nations which really did in 1870 possess the social capability for rapid industrialization; including as many nations in Baumol's sample as possible; and building as large a sample as possible. . . .

If the convergence club membership cutoff is set low enough to include all Maddison's sixteen, then nations with 1870 incomes above 300 1975 dollars are included. This sample covers half the world. All Europe including Russia, all of South America, and perhaps others (Mexico and Cuba?) were richer than Japan in 1870. This sample does not provide a fair test of convergence. The Japanese miracle is a miracle largely because there was little sign in 1870 that Japan—or any nation as poor as Japan—was a candidate for rapid industrialization.

The second poorest of Maddison's sixteen in 1870 was Finland. Taking Finland's 1870 income as a cutoff leads to a sample in which Japan is removed, while Argentina, Chile, East Germany,[4] Ireland, New Zealand, Portugal, and Spain are added. . . .

All the additional nations have strong claims to belong to the 1870 convergence club. All were well integrated into the Europe-based international economy. All had bright development prospects as of 1870. . . . Argentina, Chile, and New Zealand were grouped in the nineteenth century with Australia and Canada as countries with temperate climates, richly endowed with natural resources, attracting large-scale immigration and investment, and exporting large quantities of raw and processed agricultural commodities. They were all seen as natural candidates for the next wave of industrialization.

Ireland's economy was closely integrated with the most industrialized economy in the world. Spain and Portugal had been the technological leaders of Europe during the initial centuries of overseas expansion—their per capita incomes were still above the European mean in the 1830s (Paul Bairoch, 1981)—and had retained close trading links with the heart of industrial Europe. Coke was used to smelt iron in Asturias in the 1850s, and by 1877 3,950 miles of railroad had been built in Spain. It is difficult to see how one could exclude Portugal and Spain from the convergence club without also excluding nations like Sweden and Finland.

Baumol's sample failed to include those nations that should have belonged to any hypothetical convergence club but that nevertheless did not converge. The enlarged sample might include nations not in the 1870 convergence club. Consider Kuwait today: Kuwait is rich, yet few would take its failure to maintain its relative standard of living over the next fifty years as evidence against convergence. For Kuwait's present wealth does not necessarily carry with it the institutional capability to turn oil wealth into next generation's industrial wealth. . . .

The volume of overseas investment poured into the additional nations by investors from London and Paris between 1870 and 1913 tells us that investors thought these nations' development prospects good. Herbert Feis' (1930) standard estimates of French and British overseas investment [the interested reader should refer to Table 2, p. 1,143 of the original article] show the six non-European nations among the top ten[5] recipients of investment per capita from France and Britain, and four of the five top recipients of investment belong to the once-rich twenty-two.[6] Every pound or franc invested is an explicit bet that the recipient country's rate of profit will remain high and an implicit bet that its rate of economic growth will be rapid. The coincidence of the nations added on a per capita income basis and the nations that would have been added on a foreign investment basis is powerful evidence that these nations do belong in the potential convergence club.

Errors in estimating 1870 income are unavoidable and produce equal and opposite errors in 1870–1979 growth. These errors therefore create the appearance of convergence where it does not exist in reality. . . .[7]

From one point of view, the relatively poor quality of much of the nineteenth century data is not a severe liability for this chapter. Only if there is less measurement error than allowed for will the results be biased against convergence. A more direct check on the importance of measurement error can be performed by examining convergence starting at some later date for which income estimates are based on a firmer foundation. A natural such date is 1913.[8] The relationship between initial income and subsequent growth is examined for the period 1913–1979 in Table 19.2.

The longer 1870–1979 sample of Table 19.3 . . . is slightly more hospitable to convergence than is the 1913–1979 sample, but for neither sample do the regression lines reveal a significant inverse relationship between initial income and subsequent growth. When it is assumed that there is no measurement error in 1870 income, there is a large negative slope to the regression line. But even in this case the residual disturbance term is large. When measurement error variance is assumed equal to half disturbance variance, the slope is slightly but not significantly negative.

For the central case of equal variances growth since 1870 is unrelated to income in 1870. There is no convergence. Those countries with income edges have on average maintained them. If measurement error is assumed larger than the regression disturbance there is not convergence but divergence. Nations

Table 19.2   Maximum Likelihood Estimation for the Once-Rich Twenty-Two, 1913–1979

p	Slope Coefficient B	Standard Error of Slope	Standard Error of Regression	Standard Error in 1870 PCI
0.0	−.333	.116	.171	.000
0.5	−.140	.136	.151	.107
1.0	0.021	.158	.133	.133
2.0	0.206	.191	.106	.150
Infinity	0.444	.238	.000	.167

Source: Data from Maddison (1982).

Table 19.3   Maximum Likelihood Estimation for the Once-Rich Twenty-Two, 1870–1979

p	Slope Coefficient B	Standard Error of Slope	Standard Error of Regression	Standard Error in 1870 PCI
0.0	−.566	.144	.207	.000
0.5	−.292	.192	.192	.136
1.0	0.110	.283	.170	.170
2.0	0.669	.463	.134	.190
Infinity	1.381	.760	.000	.196

Source: Data from Maddison (1982).

Table 19.4   Standard Deviations of Log Output for Maddison's Sixteen and the Once-Rich Twenty-Two

Sample	1870	1913	1979
Maddison's 16	.411	.355	.145
Once-Rich 22	.315	.324	.329

Source: Data from Maddison (1982).

rich in 1870 or 1913 have subsequently widened relative income gaps. The evidence can be presented in other ways. The standard deviations of log income are given in Table 19.4. Maddison's sixteen do converge: the standard deviation of log income in 1979 is only 35 percent of its 1870 value. But the appearance of convergence is due to selection bias: the once-rich twenty-two have as wide a spread of relative incomes today as in 1870.

The failure of convergence to emerge for nations rich in 1870 is due to the nations—Chile, Argentina, Spain, and Portugal. In the early 1970s none of these was a democracy. Perhaps only industrial nations with democratic political systems converge. A dummy variable for democracy over 1950–80 is significant in the central ($p = 1$) case in the once-rich twenty-two regression in a at the 1 percent level, as detailed in Table 19.5.

But whether a nation is a democracy over 1950–80 is not exogenous but is partly determined by growth over the preceding century. As of 1870 it was not at all clear which nations would become stable democracies. Of the once-rich twenty-two, France, Austria (including Czechoslovakia), and Germany were empires; Britain had a restricted franchise; Spain and Portugal were semiconstitutional monarchies; the United States had just undergone a civil war; and Ireland was under foreign occupation. That all of these countries would be stable democracies by 1950 seems *ex ante* unlikely. Table 19.6 shows that shifting to an *ex ante* measure of democracy[9] removes the correlation.

Table 19.5 Democracy over 1950–1980 and Long-Run Growth for the Once-Rich Twenty-Two, 1870–1979

p	Slope Coefficient B	Standard Error of Slope	Coefficient on Democracy Variable	Standard Error	Standard Error in 1870 PCI	Standard Error of Regression
0.0	−.817	.277	.495	.085	.155	.000
0.5	−.744	.203	.476	.084	.154	.109
1.0	−.599	.208	.437	.090	.150	.150
2.0	0.104	.227	.248	.071	.131	.185
Infinity	1.137	.019	.044	.003	.000	.198

Source: Data from Maddison (1982).

Table 19.6 Democracy in 1870 and Long-Run Growth for the Once-Rich Twenty-Two, 1870–1979

p	Slope Coefficient B	Standard Error of Slope	Coefficient on Democracy Variable	Standard Error	Standard Error in 1870 PCI	Standard Error of Regression
0.0	−.567	.342	.001	.091	.207	.000
0.5	−.272	.322	−.038	.094	.192	.136
1.0	0.164	.454	−.095	.115	.169	.169
2.0	0.742	.976	−.170	.180	.131	.155
Infinity	1.231	.167	−.195	.022	.000	.194

Source: Data from Maddison (1982).

Whether a nation's politics are democratic in 1870 has little to do with growth since. The elective affinity of democracy and opulence is not one way with democracy as cause and opulence as effect.

There is one striking *ex ante* association between growth over 1870–1979 and a predetermined variable: a nation's dominant religious establishment. As Table 19.7 shows, a religious establishment variable that is one for Protestant, one-half for mixed, and zero for Catholic nations is significantly correlated with growth as long as measurement error variance is not too high.[10]

This regression is very difficult to interpret.[11] It does serve as an example of how culture may be associated with substantial divergence in growth performance. But "Protestantism" is correlated with many things—early specialization in manufacturing (for a given level of income), a high investment ratio, and a northern latitude, to name three. Almost any view—except a belief in convergence—of what determines long-run growth is consistent with this correlation between growth and religious establishment. Moreover, this correlation will not last: neither fast grower Japan nor fast grower Italy owes anything

Table 19.7 Dominant Religion in 1870 and Long-Run Growth for the Once-Rich Twenty-Two, 1870–1979

p	Slope Coefficient *B*	Standard Error of Slope	Coefficient on Democracy Variable	Standard Error	Standard Error in 1870 PCI	Standard Error of Regression
0.0	−.789	.252	.429	.088	.166	.000
0.5	−.688	.225	.403	.088	.164	.116
1.0	−.470	.248	.347	.098	.158	.158
2.0	0.375	.232	.132	.061	.132	.187
Infinity	1.199	.021	−.003	.004	.000	.197

Source: Data from Maddison (1982).

to the Protestant ethic. The main message of Table 19.7 is that, for the once-rich twenty-two, a country's religious establishment has been a surprisingly good proxy for the social capability to assimilate modern technology.

The long-run data do not show convergence on any but the most optimistic reading. They do not support the claim that those nations that should have been able to rapidly assimilate industrial technology have all converged. Nations rich among the once-rich twenty-two in 1870 have not grown more slowly than the average of the sample. And of the nations outside this sample, only Japan has joined the industrial leaders.

This is not to say that there are no forces pushing for convergence. Convergence does sometimes happen. Technology is a public good. Western Europe (except Iberia) and the British settlement colonies of Australia, Canada, and the United States are now all developed. Even Italy, which seemed outside the sphere of advanced capitalism two generations ago, is near the present income frontier reached by the richest nations. The convergence of Japan and Western Europe toward U.S. standards of productivity in the years after World War II is an amazing achievement, and this does suggest that those present at the creation of the post–World War II international order did a very good job. But others—Spain, Portugal, Ireland, Argentina, and Chile—that one would in 1870 have thought capable of equally sharing this prosperity have not done so.[12] The capability to assimilate industrial technology appears to be surprisingly hard to acquire, and it may be distressingly easy to lose.

The forces making for "convergence" even among industrial nations appear little stronger than the forces making for "divergence." The absence of convergence pushes us away from a belief that in the long run technology transfer both is inevitable and is the key factor in economic growth. It pushes us away from the belief that even the nations of the now industrial West will have roughly equal standards of living in 2090 or 2190. And the absence of convergence even among nations relatively rich in 1870 forces us to take seriously arguments like Romer's (1986) that the relative income gap between rich and poor may tend to widen.

Notes

1. Consider Baumol (1986): "Among the main observations . . . is the remarkable convergence. . . . [T]here is a strong inverse correlation between a country's productivity . . . in 1870 and its . . . productivity growth since then," and Baumol (1987): "Even more remarkable . . . is the convergence in . . . living standards of the leading industrial countries. . . . In 1870 . . . productivity in Australia, the leader, was 8 times . . . Japan's (the laggard). By 1979, the ratio . . . had fallen to about two."

2. Moses Abramovitz (1986) follows the behavior of these sixteen over time and notes that even among these nations "convergence" is almost entirely a post–World War II phenomenon. Abramovitz' remarks on how the absence of the "social capability" to grasp the benefits of the Industrial Revolution may prevent even nations that could benefit greatly from industrializing are well worth reading. Also very good on the possible determinants of the social capability to assimilate technology are Irma Adelman and Cynthia Taft Morris (1980), Gregory Clark (1987), and Richard Easterlin (1981).

3. Maddison's focus on nations that have been economically successful is deliberate; his aim in (1964), (1982), and (1987) is to investigate the features of successful capitalist development. In works like Maddison (1970, 1983) he has analyzed the long-run growth and development of less successful nations.

4. Perhaps only nations that have remained capitalist should be included in the sample, for occupation by the Red Army and subsequent relative economic stagnation have no bearing on whether the forces making for convergence among industrial capitalist economies are strong. There is only one centrally planned economy in the unbiased sample, and its removal has negligible quantitative effects on the estimated degree of convergence.

5. The foreign investment figures do provide a powerful argument for adding other Latin American nations—Mexico, Brazil, and Cuba—to the sample of those that ought to have been in the convergence club. Inclusion of these nations would weigh heavily against convergence.

6. Japan would not merit inclusion in the 1870 convergence club on the basis of foreign investment before World War I, for Japanese industrialization was not financed by British capital. Foreign investors' taste for Japan was much less, investment being equal to about one pound sterling per head and far below investment in such nations as Venezuela, Russia, Turkey, and Egypt. Admittedly, Japan was far away and not well known, but who would have predicted that Japan would have five times the measured per capita GNP of Argentina by 1979?

7. By contrast, errors in measuring 1979 per capita income induce no systematic bias in the relationship between standard of living in 1870 and growth since, although they do diminish the precision of coefficient estimates.

8. The data for 1913 are much more plentiful and solid than for other years in the early years of the twentieth century because of the concentration of historians' efforts on obtaining a pre–World War I benchmark. Beginning the sample at 1913 does mean that changes in country's "social capability" for development as a result of World War I appear in the error term in the regression. If those nations that suffered most badly in World War I were nations relatively poor in World War I, there would be cause for

alarm that the choice of 1913 had biased the sample against finding convergence when it was really present. But the major battlefields of World War I lay in and the largest proportional casualties were suffered by relatively rich nations at the core of industrial Europe.

9. Defined as inclusion of the electorate of more than half the adult male population.

10. The once-rich twenty-two are split into nations that had Protestant religious establishments in 1870 (Australia, Denmark, Finland, E. Germany, Netherlands, New Zealand, Norway, Sweden, U.K., and United States), intermediate nations—nations that either were split in established religion in 1870 or that had undergone violent and prolonged religious wars between Protestant and Catholics in the centuries after the Protestant Reformation—(Belgium, Canada, France, West Germany, and Switzerland), and nations that had solid Catholic religious establishments in 1870 (Argentina, Austria, Chile, Ireland, Italy, Portugal, and Spain). This classification is judgmental and a matter of taste: are the Netherlands one of the heartlands of the Protestant Ethic or are they one of the few nations tolerant and pluralistic on matters of religion in the seventeenth century?

11. The easy explanation would begin with the medieval maxim *homo mercato vix aut numquam placere potest Deo:* the merchant's business can never please God. Medieval religious discipline was hostile to market capitalism, the Protestant Reformation broke this discipline down in some places, and capitalism flourished most and modern democratic growth took hold strongest where this breakdown of medieval discipline had been most complete.

But this easy explanation is at best incomplete. Initially the Reformation did not see a relaxation of religious control. Strong Protestantism—Calvin's Geneva or Cromwell's Republic of the Saints—saw theology and economy closely linked in a manner not unlike the Ayatollah's Iran. And religious fanaticism is not often thought of as a source of economic growth.

Nevertheless the disapproval of self-interested profit seeking by radical Protestantism went hand-in-hand with seventeenth century economic development. And by 1800 profit seeking and accumulation for accumulation's sake had become morally praiseworthy activities in many nations with Protestant religious establishments. How was the original Protestant disapproval for the market transformed? Accounting for the evolution of the economic ethic of the Protestant West from Jean Calvin to Cotton Mather to Benjamin Franklin to Andrew Carnegie is a deep puzzle in economic history. The best analysis may still be the psychological account given by Max Weber (1958; originally published in 1905).

12. One can find good reasons—ranging from the Red Army to landlord political dominance to the legacy of imperialism—for the failure of each of the additional nations to have reached the world's achieved per capita income frontier in 1979. But the fact that there are good reasons for the relative economic failure of each of these seven nations casts substantial doubt on the claim that the future will see convergence, for "good reasons" for economic failure will always be widespread. It is a safe bet that in 2090 one will be able ex post to identify similar "good reasons" lying behind the relative economic decline of those nations that will have fallen out of the industrial core.

References

Abramovitz, M. 1986. "Catching Up, Forging Ahead, and Falling Behind," *Journal of Economic History,* June, 46: 385–406.

Adelman, I. and C. T. Morris. 1980. "Patterns of Industrialization in the Nineteenth and Early Twentieth Centuries," in Paul Uselding, ed., *Research in Economic History,* Vol. 5, Greenwich: JAI Press, 217–46.

Bairoch, P. 1981. "The Main Trends in National Economic Disparities Since the Industrial Revolution," in P. Bairoch and M. Lévy-Leboyer, eds., *Disparities in Economic Development Since the Industrial Revolution,* New York: St. Martin's Press.

Baumol, W. 1987. "America's Productivity 'Crisis,'" *The New York Times,* February 15, 3:2.

———. 1986. "Productivity Growth, Convergence, and Welfare," *American Economic Review,* December, 76: 1072–85.

Clark, G. 1987. "Why Isn't the Whole World Developed? Lessons from the Cotton Mills," *Journal of Economic History,* March, 47: 141–74.

Easterlin, R. 1981. "Why Isn't the Whole World Developed?," *Journal of Economic History,* March, 41: 1–19.

Feis, H. 1930. *Europe, The World's Banker,* New Haven: Yale.

Maddison, A. 1987. "Growth and Slowdown in Advanced Capitalist Economies," *Journal of Economic Literature,* June, 25: 649–98.

———. 1983. "A Comparison of Levels of GDP per Capita in Developed and Developing Countries, 1700–1980," *Journal of Economic History,* March, 43: 27–41.

———. 1982. *Phases of Capitalist Development,* Oxford: Oxford University Press.

———. 1970. *Economic Progress and Policy in Developing Countries,* London: Allen & Unwin.

———. 1964. *Economic Growth in the West,* New York: The Twentieth Century Fund.

Romer, P. 1986. "Increasing Returns and Long Run Growth," *Journal of Political Economy,* October, 94: 1002–37.

Weber, M. 1958. *The Protestant Ethic and the Spirit of Capitalism,* New York: Scribner's. Originally published in 1905.

Part 5

Culture and Underdevelopment

20

The Achievement Motive
in Economic Growth

David C. McClelland

In this chapter, David C. McClelland, a psychologist, expands upon ideas developed by Max Weber, who examined the relationship between the Protestant ethic and the rise of capitalism. McClelland posits a more generalized psychological attribute he calls the "need for Achievement," or n Achievement. In this discussion, which is a summary of a book on the subject, McClelland presents some very interesting historical data he believes help explain the rise and decline of Athenian civilization. Turning to the present century, he produces data that show a close association between national levels of n Achievement and rates of economic growth. In seeking to determine what produces this psychological characteristic, McClelland finds that it is not hereditary but rather is instilled in people. It is therefore possible, he claims, to teach people how to increase their need to achieve and by so doing stimulate economic growth in developing countries. McClelland has been responsible for establishing training and management programs in developing countries in hopes that a change in the psychological orientation of public officials will help speed economic growth.

FROM THE BEGINNING OF RECORDED HISTORY, MEN HAVE BEEN FASCInated by the fact that civilizations rise and fall. Culture growth, as A. L. Kroeber has demonstrated, is episodic, and sometimes occurs in quite different

Reprinted with permission of UNESCO from *Industrialization and Society,* edited by Bert F. Hoselitz and Wilbert E. Moore, pp. 74–95. Copyright © 1983 by UNESCO.

fields.[1] For example, the people living in the Italian peninsula at the time of ancient Rome produced a great civilization of law, politics, and military conquest; and at another time, during the Renaissance, the inhabitants of Italy produced a great civilization of art, music, letters, and science. What can account for such cultural flowerings? In our time we have theorists like Ellsworth Huntington, who stresses the importance of climate, or Arnold J. Toynbee, who also feels the right amount of challenge from the environment is crucial though he conceives of the environment as including its psychic effects. Others, like Kroeber, have difficulty imagining any general explanation; they perforce must accept the notion that a particular culture happens to hit on a particularly happy mode of self-expression, which it then pursues until it becomes overspecialized and sterile.

My concern is not with all culture growth, but with economic growth. Some wealth or leisure may be essential to development in other fields—the arts, politics, science, or war—but we need not insist on it. However, the question of why some countries develop rapidly in the economic sphere at certain times and not at others is in itself of great interest, whatever its relation to other types of culture growth. Usually, rapid economic growth has been explained in terms of "external" factors—favorable opportunities for trade, unusual natural resources, or conquests that have opened up new markets or produced internal political stability. But I am interested in the *internal* factors—in the values and motives men have that lead them to exploit opportunities, to take advantage of favorable trade conditions; in short, to shape their own destiny. . . .

Whatever else one thinks of Freud and the other psychoanalysts, they performed one extremely important service for psychology: once and for all, they persuaded us, rightly or wrongly, that what people said about their motives was not a reliable basis for determining what those motives really were. In his analyses of the psychopathology of everyday life and of dreams and neurotic symptoms, Freud demonstrated repeatedly that the "obvious" motives—the motives that the people themselves thought they had or that a reasonable observer would attribute to them—were not, in fact, the real motives for their often strange behavior. By the same token, Freud also showed the way to a better method of learning what people's motives were. He analyzed dreams and free associations: in short, fantasy or imaginative behavior. Stripped of its air of mystery and the occult, psychoanalysis has taught us that one can learn a great deal about people's motives through observing the things about which they are spontaneously concerned in their dreams and waking fantasies. About ten or twelve years ago, the research group in America with which I was connected decided to take this insight quite seriously and to see what we could learn about human motivation by coding objectively what people spontaneously thought about in their waking fantasies.[2] Our method was to collect such free fantasy, in the form of brief stories written about pictures, and to count the frequency with which certain themes appeared—rather as a medical technician counts the frequency with which red or white corpuscles appear in a blood sample. We were able to demonstrate that the frequency with which certain "inner concerns" appeared in these fantasies varied systematically as a function of specific experimental conditions by which we aroused or induced motivational states in the subjects. Eventually we were able to isolate several of these inner concerns, or motives, which, if present in great frequency in the fantasies of a particular person, enabled us to know something about how he would behave in many other areas of life.

Chief among these motives was what we termed "the need for Achievement" (*n* Achievement)—a desire to do well, not so much for the sake of social recognition or prestige, but to attain an inner feeling of personal accomplishment. This motive is my particular concern in this chapter. Our early laboratory studies showed that people "high" in *n* Achievement tend to work harder at certain tasks; to learn faster; to do their best work when it counts for the record, and not when special incentives, like money prizes, are introduced; to choose experts over friends as working partners; etc. Obviously, we cannot here review the many, many studies in this area. About five years ago, we became especially interested in the problem of what would happen in a society if a large number of people with a high need for achievement should happen to be present in it at a particular time. In other words, we became interested in a social-psychological question: What effect would a concentration of people with high *n* Achievement have on a society?

It might be relevant to describe how we began wondering about this. I had always been greatly impressed by the very perceptive analysis of the connection between Protestantism and the spirit of capitalism made by the great German sociologist, Max Weber.[3] He argues that the distinguishing characteristic of Protestant business entrepreneurs and of workers, particularly from the pietistic sects, was not that they had in any sense invented the institutions of capitalism or good craftsmanship, but that they went about their jobs with a new perfectionist spirit. The Calvinistic doctrine of predestination had forced them to rationalize every aspect of their lives and to strive hard for perfection in the positions in this world to which they had been assigned by God. As I read Weber's description of the behavior of these people, I concluded that they must certainly have had a high level of *n* Achievement. Perhaps the new spirit of capitalism Weber describes was none other than a high need for achievement—if so, then *n* Achievement has been responsible, in part, for the extraordinary economic development of the West. Another factor served to confirm this hypothesis. A careful study by M. R. Winterbottom had shown that boys with high *n* Achievement usually came from families in which the mothers stressed early self-reliance and mastery.[4] The boys whose mothers did not encourage their early self-reliance, or did not set such high standards of excellence, tended to develop lower need for achievement. Obviously, one of the key characteristics of the Protestant Reformation was its emphasis on self-reliance. Luther stressed the "priesthood of all believers" and translated the Bible so that every man could have direct access to God and religious thought. Calvin accentuated a rationalized perfection in this life for everyone. Certainly, the character of the Reformation seems to have set the stage, historically, for parents to encourage their children to attain earlier self-reliance and achievement. If the parents did in fact do so, they very possibly unintentionally produced the higher level of *n* Achievement in their children that was, in turn, responsible for the new spirit of capitalism.

This was the hypothesis that initiated our research. It was, of course, only a promising idea; much work was necessary to determine its validity. Very early in our studies, we decided that the events Weber discusses were probably only a special case of a much more general phenomenon—that it was *n* Achievement as such that was connected with economic development, and that the Protestant Reformation was connected only indirectly in the extent to which it had influenced the average *n* Achievement level of its adherents. If this assumption is correct, then a high average level of *n* Achievement should be equally associated with economic development in ancient Greece, in modern Japan, or in a preliterate tribe being studied by anthropologists in the South Pacific. In other words, in its most general form, the hypothesis attempts to isolate one of the key factors in the economic development, at least, of all civilizations. What evidence do we have that this extremely broad generalization will obtain? By now, a great deal has been collected—far more than I can summarize here; but I shall try to give a few key examples of the different types of evidence.

First, we have made historical studies. To do so, we had to find a way to obtain a measure of *n* Achievement level during time periods other than our own, whose individuals can no longer be tested. We have done this—instead of coding the brief stories written by an individual for a test, we code imaginative literary documents: poetry, drama, funeral orations, letters written by sea captains, epics, etc. Ancient Greece, which we studied first, supplies a good illustration. We are able to find literary documents written during three different historical periods and dealing with similar themes: the period of economic growth, 900 B.C.–475 B.C. (largely Homer and Hesiod); the period of climax, 475 B.C.–362 B.C.; and the period of decline, 362 B.C.–100 B.C. Thus, Hesiod wrote on farm and estate management in the early period; Xenophon, in the middle period; and Aristotle, in the late period. We have defined the period of "climax" in economic, rather than in cultural, terms, because it would be presumptuous to claim, for example, that Aristotle in any sense represented a "decline" from Plato or Thales. The measure of economic growth was computed from information supplied by F. Heichelheim in his *Wirtschafts-geschichte des Altertums*.[5] Heichelheim records in detail the locations throughout Europe where the remains of Greek vases from different centuries have been found. Of course, these vases were the principal instrument of Greek foreign trade, since they were the containers for olive oil and wine, which were the most important Greek exports. Knowing where the vase fragments have been found, we could compute the trade area of Athenian Greece for different time periods. We purposely omitted any consideration of the later expansion of Hellenistic Greece, because this represents another civilization; our concern was Athenian Greece.

When all the documents had been coded, they demonstrated—as predicted—that the level of *n* Achievement was highest during the period of growth prior to the climax of economic development in Athenian Greece. (See Figure 20.1.) In other words, the maximum *n* Achievement level preceded the maximum economic level by at least a century. Furthermore, that high level

Figure 20.1   Average *n* Achievement Level (plotted at midpoints of periods of growth, climax, and decline of Athenian civilization as reflected in the extent of her trade area)

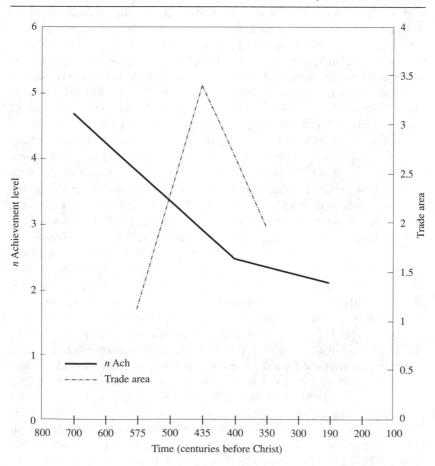

Note: Trade area measured for the sixth, fifth, and fourth centuries B.C. only.

had fallen off by the time of maximum prosperity, thus foreshadowing subsequent economic decline. A similar methodology was applied, with the same results, to the economic development of Spain in the sixteenth century[6] and to two waves of economic development in the history of England (one in the late sixteenth century and the other at the beginning of the industrial revolution, around 1800).[7] The *n* Achievement level in English history (as determined on the basis of dramas, sea captains' letters, and street ballads) rose, between 1400–1800, *twice,* a generation or two before waves of accelerated economic growth (incidentally, at times of Protestant revival). This point is significant because it shows that there is no "necessary" steady decline in a civilization's entrepreneurial energy from its earlier to its later periods. In the Spanish and English cases, as in the Greek, high levels of *n* Achievement preceded economic decline. Unfortunately, space limitations preclude more detailed discussion of these studies here.

We also tested the hypothesis by applying it to preliterate cultures of the sort that anthropologists investigate. At Yale University, an organized effort has been made to collect everything that is known about all the primitive tribes that have been studied and to classify the information systematically for comparative purposes. We utilized this cross-cultural file to obtain the two measures that we needed to test our general hypothesis. For over fifty of these cultures, collections of folk tales existed that I. L. Child and others had coded,[8] just as we coded literary documents and individual imaginative stories, for *n* Achievement and other motives. These folk tales have the character of fantasy that we believe to be so essential for getting at "inner concerns." In the meantime, we were searching for a method of classifying the economic development of these cultures, so that we could determine whether those evincing high *n* Achievement in their folk tales had developed further than those showing lower *n* Achievement. The respective modes of gaining a livelihood were naturally very different in these cultures, since they came from every continent in the world and every type of physical habitat; yet we had to find a measure for comparing them. We finally thought of trying to estimate the number of full-time "business entrepreneurs" there were among the adults in each culture. We defined "entrepreneur" as "anyone who exercises control over the means of production and produces more than he can consume in order to sell it for individual or household income." Thus an entrepreneur was anyone who derived at least 75 percent of his income from such exchange or market practices. The entrepreneurs were mostly traders, independent artisans, or operators of small firms like stores, inns, etc. Nineteen cultures were classified as high in *n* Achievement on the basis of their folk tales; 74 percent of them contained some entrepreneurs. On the other hand, only 35 percent of the twenty cultures that were classified as low in *n* Achievement contained any entrepreneurs (as we defined it) at all. The difference is highly significant statistically (Chi square = 5.97, p < .02). Hence data about primitive tribes seem to confirm the hypothesis that high *n* Achievement leads to a more advanced type of economic activity.

But what about modern nations? Can we estimate their level of *n* Achievement and relate it to their economic development? The question is obviously one of the greatest importance, but the technical problems of getting measures of our two variables proved to be really formidable. What type of literary document could we use that would be equally representative of the motivational levels of people in India, Japan, Portugal, Germany, the United States, and Italy? We had discovered in our historical studies that certain types of literature usually contain much more achievement imagery than others. This is not too serious as long as we are dealing with time changes within a given culture; but it is very serious if we want to compare two cultures, each of which may express its achievement motivation in a different literary form. At last, we decided to use children's stories, for several reasons. They exist in standard form in every modern nation, since all modern nations are involved in teaching their children to read and use brief stories for this purpose. Furthermore, the stories are imaginative; and, if selected from those used in the earliest grades, they are not often influenced by temporary political events. (We were most impressed by this when reading the stories that every Russian child reads. In general, they cannot be distinguished, in style and content, from the stories read in all the countries of the West.)

We collected children's readers for the second, third, and fourth grades from every country where they could be found for two time periods, which were roughly centered around 1925 and around 1950. We got some thirteen hundred stories, which were all translated into English. In all, we had twenty-one stories from each of twenty-three countries about 1925, and the same number from each of thirty-nine countries about 1950. Code was used on proper names, so that our scorers would not know the national origins of the stories. The tales were then mixed together, and coded for *n* Achievement (and certain other motives and values that I shall mention only briefly).

The next task was to find a measure of economic development. Again, the problem was to ensure comparability. Some countries have much greater natural resources; some have developed industrially sooner than others; some concentrate in one area of production and some in another. Economists consider national income figures in per capita terms to be the best measure available; but they are difficult to obtain for all countries, and it is hard to translate them into equal purchasing power. Ultimately, we came to rely chiefly on the measure of electricity produced: the units of measurement are the same all over the world; the figures are available from the 1920s on; and electricity is the *form* of energy (regardless of how it is produced) that is essential to modern economic development. In fact, electricity produced per capita correlates with estimates of income per capita in the 1950s around .90 anyway. To equate for differences in natural resources, such as the amount of water power available, etc., we studied *gains* in kilowatt hours produced per capita between 1925 and 1950. The level of electrical production in 1925 is, as one would expect, highly correlated with the size of the gain between then and 1950. So it was necessary to resort to a regression analysis; that is, to calculate, from the average regression of gain on level for all countries, how much gain a particular country should have shown between 1925 and 1950. The actual gain could then be compared with the expected gain, and the country could be classified as gaining more or less rapidly than would have been expected on the basis of its 1925 performance. The procedure is directly comparable to what we do when we predict, on the basis of some measure of I.Q., what grades a child can be expected to get in school, and then classify him as an "under-" or "over-achiever."

The correlation between the n Achievement level in the children's readers in 1925 and the growth in electrical output between 1925 and 1950, as compared with expectation, is a quite substantial .53, which is highly significant statistically. It could hardly have arisen by chance. Furthermore, the correlation is also substantial with a measure of gain over the expected in per capita income, equated for purchasing power by Colin Clark. To check this result more definitively with the sample of forty countries for which we had reader estimates of n Achievement levels in 1950, we computed the equation for gains in electrical output in 1952–58 as a function of level in 1952. It turned out to be remarkably linear when translated into logarithmic units, as is so often the case with simple growth functions. Table 20.1 presents the performance of each of the countries, as compared with predictions from initial level in 1952, in standard score units and classified by high and low n Achievement in 1950. Once again we found that n Achievement levels predicted significantly ($r = .43$) the countries which would perform more or less rapidly than expected in terms of the average for all countries. The finding is more striking than the earlier one, because many Communist and underdeveloped countries are included in the sample. Apparently, n Achievement is a precursor of economic growth—and not only in the Western style of capitalism based on the small entrepreneur, but also in economies controlled and fostered largely by the state.

For those who believe in economic determinism, it is especially interesting that n Achievement level in 1950 is *not* correlated either with *previous* economic growth between 1925 and 1950, or with the level of prosperity in 1950. This strongly suggests that n Achievement is a *causative* factor—a change in the minds of men which produces economic growth rather than being produced by it. In a century dominated by economic determinism, in both Communist and Western thought, it is startling to find concrete evidence for psychological determinism, for psychological developments as preceding and presumably causing economic changes.

The many interesting results which our study of children's stories yielded have succeeded in convincing me that we chose the right material to analyze. Apparently, adults unconsciously flavor their stories for young children with

Table 20.1   Rate of Growth in Electrical Output (1952–1958) and National *n* Achievement Levels in 1950

Above Expectation Growth Rate			Below Expectation Growth Rate		
National *n* Achievement levels (1950)[a]	Country	Deviation from Expected Growth Rate[b]	National *n* Achievement Levels (1950)[a]	Country	Deviations from Expected Growth Rate[b]
High *n* Achievement Countries					
3.62	Turkey	+1.38			
2.71	India[c]	+1.12			
2.38	Australia	+0.42			
2.32	Israel	+1.18			
2.33	Spain	+0.01			
2.29	Pakistan[d]	+2.75			
2.29	Greece	+1.18	3.38	Argentina	−0.56
2.29	Canada	+0.08	2.71	Lebanon	−0.67
2.24	Bulgaria	+1.37	2.38	France	−0.24
2.24	U.S.A.	+0.47	2.33	South Africa	−0.06
2.14	West Germany	+0.53	2.29	Ireland	−0.41
2.10	U.S.S.R.	+1.61	2.14	Tunisia	−1.87
2.10	Portugal	+0.76	2.10	Syria	−0.25
Low *n* Achievement Countries					
1.95	Iraq	+0.29	2.05	New Zealand	−0.29
1.86	Austria	+0.38	1.86	Uruguay	−0.75
1.67	U.K.	+0.17	1.81	Hungary	−0.62
1.57	Mexico	+0.12	1.71	Norway	−0.77
0.86	Poland	+1.26	1.62	Sweden	−0.64
			1.52	Finland	−0.08
			1.48	Netherlands	−0.15
			1.33	Italy	−0.57
			1.29	Japan	−0.04
			1.20	Switzerland[e]	−1.92
			1.19	Chile	−1.81
			1.05	Denmark	−0.89
			0.57	Algeria	−0.83
			0.43	Belgium	−1.65

Notes: Correlation of *n* Achievement level (1950) x deviations from expected growth rate = .43, $p < .01$.

a. Deviations in standard score units. The estimates are computed from the monthly average electrical production figures, in millions Kwh, for 1952 and 1958, from United Nations, *Monthly Bulletin of Statistics* (January, 1960), and *World Energy Supplies,* 1951–1954 and 1955–1958 (Statistical Papers, Series 3). The correlation between log level 1952 and log gain 1952–1958 is .976. The regression equation based on these thirty-nine countries, plus four others from the same climatic zone on which data are available (China-Taiwan, Czechoslovakia, Rumania, Yugoslavia), is: log gain (1952–1958) = .9229 log level (1952) + .0480. Standard scores deviations from mean gain predicted by the regression formula ($M = -.01831$) divided by the standard deviation of the deviations from the mean predicted gain ($SD = .159$).

b. Based on twenty-one children's stories from second-, third-, and fourth-grade readers in each country.

c. Based on six Hindi, seven Telegu, and eight Tamil stories.

d. Based on twelve Urdu and eleven Bengali stories.

e. Based on twenty-one German Swiss stories, mean = .91; twenty-one French Swiss stories, mean = 1.71; overall mean obtained by weighting German mean double to give approximately proportionate representation of the two main ethnic populations.

the attitudes, the aspirations, the values, and the motives that they hold to be most important.

I want to mention briefly two other findings, one concerned with economic development, the other with totalitarianism. When the more and less rapidly developing economies are compared on all the other variables for which we scored the children's stories, one fact stands out. In stories from those countries which had developed more rapidly in both the earlier and later periods, there was a discernible tendency to emphasize, in 1925 and in 1950, what David Riesman has called "other-directedness"—namely, reliance on the opinion of particular others, rather than on tradition, for guidance in social behavior.[9] *Public opinion* had, in these countries, become a major source of guidance for the individual. Those countries which had developed the mass media further and faster—the press, the radio, the public-address system—were also the ones who were developing more rapidly economically. I think that "other-directedness" helped these countries to develop more rapidly because public opinion is basically more flexible than institutionalized moral or social traditions. Authorities can utilize it to inform people widely about the need for new ways of doing things. However, traditional institutionalized values may insist that people go on behaving in ways that are no longer adaptive to a changed social and economic order.

The other finding is not directly relevant to economic development, but it perhaps involves the means of achieving it. Quite unexpectedly, we discovered that every major dictatorial regime which came to power between the 1920s and 1950s (with the possible exception of Portugal's) was foreshadowed by a particular motive pattern in its stories for children: namely, a low need for affiliation (little interest in friendly relationships with people) and a high need for power (a great concern over controlling and influencing other people).

The German readers showed this pattern before Hitler; the Japanese readers, before Tojo; the Argentine readers, before Perón; the Spanish readers, before Franco; the South African readers, before the present authoritarian government in South Africa; etc. On the other hand, very few countries which did not have dictatorships manifested this particular motive combination. The difference was highly significant statistically, since there was only one exception in the first instance and very few in the second. Apparently, we stumbled on a psychological index of ruthlessness—i.e., the need to influence other people (n Power), unchecked by sufficient concern for their welfare (n Affiliation). It is interesting, and a little disturbing, to discover that the German readers of today still evince this particular combination of motives, just as they did in 1925. Let us hope that this is one case where a social science generalization will not be confirmed by the appearance of a totalitarian regime in Germany in the next ten years.

To return to our main theme—let us discuss the precise ways that higher n Achievement leads to more rapid economic development, and why it should lead to economic development rather than, for example, to military or artistic development. We must consider in more detail the mechanism by which the concentration of a particular type of human motive in a population leads to a complex social phenomenon like economic growth. The link between the two social phenomena is, obviously, the business entrepreneur. I am not using the term "entrepreneur" in the sense of "capitalist": in fact, I should like to divorce "entrepreneur" entirely from any connotations of ownership. An entrepreneur is someone who exercises control over production that is not just for his personal consumption. According to my definition, for example, an executive in a steel production unit in Russia is an entrepreneur.

It was Joseph Schumpeter who drew the attention of economists to the importance that the activity of these entrepreneurs had in creating industrialization in the West. Their vigorous endeavors put together firms and created productive units where there had been none before. In the beginning, at least, the entrepreneurs often collected material resources, organized a production unit to combine the resources into a new product, and sold the product, Until recently, nearly all economists—including not only Marx, but also Western classical economists—assumed that these men were moved primarily by the "profit motive." We are all familiar with the Marxian argument that they were so driven by their desire for profits that they exploited the workingman and ultimately forced him to revolt. Recently, economic historians have been studying the actual lives of such entrepreneurs and finding—certainly to the surprise of some of the investigators—that many of them seemingly were not interested in making money as such. In psychological terms, at least, Marx's picture is slightly out of focus. Had these entrepreneurs been above all interested in money, many more of them would have quit working as soon as they had made all the money that they could possibly use. They would not have continued to risk their money in further entrepreneurial ventures. Many of them, in fact, came from pietistic sects, like the Quakers in England, that prohibited the enjoyment of wealth in any of the ways cultivated so successfully by some members of the European nobility. However, the entrepreneurs often seemed consciously to be greatly concerned with expanding their businesses, with getting a greater share of the market, with "conquering brute nature," or even with altruistic schemes for bettering the lot of mankind or bringing about the kingdom of God on earth more rapidly. Such desires have frequently enough been labeled as hypocritical. However, if we assume that these men were really motivated by a desire for achievement rather than by a desire for money as such, the label no longer fits. This assumption also simplifies further matters considerably. It provides an explanation for the fact that these entrepreneurs were interested in money without wanting it for its own sake, namely, that money served as a ready quantitative index of how well they were doing—e.g., of how much they had achieved by their efforts over the past year. The need to achieve can never be satisfied by money; but estimates of profitability in money terms can supply direct knowledge of how well one is doing one's job.

The brief consideration of the lives of business entrepreneurs of the past suggested that their chief motive may well have been a high n Achievement. What evidence have we found in support of this? We made two approaches to the problem. First, we attempted to determine whether individuals with high n Achievement behave like entrepreneurs; and second, we investigated to learn whether actual entrepreneurs, particularly the more successful ones, in a number of countries, have higher n Achievement than do other people of roughly the same status. Of course, we had to establish what we meant by "behave like entrepreneurs"—what precisely distinguishes the way an entrepreneur behaves from the way other people behave?

The adequate answers to these questions would entail a long discussion of the sociology of occupations, involving the distinction originally made by Max Weber between capitalists and bureaucrats. Since this cannot be done here, a very brief report on our extensive investigations in this area will have to suffice. First, one of the defining characteristics of an entrepreneur is *taking risks* and/or innovating. A person who adds up a column of figures is not an entrepreneur—however carefully, efficiently, or correctly he adds them. He is simply following established rules. However, a man who decides to add a new line to his business is an entrepreneur, in that he cannot know in advance whether this decision will be correct. Nevertheless, he does not feel that he is in the position of a gambler who places some money on the turn of a card. Knowledge, judgment, and skill enter into his decision making; and, if his choice is justified by future developments, he can certainly feel a sense of personal achievement from having made a successful move.

Therefore, if people with high n Achievement are to behave in an entrepreneurial way, they must seek out and perform in situations in which there is some moderate risk of failure—a risk which can, presumably, be reduced by increased effort or skill. They should not work harder than other people at routine tasks, or perform functions which they are certain to do well simply by doing what everyone accepts as the correct traditional thing to do. On the other hand, they should avoid gambling situations, because, even if they win, they can receive no sense of personal achievement, since it was not skill but luck that produced the results. (And, of course, most of the time they would lose, which would be highly unpleasant to them.) The data on this point are very clear-cut. We have repeatedly found, for example, that boys with high n Achievement choose to play games of skill that incorporate a moderate risk of failure. . . .

Another quality that the entrepreneur seeks in his work is that his job be a kind that ordinarily provides him with accurate knowledge of the results of his decisions. As a rule, growth in sales, in output, or in profit margins tells him very precisely whether he has made the correct choice under uncertainty or not. Thus, the concern for profit enters in—profit is a measure of success. We have repeatedly found that boys with a high n Achievement work more efficiently when they know how well they are doing. Also, they will not work harder for money rewards; but if they are asked, they state that greater money rewards should be awarded for accomplishing more difficult things in games of skill. In the ring-toss game, subjects were asked how much money they thought should be awarded for successful throws from different distances. Subjects with high *n* Achievement and those with low *n* Achievement agreed substantially about the amounts for throws made close to the peg. However, as the distance from the peg increased, the amounts awarded for successful throws by the subjects with high *n* Achievement rose more rapidly than did the rewards by those with low *n* Achievement. Here, as elsewhere, individuals with high *n* Achievement behaved as they must if they are to be the successful entrepreneurs of society. They believed that greater achievement should be recognized by quantitatively larger reward.

What produces high *n* Achievement? Why do some societies produce a large number of people with this motive, while other societies produce so many fewer? We conducted long series of researches into this question. I can present only a few here.

One very important finding is essentially a negative one: *n* Achievement cannot be hereditary. Popular psychology has long maintained that some races are more energetic than others. Our data clearly contradict this in connection with *n* Achievement. The changes in *n* Achievement level within a given population are too rapid to be attributed to heredity. For example, the correlation between respective *n* Achievement levels in the 1925 and 1950 samples of readers is substantially zero. Many of the countries that were high in *n* Achievement at one or both times may be low or moderate in *n* Achievement now, and vice versa. Germany was low in 1925 and is high now; and certainly the hereditary makeup of the German nation has not changed in a generation.

However, there is substantiating evidence that *n* Achievement is a motive which a child can acquire quite early in life, say, by the age of eight or ten, as a result of the way his parents have brought him up. . . . The principal results . . . indicate the differences between the parents of the "high *n* Achievement boys" and the parents of boys with low *n* Achievement. In general, the mothers and the fathers of the first group set higher levels of aspiration in a number of tasks for their sons. They were also much warmer, showing positive emotion in reacting to their sons' performances. In the area of authority or dominance, the data are quite interesting. The mothers of the "highs" were more domineering than the mothers of the "lows," but the *fathers* of the "highs" were significantly *less* domineering than the fathers of the "lows." In other words, the fathers of the "highs" set high standards and are warmly interested in their sons' performances, but they do not directly interfere. This gives the boys the chance to develop initiative and self-reliance.

What factors cause parents to behave in this way? Their behavior certainly is involved with their values and, possibly, ultimately with their religion or their general world view. At present, we cannot be sure that Protestant parents are more likely to behave this way than Catholic parents—there are too many subgroup variations within each religious portion of the community: the Lutheran father is probably as likely to be authoritarian as the Catholic father. However, there does seem to be one crucial variable discernible: the extent to which the religion of the family emphasizes individual, as contrasted with ritual, contact with God. The preliterate tribes that we studied in which the religion was the kind that stressed the individual contact had higher *n* Achievement; and in general, mystical sects in which this kind of religious self-reliance dominates have had higher *n* Achievement.

The extent to which the authoritarian father is away from the home while the boy is growing up may prove to be another crucial variable. If so, then one incidental consequence of prolonged wars may be an increase in *n* Achievement, because the fathers are away too much to interfere with their sons' development of it. And in Turkey, N. M. Bradburn found that those boys tended to have higher *n* Achievement who had left home early or whose fathers had died before they were eighteen.[10] Slavery was another factor which played an important role in the past. It probably lowered *n* Achievement—in the slaves, for whom obedience and responsibility, but not achievement, were obvious virtues; and in the slave-owners, because household slaves were often disposed to spoil the owner's children as a means for improving their own positions. This is both a plausible and a probable reason for the drop in *n* Achievement level in ancient Greece that occurred at about the time the middle-class entrepreneur was first able to afford, and obtain by conquest, as many as two slaves for each child. The idea also clarifies the slow economic development of the South in the United States by attributing its dilatoriness to a lack of *n* Achievement in its elite; and it also indicates why lower-class American Negroes, who are closest to the slave tradition, possess very low *n* Achievement.[11]

I have outlined our research findings. Do they indicate ways of accelerating economic development? Increasing the level of *n* Achievement in a country suggests itself as an obvious first possibility. If *n* Achievement is so important, so specifically adapted to the business role, then it certainly should be raised in level, so that more young men have an "entrepreneurial drive." The difficulty in this excellent plan is that our studies of how *n* Achievement originates indicate that the family is the key formative influence; and it is very hard to change on a really large scale. To be sure, major historical events like wars have taken authoritarian fathers out of the home; and religious reform movements have sometimes converted the parents to a new achievement-oriented ideology. However, such matters are not ordinarily within the policymaking province of the agencies charged with speeding economic development.

Such agencies can, perhaps, affect the general acceptance of an achievement-oriented ideology as an absolute *sine qua non* of economic development. Furthermore, this ideology should be diffused not only in business and governmental circles, but throughout the nation, and in ways that will influence the thinking of all parents as they bring up their children. As B. C. Rosen and R. G. D'Andrade found, parents must, above all, set high standards for their children. The campaign to spread achievement-oriented ideology, if possible, could also incorporate an attack on the extreme authoritarianism in fathers that impedes or prevents the development of self-reliance in their sons. This is, however, a more delicate point, and attacking this, in many countries, would be to threaten values at the very center of social life. I believe that a more indirect approach would be more successful. One approach would be to take the boys out of the home and to camps. A more significant method would be to promote the rights of women, both legally and socially—one of the ways to undermine the absolute dominance of the male is to strengthen the rights of the female! Another reason for concentrating particularly on women is that they play the leading role in rearing the next generation. Yet, while men in underdeveloped countries come in contact with new achievement-oriented values and standards through their work, women may be left almost untouched by such influences. But if the sons are to have high *n* Achievement, the mothers must first be reached.

It may seem strange that a chapter on economic development should discuss the importance of feminism and the way children are reared; but this is precisely where a psychological analysis leads. If the motives of men are the agents that influence the speed with which the economic machine operates, then the speed can be increased only through affecting the factors that create the motives. Furthermore—to state this point less theoretically—I cannot think of evinced substantial, rapid long-term economic development where women have not been somewhat freed from their traditional setting of "Kinder, Küche und Kirche" and allowed to play a more powerful role in society, specifically as part of the working force. This generalization applies not only to the Western democracies like the United States, Sweden, or England, but also to the USSR, Japan, and now China.

In the present state of our knowledge, we can conceive of trying to raise *n* Achievement levels only in the next generation—although new research findings may soon indicate *n* Achievement in adults can be increased. Most economic planners, while accepting the long-range desirability of raising *n* Achievement in future generations, want to know what can be done during the next five to ten years. This immediacy inevitably focuses attention on the process or processes by which executives or entrepreneurs are selected. Foreigners with proved entrepreneurial drive can be hired, but at best this is a temporary and unsatisfactory solution. In most underdeveloped countries where government is playing a leading role in promoting economic development, it is clearly necessary for the government to adopt rigid achievement-oriented standards of performance like those in the USSR.[12] A government manager or, for that matter, a private entrepreneur, should have to produce "or else." Production targets must be set, as they are in most economic plans; and individuals must be held responsible for achieving them, even at the plant level. The philosophy should be one of "no excuses accepted." It is common for government officials or economic theorists in underdeveloped countries to be weighed down by all the difficulties which face the economy and render its rapid development difficult or impossible. They note that there is too rapid population growth, too little capital, too few technically competent people, etc. Such obstacles to growth are prevalent, and in many cases they are immensely hard to overcome; but talking about them can provide merely a comfortable rationalization for mediocre performance. It is difficult to fire an administrator, no matter how poor his performance, if so many objective reasons exist for his doing badly. Even worse, such rationalization permits, in the private sector, the continued employment of incompetent family members as executives. If these private firms were afraid of being penalized for poor performance, they might be impelled to find more able professional managers a little more quickly. I am not an expert in the field, and the mechanisms I am suggesting may be far from appropriate. Still, they may serve to illustrate my main point: if a country short in entrepreneurial talent wants to advance rapidly, it must find ways and means of ensuring that only the most competent retain positions of responsibility. One of the obvious methods of doing so is to judge people in terms of their *performance*—and not according to their family or political connections, their skill in explaining why their unit failed to produce as expected, or their conscientiousness in following the rules. I would suggest the use of psychological tests as a means of selecting people with high *n* Achievement; but, to be perfectly frank, I think this approach is at present somewhat impractical on a large enough scale in most underdeveloped countries.

Finally, there is another approach which I think is promising for recruiting and developing more competent business leadership. It is the one called, in some circles, the "professionalization of management." Frederick Harbison and Charles A. Myers have recently completed a worldwide survey of the efforts made to develop professional schools of high-level management. They have concluded that, in most countries, progress in this direction is slow.[13] Professional management is important for three reasons: (1) It may endow a business career with higher prestige (as a kind of profession), so that business will attract more of the young men with high *n* Achievement from the elite groups in backward countries; (2) It stresses *performance* criteria of excellence in the management area—i.e., what a man can do and not what he is; (3) Advanced management schools can themselves be so achievement-oriented in their instruction that they are able to raise the *n* Achievement of those who attend them.

Applied toward explaining historical events, the results of our researches clearly shift attention away from external factors and to man—in particular, to his motives and values. That about which he thinks and dreams determines what will happen. The emphasis is quite different from the Darwinian or Marxist view of man as a creature who *adapts* to his environment. It is even different from the Freudian view of civilization as the sublimation of man's primitive urges. Civilization, at least in its economic aspects, is neither adaptation nor sublimation; it is a positive creation by a people made dynamic by a high level of *n* Achievement. Nor can we agree with Toynbee, who recognizes the importance of psychological factors as "the very forces which actually decide the issue when an encounter takes place," when he states that these factors "inherently are impossible to weigh and measure, and therefore to estimate scientifically in advance."[14] It is a measure of the pace at which the behavioral sciences are developing that even within Toynbee's lifetime we can demonstrate that he was mistaken. The psychological factor responsible for a civilization's rising to a challenge is so far from being "inherently impossible to weigh and measure" that it has been weighed and measured and scientifically estimated in advance; and, so far as we can now tell, this factor is the achievement motive.

Notes

1. A. L. Kroeber, *Configurations of Culture Growth* (Berkeley, Calif., 1944).

2. J. W. Atkinson (Ed.), *Motives in Fantasy, Action, and Society* (Princeton, N.J., 1958).

3. Max Weber, *The Protestant Ethic and the Spirit of Capitalism,* trans. Talcott Parsons (New York, 1930).

4. M. R. Winterbottom, "The Relation of Need for Achievement to Learning and Experiences in Independence and Mastery," in Atkinson, *op. cit.,* pp. 453–478.

5. F. Heichelheim, *Wirtschaftsgeschichte des Altertums* (Leiden, 1938).

6. J. B. Cortés, "The Achievement Motive in the Spanish Economy Between the Thirteenth and the Eighteenth Centuries," *Economic Development and Cultural Change,* IX (1960), 144–163.

7. N. M. Bradburn and D. E. Berlew, "Need for Achievement and English Economic Growth," *Economic Development and Cultural Change* (1961).

8. I. L. Child, T. Storm, and J. Veroff, "Achievement Themes in Folk Tales Related to Socialization Practices," in Atkinson, *op. cit.,* pp. 479–492.

9. David Riesman, with the assistance of Nathan Glazer and Reuel Denney, *The Lonely Crowd* (New Haven, Conn., 1950).

10. N. M. Bradburn, "The Managerial Role in Turkey" (unpublished Ph.D. dissertation, Harvard University, 1960).

11. B. C. Rosen, "Race, Ethnicity, and Achievement Syndrome," *American Sociological Review,* XXIV (1959), 47–60.

12. David Granick, *The Red Executive* (New York, 1960).

13. Frederick Harbison and Charles A. Myers, *Management in the Industrial World* (New York, 1959).

14. Arnold J. Toynbee, *A Study of History* (abridgment by D. C. Somervell; Vol. I; New York, 1947).

21

Underdevelopment Is a State of Mind

Lawrence E. Harrison

A fter twenty years of working for the US Agency for International
Development (USAID), Lawrence Harrison has concluded that Latin
America's culture explains its lack of development. As should be clear by
now, the cultural approach blames the poor for their poverty. According
to Harrison, Latin Americans have become so preoccupied with a belief
in the self-defeating "myths" of dependency and imperialism that they
are paralyzed to the point that they do not use the resources they have
to develop. At its heart, the process of development is one of human
creative capacity, the ability to imagine, conceptualize, and so on. If a
country is to tap the creative energy of its people, the government
must establish an environment that encourages and uses all of its
people's abilities.

What Makes Development Happen?

Development, most simply, is improvement in human well-being.[1] Most people today aspire to higher standards of living, longer lives, and fewer health problems; education for themselves and their children that will increase their earning capacity and leave them more in control of their lives; a measure of

Reprinted with permission from *Underdevelopment Is a State of Mind: The Latin American Case,* by Lawrence E. Harrison (Cambridge, MA: The Center for International Affairs, Harvard University), pp. 1–9. © 1985 by the President and Fellows of Harvard College.

stability and tranquility; and the opportunity to do the things that give them pleasure and satisfaction. A small minority will take exception to one or more of these aspirations. Some others may wish to add one or more. For the purposes of this chapter, however, I think the list is adequate.

The enormous gap in well-being between the low-income and the industrialized countries is apparent from . . . table [21.1], the source of which is the World Bank's *World Development Report* 1982. . . .

What explains the gap? What have the industrialized countries done that the low-income countries have not? Why was the Marshall Plan a monumental success, the Alliance for Progress much less successful? What makes development happen or not happen?

There are those who will say that what the industrialized countries have done that the low-income countries have not is to exploit the low-income countries; that development is a zero-sum game; that the rich countries are rich because the poor countries are poor. This is doctrine for Marxist-Leninists and it has wide currency throughout the Third World. To be sure, colonial powers often did derive great economic advantage from their colonies, and U.S. companies have made a lot of money in Latin America and elsewhere in the Third World, particularly during the first half of this century. But the almost exclusive focus on "imperialism" and "dependency" to explain underdevelopment has encouraged the evolution of a paralyzing and self-defeating mythology. The thesis of this chapter is in diametrical contrast. It looks inward rather than outward to explain a society's condition.

I believe that the creative capacity of human beings is at the heart of the development process. What makes development happen is our ability to imagine, theorize, conceptualize, experiment, invent, articulate, organize, manage, solve problems, and do a hundred other things with our minds and hands that contribute to the progress of the individual and of human-kind. Natural resources, climate, geography, history, market size, governmental policies, and many other factors influence the direction and pace of progress. But the engine is human creative capacity.

The economist Joseph Schumpeter (1883–1950) singled out the entrepreneurial geniuses—the Henry Fords of the world—as the real creators of wealth

Table 21.1   Gap in Well-Being: Low-Income and Industrialized Countries

	Low-Income Countries	Industrialized Countries
Total population (mid-1980)	2.2 billion	671 million
Annual average population growth rate (1970–80)	2.1 percent	.8 percent
Average per capita gross national product (1980)	$260	$10,320
Average life expectancy at birth (1980)	57 years	74 years
Average adult literacy (1977)	50 percent	99 percent

and progress, as indeed they must have appeared in the early years of Schumpeter's life. Economist and political scientist Everett Hagen was less elitist: "The discussion of creativity refers . . . not merely to the limiting case of genius but to the quality of creativity in general, in whatever degree it may be found in a given individual."[2]

My *own* belief is that the society that is most successful at helping its people—*all* its people—realize their creative potential is the society that will progress the fastest.

It is not just the entrepreneur who creates progress, even if we are talking narrowly about material-economic progress. The inventor of the machine employed by the entrepreneur; the scientist who conceived the theory that the inventor turned to practical use; the engineer who designed the system to mass-produce the machine; the farmer who uses special care in producing a uniform raw material to be processed by the machine; the machine operator who suggests some helpful modifications to the machine on the basis of long experience in operating it—all are contributing to growth. So is the salesman who expands demand for the product by conceiving a new use for it. So, too, are the teachers who got the scientist, the inventor, and the engineer interested in their professions and who taught the farmer agronomy.[3]

Production takes place within a broader society, and the way that society functions affects the productive process. Good government can assure stability and continuity, without which investment and production will falter. Good government can provide a variety of services that facilitate production. And the policies government pursues, e.g., with respect to taxation, interest rates, support prices for agricultural products, will importantly affect producer decisions. Thus, the creativity and skill of government officials play a key role in economic development. It can be argued, in fact, that an effective government policymaker—e.g., a Treasury Secretary—is worth many Henry Fords.[4] W. Arthur Lewis observes, "The behaviour of government plays as important a role in stimulating or discouraging economic activity as does the behaviour of entrepreneurs, or parents, or scientists, or priests."[5]

But our definition of development is far broader than just the productive dimension of human existence. It also embraces the social dimension, particularly health, education, and welfare. It is government that bears the principal responsibility for progress in these sectors, and, as with economic progress, innovation and creativity are at the root of social progress. The people who conceive the policies that expand and improve social services are thus comparable in their developmental impact to industrial entrepreneurs, as are public-sector planners, administrators, technicians, and blue-collar workers to their private-sector counterparts.

It is not difficult to see how this view of what makes development happen can be extended to virtually all forms of work, intellectual and physical, performed within a society. While it is obvious that the contribution of some will be greater than that of others, and while the role of gifted people can be enormously important, all can contribute. It is thus probably more accurate, at least in the contemporary world, to think of development as a process of millions of small breakthroughs than as a few monumental innovations, the work of geniuses. A society that smoothes the way for these breakthroughs is a society that will progress.

How does a society encourage the expression of human creative capacity? Basically, in seven ways:

1. Through creation of an environment in which people expect and receive fair treatment.
2. Through an effective and accessible education system: one that provides basic intellectual and vocational tools; nurtures inquisitiveness, critical faculties, dissent, and creativity; and equips people to solve problems.
3. Through a health system that protects people from diseases that debilitate and kill.
4. Through creation of an environment that encourages experimentation and criticism (which is often at the root of experimentation).
5. Through creation of an environment that helps people both discover their talents and interests and mesh them with the right jobs.
6. Through a system of incentives that rewards merit and achievement (and, conversely, discourages nepotism and "pull").
7. Through creation of the stability and continuity that make it possible to plan ahead with confidence. Progress is made enormously more difficult by instability and discontinuity.

Two Examples in Nicaragua

My recent experience in Nicaragua provides two examples that symbolize what societies can do to nurture or frustrate human creative capacity.

The United States ambassador to Nicaragua during my two years there was Lawrence A. Pezzullo. Larry Pezzullo grew up in the Bronx, the son of an immigrant Italian butcher. His mother, also an immigrant, was illiterate. He attended public schools in New York City, served in the U.S. Army in Europe during World War II, and returned to New York to attend Columbia University under the GI bill. Following graduation, he taught in a public high school on Long Island for six years, then joined the Foreign Service. He rose steadily through the ranks, served as deputy assistant secretary of state for congressional affairs from 1975 to 1977, and was named ambassador to Uruguay in 1977. He became ambassador to Nicaragua in July 1979, simultaneous with the installation of the revolutionary Government of National Reconstruction.

Larry Pezzullo is a person of extraordinary talent. He has great capacity for understanding complicated political processes. But he also has a flair for conceiving and orchestrating responses to the circumstances he faces, and an unerring sense of timing. He is a diplomatic entrepreneur who, in Nicaragua, was the right man in the right place at the right time. (He has since become executive director of Catholic Relief Services.)

Rosa Carballo was born into similar humble circumstances, but in Nicaragua. She is a woman in her sixties, highly intelligent, dignified, and self-disciplined. She has a profound understanding of human nature and sees well below the surface of the political process in her country. With those qualities, she might well have been a successful professional in another society. In Nicaragua she is a domestic servant. She is effectively illiterate.

I want to note in passing that, today, there are few countries that could not virtually eradicate illiteracy within a generation if the will to do so existed.

Values and Attitudes That Foster Progress

We now have to ask what values and attitudes foster the conditions that facilitate the expression of human creative capacity—and development. . . .

The society's world view is the source of its value and attitude systems. The world view is formed by a complex of influences, including geography, economic organization, and the vagaries of history. The world view and its related value and attitude systems are constantly changing, but usually at a very slow pace, measurable in decades or generations. The world view is expressed at least in part through religion.

Of crucial importance for development are: (1) the world view's time focus—past, present, or future; (2) the extent to which the world view encourages rationality; and (3) the concepts of equality and authority it propagates.

If a society's major focus is on the past—on the glory of earlier times or in reverence of ancestors—or if it is absorbed with today's problems of survival, the planning, organizing, saving, and investment that are the warp and woof of development are not likely to be encouraged. Orientation toward the future implies the possibility of change and progress. And that possibility, as Max Weber stressed in his landmark work *The Protestant Ethic and the Spirit of Capitalism,* must be realizable in this life. The Calvinist concepts of "calling" and "election" force the eyes of the faithful toward the future. So do the basic tenets of Judaism: "Judaism clings to the idea of Progress. The Golden Age of Humanity is not in the past, but in the future."[6]

If the society's world view encourages the belief that humans have the capacity to know and understand the world around them, that the universe operates according to a largely decipherable pattern of laws, and that the scientific method can unlock many secrets of the unknown, it is clearly imparting a set of attitudes tightly linked to the ideas of progress and change. If the world view explains worldly phenomena by supernatural forces, often in the form of numerous capricious gods and goddesses who demand obeisance from humans, there is little room for reason, education, planning, or progress.

Many world views propagate the idea of human equality, particularly in the theme of the Golden Rule and its variations. The idea is stressed more in some ethical systems than in others. It is obviously present in both the Protestant and Catholic ethical systems. But Weber argues that the traditional Catholic focus on the afterlife, in contrast to the Protestant (and Jewish) focus on life in this world, vitiates the force of the ethical system, particularly when that focus is accompanied by the cycle of transgression/confession/absolution.[7] One possible consequence may be a relatively stronger Protestant orientation toward equality and the community, and a relatively stronger Catholic orientation toward hierarchy and the individual.

Directly related to the idea of equality is the concept of authority. Subsequent chapters [in the original book] observe repeatedly the negative consequences of authoritarianism for growth of individuals and societies. There may well be truth in the belief of Weber and others that traditional Catholicism, with its focus on the afterlife and the crucial role of the church hierarchy and the priest, encouraged a dependency mindset among its adherents that was an obstacle to entrepreneurial activity. Martin Luther, by contrast, preached "the priesthood of all believers";[8] "every Christian had to be a monk all his life."[9]

But there are also some religions—including, to be sure, some Protestant denominations—whose basic tenets embrace the idea of inequality. Traditional Hinduism comes immediately to mind, as do Gunnar Myrdal's comments on South Asia:

> . . . Social and economic stratification is accorded the sanction of religion.
> . . . The inherited stratification implies low social and spatial mobility, little free competition in its wider sense, and great inequalities.[10]

It should be an hypothesis for further study that people in this region are not inherently different from people elsewhere, but that they live and have lived for a long time under conditions very different from those in the Western world, and that this has left its mark upon their bodies and minds. Religion has, then, become the emotional container of this whole way of life and work and by its sanction has rendered it rigid and resistant to change.[11]

The fundamental questions of future versus past orientation, encouragement or discouragement of rationality, and emphasis on equality versus emphasis on authority strongly influence three other cultural factors that play an important role in the way a society develops: (1) the extent of identification with others, (2) the rigor of the ethical system, and (3) attitudes about work.

Several of the people whose works are discussed . . . (e.g., Weber, Myrdal, David McClelland) have emphasized the importance for progress of a radius of identification and trust that embraces an entire society. There is evidence that the extended family is an effective institution for survival but an obstacle to development.[12] Weber observes, "The great achievement of ethical religions, above all of the ethical and ascetistic sects of Protestantism, was to shatter the fetters of the sib [i.e., the extended family]."[13]

The social consequences of widespread mistrust can be grave. Samuel Huntington makes the point:

> . . . the absence of trust in the culture of the society provides formidable obstacles to the creation of public institutions. Those societies deficient in stable and effective government are also deficient in mutual trust among their citizens, in national and public loyalties, and in organization skills and capacity. Their political cultures are often said to be marked by suspicion, jealousy, and latent or actual hostility toward everyone who is not a member of the family, the village, or, perhaps, the tribe. These characteristics are found in many cultures, their most extensive manifestation perhaps being in the Arab world and in Latin America. . . . In Latin America . . . traditions of self-centered individualism and of distrust and hatred for other groups in society have prevailed.[14]

A whole set of possibilities opens up when trust is extended beyond the family, possibilities that are likely to be reflected in both economic and social development. Myrdal observes, ". . . a more inclusive nationalism then becomes a force for progress . . . a vehicle for rationalism and for the ideals of planning, equality, social welfare, and perhaps democracy."[15] In such an environment, the idea of cooperation will be strengthened, with all that implies for modern production techniques, community problem-solving, and political stability. The idea of compromise, which is central to the working of a pluralistic system, is also reinforced.[16] When the idea of compromise—i.e., that a relationship is important enough to warrant seeking to avoid confrontation, even if some concession is necessary—is weak, the likelihood of confrontation is increased. Constant confrontation undermines stability and continuity, which, as noted earlier, are crucial to development.

There is a gap in all societies between the stated ethical system and the extent to which that system is honored in practice. Religions' treatment of ethical issues obviously has something to do with the size of the gap. Broad identification among the members of a society will strengthen the impact of the ethical system. Where the radius of identification and trust is small, there may effectively be no operative ethical system.

The rigor of the effective ethical system will shape attitudes about justice, which are central to several major development issues. If the members of a society expect injustice, the ideas of cooperation, compromise, stability, and continuity will be undermined. Corruption and nepotism will be encouraged. And the self-discipline necessary to keep a society working well (e.g., payment of taxes, resistance to the temptation to steal) will be weakened. The system of criminal and civil jurisprudence will be politicized and corrupted and will not be taken seriously by the citizenry. The idea of justice is also central to crucial social issues: the fairness of income distribution, availability of educational opportunities and health services, and promotion by merit.

Another link to these questions of radius of identification, rigor of the effective ethical system, and justice is the idea of dissent.[17] Its acceptance is fundamental to a functioning pluralistic political system, and it is clearly related to the idea of compromise. But it is also an important idea for creativity: what the inventor and the entrepreneur do is a kind of creative dissent.

Attitudes about work link back to several of these ideas, but particularly to future orientation. If the idea of progress is well established in the culture, there is a presumption that planning and hard work will be rewarded by increased income and improved living conditions. When the focus is on the present, on day-to-day survival, the ceiling on work may be the amount necessary to survive.

This brings us back to the seven conditions that encourage the expression of human creative capacity:

1. The expectation of fair play
2. Availability of educational opportunities
3. Availability of health services
4. Encouragement of experimentation and criticism
5. Matching of skills and jobs
6. Rewards for merit and achievement
7. Stability and continuity

Taken together, the seven conditions describe a functional modern democratic capitalist society. The extent to which countries realize their potential is determined, I believe, by the extent to which these conditions exist. . . . [T]he seven conditions substantially exist in the fifteen countries whose per-capita gross national product (GNP) is the highest in the world (excluding four oil-rich Arab countries). These same fifteen countries accounted for 83 percent of the Nobel Prize winners from 1945 to 1981. . . .

Notes

1. "Development" and "progress" are used synonymously in this chapter.
2. Everett E. Hagen, *On the Theory of Social Change. How Economic Growth Begins*, p. 88.
3. Hagen makes similar points on p. 11 of *On the Theory of Social Change*.

4. This point is elaborated in Lawrence E. Harrison, "Some Hidden Costs of the Public Investment Fixation," pp. 20–23.

5. W. Arthur Lewis, *The Theory of Economic Growth,* p. 376.

6. The words of a former Chief Rabbi of Great Britain in J. H. Hertz (ed.), *The Pentateuch and Haftorahs,* p. 196.

7. Clearly, contemporary Catholicism is moving toward the Protestant and Jewish focus on this life, particularly since Pope John XXIII.

8. Quoted in David C. McClelland, *The Achieving Society,* p. 48.

9. Max Weber, *The Protestant Ethic and the Spirit of Capitalism,* p. 121.

10. Gunnar Myrdal, *Asian Drama: An Inquiry into the Poverty of Nations,* p. 104.

11. Ibid., p. 112.

12. The conditions for human progress and happiness are still worse where trust extends no further than the nuclear family, as in Banfield's "Montegrano." In that case, both development and survival are threatened.

13. Max Weber, *The Religion of China,* p. 237.

14. Samuel P. Huntington, *Political Order in Changing Societies,* p. 28.

15. Myrdal, *Asian Drama,* p. 122.

16. It is, I believe, significant that there is no truly apt Spanish word for "compromise."

17. It also seems significant that there is no truly apt Spanish word for "dissent."

References

Hagen, E. E. 1962. *On the Theory of Social Change. How Economic Growth Begins.* Homewood, IL: Dorsey Press.

Harrison, L. E. 1970. "Some Hidden Costs of the Public Investment Fixation." *International Development Review* 12.

Hertz, J. H. (ed.). 1961. *The Pentateuch and Haftorahs.* London: Soncino Press.

Huntington, S. P. 1968. *Political Order in Changing Societies.* New York and London: Yale University Press.

Lewis, W. A. 1955. *The Theory of Economic Growth.* Homewood, IL: Richard D. Irwin, Inc.

McClelland, D. C. 1961. *The Achieving Society.* Princeton: D. Van Nostrand Co., Inc.

Myrdal, G. 1968. *Asian Drama. An Inquiry into the Poverty of Nations.* New York: Pantheon.

Weber, M. 1950. *The Protestant Ethic and the Spirit of Capitalism.* New York: Charles Scribner's Sons.

Weber, M. 1951. *The Religion of China.* New York: Macmillan.

World Bank. 1982. *World Development Report, 1982.*

22

The Effect of Cultural Values on Economic Development: Theory, Hypotheses, and Some Empirical Tests

Jim Granato, Ronald Inglehart, and David Leblang

In this chapter, Jim Granato, Ronald Inglehart, and David Leblang examine the ties between cultural values and economic development. They utilize the "achievement motive" thesis developed by McClelland as a specific empirical point of reference. The authors test the theory using the World Values Survey, a database of interviews collected in many countries around the world. In this study, data are used for twenty-five countries, and strong evidence indicates that certain cultural values help to spur economic growth. In the same journal from which this chapter was drawn, however, the findings are disputed by other authors. The jury still seems to be out on this fascinating debate.

DO CULTURAL FACTORS INFLUENCE ECONOMIC DEVELOPMENT? IF SO, CAN they be measured and their effect compared with that of standard economic factors such as savings and investment? This article examines the explanatory power of the standard endogenous growth model and compares it with that of two types of cultural variables capturing motivational factors—achievement motivation and postmaterialist values. We believe that it is not an either/or proposition: cultural and economic factors play complementary roles. This

Reprinted with permission of Blackwell Publishing from *American Journal of Political Science* 40, no. 3 (August 1996): 607–631.

belief is borne out empirically; we use recently developed econometric techniques to assess the relative merits of these alternative explanations.

Cultural factors alone do not explain all of the cross-national variation in economic growth rates. Every economy experiences significant fluctuations in growth rates from year to year as a result of short-term factors such as technological shocks or unforeseen circumstances that affect output. These could not be attributed to cultural factors, which change gradually. A society's economic and political institutions also make a difference. For example, prior to 1945, North Korea and South Korea had a common culture, but South Korea's economic performance has been far superior.

On the other hand, the evidence suggests that cultural differences are an important part of the story. Over the past five decades, the Confucian-influenced economies of East Asia outperformed the rest of the world by a wide margin. This holds true despite the fact that they are shaped by a wide variety of economic and political institutions. Conversely, during the same period most African economies experienced low growth rates. Both societal-level and individual-level evidence suggests that a society's economic and political institutions are not the only factors determining economic development; cultural factors are also important.

Traditionally, the literature presents culture and economic determinants of growth as distinct. Political economists and political sociologists view their respective approaches as mutually exclusive. One reason lies in the level of analysis employed and with this the underlying assumptions about human behavior. Another reason is that we have had inadequate measures of cultural factors. Previous attempts to establish the role of culture either infer culture from economic performance or estimate cultural factors from impressionistic historical evidence. Both factors could be important, but until cultural factors are entered into a quantitative analysis, this possibility could not be tested.

By *culture,* we refer to a system of basic common values that help shape the behavior of the people in a given society. In most preindustrial societies, this value system takes the form of a religion and changes very slowly; but with industrialization and accompanying processes of modernization, these worldviews tend to become more secular, rational, and open to change.

For reasons discussed below, the cultures of virtually all preindustrial societies are hostile to social mobility and individual economic accumulation. Thus, both medieval Christianity and traditional Confucian culture stigmatized profit-making and entrepreneurship. But (as Weber argues), a Protestant version of Christianity played a key role in the rise of capitalism—and much later—a modernized version of Confucian society encourages economic growth, through its support of education and achievement.

The theory and evidence presented in this paper are organized as follows: section one discusses theories that deal with the effect of culture on economic development. This literature emphasizes the importance of motivational factors in the growth process. Section two introduces the data. These data, based on representative national surveys of basic values, enable us to construct two measures of cultures—achievement motivation and postmaterialist values. Section three discusses the baseline endogenous growth model. We draw upon a recent paper by Levine and Renelt (1992) to specify this model, and we augment it with cultural variables. Section four is the multivariate analysis. Economic and cultural variables each explain unique aspects of the cross-national variation in economic growth. Using the *encompassing* principles we find that an improved and parsimonious explanation for economic growth comes from a model that includes both economic and cultural variables. Section four also examines the robustness of this economic-cultural model and finds that the specification is robust to alterations in the conditioning set of information, the elimination of influential cases, and variations in estimation procedure. Section five concludes.

Culture, Motivational Factors, and Economic Growth

We first discuss the literature that views achievement motivation as an essential component in the process of economic development, and then we explore how cultural measures from the World Values Survey can be used to examine the effect of motivation on growth.

The motivational literature stresses the role of cultural emphasis on economic achievement. It grows out of Weber's (1904–1905) Protestant Ethic thesis. This school of thought gave rise to the historical research of Tawney (1926, 1955), case studies by Harrison (1992), and empirical work by McClelland et al. (1953) and McClelland (1961) on achievement motivation. Inglehart (1971, 1977, 1990) extends this work by examining the shift from materialist to postmaterialist value priorities. Although previous work mainly focuses on the political consequences of these values, their emergence represents a shift away from emphasis on economic accumulation and growth. These "new" values could be viewed as the erosion of Protestant Ethic among populations that experience high levels of economic security.

We suggest that Weber is correct in arguing that the rise of Protestantism is a crucial event in modernizing Europe. He emphasizes that the Calvinist version of Protestantism encourages norms favorable to economic achievement. But we view the rise of Protestantism as one case of a more general phenomenon. It is important, not only because of the specific content of early Protestant beliefs, but because this belief system undermines a set of religious norms that inhibit economic achievement and are common to most preindustrial societies.

Preindustrial economies are zero-sum systems: they are characterized by little or no economic growth which implies that upward social mobility only comes at the expense of someone else. A society's cultural system generally reflects this fact. Social status is hereditary rather than achieved, and social norms encourage one to accept one's social position in this life. Aspirations toward social mobility are sternly repressed. Such value systems help to maintain social solidarity but discourage economic accumulation.

Weber's emphasis on the role of Protestantism seems to capture an important part of reality. The Protestant Reformation combined with the emergence of scientific logic broke the grip of the medieval Christian Worldview on a significant part of Europe. Prior to the Reformation, Southern Europe was economically more advanced than Northern Europe. During the three centuries after the Reformation, capitalism emerged, mainly among the Protestant regions of Europe and the Protestant minorities in Catholic countries. Within this cultural context, individual economic accumulation was no longer rejected.

Protestant Europe manifested a subsequent economic dynamism that moved it far ahead of Catholic Europe. Shifting trade patterns, declining food production in Southern Europe and other factors also contributed to this shift, but the evidence suggests that cultural factors played a major role. Throughout the first 150 years of the Industrial Revolution, industrial development took place almost entirely within Protestant regions of Europe, and the Protestant portions of the New World. It was only during the second half of the twentieth century that an entrepreneurial outlook emerged in Catholic Europe and in the Far East. Both now show higher rates of economic growth than Protestant Europe. In short, the concept of the Protestant Ethic would be outdated if we take it to mean something that exists in historically Protestant countries. But Weber's more general concept, that certain cultural factors influence economic growth, is an important and valid insight.

McClelland et al. (1953) and McClelland's (1961) work on achievement motivation builds on the Weberian thesis but focuses on the values that were encouraged in children by their parents, schools, and other agencies of socialization. He hypothesizes that some societies emphasize economic achievement as a positive goal while others give it little emphasis. Since it was not feasible for him to measure directly the values emphasized in given societies through representative national surveys, McClelland attempts to measure them indirectly, through content analysis of the stories and school books used to educate children. He finds that some cultures emphasize achievement in their school books more heavily than others—and that the former showed considerably higher rates of economic growth than did the latter.

McClelland's work is criticized on various grounds. It is questioned whether his approach really measures the values taught to children, or simply those of textbook writers. Subsequently, writers of the dependency school argue that any attempt to trace differences in economic growth rates to factors within a given culture, rather than to global capitalist exploitation, is simply a means of justifying exploitation of the peripheral economies. Such criticism tends to discredit this type of research but is hardly an empirical refutation.

Survey research by Lenski (1963) and Alwin (1986) finds that Catholics and Protestants in the United States show significant differences in the values they emphasize as the most important things to teach children. These differences are more or less along the lines of the Protestant Ethic thesis. Alwin also demonstrates that these differences erode over time, with Protestants and Catholics gradually converging toward a common belief system.

The Data

The World Values Survey asks representative national samples of the publics in a number of societies, "Here is a list of qualities which children can be encouraged to learn at home. Which, if any, do you consider to be especially important?" This list includes qualities that reflect emphasis on autonomy and economic achievement, such as "thrift," "saving money and things," and "determination." Other items on the list reflect emphasis on conformity to traditional social norms, such as "obedience" and "religious faith."

We construct an index of achievement motivation that sums up the percentage in each country emphasizing the first two goals minus the percentage emphasizing the latter two goals. This method of index construction controls for the tendency of respondents in some societies to place relatively heavy emphasis on all of these goals, while respondents in other countries mention relatively few of them.

Figure 22.1 shows the simple bivariate relationship between this index and rates of per capita economic growth between 1960 and 1989. The zero-point on the achievement motivation index reflects the point where exactly as many people emphasize obedience and religion, as emphasize thrift and determination. As we move to the right, the latter values are given increasing emphasis. A given society's emphasis on thrift and determination *over* obedience and religious faith has a strong bivariate linkage with its rate of economic growth over the past three decades ($r = .66$; $p = .001$).

Though often stereotyped as having authoritarian cultures, Japan, China, and South Korea emerge near the pole that emphasizes thrift more heavily than obedience. The three East Asian societies rank highest on that dimension, while the two African societies included in this survey rank near the opposite end of the continuum, emphasizing obedience and religious faith.

The publics of India and the United States also fall toward the latter end of the scale. This is *not* an authoritarianism dimension. It reflects the balance between emphasis on two types of values. One set of values—thrift and determination—support economic achievement; while the other—obedience and religious faith—tend to discourage it, emphasizing conformity to traditional authority and group norms. These two types of values are not necessarily incompatible: some societies rank relatively high on both, while others rank relatively low on both. But, the relative *priority* given to them is strongly related to its growth rate.

Do cultural factors lead to economic growth, or does economic growth lead to cultural change? We believe that the causal flow can work in both

Figure 22.1 Economic Growth Rate by Achievement Motivation Scores of Public

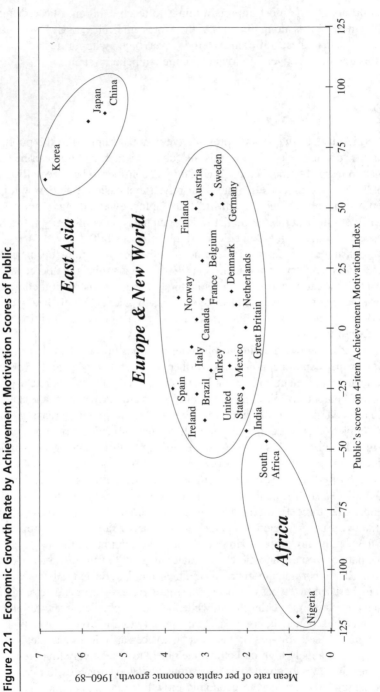

Note: Achievement Motivation Index is based on the percentage in each society who emphasized "Thrift" and "Determination" as important things for a child to learn minus the percentage emphasizing "Obedience" and "Religious Faith."

directions. For example, there is strong evidence that postmaterialist values emerge when a society attains relatively high levels of economic security. In this case, economic change reshapes culture. On the other hand, once these values become widespread, they are linked with relatively low subsequent rates of economic growth. Here, culture seems to be shaping economics—a parallel to the Weberian thesis, except that what is happening here is, in a sense, the rise of the Protestant Ethic in reverse.

Demonstrating causal connections is always difficult. In connection with our achievement motivation index, the obvious interpretation would be that emphasis on thrift and hard work, rather than on obedience and respect, is conducive to economic growth. The two most sensitive indicators of this dimension are thrift, on the one hand, and obedience on the other. For some time, economists have been aware that a nation's rate of gross domestic investment is a major influence on its long term growth rate. Investment, in turn, depends on savings. Thus, a society that emphasizes thrift produces savings, which leads to investment, and later to economic growth. We provide evidence below that this is probably the case. This does not rule out the possibility that economic growth might be conducive to thrift but this linkage is less obvious.

Emphasis on obedience is negatively linked with economic growth, for a converse reason. In preindustrial societies, obedience means conformity to traditional norms, which de-emphasize and even stigmatize economic accumulation. Obedience, respect for others, and religious faith all emphasize obligations to share with and support one's relatives, friends and neighbors. Such communal obligations are strongly felt in preindustrial societies. But from the perspective of a bureaucratized rational-legal society, these norms are antithetical to capital accumulation and conducive to nepotism. Furthermore, conformity to authority inhibits innovation and entrepreneurship.

The motivational component is also tapped by materialist/postmaterialist values, with postmaterialism having a negative relationship with economic growth. The achievement motivation variable is only modestly correlated with the materialist/postmaterialist dimension ($r = -.39$; $p = .0581$). Though both dimensions have significant linkages with economic growth, they affect it in different ways. The achievement motivation dimension seems to tap the transition from preindustrial to industrial values systems, linked with the modernization process.

The materialist/postmaterialist dimension reflects the transition to postindustrial society, linked with a shift away from emphasis on economic growth, toward increasing emphasis on protection of the environment and on the quality of life more generally. Previous research demonstrates that: (1) a gradual shift from materialist toward postmaterialist goals has been taking place throughout advanced industrial society; (2) that this shift is strongly related to the emergence of democracy ($r = .71$); but (3) that it has a tendency to be negatively linked with economic growth (Abramson and Inglehart 1995).

Multivariate Analysis

Our empirical approach is straightforward: we begin by estimating (via OLS) a baseline endogenous growth model that includes variables identified by Levine and Renelt (1992) as having robust partial correlations with economic growth. Using data for 25 countries[1] we first test the endogenous growth specification (Model 1 in Table 22.1). Following Equation [1], a nation's rate of per capita economic growth is regressed on its initial level of per capita income and human capital investment (education spending) as well as on its rate of physical capital accumulation. As expected, the results are quite compatible with the expectations of endogenous growth theory. The results of Model 1 are summarized as follows: (1) the significant negative coefficient on the initial level of per capita income indicates that there is evidence of "conditional convergence." That is, controlling for human and physical capital investment, poorer nations grow faster than richer nations; (2) investment in human capital (education spending) has a positive and statistically significant effect on subsequent

Table 22.1   OLS Estimation of Economic Growth Models Dependent Variable: Mean Rate of per Capita Economic Growth (1960–1989)

Model Variable	Model 1	Model 2	Model 3	Model 4
Constant	−0.70	7.29*	3.16	2.40*
	(1.08)	(1.49)	(1.94)	(0.77)
Per Capita GDP in 1960	−0.63*		−0.42*	−0.43*
	(0.14)		(0.14)	(0.10)
Primary Education in 1960	2.69*		2.19*	2.09*
	(1.22)		(1.06)	(0.96)
Secondary Education	3.27*		1.21	
	(1.01)		(1.08)	
Investment	8.69*		3.09	
	(4.90)		(4.40)	
Achievement Motivation		2.07*	1.44*	1.88*
		(0.37)	(0.48)	(0.35)
Postmaterialism		−2.24*	−1.07	
		(0.77)	(1.03)	
R^2 Adjusted	.55	.59	.69	.70
SEE	.86	.83	.72	.71
LM (x^2[1])	.42	.65	.68	.87
Jarque-Bera (x^2[2])	.05	.30	.18	.57
White (x^2[1])	.28	.24	.37	.18
SC	.119	−.117	−.095	−.352

Notes: Mean of dependent variable: 3.04; N is 25 for all models; standard errors in parentheses.

*t test: $p < .05$

economic growth; and (3) increasing the rate of physical capital accumulation increases a nation's rate of economic growth.

Overall this baseline economic model performs well: it accounts for 55% of the variation in cross-national growth rates and is consistent with prior cross-national tests of the conditional convergence hypothesis (e.g., Barro 1991; Mankiw, Romer, and Weil 1992). Model 1 also passes all diagnostic tests, indicating that the residuals are not serially correlated[2] (LM test), are normally distributed (Jarque-Bera test), and homoskedastic (White test).

Model 2 in Table 22.1 regresses the rate of per capita economic growth on a constant and the two cultural variables. As expected, both achievement motivation and postmaterialism are significant predictors of economic growth and have the expected sign. Thus, the arguments of both Protestant Ethic and postmaterialist type theories cannot be rejected by this evidence. In addition, these variables, taken by themselves, do fairly well, accounting for 59% of the variance in growth rates. A glance at the diagnostics also indicates that the residuals are well behaved.

Comparing Competing Empirical Models: Encompassing Results

Both the economic and cultural models give similar goodness-of-fit performance. Each model's regressors are statistically significant. Yet, which model is superior? Or do both models possess explanatory factors that are missing in the other? . . .

In short, both models explain aspects of growth that the rival cannot. The implication is straightforward: growth rates are best understood as a consequence of both economic and cultural factors.

What happens when we combine the economic model with the cultural model? The results of this experiment are contained in Model 3. Beginning with the endogenous growth variables, adding the variables from Model 2 significantly alters the parameter estimates and standard errors on secondary education spending and physical capital investment. In fact, the coefficient on the physical capital investment variable changes dramatically. It decreases from 8.69 in Model 1 to 3.09 in Model 3. While this coefficient still has the expected sign, it is now far from significant.

Why is physical capital investment, a variable "robustly" correlated with economic growth in a number of other studies, now insignificant? Achievement motivation quite possibly is conducive to economic growth at least partly because it encourages relatively high rates of investment. Achievement motivation also has an important direct effect on economic growth rates, quite apart from its tendency to increase investment. Presumably the direct path from culture to economic growth reflects the effect of motivational factors on entrepreneurship and effort.

Returning to the analysis of Model 3 in Table 22.1, we now examine the direct effect of cultural values, particularly achievement motivation, on economic growth. As in Model 2, achievement motivation is positively and significantly related to economic growth. Combining Model 2 and Model 3 results in postmaterialism now being insignificant, however. This is probably due to the fact that countries with postmaterialist values are already fairly rich; the bivariate correlation between the initial level of wealth and postmaterialism is .75 and is significant at the .0000 level. Combining the regressors of these models (Model 3) we again have a model that does not violate any diagnostic test. In addition, the fit is more accurate (SEE).

Sensitivity Analysis

Table 22.1 contains an additional specification. In Model 4 we eliminate the three insignificant variables from Model 3—those for postmaterialism, investment, and secondary school enrollment—to check the stability of the remaining parameters. Model 4 is the most parsimonious and efficient model, explaining 70 percent of the variance in per capita growth rates with only three variables. . . .

Conclusion

The idea that economic growth is partly shaped by cultural factors has encountered considerable resistance. One reason for this resistance is because cultural values have been widely perceived as diffuse and permanent features of given societies: if cultural values determine economic growth, then the outlook for economic development seems hopeless, because culture cannot be changed. Another reason for opposition is that standard economic arguments supposedly suffice for international differences in savings and growth rates. For example, the standard life cycle model and not cultural arguments explains the difference in savings rates and growth rates between, say, Germany, Japan, and the United States.[3]

When we approach culture as something to be measured on a quantitative empirical basis, the illusion of diffuseness and permanence disappears. We no longer deal with gross stereotypes, such as the idea that "Germans have always been militaristic," or "Hispanic culture is unfavorable to development." We can move to the analysis of specific components of a given culture at a given time and place. Thus, we find that, from 1945 to 1975, West German political culture underwent a striking transformation from being relatively authoritarian to becoming increasingly democratic and participant (Baker, Dalton, and Hildebrandt 1981). And we find that, from 1970 to 1993, the United States and a number of West European societies experienced a gradual intergenerational shift from having predominantly materialist toward increasingly postmaterialist value priorities (Abramson and Inglehart 1995). Though these changes have been gradual, they demonstrate that central elements of culture can and do change.

Furthermore, empirical research can help identify specific components of culture that are relevant to economic development. One need not seek to change a society's entire way of life. The present findings suggest that one specific dimension—achievement motivation—is highly relevant to economic growth rates. In the short run, to change even a relatively narrow and well-defined cultural component such as this is not easy, but it should be far easier than attempting to change an entire culture. Furthermore, empirical research demonstrates that culture can and does change. Simply making parents, schools and other organizations aware of the potentially relevant factors may be a step in the right direction.

We find that economic theory already is augmented with "social norms" and "cultural" factors (Cole, Malaith, and Postlewaite 1992; Elster 1989; Fershtman and Weiss 1993). Where would cultural values fit theoretically in growth models? The economics literature is replete with models of savings behavior that focus on the "life cycle" and, more specifically, the bequest motive. Cultural variables matter here. Since savings and investment behavior holds an important place in growth models, a determination of how cultural and motivational factors can be used to augment these existing economic models, it seems to us, is the next step to uncovering a better understanding of economic growth.[4]

In the end, however, these arguments can only be resolved on the empirical battlefield. We use ordinary least squares regression to test economic and cultural models of growth on a cross section of 25 countries. We find that economic and cultural factors affect growth. . . .

The results in this article demonstrate that *both* cultural and economic arguments matter. Neither supplants the other. Future theoretical and empirical work is better served by treating these "separate" explanations as complementary.

Notes

1. The nations included in the multivariate analysis are: Austria, Belgium, Brazil, Canada, China, Denmark, Finland, France, Germany, Great Britain, India, Ireland, Italy, Japan, Korea, Mexico, Netherlands, Nigeria, Norway, South Africa, Spain, Sweden, Switzerland, Turkey, United States.

2. This is a check for spatial correlation between the errors of the cases.

3. In the post–World War II period, the life cycle model argues that since Japan and Germany had a substantial portion of their capital stock destroyed, the "permanent income" of the population was going to be less than was expected at the onset of the

war. The lower capital-labor ratio contributes to lower real wages and higher interest rates. In response the public raised its savings rate to "smooth" its postretirement income. The United States, on the other hand, saw a significant increase in its capital stock as a result of the war. This had the opposite effect since the higher capital-labor ratio depresses interest rates and raises real wages. The public's savings rate falls in this case since "permanent income" increases, while current consumption rises.

4. Institutional factors such as regime type and property rights have also been suggested as important determinants of economic growth (Helliwell 1994; Leblang 1996).

References

Abramson, Paul, and Ronald Inglehart. 1995. *Value Change in Global Perspective.* Ann Arbor: University of Michigan Press.

Achen, Christopher. 1982. *Interpreting and Using Regression.* Beverly Hills: Sage.

Alwin, Duane F. 1986. "Religion and Parental Child-Rearing Orientations: Evidence of a Catholic-Protestant Convergence." *American Journal of Sociology* 92:412–40.

Baker, Kendall L., Russell Dalton, and Kai Hildebrandt. 1981. *Germany Transformed.* Cambridge: Harvard University Press.

Barro, Robert. 1991. "Economic Growth in a Cross Section of Countries." *Quarterly Journal of Economics* 106:407–44.

Bollen, Kenneth, and Robert Jackman. 1985. "Regression Diagnostics. An Expository Treatment of Outliers and Influential Cases." *Sociological Methods and Research* 13:510–42.

Chatterjee, S., and A. S. Hadi. 1988. *Sensitivity Analysis in Linear Regression.* New York: John Wiley.

Cole, Harold, George Malaith, and Andrew Postlewaite. 1992. "Social Norms, Savings Behavior, and Growth." *Journal of Political Economy* 100:1092–125.

Cook, R. D., and S. Weisberg. 1982. *Residuals* and *Influence in Regression.* London: Chapman and Hall.

Davidson, Ronald, and James MacKinnon. 1991. "Several Tests for Model Specification in the Presence of Alternative Hypotheses." *Econometrica* 49:781–93.

Elster, Jon. 1989. "Social Norms and Economic Theory." *Journal of Economic Perspectives* 3:99–117.

Fershtman, Chaim, and Yoram Weiss. 1993. "Social Status, Culture, and Economic Performance." *The Economic Journal* 103:946–59.

Fox, John. 1991. *Regression Diagnostics: An Introduction.* Sage University Paper Series on Quantitative Applications in the Social Sciences, 07-079. Newbury Park, CA: Sage.

Godfrey, Leslie. 1984. "On the Uses of Misspecification Checks and Tests of Nonnested Hypotheses in Empirical Econometrics." *Economic Journal* Supplement 96:69–81.

Granato, Jim, and Motoshi Suzuki. N.d. "The Use of the Encompassing Principle to Resolve Empirical Controversies in Voting Behavior: An Application to Voter Rationality in Congressional Elections." *Electoral Studies.* Forthcoming.

Hamilton, Lawrence. 1992. *Regression with Graphics: A Second Course in Applied Statistics.* Pacific Grove, CA: Brooks/Cole Publishing.

Harrison, Lawrence E. 1992. *Who Prospers? How Cultural Values Shape Economic and Political Success.* New York: Basic Books.

Helliwell, J. F. 1994. "Empirical Linkages Between Democracy and Growth." *British Journal of Political Science* 24:225–48.

Hendry, David, and Jean-Francois Richard. 1989. "Recent Developments in the Theory of Encompassing." In *Contributions to Operations Research and Econometrics: The XXth Anniversary of CORE,* ed. B. Comet and H. Tulkens. Boston: MIT Press.

Inglehart, Ronald. 1971. "The Silent Revolution in Europe." *American Political Science Review* 4:991–1017.

Inglehart, Ronald. 1977. *The Silent Revolution: Changing Values and Political Styles.* Princeton: Princeton University Press.

Inglehart, Ronald. 1990. *Culture Shift in Advanced Industrial Society.* Princeton: Princeton University Press.

Jackman, Robert. 1987. "The Politics of Economic Growth in Industrialized Democracies, 1974–1980." *Journal of Politics* 49:242–56.

Leamer, Edward. 1983. "Let's Take the 'Con' Out of Econometrics." *American Economic Review* 73:31–43.

Leblang, David. 1996. "Property Rights, Democracy, and Economic Growth." *Political Research Quarterly* 49:5–26.

Lenski, Gerhard. 1963. *The Religious Factor.* New York: Anchor-Doubleday.

Levine, Ross, and David Renelt. 1992. "A Sensitivity Analysis of Cross-Country Growth Regressions." *American Economic Review* 82:942–63.

Lucas, Robert. 1988. "On the Mechanics of Economic Development." *Journal of Monetary Economics* 1:3–32.

Mankiw, N. Gregory, David Romer, and David Weil. 1992. "A Contribution to the Empirics of Economic Growth." *Quarterly Journal of Economics* 152:407–37.

McClelland, David. 1961. *The Achieving Society.* Princeton: Van Nostrand.

McClelland, David, et al. 1953. *The Achievement Motive.* New York: Appleton-Century-Crofts.

Mizon, Grayham, and Jean-Francois Richard. 1986. "The Encompassing Principle and Its Application to Non-nested Hypothesis Tests." *Econometrica* 54:657–78.

Mooney, Christopher, and Robert Duval. 1993. *Bootstrapping: A Nonparametric Approach to Statistical Inference.* Sage University Paper Series on Quantitative Applications in the Social Sciences, 07-095. Newbury Park, CA: Sage.

Romer, Paul. 1990. "Endogenous Technological Change." *Journal of Political Economy* 98:71–102.

Solow, Robert. 1956. "A Contribution to the Theory of Economic Growth." *Quarterly Journal of Economics* 70:65–94.

Stine, Robert. 1990. "An Introduction to Bootstrap Methods." *Sociological Methods and Research* 18:243–91.

Swan, Trevor. 1956. "Economic Growth and Capital Accumulation." *Economic Record* 22:334–61.

Tawney, Richard. 1926. *Religion and the Rise of Capitalism: A History.* Gloucester, MA: P. Smith.

Tawney, Richard. [1922] 1955. *The Acquisitive Society.* Reprint. New York: Harcourt Brace.

Welsch, Roy. 1980. "Regression Sensitivity Analysis and Bounded-Influence Estimation." In *Evaluation of Econometric Models,* ed. Jan Kmenta and James Ramsey. New York: Academic Press.

Part 6

Dependency and World Systems Theory: Still Relevant?

23

The Development
of Underdevelopment

Andre Gunder Frank

*T*his chapter is the classic work that initiated what would eventually
grow into a tidal wave of "dependency theory" research. In it, the
author argues against the classical theory of economics, as articulated in
works such as W. W. Rostow's The Stages of Economic Growth (see this
volume, Chapter 17), in which all countries will eventually become
developed. Gunder Frank takes a very long-term view, as do Diamond
(Chapter 8) and Acemoglu et al. (Chapter 10), but from his perspective
the cause of underdevelopment is that great colonial powers became
wealthy at the expense of the colonies that they exploited and continued
to exploit even after the formal colonial period ended.

WE CANNOT HOPE TO FORMULATE ADEQUATE DEVELOPMENT THEORY
and policy for the majority of the world's population who suffer from underdevelopment without first learning how their past economic and social history
gave rise to their present underdevelopment. Yet most historians study only the
developed metropolitan countries and pay scant attention to the colonial and
underdeveloped lands. For this reason most of our theoretical categories and
guides to development policy have been distilled exclusively from the historical experience of the European and North American advanced capitalist
nations.

Excerpted from Andre Gunder Frank, *Latin America: Underdevelopment or Revolution?* (New York: Monthly Review Press, 1969). Reprinted with permission from the
Monthly Review Foundation.

Since the historical experience of the colonial and underdeveloped countries has demonstrably been quite different, available theory therefore fails to reflect the past of the underdeveloped part of the world entirely, and reflects the past of the world as a whole only in part. More important, our ignorance of the underdeveloped countries' history leads us to assume that their past and indeed their present resembles earlier stages of the history of the now developed countries. This ignorance and this assumption lead us into serious misconceptions about contemporary underdevelopment and development. Further, most studies of development and underdevelopment fail to take account of the economic and other relations between the metropolis and its economic colonies throughout the history of the world-wide expansion and development of the mercantilist and capitalist system. Consequently, most of our theory fails to explain the structure and development of the capitalist system as a whole and to account for its simultaneous generation of underdevelopment in some of its parts and economic development in others.

It is generally held that economic development occurs in a succession of capitalist stages and that today's underdeveloped countries are still in a stage, sometimes depicted as an original stage of history, through which the now developed countries passed long ago. Yet even a modest acquaintance with history shows that underdevelopment is not original or traditional and that neither the past nor the present of the underdeveloped countries resembles in any important respect the past of the now developed countries. The now developed countries were never underdeveloped, though they may have been undeveloped. It is also widely believed that the contemporary underdevelopment of a country can be understood as the product or reflection solely of its own economic, political, social, and cultural characteristics or structure. Yet historical research demonstrates that contemporary underdevelopment is in large part the historical product of past and continuing economic and other relations between the satellite underdeveloped and the now developed metropolitan countries. Furthermore, these relations are an essential part of the structure and development of the capitalist system on a world scale as a whole. A related and also largely erroneous view is that the development of these underdeveloped countries and, within them of their most underdeveloped domestic areas, must and will be generated or stimulated by diffusing capital, institutions, values, etc., to them from the international and national capitalist metropoles. Historical perspective based on the underdeveloped countries' past experience suggests that, on the contrary, in the underdeveloped countries economic development can now occur only independently of most of these relations of diffusion.

Evident inequalities of income and differences in culture have led many observers to see "dual" societies and economies in the underdeveloped countries. Each of the two parts is supposed to have a history of its own, a structure, and a contemporary dynamic largely independent of the other. Supposedly, only one part of the economy and society has been importantly affected by intimate economic relations with the "outside" capitalist world; and that part, it is held, became modern, capitalist, and relatively developed precisely because of this contact. The other part is widely regarded as variouly isolated, subsistence-based, feudal, or precapitalist, and therefore more underdeveloped.

I believe on the contrary that the entire "dual society" thesis is false and that the policy recommendations to which it leads will, if acted upon, serve only to intensify and perpetuate the very conditions of underdevelopment they are supposedly designed to remedy.

A mounting body of evidence suggests, and I am confident that future historical research will confirm, that the expansion of the capitalist system over the past centuries effectively and entirely penetrated even the apparently most isolated sectors of the underdeveloped world. Therefore, the economic, political, social, and cultural institutions and relations we now observe there are the products of the historical development of the capitalist system no less than are the seemingly more modern or capitalist features of the national metropoles of these underdeveloped countries. Analogously to the relations between development and underdevelopment on the international level, the contemporary underdeveloped institutions of the so-called backward or feudal domestic areas of an underdeveloped country are no less the product of the single historical process of capitalist development than are the so-called capitalist institutions of the supposedly more progressive areas. In this paper I should like to sketch the kinds of evidence which support this thesis and at the same time indicate lines along which further study and research could fruitfully proceed.

The Secretary General of the Latin American Center for Research in the Social Sciences writes in that Center's journal: "The privileged position of the city has its origin in the colonial period. It was founded by the Conqueror to serve the same ends that it still serves today; to incorporate the indigenous population into the economy brought and developed by that Conqueror and his descendants. The regional city was an instrument of conquest and is still today an instrument of domination."[1] The Instituto Nacional Indigenista (National Indian Institute) of Mexico confirms this observation when it notes that "the mestizo population, in fact, always lives in a city, a center of an intercultural region, which acts as the metropolis of a zone of indigenous population and which maintains with the underdeveloped communities an intimate relation which links the center with the satellite communities."[2] The Institute goes on to point out that "between the mestizos who live in the nuclear city of the region and the Indians who live in the peasant hinterland there is in reality a closer economic and social interdependence than might at first glance appear" and that the provincial metropoles "by being centers of intercourse are also centers of exploitation."[3]

Thus these metropolis-satellite relations are not limited to the imperial or international level but penetrate and structure the very economic, political, and social life of the Latin American colonies and countries. Just as the colonial and national capital and its export sector become the satellite of the Iberian (and later of other) metropoles of the world economic system, this satellite immediately becomes a colonial and then a national metropolis with respect to the productive sectors and population of the interior. Furthermore, the provincial capitals, which thus are themselves satellites of the national metropolis—and through the latter, of the world metropolis—are in turn provincial centers around which their own local satellites orbit. Thus, a whole chain of constellations of metropoles and satellites relates all parts of the whole system from its metropolitan center in Europe or the United States to the farthest outpost in the Latin American countryside.

When we examine this metropolis-satellite structure, we find that each of the satellites, including now underdeveloped Spain and Portugal, serves as an instrument to suck capital or economic surplus out of its own satellites and to channel part of this surplus to the world metropolis of which all are satellites. Moreover, each national and local metropolis serves to impose and maintain the monopolistc structure and exploitative relationship of this system (as the Instituto Nacional Indigenista of Mexico calls it) as long as it serves the interests of the metropoles which take advantage of this global, national, and local structure to promote their own development and the enrichment of their ruling classes.

These are the principal and still surviving structural characteristics which were implanted in Latin America by the Conquest. Beyond examining the establishment of this colonial structure in its historical context, the proposed approach calls for study of the development—and underdevelopment—of these metropoles and satellites of Latin America throughout the following and still continuing historical process. In this way we can understand why there were and still are tendencies in the Latin American and world capitalist structure which seem to lead to the development of the metropolis and the underdevelopment of the satellite and why, particularly, the satellized national, regional, and local metropoles in Latin America find that their economic development is at best a limited or underdeveloped development.

That present underdevelopment of Latin America is the result of its centuries-long participation in the process of world capitalist development, I believe I have shown in my case studies of the economic and social histories of Chile and Brazil.[4] My study of Chilean history suggests that the Conquest not only incorporated this country fully into the expansion and development of the world mercantile and later industrial capitalist system but that it also introduced the monopolistic metropolis-satellite structure and development of capitalism into the Chilean domestic economy and society itself. This structure then penetrated and permeated all of Chile very quickly. Since that time and in the course of world and Chilean history during the epochs of colonialism, free trade, imperialism, and the present, Chile has become increasingly marked by the economic, social, and political structure of satellite underdevelopment. This development of underdevelopment continues today, both in Chile's still in-creasing satellization by the world metropolis and through the ever more acute polarization of Chile's domestic economy.

The history of Brazil is perhaps the clearest case of both national and re-gional development of underdevelopment. The expansion of the world econ-omy since the beginning of the sixteenth century successively converted the Northeast, the Minas Gerais interior, the North, and the Center-South (Rio de Janeiro, São Paulo, and Paraná) into export economies and incorporated them into the structure and development of the world capitalist system. Each of these regions experienced what may have appeared as economic development during the period of its respective golden age. But it was a satellite development which was neither self-generating nor self-perpetuating. As the market or the produc-tivity of the first three regions declined, foreign and domestic economic interest in them waned; and they were left to develop the underdevelopment they live today. In the fourth region, the coffee economy experienced a similar though not yet quite as serious fate (though the development of a synthetic coffee sub-stitute promises to deal it a mortal blow in the not too distant future). All of this historical evidence contradicts the generally accepted theses that Latin America suffers from a dual society or from the survival of feudal institutions and that these are important obstacles to its economic development.

During the First World War, however, and even more during the Great De-pression and the Second World War, São Paulo began to build up an industrial establishment which is the largest in Latin America today. The question arises whether this industrial development did or can break Brazil out of the cycle of satellite development and underdevelopment which has characterized its other regions and national history within the capitalist system so far. I believe that the answer is no. Domestically the evidence so far is fairly clear. The development of industry in São Paulo has not brought greater riches to the other regions of Brazil. Instead, it converted them into internal colonial satellites, de-capitalized them further, and consolidated or even deepened their underdevelopment. There is little evidence to suggest that this process is likely to be reversed in the foreseeable future except insofar as the provincial poor migrate and become the poor of the metropolitan cities. Externally, the evidence is that although the ini-tial development of São Paulo's industry was relatively autonomous it is being increasingly satellized by the world capitalist metropolis and its future devel-opment possibilities are increasingly restricted.[5] This development, my studies lead me to believe, also appears destined to limited or underdeveloped devel-opment as long as it takes place in the present economic, political, and social framework.

We must conclude, in short, that underdevelopment is not due to the sur-vival of archaic institutions and the existence of capital shortage in regions that have remained isolated from the stream of world history. On the contrary, un-derdevelopment was and still is generated by the very same historical process which also generated economic development: the development of capitalism itself. This view, I am glad to say, is gaining adherents among students of Latin America and is proving its worth in shedding new light on the problems of the area and in affording a better perspective for the formulation of theory and policy.[6]

The same historical and structural approach can also lead to better development theory and policy by generating a series of hypotheses about development and underdevelopment such as those I am testing in my current research. The hypotheses are derived from the empirical observation and theoretical assumption that within this world-embracing metropolis-satellite structure the metropoles tend to develop and the satellites to underdevelop. The first hypothesis has already been mentioned above: that in contrast to the development of the world metropolis which is no one's satellite, the development of the national and other subordinate metropoles is limited by their satellite status. It is perhaps more difficult to test this hypothesis than the following ones because part of its confirmation depends on the test of the other hypotheses. Nonetheless, this hypothesis appears to be generally confirmed by the non-autonomous and unsatisfactory economic and especially industrial development of Latin America's national metropoles, as documented in the studies already cited. The most important and at the same time most confirmatory examples are the metropolitan regions of Buenos Aires and São Paulo whose growth only began in the nineteenth century, was therefore largely untrammeled by any colonial heritage, but was and remains a satellite development largely dependent on the outside metropolis, first of Britain and then of the United States.

A second hypothesis is that the satellites experience their greatest economic development and especially their most classically capitalist industrial development if and when their ties to their metropolis are weakest. This hypothesis is almost diametrically opposed to the generally accepted thesis that development in the underdeveloped countries follows from the greatest degree of contact with and diffusion from the metropolitan developed countries. This hypothesis seems to be confirmed by two kinds of relative isolation that Latin America has experienced in the course of its history. One is the temporary isolation caused by the crises of war or depression in the world metropolis. Apart from minor ones, five periods of such major crises stand out and seem to confirm the hypothesis. These are: the European (and especially Spanish) depression of the seventeenth century, the Napoleonic Wars, the First World War, the depression of the 1930s, and the Second World War. It is clearly established and generally recognized that the most important recent industrial development—especially of Argentina, Brazil, and Mexico, but also of other countries such as Chile—has taken place precisely during the periods of the two World Wars and the intervening depression. Thanks to the consequent loosening of trade and investment ties during these periods, the satellites initiated marked autonomous industrialization and growth. Historical research demonstrates that the same thing happened in Latin America during Europe's seventeenth-century depression. Manufacturing grew in the Latin American countries, and several of them such as Chile became exporters of manufactured goods. The Napoleonic Wars gave rise to independence movements in Latin America, and these should perhaps also be interpreted as in part confirming the development hypothesis.

The other kind of isolation which tends to confirm the second hypothesis is the geographic and economic isolation of regions which at one time were relatively weakly tied to and poorly integrated into the mercantilist and capitalist system. My preliminary research suggests that in Latin America it was these regions which initiated and experienced the most promising self-generating economic development of the classical industrial capitalist type. The most important regional cases probably are Tucumán and Asunción, as well as other cities such as Mendoza and Rosario, in the interior of Argentina and Paraguay during the end of the eighteenth and the beginning of the nineteenth centuries. Seventeenth- and eighteenth-century São Paulo, long before coffee was grown there, is another example. Perhaps Antioquia in Colombia and Puebla and Querétaro in Mexico are other examples. In its own way, Chile was also an example since, before the sea route around the Horn was opened, this country was relatively isolated at the end of the long voyage from Europe via Panama. All of these regions became manufacturing centers and even exporters, usually of textiles, during the periods preceding their effective incorporation as satellites into the colonial, national, and world capitalist system.

Internationally, of course, the classic case of industrialization through non-participation as a satellite in the capitalist world system is obviously that of Japan after the Meiji Restoration. Why, one may ask, was resource-poor but unsatellized Japan able to industrialize so quickly at the end of the century while resource-rich Latin American countries and Russia were not able to do so and the latter was easily beaten by Japan in the War of 1904 after the same forty years of development efforts? The second hypothesis suggests that the fundamental reason is that Japan was not satellized either during the Tokugawa or the Meiji period and therefore did not have its development structurally limited as did the countries which were so satellized.

A corollary of the second hypothesis is that when the metropolis recovers from its crisis and reestablishes the trade and investment ties which fully reincorporate the satellites into the system, or when the metropolis expands to incorporate previously isolated regions into the world-wide system, the previous development and industrialization of these regions is choked off or channelled into directions which are not self-perpetuating and promising. This happened after each of the five crises cited above. The renewed expansion of trade and the spread of economic liberalism in the eighteenth and nineteenth centuries choked off and reversed the manufacturing development which Latin America had experienced during the seventeenth century, and in some places at the beginning of the nineteenth. After the First World War, the new national industry of Brazil suffered serious consequences from American economic invasion. The increase in the growth rate of Gross National Product and particularly of industrialization throughout Latin America was again reversed and industry became increasingly satellized after the Second World War and especially after the post–Korean War recovery and expansion of the metropolis. Far from having become more developed since then, industrial sectors of Brazil and most conspicuously of Argentina have become structurally more and more underdeveloped and less and less able to generate continued industrialization and/or sustain development of the economy. This process, from which India also suffers, is reflected in a whole gamut of balance of payments, inflationary, and other economic and political difficulties, and promises to yield to no solution short of far-reaching structural change.

Our hypothesis suggests that fundamentally the same process occurred even more dramatically with the incorporation into the system of previously unsatellized regions. The expansion of Buenos Aires as a satellite of Great Britain and the introduction of free trade in the interest of the ruling groups of both metropoles destroyed the manufacturing and much of the remainder of the economic base of the previously relatively prosperous interior almost entirely. Manufacturing was destroyed by foreign competition, lands were taken and concentrated into latifundia by the rapaciously growing export economy, intraregional distribution of income became much more unequal, and the previously developing regions became simple satellites of Buenos Aires and through it of London. The provincial centers did not yield to satellization without a struggle. This metropolis-satellite conflict was much of the cause of the long political and armed struggle between the Unitarists in Buenos Aires and the Federalists in the provinces, and it may be said to have been the sole important cause of the War of the Triple Alliance in which Buenos Aires, Montevideo, and Rio de Janeiro, encouraged and helped by London, destroyed not only the autonomously developing economy of Paraguay but killed off nearly all of its population which was unwilling to give in. Though this is no doubt the most spectacular example which tends to confirm the hypothesis, I believe that historical research on the satellization of previously relatively independent yeoman-farming and incipient manufacturing regions such as the Caribbean islands will confirm it further.[7] These regions did not have a chance against the forces of expanding and developing capitalism, and their own development had to be sacrificed to that of others. The economy and industry of Argentina, Brazil, and other countries which have experienced the effects of metropolitan recovery since the Second World War are today suffering much the same fate, if fortunately still in lesser degree.

A third major hypothesis derived from the metropolis-satellite structure is that the regions which are the most underdeveloped and feudal-seeming today are the ones which had the closest ties to the metropolis in the past. They are the regions which were the greatest exporters of primary products to and biggest sources of capital for the world metropolis and which were abandoned by the metropolis when for one reason or another business fell off. This hypothesis also contradicts the generally held thesis that the source of a region's underdevelopment is its isolation and its pre-capitalist institutions.

This hypothesis seems to be amply confirmed by the former super-satellite development and present ultra-underdevelopment of the once sugar-exporting West Indies, Northeastern Brazil, the ex-mining districts of Minas Gerais in Brazil, highland Peru, and Bolivia, and the central Mexican states of Guanajuato, Zacatecas, and others whose names were made world famous centuries ago by their silver. There surely are no major regions in Latin America which are today more cursed by underdevelopment and poverty; yet all of these regions, like Bengal in India, once provided the life blood of mercantile and industrial capitalist development—in the metropolis. These regions' participation in the development of the world capitalist system gave them, already in their golden age, the typical structure of underdevelopment of a capitalist export economy. When the market for their sugar or the wealth of their mines disappeared and the metropolis abandoned them to their own devices, the already existing economic, political, and social structure of these regions prohibited autonomous generation of economic development and left them no alternative but to turn in upon themselves and to degenerate into the ultra-underdevelopment we find there today.

These considerations suggest two further and related hypotheses. One is that the latifundium, irrespective of whether it appears as a plantation or a hacienda today, was typically born as a commercial enterprise which created for itself the institutions which permitted it to respond to increased demand in the world or national market by expanding the amount of its land, capital, and labor and to increase the supply of its products. The fifth hypothesis is that the latifundia which appear isolated, subsistence-based, and semi-feudal today saw the demand for their products or their productive capacity decline and that they are to be found principally in the above-named former agricultural and mining export regions whose economic activity declined in general. These two hypotheses run counter to the notions of most people, and even to the opinions of some historians and other students of the subject, according to whom the historical roots and socioeconomic causes of Latin American latifundia and agrarian institutions are to be found in the transfer of feudal institutions from Europe and/or in economic depression.

The evidence to test these hypotheses is not open to easy general inspection and requires detailed analyses of many cases. Nonetheless, some important confirmatory evidence is available. The growth of the latifundium in nineteenth-century Argentina and Cuba is a clear case in support of the fourth hypothesis and can in no way be attributed to the transfer of feudal institutions during colonial times. The same is evidently the case of the postrevolutionary and contemporary resurgence of latifundia particularly in the north of Mexico, which produce for the American market, and of similar ones on the coast of Peru and the new coffee regions of Brazil. The conversion of previously yeoman-farming Caribbean islands, such as Barbados, into sugar-exporting economies at various times between the seventeenth and twentieth centuries and the resulting rise of the latifundia in these islands would seem to confirm the fourth hypothesis as well. In Chile, the rise of the latifundium and the creation of the institutions of servitude which later came to be called feudal occurred in the eighteenth century and have been conclusively shown to be the result of and response to the opening of a market for Chilean wheat in Lima.[8] Even the growth and consolidation of the latifundium in seventeenth-century Mexico—which most expert students have attributed to a depression of the economy caused by the decline of mining and a shortage of Indian labor and to a consequent turning in upon itself and ruralization of the economy—occurred at a time when urban population and demand were growing, food shortages became acute, food prices skyrocketed, and the profitability of other economic activities such as mining and foreign trade declined.[9] All of these and other factors rendered hacienda agriculture more profitable. Thus, even this case would seem to confirm the hypothesis that the growth of the latifundium and its feudal-seeming conditions of servitude in Latin America has always been and still is the commercial response to increased demand and that it does not represent the transfer or survival of alien institutions that have remained beyond the reach of capitalist development. The emergence of latifundia, which today really are more or less (though not entirely) isolated, might then be attributed to the causes advanced in the fifth hypothesis—i.e., the decline of previously profitable agricultural enterprises whose capital was, and whose currently produced economic surplus still is, transferred elsewhere by owners and merchants who frequently are the same persons or families. Testing this hypothesis requires still more detailed analysis, some of which I have undertaken in a study on Brazilian agriculture.[10]

All of these hypotheses and studies suggest that the global extension and unity of the capitalist system, its monopoly structure and uneven development throughout its history, and the resulting persistence of commercial rather than industrial capitalism in the underdeveloped world (including its most industrially advanced countries) deserve much more attention in the study of economic development and cultural change than they have hitherto received. Though science and truth know no national boundaries, it is probably new generations of scientists from the underdeveloped countries themselves who most need to, and best can, devote the necessary attention to these problems and clarify the process of underdevelopment and development. It is their people who in the last analysis face the task of changing this no longer acceptable process and eliminating this miserable reality.

They will not be able to accomplish these goals by importing sterile stereotypes from the metropolis which do not correspond to their satellite economic reality and do not respond to their liberating political needs. To change their reality they must understand it. For this reason, I hope that better confirmation of these hypotheses and further pursuit of the proposed historical, holistic, and structural approach may help the peoples of the underdeveloped countries to understand the causes and eliminate the reality of their development of underdevelopment and their underdevelopment of development.

Notes

1. *America Latina,* Año 6, No. 4, October–December 1963, p. 8.
2. Instituto Nacional Indigenista, *Los centros coordinadores indigenistas,* Mexico, 1962, p. 34.
3. Ibid., pp. 33–34, 88.
4. "Capitalist Development and Underdevelopment in Chile" and "Capitalist Development and Underdevelopment in Brazil," in *Capitalism and Underdevelopment in Latin America,* New York, Monthly Review Press, 1967.
5. Also see, "The Growth and Decline of Import Substitution," *Economic Bulletin for Latin America,* New York, IX, No. 1, March 1964, and Celso Furtado, *Dialectica do Desenvolvimiento,* Rio de Janeiro, Fundo de Cultura, 1964.
6. Others who use a similar approach, though their ideologies do not permit them to derive the logically following conclusions, are Anibal Pintos S.C., *Chile: Un caso de desarrollo frustado,* Santiago, Editorial Universitaria, 1957; Celso Furtado, *A formacao economica do Brasil,* Rio de Janeiro, Fundo de Cultura, 1959 (translated into English and published under the title *The Economic Growth of Brazil* by the University of California Press); and Caio Prado Junior, *Historia economica do Brasil,* São Paulo, Editora Brasiliense, 7th ed., 1962.
7. See, for instance, Ramon Guerra y Sanchez, *Azucar y poblacion en las Antillas,* Havana 1942, 2nd ed., also published as *Sugar and Society in the Caribbean,* New Haven, Yale University Press, 1964.
8. Mario Gongora, *Origen de los "inquilinos" de Chile central,* Santiago, Editorial Universitaria, 1960; Jean Borde and Mario Gongora, *Evolucion de la propiedad rural en el Valle del Puango,* Santiago, Instituto de Sociologia de la Universidad de Chile; Sergio Sepulveda, *El trigo chileno en el mercado mundial,* Santiago, Editorial Universitario, 1959.
9. Woodrow Borah makes depression the centerpiece of his explanation in "New Spain's Century of Depression," *Ibero-Americana,* Berkeley, No. 35, 1951. François Chevalier speaks of turning upon itself in the most authoritative study of the subject, "La formacion de los grandes latifundios en Mexico," Mexico, *Problemas Agricolas e Industriales de Mexico,* VIII, No. 1, 1956 (translated from the French and recently published by the University of California Press). The data which provide the basis for my contrary interpretation are supplied by these authors themselves. This problem is discussed in my "Con que modo de produccion convierte la gallina maiz en huevos de oro?" *El Gallo Illustrado, Suplemento de El Dia,* Mexico, Nos. 175 and 179, October 31 and November 28, 1965; and it is further analyzed in a study of Mexican agriculture under preparation by the author.
10. "Capitalism and the Myth of Feudalism in Brazilian Agriculture," in *Capitalism and Underdevelopment in Latin America,* cited footnote 4 above.

24

American Penetration and Canadian Development: A Case Study of Mature Dependency

Heather-Jo Hammer and John W. Gartrell

*D*ependency theorists have found that extensive foreign capital penetration dampens long-term economic growth, but, in a previous edition of this volume, Edward Muller asserted that up to that point, dependency theory had been unable to explain how Canada—a country highly penetrated by foreign investment—could be wealthy, fast growing, and experiencing relatively low levels of income inequality. In this chapter, Heather-Jo Hammer and John Gartrell argue that dependency theorists had failed to acknowledge that a country could be both a member of the core and a dependent country. After noting some similarities between mature dependency and Peter Evans's dependent development, the authors provide a model for Canada's mature dependence and offer evidence of a negative long-term effect of change in American direct investment on change in Canadian economic growth.

THE DEPENDENCY PERSPECTIVE ON THE SOCIOLOGY OF DEVELOPMENT HAS had difficulties in coming to terms with the Canadian situation. Canada seems to fall between types of social formations, displaying the social relations of advanced capitalism and the economic structure of dependency (Drache 1983, 36). Indeed, the Innisian tradition of Canadian political economy[1] stems from a perceived need for both original theory and distinctive methodology in the

Reprinted with permission of the American Sociological Association and the authors from *American Sociological Review* 51, no. 2 (April 1986): 201–213.

explanation of Canadian development (Drache 1983, 38). There is little doubt within the dependency perspective that Canada is "profoundly dependent" in the critical sense that it is extensively penetrated by American direct investment. Nevertheless, Canadian dependency is of a "different genre" than classic peripheral dependency (Portes 1976, 78). . . .

As a theory of development, dependency cannot adequately explain why core economies are not susceptible to the negative consequences of penetration as long as dependency is defined as a structural distortion that is evident exclusively in peripheral modes of development. We think that a demonstration of the negative structural effect of dependency is possible in the case of extensively penetrated core countries. The situation of "relative" core underdevelopment is described with the concept "mature dependency" (Hammer 1982, 1984a, 1984b). The differentiation of mature dependency from other forms of economic power dependency requires that the theory be liberated from its focus on the periphery and the semi-periphery, and the empirical studies be liberated from cross-national analysis. Our endeavour to specify a model of the structural effect of mature dependency on economic growth in Canada reflects Duvall's suggestion to merge dialectical analysis with time series methodology (Duvall 1978).

Mature Dependency and Canadian Development: Reformulating Dependency Theory

Dialectical analysis requires that each new situation of dependency be specified in a "search for differences and diversity" (Cardoso and Faletto 1979, xiii). Contrary to Caporaso and Zare (1981, 47) who state that "The questions of identification and measurement must be answered before theoretical ones can be raised," the dialectical method suggests that ". . . before measuring, previous elaboration of adequate theories and categories is required to give sense to the data" (Cardoso and Faletto 1979, xiii). In brief, Cardoso and Faletto's strategy is to establish the evidence on theoretical grounds and to interpret the data historically. Shifting to the language of empirical models, historical arguments must be interpreted in terms of the important context-defining variables that specify the form of dependency (Duvall 1978, 74).

The existing form of dependency that is most relevant to the Canadian case is Evans's (1979) statement of dependent development. There are some striking similarities between the Canadian and Brazilian developmental histories, particularly in relation to changes in the concentration of foreign capital. In both countries there is an historical shift from British portfolio to American direct investment, and from concentration in resources to concentration in industry. The key difference rests with the timing of the changes and the initial mode of incorporation into the world economy. During the period of Canada's initial industrialization at the end of the nineteenth century, American direct investment in Canadian manufacturing accounted for about 34 percent of total manufacturing investment, compared to less than 4 percent in Brazil. The proportion of American to total direct investment in Canadian manufacturing was 55.6 percent by 1924 (Lewis 1938); in Brazil, by 1929, American direct investment accounted for only 24 percent of total manufacturing investment (Evans 1979, 78). It was not until the 1950s that American direct investment in Brazilian manufacturing attained the concentration levels evident in Canada before the 1920s.

Most of the American [multinational enterprises] MNEs that are currently dominant in Canada had already been established by the end of 1920 (Gonick 1970, 62). By 1897, Canada accounted for about 25 percent of total American direct investment abroad. By 1913, there were 450 American branch plants in Canada, including such giants as Singer, Bell, and Houston Electric (now General Electric) (Field 1914). When the American MNEs asserted their interests in Canadian manufacturing, Canada was the eighth largest manufacturing country in the world, not a peripheral country in transition (Maizels 1963). In 1870, manufacturing accounted for 19 percent of Canada's gross national product, with the production of iron and steel leading the composition.

"Production moves to the periphery only after the technology has become routinized" (Evans 1979, 28). Therefore, the comparative advantage of the periphery in the international market becomes the low cost of its labor (Evans 1979, 28). In addition to the economic disarticulation that results from the lack of integration between subsidiary firms,[2] there exists a disarticulation between technology and social structure. The problem is evident in the failure of imported technology to absorb the huge reserves of underemployed agricultural labor that have been excluded from urban industrialization (Evans 1979, 29). For the elite, disarticulation is an obstacle to self-sustained, autocentric accumulation (Evans 1979, 29). For the masses, economic exclusion is followed by political repression in order to prevent a rise in wages that would mean a loss in comparative advantage (Evans 1979, 48). Evans (1979, 29) describes both exclusion and disarticulation as the constant features of dependency, in the case of dependent development.[3]

Certainly, there is evidence of internal economic disarticulation in Canada. The establishment and protection of foreign technology and the control of the market by oligopolistic MNEs has resulted in a miniature replica effect. The Canadian goods market is fragmented due to an excess of buyers and sellers relative to size, and the concentration of MNEs in central Canada has resulted in regional disparity (Britton and Gilmour 1978, 93–96). However, the only way one can argue for the exclusion of the Canadian masses is in a relative sense, and only in comparison to the U.S. Historically, the wage levels of Canadian workers have been considerably higher than the wage levels of European workers. In fact, when American direct investment moved into Canadian industry at the end of the 1800s, Canada was at a comparative "disadvantage" because of its high wage levels. Where the wage differential does show up is in comparison to American industrial wages which were 60 percent higher than those in Canada during the period (Logan 1937, 90). Firestone's (1958) research suggests that real productivity in Canada outstripped real wages, but this relationship was reversed in the 1930s.

Canada had a reserve army of unskilled labor working in resources, construction and agriculture, whose wage rates were tied to the boom-bust cycle of export-led growth rather than to the import of technology (Drache 1983). This relation is accounted for by Canada's unique situation of being extensively penetrated by MNE investment simultaneously in resource extraction and manufacturing (Gherson 1980). In this sense the Canadian economy remains classically dependent, in that its export composition is predominated by primary resources.[4] In 1913, Canada was exporting an average of 31 percent less finished manufactures than the largest seven manufacturing countries (Maizels 1963). It was not the case that Canada lacked domestic savings for investment in the technology needed to further develop the manufacturing sector. Instead, Canadian funds were being directed into an elaborate banking and financial system to support the domestic transportation and utilities infrastructure needed for the export of wheat (Laxer 1984).

Technology was being imported at a much faster rate than manufactured goods were being exported. Consequently, foreign capital inflows were solicited to maintain the overall rate of economic growth (Ingram 1957). Gonick (1970, 70) argues that the import-substitution mentality implicit in the Canadian National Policy of 1897 was motivated by the commercial capitalists' concern with protecting their trade monopoly in staple exports. The policy of establishing a tariff barrier around Canadian manufacturing was intended to force the American MNEs to finance the Canadian industrial sector in order to penetrate the Canadian market. Apart from sidestepping the Canadian tariff, the opportunity to compete under the terms of British preference in export trade was a further attraction to American direct investment. In addition, the MNEs were able to take advantage of tax benefits and offers of free land that were a result of the regional competition within Canada to attract investment (Scheinberg 1973, 85).

The Canadian railway and financial capitalists were the same central Canadian capitalists who stood to gain from the protection of Canadian manufacturing and from government assistance to the Canadian Pacific Railway. Levitt (1970, 50–51) explains that Canadian private capital flowed freely from railway enterprises into the financial sector and manufacturing industries. In dependent development, the industrial bourgeoisie has no choice but to ally with the state and foreign capital (Evans 1979), whereas in mature dependency, the position and privileges of the commercial industrialists are not contingent upon the tripartite alliance. The alliance is formed by invitation, not necessity.

Innis (1956) argues that even though Canada had liberal democratic institutions, it lacked "strong" popular and democratic traditions. He suggests that this anomaly is linked to Canada's historical dependence and the way Canada was settled. The white settlers who colonized Canada were either fleeing revolution or were exiled when their revolution failed. "It was the presence of a deeply entrenched counter-revolutionary tradition which fundamentally altered not only the liberal democratic character and institutions of Canada but class relations as well" (Drache 1983, 44). Nevertheless, the history of democratic government in Canada can hardly be described as repressive, particularly in comparison to the history of Brazilian government. Thus, the two constant features of dependent development, exclusion of the masses and disarticulation, are evident in Canada, but to a relatively small degree. We suggest that the historical evidence does not support the argument that Canada has experienced dependent development. Rather, Canadian dependency is mature.

Mature dependency diverges from dependent development in the following respects:

1. The mature dependent's economy is functionally complete at the time when the tripartite alliance is formed. External capital inputs are invited, not essential.
2. The economic disarticulation associated with MNE investment is superimposed upon an intact economy that has demonstrated the capacity for self-sustained, autocentric accumulation. Mature dependency is a concrete historical alternative to classic autocentric development rather than an advanced phase of dependent development.
3. Mature dependency does not require economic exclusion of the masses, nor does it result in the associated conditions of political repression.
4. Mature dependency is the condition that causes rich, industrialized core countries to exhibit relative underdevelopment vis-à-vis some of the other core countries on some criteria. The variability in relative status is determined, to a large extent, by the effectiveness of a state's development policy.

In contrast to its non-core counterparts, the mature dependent has abundant social, economic, and political resources that can be mobilized to regulate the negative effects of dependency (Duvall 1978, 69; Bornschier 1980, 166–67). The contemporary features of mature dependency reflect a slow, historical process that has extended over a period of at least 120 years. Similar to dependent development, mature dependency emerged during the period of classic colonial dependence on staple-export growth. The continuity between Canada's early reliance on staple exports and contemporary mature dependency is a result of the continued interest of the Canadian state and the dominant capital interests in the encouragement of American MNE investment.

The difficulty in modeling mature dependency empirically is that we do not expect that the negative structural effects associated with MNE penetration will be evident in a rich, industrialized host until after the division of labor within the multinationals has come to dominate economic structure and growth. The actual effect, according to the decapitalization thesis, will appear only when inflows of fresh foreign capital slow down, or as we will demonstrate for the Canadian case, in combination with actual disinvestment. Although 80 percent of total direct investment in Canada has been American (Government of Canada 1981, 10), British portfolio investment was the primary source of foreign long-term investment capital until 1926.

Circa 1926, American portfolio investment split the market with the U.K., and by 1933, total American long-term investment came to exceed total British investment. Yet, at the onset of World War I, American direct investment accounted for only 13.5 percent of total foreign long-term investment in Canada. Fully 73.2 percent of all foreign long-term investment capital in Canada was in the form of British portfolio investment, imported by the sale of government-guaranteed railway bonds in order to subsidize Canadian investments.

American economic domination was not perceived as a threat to the Canadian state (Marshall et al. 1976, 15), because of its relatively small proportion and because it was complementary to British and Canadian investment (Behrman 1970). Moreover, for the period 1930–1946, portfolio investment (American and British) accounted for twice as much foreign long-term investment as did American direct investment. Flows of portfolio capital generally contribute to economic growth whereas the structural effects of foreign direct investment reduce growth (Behrman 1970, 19). Direct investments are those in which control lies with the foreign investor (Aitken 1961, 24). The organizational form of foreign direct investment is the multinational (Evans 1979, 38). In contrast, portfolio investments involve the acquisition of foreign securities by individuals or institutions with limited control over the companies concerned. In fact, there is considerable agreement that portfolio investment does not involve foreign control at all (Aitken 1961, 24; Hood and Young 1979, 9; Levitt 1970, 58; Gonick 1970, 50). As an economy expands, the foreign sector recedes (Gonick 1970, 50), whereas foreign direct investment may well expand faster than the general economy due to its concentration in the most dynamic and profitable sectors.

World War II changed the balance of foreign capital investments in Canada. Prior to the war, foreign portfolio investment accounted for an average of 71 percent of total foreign capital investment. After World War II, the average dropped to 34.8 percent. American direct investment, which had accounted for only 19.3 percent of the pre-war average, increased to 42.9 percent of foreign long-term investment for the period after 1946. Although American direct exceeded British portfolio investment as a proportion of total foreign long-term investment for the first time in 1946, it took about six more years for American direct investment to emerge as the primary source of foreign capital investment in Canada. While World War II facilitated an important increase in Canadian-owned manufacturing, it also brought closer economic ties with the U.S. Prior to 1950, American direct investment was linked closely to changes in the Canadian economy, accelerating during periods of high tariffs and decelerating during periods of recession (Marshall et al. 1976, 21). Pope (1971, 24) and Aitken (1961, 104) suggest that by 1950, American direct investment had become so large that it not only exploited opportunities, it created them by molding the Canadian economic structure.

The acceleration of American direct investment in Canada during the postwar boom period (1946–1960) is related to both the loss of Canadian access to British portfolio investment and markets and the ascent of the American economy to world economic hegemony. However, the crucial years, according to Grant (1970, 8), were the early 1940s when it was decided that Canada would become a branch plant economy. Both the organization of the war and the postwar construction were carried out under the assumption that government supported business interests in all national economic decisions. World War II brought the Ogdensburg agreements of 1940 to establish a joint defense board, the Hyde Park Declaration on the specialization of munitions production in 1941, a Joint War Production Committee, and Article VII of the Lend-Lease Law, which provided for a reduction in trade barriers. At this point, states Scheinberg (1973), Canadian leaders did perceive a threat to sovereignty, but were not prepared to change course in a period of accelerated wartime production.

Levitt (1970) describes how American direct investment continued to flow into the Canadian economy after the recession of 1957–1958, despite rising rates of unemployment and a slowing of Canadian output. The most important feature of the post-recession expansion was that only a very small proportion of foreign investment actually involved the importation of foreign savings (Gonick 1970, 64). American direct investment was financed largely from corporate capital raised in Canada through the sale of Canadian resources extracted and processed by Canadian labor, or from the sale of branch plant manufactures back to Canadian consumers at tariff-protected prices (Levitt 1970, 63).

Levitt (1970, 63–64) estimates that between 1957 and 1964, American direct investment in manufacturing, petroleum and natural gas, and mining and smelting secured 73 percent of investment funds from retained earnings and depreciation reserves. The strongest cross-national evidence (Bornschier 1980a, 161) of the negative impact of MNE penetration on specific economic sectors is evident in two of the three areas of American concentration in Canada, manufacturing and mining and smelting.

Although the proportion of American direct investment declined in the late 1970s, Canada's liabilities to the U.S. continued to rise through the reinvestment of retained earnings. Since 1975, almost 90 percent of the net increase in the book value of the stock of foreign direct investment in Canada has been accounted for by this process (Government of Canada 1981, 10).

Within the post-war period, both Grant and Levitt select 1960 as an important turning point in Canadian economic history. Grant (1970, 8) argues that since 1960, Canada has developed as a "northern extension" of the continental economy. Levitt (1970, 65) divides the post-war period into a boom period followed by a period of stabilization and disinvestment that she dates precisely to 1960. Levitt describes the latter phase of Canadian economic history as the period of "American Corporate Imperialism." In our analysis, the specification of this structural break is critical in the demonstration of the long-term negative effect of American direct investment on Canadian economic growth. Bergesen (1982) emphasizes the importance of considering structural breaks in world economic development as parameters that delineate the time frame of analysis. World wars are structural breaks, and in the context of dependency analysis World War II takes on particular significance as the demarcation of the emergence of the MNEs as the basic organizational units of world production (Bergesen 1982, 33; Bornschier and Ballmer-Cao 1979, 488; Blake and Walters 1983, 87; Hood and Young 1979, 18), and the establishment of American direct investment as the dominant form of foreign investment capital in Canada. Our restriction of the time series analysis to the post–World War II period is consistent with the literature. . . .

Results

The results of the time series regression analysis support our hypothesis. Change in American direct investment for the post-war period has a negative effect on change in Canadian GNP after a lag of nine years. This effect is evident after 1960. The equation is reported in Table 24.1.

According to the full equation with all the variables included, IL9USDI has a negative effect on GNP of −1.88. As indicated by the value of the Durbin-Watson statistic (2.14), the model is free of autocorrelation. The coefficient for the long-term negative effect, specified as an interaction, is significant at the .025 level. The main effect of the lagged change in American direct investment (L9USDI) is small, negative and not significant for the entire post-war period. There is no evidence of a negative effect for the boom period (this run is not reported). The difference between the pre- and post-1960 series is significant at the .005 level. This difference . . . is equal to $4,709 million. Also significant at this level are the coefficients for the short-term (synchronous) effect of GFCF and USDI. As predicted by dependency theory, these effects are positive, and the immediate effect of change in American direct investment on change in Canadian economic growth is .42 larger than the GFCF coefficient. The main effect of the interaction term (IUSDI) is negative and not significant.

Although the Durbin-Watson statistic does not call for reestimation of the full equation, the variables are taken as first differences; therefore, the

Table 24.1   Change in American Direct Investment and Change in Canadian Gross National Product: Ordinary Least Squares Time Series Estimates for the Period 1947–1978

Variable	Estimated Coefficient	Standard Error	T
DIFF	4709.16	882.282	5.33748
GFCF	.992951	.253596	3.91549
USDI	1.31187	.441842	2.96909
L9USDI	−.118747	.207940	−.571065
IUSDI	−.560369	.615555	−.910347
IL9USDI	−1.87526	.899004	−2.08593

Sum of the squared residuals = .321235E+08.
Standard error of the regression = −1111.54.
Mean of the dependent variable = −3066.78.
Standard deviation = 1893.11.
Log of the likelihood function = −266.516.
Number of observations = 32.
Sum of the residuals = 3486.96.
Durbin-Watson statistic = 2.1452.

time-series procedure does not calculate in R^2. For this reason, the Cochrane-Orcutt iterative procedure (see Pindyck and Rubinfeld 1981, 157) has been performed on the equation as a check on the amount of variance explained. The R^2 and the R^2 adjusted both exceed .90. Various specifications of this full model have been estimated, eliminating the nonsignificant variables. What is most remarkable about the restricted equations is the stability of the coefficients and reported statistics across the different models. In the equation that includes only the difference between the periods, GFCF, USDI and IL9USDI, the estimated long-term negative effect for the post-1960 period is −1.92, compared to −1.88 in the full model. The other statistics are comparably close (results are not reported).

The argument could be made that the negative effect of change in USDI is simply a reflection of an underlying business cycle of the Juglar type (7–10 years). If this were the case, it is likely that a similarly lagged GFCF would show a negative effect on change in GNP. In the equation which estimates both main and interaction effects, the Durbin-Watson statistic indicates a problem of autocorrelation (D.W. = 1.54). The Cochrane-Orcutt estimation indicates that the period difference and the short-term effect of change in GFCF are both significant at the .005 level. The coefficient for GFCF is 1.77. These are the only significant effects in the equation. The other coefficients are estimated with enormous standard errors. The R^2 and adjusted R^2 are reduced to .83 and .81 respectively.

American direct investment in Canada is part of the composite measure of total American long-term investment. If the structural effect of mature dependency is related to the organization of the multinationals, we would expect to see a similar structure in total American long-term investment, to the extent that direct investment is proportionally dominant. The other two components of total long-term investment, portfolio and miscellaneous investments, should not exhibit the dependency effect on growth when they are disaggregated from the composite. Because American miscellaneous investment in Canada has accounted for only about 2.7 percent of total American long-term investment since 1926 (Government of Canada 1978), we will elaborate on the total of investment and on portfolio investment disaggregated.

Again, the analyses support our hypotheses about the nature of mature dependency. Comparing the lagged effects of American long-term and American direct investment, there is a similarity in the magnitudes and relative size of the coefficients, although the lagged effect is not significant. The portfolio estimates exhibit very little similarity to the direct investment estimates, and the short-term effect of portfolio investment is not significant. In fact, there is no significant effect for any of the portfolio variables when the American direct investment model is used to structure the equation. The evidence suggests that foreign direct investment is the only component of foreign long-term capital investments that has a long-term negative effect on the growth of the host economy. Granted, the empirical demonstration of a structural economic effect of dependency is a narrow delineation of the complexity of the alliance of social forces whose coincidence of interests causes the internalization of MNE investment. In fact, Portes (1976, 77) describes the internal impact of the multinationals as a remolding of the domestic social structure. Although our demonstration is limited to the transformation of the domestic economic structure, the specificities of our model are clearly defined by the contextual specificity of the larger social structure.

The importance of the findings is enhanced by their application to Canada, a dependent and yet non-peripheral economy. In this sense the findings and the historical evidence upon which they are based, suggest that dependency theory requires some modification. According to economic theories of the internal markets of MNEs, it is possible for core countries to experience MNE-based dependency. The implications for the social structure of the dependent mature economy are not as devastating as they are in the periphery and the semi-periphery, but the structural effect on long-term economic growth is precisely the same.

Discussion and Conclusions

For the researcher interested in the demonstration of dependency effects in non-peripheral countries, model specification is the key directive in research design. Duvall (1978, 74) argues that the design of dependency research must incorporate the notion that context affects causal relations. "To effectuate this requirement, it is necessary to interpret verbal historicist arguments in terms of the important context-defining variables that are implied in the contextually-specific analysis" (Duvall 1978, 74). The context of mature dependency is provided by both history and theory. The historical legacy of the process of incorporation into the world economy has resulted in a hierarchical division of labor that requires both the measurement of variation between different structural positions and the measurement of variations within positions.

The restriction of current empirical studies of dependency to comparative non–time series designs has meant that events which are major sources of variation in independent variables have been largely ignored (Esteb 1977, 13). In the case of Canada's mature dependency, a time series design is required to capture the structural break that occurs in 1960. Moreover, the cross-national analysis of core countries as a block has obscured the structural distinctions that differentiate Canada from other developed countries.

Dependency theory suggests that extensive foreign capital penetration will have a long-term negative effect on the host's economic growth. The critical importance of theory in the design of dependency research is evident in variable selection, specification of the functional form of the relationship between variables, and the identification of the structure of lagged effects. Dependency theory has integrated organizational economics to explain how the dominance of multinational enterprises has changed the structure of the postwar world economy (see Evans 1979; dos Santos 1970; Cardoso and Faletto 1979). However, dependency theory has not seriously considered the implications of cross-penetration within the core for the structure of developed economies.

New theories addressing the organizational economics of multinational enterprises suggest that the structural effect associated with dependency need not be confined to the peripheral economies of the world system. The couching of dependency arguments in terms of peripheral modes of development does not accommodate "deviant" case analyses without some modification to the theory. Although Wallerstein himself waivers between essays, he classifies Canada, Australia and New Zealand as members of the semi-periphery in order to deal with the "doubtful" economic structures of these countries (see Wallerstein 1974; 1976). Evans (1979, 293) does the same. On this point, we must disagree with both theorists.

The theoretical definition of what constitutes the semi-periphery is admittedly imprecise; however, the term is used as a catch-all category for those countries which cannot simply be considered "peripheral" and yet are structurally distinguishable from center countries (Evans 1979, 291; Wallerstein 1976). Wallerstein (1974) suggests that the coherence of the category is derived from the fact that the semi-periphery is formed by the more advanced exemplars of dependent development. According to Evans's (1979) theory of dependent development, Canada does not fit the category.

The resolution of the issue of Canada's status requires both theoretical and methodological innovation. We suggest that a country can be both a member of the core and dependent. The situation has been described by the concept "mature dependency." The demonstration of a negative long-term effect of change in American direct investment on change in Canadian economic growth provides strong evidence for the existence of mature dependency as a variation in core development. We suggest that future empirical research be directed into case-by-case analyses of core country dependency. Portes (1976) suggests that Australia may be a good candidate for analysis. The Canadian case was a good place to start, particularly because of the significance of retained earnings in Canada, a characteristic which sets Canada apart from other American dependencies (see Hood and Young 1979, 39). In conclusion, we may have inadvertently bridged the rift between the dialectical method of analysis and empirical dependency research. As we have demonstrated in this paper, theoretically and historically informed time series analysis is the appropriate design for modeling the contextual specificity of variations in dependency.

Notes

1. The Innisian tradition began with the work of Harold Innis in the 1930s. He explained Canadian development in terms of its domination by staple-export-led growth. The tradition is a reformulation of Marxism tailored to Canada's mode of capitalist accumulation. It negates the liberal argument [that] Canada's development has been principally autonomous, introverted and autocentric (Drache 1983, 27).
2. "Firms in dependent countries buy their equipment and other capital goods from outside. so that the 'multiplier effect' of new investments is transferred back to the center" (Evans 1979, 28).
3. Because the masses are effectively barred from economic participation, "to allow them political participation would be disruptive. Social and cultural exclusion follow from political and economic exclusion" (Evans 1979, 29).
4. See Richards and Pratt (1979) on "advanced resource capitalism."

References

Aitken, Hugh G.J. 1961. *American Capital and Canadian Resources*. Cambridge, MA: Harvard University Press.

Behrman, Jack N. 1970. *National Interests and the Multinational Enterprise: Tensions Among the North Atlantic Countries*. Englewood Cliffs, NJ: Prentice-Hall.

Bergesen, Albert. 1982. "The Emerging Science of the World-System." *International Social Science Journal* 34:23–25.

Blake, David H. and Robert S. Walters. 1983. *The Politics of Global Economic Relations*. Englewood Cliffs, NJ: Prentice-Hall.

Bornschier, Volker. 1980. "Multinational Corporations, Economic Policy and National Development in the World System." *International Social Sciences Journal* 32:158–72.

Bornschier, Volker and Thanh-Huyen Ballmer-Cao. 1979. "Income Inequality: A Cross-national Study of the Relationship Between MNC-Penetration, Dimensions of the Power Structure and Income Distribution." *American Sociological Review* 44:487–506.

Britton, John H. and James A. Gilmour. 1978. *The Weakest Link—A Technological Perspective on Canadian Industrial Underdevelopment*. Ottawa: Science Council of Canada.

Caporaso, James A. and Behrouz Zare. 1981. "An Interpretation and Evaluation of Dependency Theory." 43–56 in *From Dependency to Development: Strategies to Overcome Underdevelopment and Inequality*, edited by Herald Manoz. Boulder, CO: Westview Press.

Cardoso, Fernando Henrique and Enzo Faletto. 1979. *Dependency and Development in Latin America*. Berkeley, CA: University of California Press.

dos Santos, Theotonio. 1970. "The Structure of Dependence." *American Economic Review* 60:231–36.

Drache, Daniel. 1983. "The Crisis of Canadian Political Economy Dependency Theory Versus the New Orthodoxy." *Canadian Journal of Political and Social Theory* 7:25–49.

Duvall, Raymond. 1978. "Dependency and Dependencia Theory: Notes Towards Precision of Concept and Argument." *International Organization* 32:51–78.

Duvall, Raymond and John Freeman. 1981. "The State and Dependent Capitalism." *International Studies Quarterly* 25:99–118.

Esteb, Nancy. 1977. "Methods for World System Analysis: A Critical Appraisal." Paper presented at the 72nd annual meeting of the American Sociological Association in Chicago, September 5–9.

Evans, Peter. 1979. *Dependent Development: The Alliance of Multinational, State, and Local Capital in Brazil*. Princeton, NJ: Princeton University Press.

Field, F. W. 1914. *Capital Investments in Canada*. Montreal: The Monetary Times of Canada.

Firestone, O. John. 1958. *Canada's Economic Development, 1867–1953*. London: Bowes and Bowes.

Gherson, Joan. 1980. "U.S. Investment in Canada." *Foreign Investment Review* 3:11–14.

Gonick, Cyril Wolfe. 1970. "Foreign Ownership and Political Decay." 44–73 in *Close the 49th Parallel etc.: The Americanization of Canada*, edited by Ian Lumsden. Toronto: University of Toronto Press.

Government of Canada. 1978. *Canada's International Investment Position 1978*. Ottawa: Minister of Supply and Services (catalogue no. 67-202).

———. 1981. *Canada's International Investment Position 1981*. Ottawa: Minister of Supply and Services (catalogue no. 67-202).

———. Statistics Canada. 1983. *National Income and Expenditure Accounts 1965–1982*. Ottawa: Minister of Supply and Services (catalogue no. 13-201).

Grant, George. 1970. *Lament for a Nation*. Toronto: McClelland and Stewart.

Hammer, Heather-Jo. 1982. "Multinational Corporations and National Development: American Direct Investment in Canada." Paper presented at the 10th annual congress meeting of the International Sociological Association in Mexico City, August 16–21.

———. 1984a. Comment on "Dependency Theory and Taiwan: Analysis of a Deviant Case." *American Journal of Sociology* 89:932–36.

———. 1984b. "Mature Dependency: The Effects of American Direct Investment on Canadian Economic Growth." Unpublished Ph.D. dissertation. Department of Sociology, University of Alberta, Edmonton, Canada.

Hood, Neil and Stephen Young. 1979. *The Economics of Multinational Enterprise.* London: Longman Group Limited.

Ingram, James C. 1957. "Growth in Capacity in Canada's Balance of Payments." *American Economic Review* 47:93–104.

Innis, Harold. 1956. *Essays in Canadian Economic History.* Toronto: Toronto University Press.

Laxer, Gordon. 1984. "Foreign Ownership and Myths About Canadian Development." *Review of Canadian Sociology and Anthropology* 22:311–45.

Levitt, Kari. 1970. *Silent Surrender: The Multinational Corporation in Canada.* Toronto: Macmillan.

Lewis, Cleona. 1938. *America's Stake in International Investments.* Washington, DC: Brookings Institution.

Logan, Harold. 1937. "Labour Costs and Labour Standards." 63–97 in *Labour in Canadian-American Relations,* edited by H. Innis. Toronto: University of Toronto Press.

Maizels, Alfred. 1963. *Industrial Growth and World Trade.* London: Cambridge University Press.

Marshall, Herbert, Frank A. Southard Jr. and Kenneth W. Taylor. 1976. *Canadian-American Industry: A Study in International Investment.* New Haven: Yale University Press.

Pindyck, Robert S. and Daniel Rubinfeld. 1981. *Econometric Methods and Economic Forecasting.* New York: McGraw-Hill.

Pope, William H. 1971. *The Elephant and the Mouse.* Toronto: McClelland and Stewart.

Portes, Alejandro. 1976. "On the Sociology of National Development: Theories and Issues." *American Journal of Sociology* 82:55–85.

Richards, John and Larry Pratt. 1979. *Prairie Capitalism: Power and Influence in the New West.* Toronto: McClelland and Stewart.

Scheinberg, Stephen. 1973. "Invitation to Empire: Tariffs and American Economic Expansion in Canada." 80–100 in *Enterprise and National Development: Essays on Canadian Business and Economic History,* edited by Glenn Porter and Robert D. Cuff. Toronto: Hakkert.

Stoneman, Colin. 1975. "Foreign Capital and Economic Growth." *World Development* 3:11–26.

Wallerstein, Immanuel. 1974. "Dependence in an Interdependent World: The Limited Possibilities of Transformation Within the Capitalist World Economy." *African Studies Review* 17:1–26.

———. 1976. "Semi-Peripheral Countries and the Contemporary World Crisis." *Theory and Society* 3:461–83.

25

New Paths: Globalization in a Historical Perspective

Fernando Henrique Cardoso
President of Brazil (1995–2003)

*A*s coauthor of the enormously important book Dependency
and Development in Latin America, *Fernando Henrique Cardoso*
used structural analysis to argue that Latin America was then facing a
new form of political and economic dependence. This new form of
dependence morphed and changed as alliances between domestic
and international forces, both market and political, were forged
and matured. After four decades and two terms as the president of
Brazil, Cardoso offers a new structural analysis of Latin America's
development. Given the collapse of the Soviet Union, Cardoso argues
that one of the great challenges is the adoption of true democracy.
Cardoso analyzes the evolution of civic cultures in Latin America and how
varying alliances and understandings of democracy resulted in different
political structures and outcomes. The second great challenge has been
Latin America's insertion into the international capitalist market. This
required the region to abandon its fondness for the various policies
known collectively as import substitution industrialization.

FORTY YEARS AGO, IN 1967, I COMPLETED WITH ENZO FALETTO, IN SANTI-
ago de Chile, the draft of a book, *Dependency and Development in Latin America*. The book discussed the main interpretations on the theme of development.
At that time, both of us worked at the Economic Commission for Latin America

Reprinted with permission from *International Journal of International Communication*
2 (2008): 385–395.

(ECLA) better known in the region by its Spanish acronym, CEPAL, the UN institution that proposed an approach to the studies on economic development known as *Latin American structuralism*. The main architect of this theory was the Argentinean economist, Raul Prebisch, but it underwent several developments.

Prebisch defined the region's underdevelopment as being structural. Based on the statistical analysis by Hans Singer, an important UN economist, Prebisch highlighted that there was a process of ongoing loss in international trade that limited the chances of growth for underdeveloped countries. This happened because international trade was limited to imports by underdeveloped countries of manufactured goods and the exports of raw materials and agricultural products, the so-called commodities. These commodities had low technological content and the wages paid to the workers for their production were low. On the other hand, despite the high technological component embedded in manufactured goods that should make them cheaper, unions and other organized sectors of the developed societies withheld the productivity gains. These were the social and political foundations for the existence of a growing gap between the countries in the Center and in the Periphery. This gap was structural and could not be explained solely by short-term factors linked to price fluctuations. . . .

In this essay, I do not wish to follow, step-by-step, the relation between Center and Periphery as we saw it in the past compared with today's relationship between advanced economies and emerging economies, to use the current fashionable term. I just want to emphasize that ECLA had then a "vision" that stressed the structural differences between Center and Periphery and the fact that my book with Faletto did not deviate from it. It added the historical dimension to show how the diverse situations of dependency came into being. We did this through an integrated approach of the economic, social and political factors in the formation of capitalism in the periphery. And more importantly, the book revealed that there were differences between countries concerning the opportunities for growth and integration in the international market. It downplayed the relative weight of the external factors in the interplay of the indigenous social classes among themselves and in their relations with the countries of the Center. It also analyzed the changes that occurred in the countries of the region as the overall conditions of capitalism evolved. . . .

Forty years later, where do we stand? . . .

At the domestic level, the first challenge that Latin America had to confront after the end of the Cold War and the ensuing withering away of the two opposing blocks was the full-fledged adoption of democracy. There was neither space for the survival of military dictatorships in the region nor any support for them from the dominant poles. The transition to democracy, in one way or another, has been accomplished.

This happened, however, without the strengthening of the very foundations of democracy. I refer here to a greater equality (at least in terms of opportunities) and to the existence of a truly democratic civic culture. Many sectors of Latin America still lack those lodestones of a capitalist-democratic culture, so eloquently praised by Tocqueville: the communal solidarity of protestant inspiration and the American's sense of personal responsibility. But the architecture of democracy is present. Political parties, elections and even this essential component of the democratic ideals—the taste of freedom—have spread throughout the region with one caveat: freedom is mixed up with non-compliance with the law and the arbitrariness of the powerful that follow the dictum "to enemies, the law, to friends, forgiveness." We created the infra-structure of democracy but the soul is missing: we still lack the "due respect to the legal process," the prevalence of the "rule of law." We keep moving back and forth between institutions and personalism. Charisma threatens the compliance with the rules and the citizen still runs the risk of being treated as a client, as a dependent, entitled to receiving gifts rather than to exercising rights.

The second challenge that globalization brought to the region was its in-sertion in the global competitive capitalism. It is essential to take into account these two challenges together—to build democracy, even though in an incom-plete way, and to come to grips with globalization—to grasp what is happen-ing now. Integration to the global market implied breaking with high protec-tive tariffs and limiting state interventions over the market. These traditional instruments of protection against external competition and of promotion of a development *hacia adentro* had become inefficient. On the other hand, the rules for the attraction of international capital are clear: respect for contracts and reduced arbitrariness in interpretation of the law. To these conditions should be added economic predictability, excluding inflationary indulgences and, hence, a greater control of public spending, and so forth. If we recall that in the 1980s oil crises affected many countries of the region and, combined with inflation, led treasuries to the verge of bankruptcy or to huge debts, we have another factor leading to drastic change in the action of states: the time for privatization had come. Privatization was undertaken less as the conse-quence of a neo-liberal–inspired ideological decision and more to help the ad-justment of the government accounts and to provide market mobility to the large, previously state-run, corporations as well as to build the modern infra-structure needed for economic development. Even the companies that by po-litical decision remained under state control started to operate in the market as large private corporations, having in the quest for profit, compliance with the law and transparency in decisions an ideal that, even when not fully attained, did limit the level of interference by political and partisan interests.

These overlapping processes generated a contradiction or, at least, an am-biguity between traditional interests rooted in the political system, with in-fluence on the state apparatus and rules of the market, increasingly more ho-mogeneous at the international level, due to the global standards of quality required for the operation of the productive system, especially in the case of exports of industrial goods. Moreover, the slow resumption of economic growth (which only from 2003 onwards received incentives from the international market) and the growing demands from the masses created a cauldron of pressures. This situation led in several countries to political crises or, at least, to the electoral defeat of proponents of the modernization required for adjustment to the global economy. In some cases, democracy itself, not only the economy, started to be blamed for the failure to respond promptly to popular demands.

Not all countries of the region had the conditions for an insertion in the new world order with opportunities for economic development and better well-being for the people. In a nutshell, the hurricane of macro-economic adjustments that swept the continent in the last decade of the past century (known, unjustly, as the application of the Washington Consensus agenda) took different forms and met with different political, economic and social situations. By and large, countries lacking a diversified economy, especially those with characteristics similar to the old economies of enclave (Bolivia, Ecuador, Venezuela and some countries of Central America) experienced a greater difficulty to adjust positively than countries whose economies and societies had undergone processes of diversification and had developed an urban industrial base that complemented the agro-exporting sector.

The climate of political freedom and the continuity of elections enabled previously marginalized sectors gradually to enter the stage. There was a resurgence or emergence, all over the continent, of peasant demands as well as a growing pressure by urban masses. In the first stages of globalization, there were protest movements of Cuban or Maoist inspiration. In one particular case, that of Allende's Chile, the demand for profound social change was supported by the popular vote and gained power. After the downfall of Allende, a process that had the participation of the international forces fighting the Soviet block, and after the smothering of the strongest guerrilla movements, such as *Sendero Luminoso,* the *Tupamaros* and the *Montoneros,* or of their containment, like in Colombia, the high-pitched rhetoric for change was not followed by transformative action. The nonexistence of "another bloc," with the demise of the Soviet Union, limited the transfer of the revolutionary myth into reality.

This does not mean that the revolutionary myth has disappeared from the ideological amalgam of political movements active in many parts of the region. The appeal of a radical structural transformation remains alive in many of them, from the neo-*zapatistas* of *comandante* Marcos, through the Bolivarianistas's proclamations of the Venezuelan leadership, to the Bolivian *indigenismo* and the rebel movements in Guatemala. The same is true for Colombia, where the *narco-guerrilleros* still see themselves as revolutionaries. In other cases, like in the Landless Movement (MST) in Brazil, the overall situation of the country is so removed from the revolutionary rhetoric that it is hard to assume it publicly, even though the dream of "another society" remains alive.

More recently, the political challenge to the established order took a new shape.

Many have used the notion of populism or neo-populism to characterize the policy of countries like Venezuela, Bolivia or even Argentina, given the charisma of the leader and the "distributivism" of these countries' social policies. What emerges from these experiences, however, is above all the mistrust of markets and the return to statism. The new populist situations emerged in reaction to the adjustment policies, blamed for all the evils of the present. Hence, the regressive component of the rhetoric that supports them. Their leaders do not propose new forms of social or economic organization. Their rhetoric is negativist. They give voice to an anti-American and anti-globalization message, but abstain from defining the utopian way towards a future of greater equality and economic prosperity. *Pari passu* with the messianic attitude of the Bush government that imposes political regime change and sustains the legitimacy of preventive wars, anti-Americanism is the magnet for the new Latin American populism. An external enemy is singled out to justify the national-statist rhetoric in a way that is immediately understood by the masses, increasingly disgusted with the arrogance of Bush's America.

Though these patterns of political behavior have been qualified as populist (even in the case of Lula in Brazil who, from time to time, is defined in those terms), they differ significantly from the classical populism. We are living through situations that are different from former populist processes, of a Varguista or Peronista type, or whatever other name they may have had. Those appealed directly to the masses, partially incorporating them in society. They despised representative democracy, promoted the redistribution of resources but did not seek to change the prevailing social and economic order. Anti-Americanism was strong with Perón, but was not a characteristic of Vargas. And both never entertained an anti-market stance. Their statism, especially in the Vargas democratic period, was more pragmatic—as is today's privatizing wave—than ideological. The new populism, of Chávez or Morales, has in common with their predecessors the policies of income distribution. However, it is much more anti than in favor of, and does not hide its hostility towards the markets. In Morales's case, there is still the *indigenista* component that drives the rhetoric toward the proposal of another society, based on non-Western values.

Each country implemented the agenda of adjustments to the global order according to its specific situation. In countries with an economy with little differentiation and dependency on one basic export commodity, like Bolivia, the consequences of the adjustment were traumatic. There was an outright crisis of the political system and the rise of a leadership with indigenous roots strongly influenced by the negativism typical of the anti-globalization reaction. In Ecuador, the same conditions generated a situation of profound instability, with indigenous communities playing an active role in political pressure. It would, therefore, be simplistic to explain the dynamics of these countries just as the result of a lack of economic alternatives in the globalized world. These factors interacted with the demands of cultural identity expressed by indigenous masses, previously marginalized from influence in society (in Bolivia, for instance, more than 60% of the population declares to be indigenous). The same is true of other countries where the original populations conserved their cultures and are in sufficient number to exercise political power in times of democratic affirmation.

The difficulty to accommodate democratic demands to the macroeconomic adjustments in countries with few productive alternatives characterized Venezuela already under President Caldera. They paved the way for Hugo Chávez's successive armed or electoral victories, with the difference that Venezuela controls an important tool for success in the global world, oil. Fujimori's Peru (still at the time of Sendero Luminoso's revolutionary illusions and before the end of bipolarity) escaped this dilemma. Thanks to the liberalizing reforms that were pursued by President Toledo, Peru achieved high rates of economic growth and a certain differentiation of its productive base. This opened space for a modest incorporation of segments of the impoverished masses.

Let me again restate the importance of avoiding simplifications. It was not only the inconsistency between the modernizing pressures of the globalized economy and the scant productive differentiation of these countries that led them to political crises. There was also a fraying of pre-existing democratic institutions, undermined by corruption and by inefficiency, as occurred in Venezuela prior to Caldera and in Peru. And it was not a hazard that in both Venezuela and Peru what happened was the tearing down of relatively old democratic experiences, not military dictatorships.

Chile represents a different and specific case. Since the pre-globalization period, Chile, although crucially dependent on the export of copper, presented a more diversified economy. On the other hand, the beginnings of the Chilean adjustment took place (without the reward of economic growth, let it be said) still during Pinochet's government. Later, with the redemocratization, Chile achieved what few countries could, a consensual agenda supported by government and opposition—moreover, a consensual policy embedded in society itself. This led to the strengthening of democratic institutions and the promotion of economic growth. Pinochet's violence produced antibodies in a society with a history of deeply rooted values of respect for the institutions.

Nothing was written or pre-ordained, of course. Political options evidently depend on leadership and Chile had competent leaders. Competent and capable of understanding that, in the global economy, the brand, the design, the circuits of commercialization, together with efficiency and compliance with the rules, are as important as abundant natural resources, labor force and capital to accomplish a full economic circuit in the framework of the national frontiers. In other words, we no longer live in a time where the Prussian economic model *á la* Frederich Lizt, or even of the industrialization driven by import substitution, was seen as the only path toward GDP growth. Exporting oysters, salmon, wine or fruits, provided that is in accordance with the quality requirements of the global market, adds value to products and leads to an international insertion appropriate for a country with a relatively small economy and population.

This strategy highlighted the value of a political model that might be called "globalized social democracy," which does not fear the external market. Rather, it values the institutions, the responsibility of citizens and is aware that the stability of the democratic process depends on some measure of economic progress. But also, a great deal depends on active policies geared to reducing poverty and enhancing social well-being. Somehow, this application in our continent under other conditions, referred to in Europe as *market social economy,* with the difference that, besides respecting the rules of the local market, there is an engagement with the global market and the promotion of social and economic policies that stimulate social action by governments and society. In countries marked by an Iberian cultural tradition, like ours, possessive individualism and the belief that competition in the market lead to common good have never been assimilated. This facilitates the acceptance of the new version of the social democracy. It promotes economic modernization and, at the same time, paves the way for action by government in the social and productive areas. It also stimulates an active civil society. Far from praising individualism, this philosophy values people's engagement in society, imparting them with responsibilities, especially in the struggle against poverty and inequality.

This was also the path followed by Brazil, a country with a greater degree of economic diversification than any other in the region, facing obstacles like none other to overcome poverty and social inequality. Brazil underwent the opening of the economy, the reforms of the state (still incomplete), taking forward its democratization despite relatively low growth rates of its domestic product over the last 15 years. The resilience of economic structures and democratic institutions, combined with the existence of a vibrant civil society led to significant progress in response to the dual challenge of building a democracy and participating in the global market. In contrast with the Chilean experience, based on consensus, the Brazilian case's political disputes between the two polarizing parties, Partido dos Trabalhadores (PT) and Partido da Social Democracia Brasileira (PSDB), did not hinder the pursuit of both processes. The differences between the parties finally proved to be less of an ideological nature than linked to the struggle for political power. There was one fundamental difference: the belief in the values and practices of democracy is stronger in the PSDB, while the Leninist vision of the path political party—state controlled by militants—with the goal (or excuse) to promote far-reaching reforms, remains alive, even though somewhat faded, in the PT. Once in government, the PT pursued, in broad terms, the same policies adopted by PSDB. It may eventually reduce their impetus or introduce changes here and there, but nothing that undermines the path followed since the previous government, insofar as such path was not arbitrarily chosen by one government but embodied what was needed to adapt the country to the challenges of reality.

What I said earlier about Chile can be repeated for the Brazilian case. Much more than following a neo-liberal model, the policy adopted in Brazil followed the model of a globalized social democracy. Brazil seized the opportunities of the global market, deepened the economic transformations that came from previous decades and what seemed an impossibility in the past is today a reality. The country became an exporter of sophisticated industrial products (such as airplanes or cell phones), developed autonomous technologies (for instance, deep-water oil drilling), revolutionized its agro-industry with new technologies and is seeing some of its companies become global players. Simultaneously, it launched ambitious social programs, both with a universal scope (health and education) and targeted to specific groups (land reform, social protection networks and direct income distribution). The levels of poverty and even, incrementally, those of inequality have started to fall since the nineties.

In Argentina, events followed a different course. There was no correlation between the economic advances in the period prior to globalization and an effort aimed at productive diversification. The preexisting industrial investment was not the basis for the country's integration in the new phase of the world market. Since the 19th century, the Argentinean economy was internationally integrated through agriculture. With globalization, linkages were deepened in the same way.

The adjustment undertaken in the time of President Menem and Minister Cavallo—this, indeed, a truly neo-liberal one—did not prevent Argentina from being more severely hit than other countries by the consequences of the world financial crises. The way government controlled inflation, pegging the peso to the dollar, led the economy to default as soon as the speculative international tornado turned against the local currency. Argentinean democracy, however, remained afoot even though reeling (De la Rua resigned the presidency; there was a succession of interim presidents until Eduardo Duhalde took power). With the election of President Kirchner, due to the action of the minister of Finance, Roberto Lavagna, the government managed to control the crisis, without having to accept the negotiation of the foreign debt on the traditional terms proposed by the IMF.

Having reestablished the control over the economy, the Kirchner government opted for an intermediary path between the neo-liberal position of his predecessors and the strengthening of the internal market to stimulate industrialization and growth of domestic product. It raised custom tariffs, imposed price controls and, fearful of Brazilian competition, reneged on some integrationist measures that the Mercosul had adopted. Argentina remained, therefore, to a certain extent on the sidelines of the more dynamic international market.

The success of the adopted policies is based on the high rates of economic growth allowing the government to mitigate the demands of the popular classes, highly repressed in the previous period. These rates were achieved due to the expansion of international agricultural commerce, accelerated by China's entry in it, and to measures protecting local production. It was in this context that the president asserted his popular leadership, in this case with a higher resemblance with the past, even though without the fiery anti-Americanism of early Peronism.

To conclude these considerations, we have to mention another important country of the region, Mexico. If there was one country hard-pressed to rebuild its policies and institutions to respond to the dual challenge of the globalizing modernization and of democracy, that was Mexico. Heir to a political system stemming from a popular revolution which had withered away in bureaucratism from a single ruling party and in a strong state intervention in the economy, Mexico did not seem poised to engage constructively with the changing times. The regime of the Institutionalized Revolution had achieved marked economic progress but had also created all kinds of difficulties for the flourishing of a competitive market, opening of the economy, political power alternatives and democratic transparency.

I recall the conversation I had with the present Italian Prime Minister Romano Prodi, when he exercised this same function before the effective entrance of Italy in the Maastricht rules and fiscal disorder prevailed in the country. I asked him how it would be possible to fulfill the obligations in terms of fiscal and budgetary control for Italy to integrate with the European Union. He answered: there is only one way—to sign the engagements and impose the discipline from the outside in. That is what happened with Mexico. By signing the integration agreements with the USA and Canada, the country entered into a straitjacket. The NAFTA can be contested by the opposition but, for better or worse, it set the parameters for the Mexican economy and opened new perspectives for the country.

The previous economic diversification already signaled in the direction of an industrialization complementary to the American economy. The *maquila* was already in place, based on the local assemblage of components of durable consumption goods geared to the North American market. The production expanded and became differentiated. Today, Monterrey, center of the area of greatest industrial dynamism in the country, became an important pole, even hosting (as in the Brazilian case) global companies, for example, in the cement sector. There was a partial privatization of public companies, as in the case of telecommunications (with less emphasis on regulatory agencies and competition than in Brazil); power companies stayed in government hands and the financial system (contrary to Brazil) was denationalized.

The impression one has is that, in the Mexican case, there was a one-way integration in the North American market. Statistics show the enormous proportion of export products going in that direction (circa 90%). Economic growth accelerated in the initial phase of globalization, lost impetus later on and, as in Brazil, employment demand did not match employment supply, which explains the persistence of the migratory flow to the United States. Mexico still has indigenous populations with a relatively low level of integration into the national society and suffers from a lack of transparency in the political system (despite the democratizing efforts that started electoral reforms in the seventies and were deepened during President Ernesto Zedillo's government). The Mexican answer to the globalization challenges generated a significant level of economic growth but was obtained thanks to the growing links with a single large market. The political process, even though advancing, has not yet fully consolidated the democratic practices. This is reflected in the electoral rhetoric that keeps emphasizing nationalist values (to warn against the risks of an umbilical link with the American economy) and has not yet disassociated itself from the anti-globalization and anti-American debate, as expressed in the recent campaign by López Obrador, defeated by President Calderón by a slim margin of votes.

As the purpose of this lecture is not to analyze exhaustively each country, I will abstain from making specific references to many of them. Some, given the small dimension of their economies, keep looking for some trade agreement opening space for their exports (as is the case of Uruguay and Paraguay). They respond to the challenges of democracy according to their history and tradition. Uruguay, for instance, ruled today by a Left coalition, preserved its democratic tradition.

If I had to qualify the Uruguayan political system, I would say that it is closer to the Chilean-style contemporary social-democracy than to the anti-market and anti-globalization positions adopted by the countries of the old economies of enclave.

Paraguay, in turn, characterized by a political system with a strong patrimonialist and clientelistic tradition, has not moved away from this pattern and has not found a way toward economic growth that would release it from the grip of underdevelopment. Paraguay has therefore more possibilities to follow the paths of today's anti-liberal and anti-American populism than to attempt a different alternative.

The countries of Central America represent a fairly specific case. In all of them, representative democracy is afoot in its traditional form, that is, without the complement of active civil societies capable of stimulating citizen social participation and reducing clientelism. This happens, of course, at variable levels. In Costa Rica as well as in Panama and Santo Domingo, the landscape is more dynamic. In other countries, like Nicaragua, we are witnessing the return to power of leaders that, in the past, seemed closer to the Cuban ideals. If, today, they still cling to them, it is in a watered-down way, given the changes that took place in the world and in their own local economies. Taken as a whole, Central American economies have found some relief thanks to commercial agreements with the United States that opened market shares to their few export products, while deepening the traditional links of dependency. Globalization here, more than in Mexico, that has at its disposal a larger array of productive resources, is synonymous with a growing and unequal relationship with the United States.

There are, however, some trends that qualify the Central American situation. The main one is the migration to the United States that generates a huge volume of income remittances to the families that stayed in the countries of origin. One out of each three Salvadorans lives abroad, 2.5 million of them in the United States alone. The same happens in neighboring Mexico, with many millions living in the United States and sending money back to their families, even though the dimension of the phenomenon is smaller given the size of the Mexican economy and population.

Not only the people of El Salvador, but also the Colombians, the Ecuadorians (many of them in Spain), Dominicans, etc., migrate and create attachments of a different nature with the host country. Their remittances have a huge economic impact in the countries of origin. It is easy to imagine the complexity of the relationship thus established between them and the United States, made, at the same time, of reaction against and cultural and financial amalgamation. All this leads to a scenario that is quite diverse from what happens in the relations between the Southern cone of South America and the United States.

It is time to conclude. I tried to demonstrate in this essay that the historical-structural framework of analysis is still useful to describe the transformations generated by globalization in the underdeveloped countries, provided that it is used with the subtlety needed to avoid reductionism in the analysis. Globalization, in the same way as *dependencia,* is nothing more than an enfoldment of the capitalist system in today's historical conditions.

The standpoint of the structural analysis conditions, but does not determine, the shape taken by economic and political processes. Political strategies of insertion in the global economy have a certain margin of autonomy, even though they depend on factors that differ from country to country, such as the local capacity of income accumulation, the presence of direct foreign investment, the mix between nationally controlled production and the one controlled by multinationals, the participation of the public sector in production, the capacity of the leadership, the prevailing ideologies, and so forth. In other words, there are alternative paths, not all or any of them, of course, nor with the same chances of success in every country. The choice of the alternatives and their ultimate success depend as much on the structural basis as on the political capacity of the leadership, and even on the institutions and political culture in the broader sense.

In the recent history of Latin America, at least three countries achieved a more favorable integration in the globalized market and provided more or less acceptable, even though still insufficient responses to the demands of their populations: Chile, Brazil and Mexico. Others developed a strategy of *exit,* rather of withdrawal, like Argentina, while the majority, like the countries of Central America, Uruguay and Paraguay, lacking the resources to accelerate the transformation of the economic base needed to achieve a qualitative leap, designed survival strategies looking for niches in the global market for their traditional production. And there are those that disposing of a global value commodity, but lacking the other resources needed for bolder globalizing leaps, defined a *voice* strategy: they vocalize their discontent with globalization as a whole and, in less clear terms, also with representative democracy. Not to speak of countries like Peru and Colombia that, even though with less resources than the three forerunners in terms of globalization, dispose of enough resources to give them, in time, better chances to face the challenges of the new world order.

The failure to take into account these multiple paths and alternatives would be similar to not acknowledging the structural limits (even though changeable across time) imposed on developing countries. Globalization, as I have insisted, implies in the extension to the planetary scale of the financial links and the rapid diffusion of new productive techniques that create the so-called knowledge economy. Both processes remain, by and large, under the control of the great multinational corporations or the megafinancial organizations, based in a handful of countries. These remain the dominant players in the global economy.

However, the number of main partners is not static; suffice to see what is happening with China. It is also clear that the path to enlarge the chances for creation and diffusion of new technologies and access to capital is an arduous one. Even though, to mention just the countries with the largest populations, Brazil, Russia and India, not to speak of China that has taken the lead, the so-called BRIC are right now engaged in a course against time to see who gets there.

Everything will depend not only on the economy but also on the world political scene, and mainly, on the capacity of local societies and their leaders to frame policies, as much as possible consensual, that seize opportunities—and not only economic ones—and make the effects of globalization and democracy more favorable to the developing countries and to their peoples.

Part 7

The Role of Institutions

26

Big Bills Left on the Sidewalk: Why Some Nations Are Rich and Others Poor

Mancur Olson Jr.

During his lifetime Mancur Olson Jr. was one of the most influential champions of rational choice theory. Here he dismisses many of the proposed causes of the gap between rich and poor countries offered throughout this volume—access to productive knowledge, access to capital markets, population stresses, lack of natural resources, quality of human capital, culture, and so on—declaring that the cause is the quality of institutions and economic policies. Olson argues that all governments and policies are not made equally and countries do not produce as much as their natural endowments permit, but rather strong institutions that get the policy right are the decisive factor in a country's economic performance. According to Olson, convergence theorists are not right about convergence because most poor countries, despite having a higher propensity to grow than richer countries, have poorer economic policies and institutions than richer countries.

THERE IS ONE METAPHOR THAT NOT ONLY ILLUMINATES THE IDEA BEHIND many complex and seemingly disparate articles, but also helps to explain why many nations have remained poor while others have become rich. This metaphor grows out of debates about the "efficient markets hypothesis" that all pertinent publicly available information is taken into account in existing stock market prices, so that an investor can do as well by investing in randomly chosen stocks

Reprinted with permission of the American Economic Association from the *Journal of Economic Perspectives* 10, no. 2 (1996): 3–24.

as by drawing on expert judgment. It is embodied in the familiar old joke about the assistant professor who, when walking with a full professor, reaches down for the $100 bill he sees on the sidewalk. But he is held back by his senior colleague, who points out that if the $100 bill were real, it would have been picked up already. This story epitomizes many articles showing that the optimization of the participants in the market typically eliminates opportunities for supranormal returns: big bills aren't often dropped on the sidewalk, and if they are, they are picked up very quickly.

Many developments in economics in the last quarter century rest on the idea that any gains that can be obtained are in fact picked up. Though primitive early versions of Keynesian macroeconomics promised huge gains from activist fiscal and monetary policies, macroeconomics in the last quarter century has more often than not argued that rational individual behavior eliminates the problems that activist policies were supposed to solve. If a disequilibrium wage is creating involuntary unemployment, that would mean that workers had time to sell that was worth less to them than to prospective employers, so a mutually advantageous employment contract eliminates the involuntary unemployment. The market ensures that involuntarily unemployed labor is not left pacing the sidewalks.

Similarly, profit-maximizing firms have an incentive to enter exceptionally profitable industries, which reduces the social losses from monopoly power. Accordingly, a body of empirical research finds that the losses from monopoly in U.S. industry are slight: Harberger triangles are small. In the same spirit, many economists find that the social losses from protectionism and other inefficient government policies are only a minuscule percentage of the GDP [gross domestic product].

The literature growing out of the Coase theorem similarly suggests that even when there are externalities, bargaining among those involved can generate socially efficient outcomes. As long as transactions costs are not too high, voluntary bargaining internalizes externalities, so there is a Pareto-efficient outcome whatever the initial distribution of legal rights among the parties. Again, this is the idea that bargainers leave no money on the table.

Some of the more recent literature on Coaseian bargains emphasizes that transactions costs use up real resources and that the value of these resources must be taken into account in defining the Pareto frontier. It follows that, if the bargaining costs of internalizing an externality exceed the resulting gains, things should be left alone. The fact that rational parties won't leave any money on the table automatically insures that laissez faire generates Pareto efficiency.

More recently, Gary Becker (1983, 1985) has emphasized that government programs with deadweight losses must be at a political disadvantage. Some economists have gone on to treat governments as institutions that reduce transactions costs, and they have applied the Coase theorem to politics. They argue, in essence, that rational actors in the polity have an incentive to bargain politically until all mutual gains have been realized, so that democratic government, though it affects the distribution of income, normally produces socially efficient results (Stigler, 1971, 1992; Wittman, 1989, 1995; Thompson and Faith, 1981; Breton, 1993). This is true even when the policy chosen runs counter to the prescriptions of economists: if some alternative political bargain would have left the rational parties in the polity better off, they would have chosen it! Thus, the elemental idea that mutually advantageous bargaining will obtain all gains that are worth obtaining—that there are no bills left on the sidewalk—leads to the conclusion that, whether we observe laissez faire or rampant interventionism, we are already in the most efficient of all possible worlds.

The idea that the economies we observe are socially efficient, at least to an approximation, is not only espoused by economists who follow their logic as far as it will go, but is also a staple assumption behind much of the best-known empirical work. In the familiar aggregate production function or growth accounting empirical studies, it is assumed that economies are on the frontiers of their aggregate production functions. Profit-maximizing firms use capital and other factors of production up to the point where the value of the marginal product equals the price of the input, and it is assumed that the marginal private product of each factor equals its marginal social product. The econometrician can then calculate how much of the increase in social output is attributable to the accumulation of capital and other factors of production and treat any increases in output beyond this—"the residual"—as due to the advance of knowledge. This procedure assumes that output is as great as it can be, given the available resources and the level of technological knowledge.

If the ideas evoked here are largely true, then the rational parties in the economy and the polity ensure that the economy cannot be that far from its potential, and the policy advice of economists cannot be especially valuable. Of course, even if economic advice increased the GDP by just 1 percent, that would pay our salaries several times over. Still, the implication of the foregoing ideas and empirical assumptions is that economics cannot save the world, but at best can only improve it a little. In the language of Keynes' comparison of professions, we are no more important for the future of society than dentists.

The Boundaries of Wealth and Poverty

How can we find empirical evidence to test the idea that the rationality of individuals makes societies achieve their productive potential? This question seems empirically intractable. Yet there is one type of place where evidence abounds: the borders of countries. National borders delineate areas of different economic policies and institutions, and so—to the extent that variations in performance across countries cannot be explained by the differences in their endowments—they tell us something about the extent to which societies have attained their potentials.

Income levels differ dramatically across countries. According to the best available measures, per capita incomes in the richest countries are more than 20 times as high as in the poorest. Whatever the causes of high incomes may be, they are certainly present in some countries and absent in others. Though rich and poor countries do not usually share common borders, sometimes there are great differences in per capita income on opposite sides of a meandering river, like the Rio Grande, or where opposing armies happened to come to a stalemate, as between North and South Korea, or where arbitrary lines were drawn to divide a country, as not long ago in Germany.

At the highest level of aggregation, there are only two possible types of explanations of the great differences in per capita income across countries that can be taken seriously.

The first possibility is that, as the aggregate production function methodology and the foregoing theories suggest, national borders mark differences in the scarcity of productive resources per capita: the poor countries are poor because they are short of resources. They might be short of land and natural resources, or of human capital, or of equipment that embodies the latest technology, or of other types of resources. On this theory, the Coase theorem holds as much in poor societies as in rich ones: the rationality of individuals brings each society reasonably close to its potential, different as these potentials are. There are no big bills on the footpaths of the poor societies, either.

The second possibility is that national boundaries mark the borders of public policies and institutions that are not only different, but in some cases better and in other cases worse. Those countries with the best policies and institutions achieve most of their potential, while other countries achieve only a tiny fraction of their potential income. The individuals and firms in these societies may display rationality, and often great ingenuity and perseverance, in eking out a living in extraordinarily difficult conditions, but this individual achievement does not generate anything remotely resembling a socially efficient outcome. There are hundreds of billions or even trillions of dollars that could be—but are not—earned each year from the natural and human resources of these countries. On this theory, the poorer countries do not have a structure of incentives that brings forth the productive cooperation that would pick up the big bills, and the reason they don't have it is that such structures do not emerge automatically as a consequence of individual rationality. The structure of incentives depends not only on what economic policies are chosen in each period, but also on the long run or institutional arrangements: on the legal systems that enforce contracts and protect property rights and on political structures, constitutional provisions, and the extent of special-interest lobbies and cartels.

How important are each of the two foregoing possibilities in explaining economic performance? This question is extraordinarily important. The answer must not only help us judge the theories under discussion, but also tell us about the main sources of economic growth and development.

I will attempt to assess the two possibilities by aggregating the productive factors in the same way as in a conventional aggregate production function or growth-accounting study and then consider each of the aggregate factors in turn. That is, I consider separately the relative abundance or scarcity of "capital," of "land" (with land standing for all natural resources) and of "labor" (with labor including not only human capital in the form of skills and education, but also culture). I will also consider the level of technology separately, and I find some considerations and evidence that support the familiar assumption from growth-accounting studies and Solow-type growth theory that the same level of technological knowledge is given exogenously to all countries. With this conventional taxonomy and the assumption that societies are on the frontiers of their aggregate neoclassical production functions, we can derive important findings with a few simple deductions from familiar facts.

The next section shows that there is strong support for the familiar assumption that the world's stock of knowledge is available at little or no cost to all the countries of the world. I next examine the degree to which the marginal productivity of labor changes with large migrations and evidence on population densities, and I show that diminishing returns to land and other natural resources cannot explain much of the huge international differences in income. After that, I borrow some calculations from Robert Lucas on the implications of the huge differences across countries in capital intensity—and relate them to facts on the direction and magnitude of capital flows—to show that it is quite impossible that the countries of the world are anywhere near the frontiers of aggregate neoclassical production functions. I then examine some strangely neglected natural experiments with migrants from poor to rich countries to estimate the size of the differences in endowments of human capital between the poor and rich countries, and I demonstrate that they are able to account for only a small part of the international differences in the marginal product of labor.

Since neither differences in endowments of any of the three classical aggregate factors of production nor differential access to technology explain much of the great variation in per capita incomes, we are left with the second of the two (admittedly highly aggregated) possibilities set out above: that much the most important explanation of the differences in income across countries is the difference in their economic policies and institutions. There will not be room here to set out many of the other types of evidence supporting this conclusion, nor to offer any detailed analysis of what particular institutions and policies best promote economic growth. Nonetheless, by referring to other studies—and by returning to something that the theories with which we began overlook—we shall obtain some sense of why variations in institutions and policies are surely the main determinants of international differences in per capita incomes. We shall also obtain a faint glimpse of the broadest features of the institutions and policies that nations need to achieve the highest possible income levels.

The Access to Productive Knowledge

Is the world's technological knowledge generally accessible at little or no cost to all countries? To the extent that productive knowledge takes the form of un-patentable laws of nature and advances in basic science, it is a non-excludable public good available to everyone without charge. Nonpurchasers can, however, be denied access to many discoveries (in countries where intellectual property rights are enforced) through patents or copyrights, or because the discoveries are embodied in machines or other marketable products. Perhaps most advances in basic science can be of use to a poor country only after they have been combined with or embodied in some product or process that must be purchased from firms in the rich countries. We must, therefore, ask whether most of the gains from using modern productive knowledge in a poor country are mainly captured by firms in the countries that discovered or developed this knowledge.

Since those third world countries that have been growing exceptionally rapidly must surely have been adopting modern technologies from the first world, I tried (with the help of Brendan Kennelly) to find out how much foreign technologies had cost some such countries. As it happens, there is a study with some striking data for South Korea for the years from 1973 to 1979 (Koo, 1982). In Korea during these years, royalties and all other payments for dis-embodied technology were minuscule—often less than one-thousandth of GDP. Even if we treat all profits on foreign direct investment as solely a payment for knowledge and add them to royalties, the total is still less than 1.5 percent of the *increase* in Korea's GDP over the period. Thus the foreign owners of productive knowledge obtained less than a fiftieth of the gains from Korea's rapid economic growth.

The South Korean case certainly supports the long-familiar assumption that the world's productive knowledge is, for the most part, available to poor countries, and even at a relatively modest cost. It would be very difficult to explain much of the differences in per capita incomes across countries in terms of differential access to the available stock of productive knowledge.

Overpopulation and Diminishing Returns to Labor

Countries with access to the same global stock of knowledge may nonetheless have different endowments, which in turn might explain most of the differences in per capita income across countries. Accordingly, many people have supposed that the poverty in the poor countries is due largely to overpopulation, that is, to a low ratio of land and other natural resources to population. Is this true?

There is some evidence that provides a surprisingly persuasive answer to this question. I came upon it when I learned through Bhagwati (1984) of Hamilton and Whalley's (1984) estimates about how much world income would change if more workers were shifted from low-income to high-income countries. The key is to examine how much migration from poorer to richer countries *changes* relative wages and the marginal productivities of labor.

For simplicity, suppose that the world is divided into only two regions: North and South, and stick with the conventional assumption that both are on the frontiers of their aggregate production functions. As we move left to right from the origin of Figure 26.1, we have an ever larger workforce in the North until, at the extreme right end of this axis, all of the world's labor force is there. Conversely, as we move right to left from the right-hand axis, we have an ever larger workforce in the South. The marginal product of labor or wage in the rich North is measured on the vertical axis at the left of Figure 26.1. The curve MPL_N gives the marginal product or wage of labor in the North, and, of course, because of diminishing returns, it slopes downward as we move to the right. The larger the labor force in the South, the lower the marginal product of labor in the South, so MPL_S, measured on the right-hand vertical axis, slopes down as we move to the left. Each point on the horizontal axis will specify a distribution of the world's

Figure 26.1   Population Distribution and Relative Wages

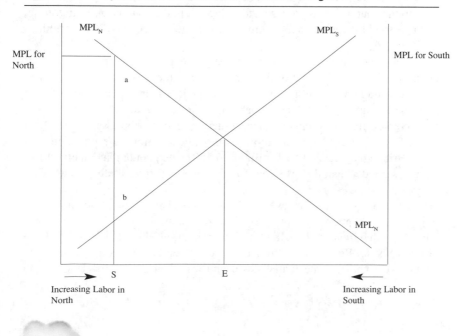

population between the North and the South. A point like S represents the status quo. At S, there is relatively little labor and population in relation to resources in the North, and so the Northern marginal product and wage are high. The marginal product and wage in the overpopulated South will be low, and the marginal product of labor in the North exceeds that in the South by a substantial multiple.

This model tells us that when workers migrate from the low-wage South to the high-wage North, world income goes up by the difference between the wage the migrant worker receives in the rich country and what that worker earned in the poor country, or by amount ab. Clearly, the world as a whole is not on the frontier of its aggregate production, even if all of the countries in it are: some big bills have not been picked up on the routes that lead from poor to rich countries. Of course, the argument that has just been made is extremely simple, and international migration involves many other considerations. We can best come to understand these considerations—as well as other matters— by staying with this simple factor proportions story a while longer.

The Surprising Results of Large Migrations

This elementary model reminds us that, if it is diminishing returns to land and other natural resources that mainly explain international differences in per capita incomes, then large migrations from poorer to richer societies will, if other things (like the stocks of capital) remain equal, necessarily reduce income differentials. Such migration obviously raises the resource-to-population ratio in the country of emigration and reduces it in the country of immigration, and if carried far enough will continue until wages are equalized, as at point E in Figure 26.1.

Now consider Ireland, the country that has experienced much of the highest proportion of outmigration in Europe, if not the world. In the census of 1821, Ireland had 5.4 million people, and Great Britain a population of 14.2 million. Though the Irish have experienced the same rates of natural population increase that have characterized other European peoples since 1821, in 1986, Ireland had only 3.5 million people. By this time, the population of Great Britain had reached 55.1 million. In 1821, the population density of Ireland was greater than that of Great Britain; by 1986, it was only about a fifth as great.

If the lack of "land" or overpopulation is decisive, Ireland ought to have enjoyed an exceptionally rapid growth of per capita income, at least in comparison with Great Britain, and the outmigration should eventually have ceased. Not so. Remarkably, the Irish level of per capita income is still only about five-eighths of the British level and less than half of the level in the

United States, and the outmigration from Ireland is still continuing. As we shall see later, such large disparities in per capita income cannot normally be explained by differences in human capital. It is clear that in the United States, Britain and many other countries, immigrants from Ireland tend to earn as much as other peoples, and any differences in human capital could not explain the *increase* in wage that migrants receive when they go to a more productive country. Thus we can be sure that it is not the ratio of land to labor that has mainly determined per capita income in Ireland.

Now let us took at the huge European immigration to the United States between the closing of the U.S. frontier in about 1890 and the imposition of U.S. immigration restrictions in the early 1920s. If diminishing returns to labor were a substantial part of the story of economic growth, this vast migration should have caused a gradual reduction of the per capita income differential between the United States and Europe. In fact, the United States had a bigger lead in per capita income over several European countries in 1910 and 1920 than it had in the nineteenth century. Although many European countries did *not* narrow the gap in per capita incomes with the United States in the nineteenth century when they experienced a large outmigration to the United States, many of these same countries did nearly close that gap in the years after 1945, when they had relatively little emigration to the United States, and when their own incomes ought to have been lowered by a significant inflow of migrants and guest workers. Similarly, from the end of World War II until the construction of the Berlin wall, there was a considerable flow of population from East to West Germany, but this flow did not equalize income levels.

Consider also the irrepressible flow of documented and undocumented migration from Latin America to the United States. If diminishing returns to land and other natural resources were the main explanation of the difference in per capita incomes between Mexico and the United States, these differences should have diminished markedly at the times when this migration was greatest. They have not.

Several detailed empirical studies of relatively large immigration to isolated labor markets point to the same conclusion as the great migrations we have just considered. Card's (1990) study of the Mariel boatlift's effect on the wages of natives of Miami, Hunt's (1992) examination of the repatriation of Algerian French workers to Southern France, and Carrington and De Lima's (1996) account of the repatriates from Angola and Mozambique after Portugal lost its colonies all suggest that the substantial immigration did not depress the wages of natives.

Perhaps in some cases the curves in Figure 26.1 would cross when there was little population left in a poor country. Or maybe they would not cross at all: even that last person who turned the lights out as he left would obtain a higher wage after migrating.

Surprising Evidence on Density of Population

Let us now shift focus from changes in land/labor ratios due to migration to the cross-sectional evidence at given points in time on ratios of land to labor. Ideally, one should have a good index of the natural resource endowments of each country. Such an index should be adjusted to take account of changes in international prices, so that the value of a nation's resources index would change when the prices of the resources with which it was relatively well endowed went up or down. For lack of such an index, we must here simply examine density of population. Fortunately, the number of countries on which we have data on population and area is so large that population density alone tells us something.

Many of the most densely settled countries have high per capita incomes, and many poor countries are sparsely settled. Argentina, a country that fell from having one of the highest per capita incomes to third world status, has only 11 persons per square kilometer; Brazil, 16; Kenya, 25; and Zaire, 13. India, like most societies with a lot of irrigated agriculture, is more densely settled, with 233 people per square kilometer. But high-income West Germany, with 246 people per square kilometer, is more densely settled than India. Belgium and Japan have half again more population density than India, with 322 and 325 people per square kilometer, and Holland has still more density with 357. The population of Singapore is 4,185 per square kilometer; that of Hong Kong, over 5,000 persons per square kilometer (United Nations, 1986). These two densely settled little fragments of land also have per capita incomes 10 times as high as the poorest countries (and as of this writing they continue, like many other densely settled countries, to absorb migrants, at least when the migrants can sneak through the controls).

The foregoing cases could be exceptions, so we need to take all countries for which data are available into account and summarily describe the overall relationship between population density and per capita income. If we remember that the purpose is description and are careful to avoid drawing causal inferences, we can describe the available data with a univariate regression in which the natural log of real per capita income is the left-hand variable, and the natural log of population per square kilometer is the "explanatory" variable. Obviously, the per capita income of a country depends on many things, and any statistical test that does not take account of all important determinants is misspecified, and thus must be used only for descriptive and heuristic purposes. It is nonetheless interesting—and for most people surprising—to find that there is a positive and even a statistically significant relationship between these two variables: the greater the number of people per square kilometer the higher per capita income.

The law of diminishing returns is indisputably true: it would be absurd to suppose that a larger endowment of land makes a country poorer. This consideration by itself would, of course, call for a negative sign on population density.

Thus, it is interesting to ask what might account for the "wrong" sign and to think of what statistical tests should ultimately be done. Clearly, there is a simultaneous two-way relationship between population density and per capita income: the level of per capita income affects population growth just as population, through diminishing returns to labor, affects per capita income.

The argument offered here suggests that perhaps countries with better economic policies and institutions come to have higher per capita incomes than countries with inferior policies and institutions, and that these higher incomes bring about a *higher population* growth through more immigration and lower death rates. In this way, the effect of better institutions and policies in raising per capita income swamps the tendency of diminishing returns to labor to reduce it. This hypothesis also may explain why many empirical studies have not been able to show a negative association between the rate of population growth and increases in per capita income.

One reason why the ratio of natural resources to population does not account for variations in per capita income is that most economic activity can now readily be separated from deposits of raw materials and arable land. Over time, transportation technologies have certainly improved, and products that have a high value in relation to their weight, such as most services and manufactured goods like computers and airplanes, may have become more important. The Silicon Valley is not important for the manufacture of computers because of deposits of silicon, and London and Zurich are not great banking centers because of fertile land. Even casual observation suggests that most modern manufacturing and service exports are not closely tied to natural resources. Western Europe does not now have a *high* ratio of natural resources to population, but it is very important in the export of manufactures and services. Japan has relatively little natural resources per capita, but it is a great exporter of manufactures. Certainly the striking successes in manufactures of Hong Kong and Singapore cannot be explained by their natural resources.

Diminishing Returns to Capital

We have seen that large migrations of labor do not change the marginal productivities of labor the way that they would if societies were at the frontiers of aggregate neoclassical production functions and that there is even evidence that labor is on average more *highly paid* where it is combined with less land. We shall now see that the allocation of capital across countries— and the patterns of investment and migration of capital across countries of *high and low* capital intensities—contradict the assumption that countries are on the frontiers of aggregate neoclassical production functions in an even more striking way.

This is immediately evident if we return to Figure 26.1 and relabel its coordinates and curves. If we replace the total world labor supply given along the horizontal axis of Figure 26.1 with the total world stock of capital and assume that the quantity of labor as well as natural resources in the North and South do not change, we can use Figure 26.1 to analyze diminishing returns to capital in the same way we used it to consider diminishing returns to labor.

As everyone knows, the countries with *high* per capita incomes have incomparably *higher capital* intensities of production than do those with low incomes. The countries of the third world use relatively little capital, and those of the first world are capital rich: most of the world's stock of capital is "crowded" into North America, western Europe and Japan.

If the countries of the world were on the frontiers of neoclassical production functions, the marginal product of capital would therefore be many times higher in the low-income than in the high-income countries. Robert Lucas (1990) has calculated, albeit in a somewhat different framework, the marginal product of capital that should be expected in the United States and in India. Lucas estimated that if an Indian worker and an American worker supplied the same quantity and quality of labor, the marginal product of capital in India should be 58 times as great as in the United States. Even when Lucas assumed that it took five Indian workers to supply as much labor as one U.S. worker, the predicted return to capital in India would still be a multiple of the return in the United States.

With portfolio managers and multinational corporations searching for more profitable investments for their capital, such gigantic differences in return should generate huge migrations of capital from the high-income to the low-income countries. Capital should be struggling at least as hard to get into the third world as labor is struggling to migrate into the high-wage countries. Indeed, since rational owners of capital allocate their investment funds across countries so that the risk-adjusted return at the margin is the same across countries, capital should be equally plentiful in all countries. (As we know from the Hecksher-Ohlin-Stolper-Samuelson discovery, if all countries operate on the same aggregate production functions, free trade alone is sometimes enough to equalize factor price ratios and thus factor intensities even in the absence of capital flows.)

Obviously, the dramatically uneven distribution of capital around the world contradicts the familiar assumption that all countries are on the frontiers of aggregate neoclassical production functions. A country could not be Pareto efficient and thus could not be on the frontier of its aggregate production unless it had equated the marginal product of capital in the country to the world price of capital. If it were not meeting this law-of-one-price condition, it would be passing up the gains that could come from borrowing capital abroad at the world rate of interest, investing it at home to obtain the higher marginal product of capital and pocketing the difference—it would be leaving large bills on the sidewalk. Accordingly, the strikingly unequal allocation of the world's stock of capital across nations proves that the poor countries cannot be anywhere near the frontiers of their aggregate production functions.

Sometimes the shortcomings of the economic policies and institutions of the low-income countries keep capital in these countries from earning rates of return appropriate to its scarcity, as we may infer from Harberger's (1978) findings and other evidence. Sometimes the shortcomings of the economic policies and institutions of poor countries make foreign investors and foreign firms unwelcome, or provoke the flight of locally owned capital, or make lending to these countries exceedingly risky. Whether the institutional and policy shortcomings of a country keep capital from having the productivity appropriate to its scarcity or discourage the investments and lending that would equalize the marginal product of capital across countries, they keep it from achieving its potential.

On top of all this, it is not rare for capital and labor to move *in the same direction:* both capital and labor are sometimes trying to move out of some countries and into some of the same countries. Of course, in a world where countries are on the frontiers of their aggregate production functions, capital and labor move in opposite directions.

Given the extraordinarily uneven allocation of capital across the countries of the world and the strong relationship between capital mobility and the economic policies and institutions of countries, the stock of capital cannot be taken to be exogenous in any reasonable theory of economic development.

Distinguishing Private Good and Public Good Human Capital

The adjustment of the amount of human capital per worker in Lucas's (1990) foregoing calculation for India and the United States raises a general issue: can the great differences in per capita income be mainly explained by differences in the third aggregate factor, labor, that is, by differences in the *human* capital per capita, broadly understood as including the cultural or other traits of different peoples as well as their skills? The average level of human capital in the form of occupational skills or education in a society can obviously influence the level of its per capita income.

Many people also argue that the high incomes in the rich countries are due in part to cultural or racial traits that make the individuals in these countries adept at responding to economic opportunities: they have the "Protestant ethic" or other cultural or national traits that are supposed to make them hard workers, frugal savers and imaginative entrepreneurs. Poor countries are alleged to be poor because they lack these traits. The cultural traits that perpetuate poverty are, it is argued, the results of centuries of social accumulation and cannot be changed quickly.

Unfortunately, the argument that culture is important for economic development, though plausible, is also vague: the word "culture," even though it is widely used in diverse disciplines, has not been defined precisely or in a way that permits comparison with other variables in an aggregate production function. We can obtain conceptions of culture that are adequate for the present purpose by breaking culture down into two distinct types of human capital.

Some types of human capital are obviously marketable: if a person has more skill, or a propensity to work harder, or a predilection to save more, or a more entrepreneurial personality, this will normally increase that individual's money income. Let us call these skills, propensities, or cultural traits that affect the quality or the quantity of productive inputs that an individual can sell in the marketplace "marketable human capital" or, synonymously, "personal culture." Max Weber's analysis of what he called the Protestant ethic was about marketable human capital or personal culture.

The second type of culture or human capital is evident when we think of knowledge that individuals may have about how they should vote: about what public policies will be successful. If enough voters acquire more knowledge about what the real consequences of different public policies will be, public policies will improve and thereby increase real incomes in the society. But this better knowledge of public policy is usually not marketable: in a society with given economic policies and institutions, the acquisition of such knowledge would not in general have any effect on an individual's wage or income. Knowledge about what public policy should be is a public good rather than a private or marketable good. Thus this second kind of human capital is "public good human capital" or "civic culture." Whereas marketable human capital or personal culture increases an individual's market income under given institutions and public policies, public good human capital or civic culture is not normally marketable and only affects incomes by influencing public policies and institutions.

With the aid of the distinction between marketable and public good human capital, we can gain important truths from some natural experiments.

Migration as an Experiment

As it happens, migration from poor to rich countries provides researchers with a marvelous (and so far strangely neglected) natural experiment. Typically, the number of individuals who immigrate to a country in any generation is too small to bring about any significant change in the electorate or public policies of the host country. But the migrant who arrives as an adult comes with the marketable human capital or personal culture of the country of origin; the Latin American who swims the Rio Grande is not thereby instantly baptized with the Protestant ethic. Though the migrant may in time acquire the culture of the host country, the whole idea behind the theories that emphasize the cultural or other characteristics of peoples is that it takes time to erase generations of socialization: if the cultural or other traits of a people could be changed overnight, they could not be significant barriers to development. Newly arrived immigrants therefore have approximately the same marketable human capital or personal culture they had before they migrated, but the institutions and public policies that determine the opportunities that they confront are those of the host country. In the case of the migration to the United States, at least, the data about newly arrived migrants from poor countries are sufficient to permit some immediate conclusions.

Christopher Clague (1991), drawing on the work of Borjas (1987), has found that individuals who had just arrived in the United States from poor countries, in spite of the difficulties they must have had in adjusting to a new environment with a different language and conditions, earned about 55 percent as much as native Americans of the same age, sex and years of schooling. New immigrants from countries where per capita incomes are only a tenth or a fifth as large as in the United States have a wage more than half as large as comparable American workers. Profit-maximizing firms would not have hired these migrants if they did not have a marginal product at least as large as their wage. The migrant's labor is, of course, combined with more capital in the rich than in the poor country, but it is not an accident that the owners of capital chose to invest it where they did: as the foregoing argument showed, the capital-labor ratio in a country is mainly determined by its institutions and policies.

Migrants might be more productive than their compatriots who did not migrate, so it might be supposed that the foregoing observations on immigrants are driven by selection bias. In fact, no tendency for the more productive people in poor countries to be more likely to emigrate could explain the huge increases in wages and marginal products of the migrants themselves. The migrant earns and produces much more in the rich country than in the poor country, so no tendency for migrants to be more productive than those who did not migrate could explain the increase in the migrant's marginal product when he or she moves from the poor to the rich country. In any event, developing countries often have much more unequal income distributions than developed nations, and the incentive to migrate from these countries is greatest in the least successful half of their income distributions. In fact, migrants to the United States are often drawn from the lower portion of the income distribution of underdeveloped countries (Borjas, 1990).

It is also instructive to examine the differences in productivity of migrants from poor countries with migrants from rich countries and then to see how much of the difference in per capita incomes in the countries of origin is likely to be due to the differences in the marketable human capital or personal culture of their respective peoples. Compare, for example, migrants to the United States from Haiti, one of the world's least successful economies, with migrants from West Germany, one of the most successful. According to the 1980 U.S. Census, self-employed immigrants from Haiti earned $18,900 per year, while those from West Germany earned $27,300; salaried immigrants from Haiti earned $10,900, those from West Germany, $21,900. Since the average Haitian immigrants earned only two-thirds or half as much as their West German counterparts in the same American environment, we may suspect that the Haitians had, on average, less marketable human capital than the West Germans.

So now let us perform the thought experiment of asking how much West Germans would have produced if they had the same institutions and economic policies as Haiti, or conversely how much Haitians would have produced had they had the same institutions and economic policies as West Germany. If we infer from the experience of migrants to the United States that West Germans have twice as much marketable capital as the Haitians, we can then suppose that Haiti with its present institutions and economic policies, but with West German levels of marketable human capital, would have about twice the per capita income that it has. But the actual level of Haitian per capita income is only about a tenth of the West German level, so Haiti would still, under our thought experiment, have less than one-fifth of the West German per capita income. Of course, if one imagines Haitian levels of marketable human capital operating with West German institutions and economic policies, one comes up with about half of the West German per capita income, which is again many times larger than Haiti's actual per capita income.

Obviously, one of the reasons for the great disparity implied by these thought experiments is the different amounts of tangible capital per worker in the two countries. Before taking this as given exogenously, however, the reader should consider investing his or her own money in each of these two countries. It is also possible that different selection biases for immigrants from different countries help account for the results of the foregoing thought experiments. Yet roughly the same results hold when one undertakes similar comparisons from migrants from Switzerland and Egypt, Japan and Guatemala, Norway and the Philippines, Sweden and Greece, the Netherlands and Panama, and so on. If, in comparing the incomes of migrants to the United States from poor and rich countries, one supposes that selection bias leads to an underestimate of the differences in marketable human capital between the poor and rich countries, and then makes a larger estimate of this effect than anyone is likely to think plausible, one still ends up with the result that the rich countries have vastly larger leads over poor countries in per capita incomes than can possibly be explained by differences in the marketable human capital of their populations. Such differences in personal culture can explain only a small part of the huge differences in per capita income between the rich and the poor countries.

History has performed some other experiments that lead to the same conclusion. During most of the postwar period, China, Germany and Korea have been divided by the accidents of history, so that different parts of nations with about the same culture and group traits have had different institutions and economic policies. The economic performances of Hong Kong and Taiwan, of West Germany and of South Korea have been incomparably better than the performances of mainland China, East Germany and North Korea. Such great differences in economic performance in areas of very similar cultural characteristics could surely not be explained by differences in the marketable human capital of the populations at issue.

It is important to remember that the foregoing experiments involving migration do not tell us anything about popular attitudes or prejudices in different countries regarding what public policy should be. That is, they do not tell us anything about the public good human capital or civic cultures of different peoples. As we know, the migrants from poor to rich countries are normally tiny minorities in the countries to which they migrate, so they do not usually change the public policies or institutions of the host countries. The natural experiments that we have just considered do not tell us what would happen if the civic cultures of the poor countries were to come to dominate the rich countries. For example, if traditional Latin American or Middle Eastern beliefs about how societies should be organized came to dominate North America or western Europe, institutions and economic policies—and then presumably also economic performance—would change.

The Overwhelming Importance of Institutions and Economic Policies

If what has been said so far is correct, then the large differences in per capita income across countries cannot be explained by differences in access to the world's stock of productive knowledge or to its capital markets, by differences in the ratio of population to land or natural resources, or by differences in the quality of marketable human capital or personal culture. Albeit at a high level of aggregation, this eliminates each of the factors of production as possible explanations of most of the international differences in per capita income. The only remaining plausible explanation is that the great differences in the wealth of nations are mainly due to differences in the quality of their institutions and economic policies.

The evidence from the national borders that delineate different institutions and economic policies not only contradicts the view that societies produce as much as their resource endowments permit, but also directly suggests that a country's institutions and economic policies are decisive for its economic performance. The very fact that the differences in per capita incomes across countries—the units with the different policies and institutions—are so large in relation to the differences in incomes across regions of the same country supports my argument. So does the fact that national borders sometimes sharply divide areas of quite different per capita incomes.

Old Growth Theory,
New Growth Theory and the Facts

The argument offered here also fits the relationships between levels of per capita income and rates of growth better than does either the old growth theory or the new. As has often been pointed out, the absence of any general tendency for the poor countries with their opportunities for catch-up growth to grow faster than the rich countries argues against the old growth theory. The new or endogenous growth models feature externalities that increase with investment or with stocks of human or tangible capital and can readily explain why countries with high per capita incomes can grow as fast or faster than low-income countries.

But neither the old nor the new growth theories predict the relationship that is actually observed: *the fast-growing countries are never the countries with the highest per capita incomes but always a subset of the lower-income countries.* At the same time that low-income countries as a whole fail to grow any faster than high-income countries, a subset of the lower-income countries grows far faster than *any* high-income country does. The argument offered here suggests that poor countries on average have poorer economic policies and institutions than rich countries, and, therefore, in spite of their opportunity for rapid catch-up growth, they need not grow faster on average than the rich countries.

But any poorer countries that adopt relatively good economic policies and institutions enjoy rapid catch-up growth: since they are far short of their potential, their per capita incomes can increase not only because of the technological and other advances that simultaneously bring growth to the richest countries, but also by narrowing the huge gap between their actual and potential income (Barro, 1991). Countries with the highest per capita incomes do not have the same opportunity.

Thus the argument here leads us to expect what is actually observed: no necessary connection between low per capita incomes and more rapid rates of growth, but much the highest rates of growth in a subset of low-income countries—the ones that adopt better economic policies and institutions. During the 1970s, for example, South Korea grew seven times as fast as the United States. During the 1970s, the four countries that (apart from the oil-exporting countries) had the fastest rates of growth of per capita income grew on average 6.9 percentage points faster per year than the United States—more than five times as fast. In the 1980s, the four fastest growers grew 5.3 percentage points faster per year than the United States—four times as fast. They outgrew the highest income countries as a class by similarly large multiples. All of the four of the fastest-growing countries in each decade were low-income countries.

In general, the endogenous growth models do not have anything in their structures that predicts that the most rapid growth will occur in a subset of low-income countries, and the old growth theory is contradicted by the absence of general convergence.

Note also that, as the gap in per capita incomes between the relatively poor and relatively rich countries has increased over time, poor countries have also fallen further behind their potential. Therefore, the argument offered here predicts that the maximum rate of growth that is possible for a poor country—and the rate at which it can gain on the highest per capita income countries—is increasing over time. This is also what has been observed. In the 1870s, the four continental European countries with the fastest growth of per capita incomes grew only 0.3 of 1 percent per annum faster than the United Kingdom. The top four such countries in the 1880s also had the same 0.3 percent gain over the United Kingdom. As we have seen, the top four countries in the 1970s grew 6.9 percentage points faster than the United States, and the top four in the 1980s, 5.3 percentage points faster. Thus, the lead of the top four in the 1970s was 23 times as great as the lead of the top four in the 1870s, and the lead of the top four in the 1980s was more than 17 times as great as the top four a century before.

Thus neither the old nor the new growth theory leads us to expect either the observed overall relationship between the levels and rates of growth of per capita incomes or the way this relationship has changed as the absolute gap in per capita incomes has increased over time. The present theory, by contrast, suggests that there should be patterns like those we observe.

Picking Up the Big Bills

The best thing a society can do to increase its prosperity is to wise up. This means, in turn, that it is very important indeed that economists, inside government and out, get things right. When we are wrong, we do a lot of harm. When we are right—and have the clarity needed to prevail against the special interests and the quacks—we make an extraordinary contribution to the amelioration of poverty and the progress of humanity. The sums lost because the poor countries obtain only a fraction of—and because even the richest countries do not reach—their economic potentials are measured in the trillions of dollars.

None of the familiar ideologies is sufficient to provide the needed wisdom. The familiar assumption that the quality of a nation's economic institutions and policies is given by the smallness, or the largeness, of its public sector—or by the size of its transfers to low-income people—does not fit the facts very well (Levine and Remit, 1992; Rubinson, 1977; Olson, 1986).

But the hypothesis that economic performance is determined mostly by the structure *of* incentives—and that it is mainly national borders that mark the boundaries of different structures of incentives—has far more evidence in its favor. This lecture has set out only one of the types of this evidence; there is also direct evidence of the linkage between better economic policies and institutions and better economic performance. Though it is not feasible to set out this direct evidence here, it is available in other writings (Clague, Keefer, Knack and Olson, 1995; Olson, 1982, 1987a, 1987b, 1990).

We can perhaps obtain a glimpse of another kind of logic and evidence in support of the argument here—and a hint about what kinds of institutions and economic policies generate better economic performance—by returning to the theories with which we began. These theories suggested that the rationality of the participants in an economy or the parties to a bargain implied that there would be no money left on the table. We know from the surprisingly good performance of migrants from poor countries in rich countries, as well as from other evidence, that there is a great deal of rationality, mother wit and energy among the masses of the poor countries: individuals in these societies can pick up the bills on the sidewalk about as quickly as we can.

The problem is that the really big sums cannot be picked up through uncoordinated individual actions. They can only be obtained through the efficient cooperation of many millions of specialized workers and other inputs: in other words, they can only be attained if a vast array of gains from specialization and trade are realized. Though the low-income societies obtain most of the gains from self-enforcing trades, they do not realize many of the largest gains from specialization and trade. They do not have the institutions that enforce contracts impartially, and so they lose most of the gains from those transactions (like those in the capital market) that require impartial third-party enforcement. They do not have institutions that make property rights secure over the long run, so they lose most of the gains from capital-intensive production. Production and trade in these societies is further handicapped by misguided economic policies and by private and public predation. The intricate social cooperation that emerges when there is a sophisticated array of markets requires far better institutions and economic policies than most countries have. The effective correction of market failures is even more difficult.

The spontaneous individual optimization that drives the theories with which I began is important, but it is not enough by itself. If spontaneous Coase-style bargains, whether through laissez faire or political bargaining and government, eliminated socially wasteful predation and obtained the institutions that are needed for a thriving market economy, then there would not be so many grossly inefficient and poverty stricken societies. The argument presented here shows that the bargains needed to create efficient societies are not, in fact, made. Though that is another story, I can show that in many cases such bargains are even logically inconsistent with rational individual behavior. Some important trends in economic thinking, useful as they are, should not blind us to a sad and all-too-general reality: as the literature on collective action demonstrates (Olson,

1965; Hardin, 1982; Sandler, 1992; and many others), individual rationality is very far indeed from being sufficient for social rationality.

References

Barro, Robert J., "Economic Growth in a Cross Section of Countries," *Quarterly Journal of Economics,* May 1991, 106:2, 407–43.

Becker, Gary, "A Theory of Competition Among Pressure Groups for Political Influence," *Quarterly Journal of Economics,* August 1983, 98, 371–400.

Becker, Gary, "Public Policies, Pressure Groups, and Dead Weight Costs," *Journal of Public Economics,* December 1985, 28:3, 329–47.

Bhagwati, Jagdish, "Incentives and Disincentives: International Migration," *Weltwirtschaftliches Archiv,* 1984, 120, 678–701.

Borjas, George, "Self-Selection and the Earnings of Immigrants," *American Economic Review,* September 1987, 77, 531–53.

Borjas, George, *Friends or Strangers: The Impact of Immigrants on the U.S. Economy.* New York: Basic Books, 1990.

Breton, A., "Toward a Presumption of Efficiency in Politics," *Public Choice,* September 1993, 77:1, 53–65.

Card, David, "The Impact of the Mariel Boatlift on the Miami Labor Market," *Industrial and Labor Relations Review,* January 1990, 43:2, 245–57.

Carrington, William J., and Pedro J. F. De Lima, "The Impact of 1970s Repatriates from Africa on the Portuguese Labor Market," *Industrial and Labor Relations Review,* January 1996, 49:2, 330–47.

Clague, Christopher, "Relative Efficiency, Self-Containment and Comparative Costs of Less Developed Countries," *Economic Development and Cultural Change,* April 1991, 39:3, 507–30.

Clague, Christopher, P. Keefer, S. Knack, and Mancur Olson, "Contract-Intensive Money: Contract Enforcement, Property Rights, and Economic Performance." IRIS Working Paper No. 151, University of Maryland, 1995.

Great Britain Central Statistical Office, *Annual Abstract of Statistics.* London: H.M.S.O., 1988.

Hamilton, Bob, and John Whalley, "Efficiency and Distributional Implications of Global Restrictions on Labour Mobility Calculations and Policy Implications," *Journal of Development Economics,* January/February 1984, 14, 61–75.

Harberger, Arnold, "Perspectives on Capital and Technology in Less Developed Countries." In Artis, M., and A. Nobay, eds., *Contemporary Economic Analysis.* London: Croom Helm, 1978, pp. 12–72.

Hardin, Russell, *Collective Action.* Baltimore: Johns Hopkins University Press, 1982.

Hunt, Jennifer, "The Impact of the 1962 Repatriates from Algeria on the French Labor Market," *Industrial and Labor Relations Review,* April 1992, 45:3, 556–72.

Ireland Central Statistics Office, *Statistical Abstract.* Dublin: Stationery Office, 1986.

Koo, Bohn-Young, "New Forms of Foreign Direct Investment in Korea." Korean Development Institute Working Paper No. 82-02, June 1982.

Krueger, Alan B., and Jörn-Steffen Pischke, "A Comparative Analysis of East and West German Labor Markets." In Freeman, Richard, and Lawrence Katz, eds., *Differences and Changes in Wage Structures.* Chicago: University of Chicago Press, 1995, pp. 405–45.

Landes, David, "Why Are We So Rich and They So Poor?," *American Economic Review,* May 1990, 80, 1–13.

Levine, Ross, and David Remit, "A Sensitivity Analysis of Cross-Country Growth Regressions," *American Economic Review,* September 1992, 82, 942–63.

Lucas, Robert, "Why Doesn't Capital Flow from Rich to Poor Countries?," *American Economic Review,* May 1990, 80, 92–96.

Mitchell, Brian R., *Abstract of British Historical Statistics.* Cambridge, UK: Cambridge University Press, 1962.

Mitchell, Brian R., and H. G. Jones, *Second Abstract of British Historical Statistics.* Cambridge, UK: Cambridge University Press, 1971.

Mokyr, Joel, *My Ireland Starved: A Quantitative and Analytical History of the Irish 1800–1850.* London and Boston: Allen & Unwin, 1983.

Olson, Mancur, *The Logic of Collective Action.* Cambridge: Harvard University Press, 1965.

Olson, Mancur, *The Rise and Decline of Nations.* New Haven: Yale University Press, 1982.

Olson, Mancur, "Supply-Side Economics, Industrial Policy, and Rational Ignorance." In Barfield, Claude E., and William A. Schambra, eds., *The Politics of Industrial Policy.* Washington: American Enterprise Institute for Public Policy Research, 1986, pp. 245–69.

Olson, Mancur, "Diseconomies of Scale and Development," *The Cato Journal,* Spring/Summer 1987a, 7:1, 77–97.

Olson, Mancur, "Economic Nationalism and Economic Progress, the Harry Johnson Memorial Lecture," *The World Economy,* September 1987b, 10:3, 241–64.

Olson, Mancur, "The IRIS Idea," IRIS, University of Maryland, 1990.

Olson, Mancur, "Transactions Costs and the Coase Theorem: Is This Most Efficient of All Possible Worlds?" Working paper, 1995.

Rubinson, Richard, "Dependency, Government Revenue, and Economic Growth, 1955–1970," *Studies in Comparative Institutional Development,* Summer 1977, 12:2, 3–28.

Sandler, Todd, *Collective Action.* Ann Arbor: University of Michigan Press, 1992.

Stigler, George J., "The Theory of Economic Regulation," *Bell Journal of Economics and Management Science,* Spring 1971, 2, 3–21.

Stigler, George J., "Law or Economics?," *The Journal of Law and Economics,* October 1992, 35:2, 455–68.

Thompson, Earl, and Roger Faith, "A Pure Theory of Strategic Behavior and Social Institutions," *American Economic Review,* June 1981, 71:3, 366–80.

United Nations, *Demographic Yearbook.* New York: United Nations, 1986.

Wittman, Donald, "Why Democracies Produce Efficient Results," *Journal of Political Economy,* December 1989, 97:6, 1395–424.

Wittman, Donald, *The Myth of Democratic Failure. Why Political Institutions Are Efficient.* University of Chicago Press, 1995.

27

Urban Bias and Inequality

Michael Lipton

*M*ichael Lipton is the principal advocate of the thesis that the
primary explanation for the internal gap between rich and poor
is "urban bias." He argues that even though leaders of developing
countries sympathize with the plight of the rural poor, they consistently
concentrate scarce development resources in the urban sector. The result
is that the urban sectors, which are already well-off in a comparative
sense, get an increasing share of national income, which exacerbates the
inequalities. In the book from which this chapter is drawn, Lipton tries
to show that it is in the interests of the elites of developing countries
to maintain this urban bias because they benefit directly from it. Critics
of Lipton's thesis claim that historically there has been a rural bias in
development and that much political power continues to reside in the
hands of the rural elite. One might also ask if there is anything about
the cultures found in developing nations that encourages policies
favoring one sector over another; rural or urban biases (if they truly
exist) might be a function of conditions estsablished by the international
environment.

THE MOST IMPORTANT CLASS CONFLICT IN THE POOR COUNTRIES OF THE
world today is not between labor and capital. Nor is it between foreign and national interests. It is between the rural classes and the urban classes. The rural

Reprinted with permission of Ashgate Publishing Ltd. from *Why Poor People Stay Poor: A Study of Urban Bias in World Development*, by Michael Lipton.

sector contains most of the poverty, and most of the low-cost sources of potential advance; but the urban sector contains most of the articulateness, organization, and power. So the urban classes have been able to "win" most of the rounds of the struggle with the countryside; but in so doing they have made the development process needlessly slow and unfair. Scarce land, which might grow millets and beansprouts for hungry villagers, instead produces a trickle of costly calories from meat and milk, which few except the urban rich (who have ample protein anyway) can afford. Scarce investment, instead of going into water-pumps to grow rice, is wasted on urban motorways. Scarce human skills design and administer, not village wells and agricultural extension services, but world boxing championships in showpiece stadia. Resource allocations, within the city and the village as well as between them, reflect urban priorities rather than equity or efficiency. The damage has been increased by misguided ideological imports, liberal and Marxian, and by the town's success in buying off part of the rural elite, thus transferring most of the costs of the process to the rural poor.

But is this urban bias really damaging? After all, since 1945 output per person in the poor countries has doubled; and this unprecedented growth has brought genuine development. Production has been made more scientific: in agriculture, by the irrigation of large areas, and more recently by the increasing adoption of fertilizers and of high-yield varieties of wheat and rice; in industry, by the replacement of fatiguing and repetitive effort by rising levels of technology, specialization and skills. Consumption has also developed, in ways that at once use and underpin the development of production; poor countries now consume enormously expanded provisions of health and education, roads and electricity, radios and bicycles. Why, then, are so many of those involved in the development of the Third World—politicians and administrators, planners and scholars—miserable about the past and gloomy about the future? Why is the United Nations' "Development Decade" of the 1960s, in which poor countries as a whole exceeded the growth target,[1] generally written off as a failure? Why is aid, which demonstrably contributes to a development effort apparently so promising in global terms, in accelerating decline and threatened by a "crisis of will" in donor countries?[2]

The reason is that since 1945 growth and development, in most countries, have done so little to raise the living standards of the poorest people. It is scant comfort that today's mass-consumption economies, in Europe and North America, also featured near-stagnant mass welfare in the early phases of their economic modernization. Unlike today's poor countries, they carried in their early development the seeds of mass consumption later on. They were massively installing extra capacity to supply their people with simple goods: bread, cloth, and coal, not just luxury housing, poultry, and airports. Also the nineteenth-century "developing countries," including Russia, were developing not just market requirements but class structures that practically guaranteed subsequent "trickling down" of benefits. The workers even proved able to raise their share of political power and economic welfare. The very preconditions of such trends are absent in most of today's developing countries. The sincere egalitarian rhetoric of, say, Mrs. Indira Gandhi or Julius Nyerere was—allowing for differences of style and ideology—closely paralleled in Europe during early industrial development: in Britain, for example, by Henry Brougham and Lord Durham in the 1830s.[3] But the rural masses of India and Tanzania, unlike the urban masses of Melbourne's Britain, lack the power to organize the pressure that alone turns such rhetoric into distributive action against the pressure of the elite.

Some rather surprising people have taken alarm at the persistently unequal nature of recent development. Aid donors are substantially motivated by foreign-policy concerns for the stability of recipient governments; development banks, by the need to repay depositors and hence to ensure a good return on the projects they support. Both concerns coalesce in the World Bank, which raises and distributes some £3,000 million of aid each year. As a bank it has advocated—and financed—mostly "bankable" (that is, commercially profitable) projects. As a channel for aid donors, it has concentrated on poor countries that are relatively "open" to investment, trade and economic advice from those donors. Yet the effect of stagnant mass welfare in poor countries, on the well-intentioned and perceptive people who administer World Bank aid, has gradually overborne these traditional biases. Since 1971 the president of the World Bank, Robert McNamara, has in a series of speeches focused attention on the stagnant or worsening lives of the bottom 40 percent of people in poor countries.[4] Recently this has begun to affect the World Bank's projects, though its incomplete engagement with the problem of urban bias restricts the impact. For instance, an urban-biased government will prepare rural projects less well than urban projects, will manipulate prices to render rural projects less apparently profitable (and hence less "bankable"), and will tend to cut down its own effort if donors step up theirs. Nevertheless, the World Bank's new concern with the "bottom 40 percent" is significant.

These people—between one-quarter and one-fifth of the people of the world—are overwhelmingly rural: landless laborers, or farmers with no more than an acre or two, who must supplement their incomes by wage labor. Most of these countryfolk rely, as hitherto, on agriculture lacking irrigation or fertilizers or even iron tools. Hence they are so badly fed that they cannot work efficiently, and in many cases are unable to feed their infants well enough to prevent physical stunting and perhaps even brain damage. Apart from the rote-learning of religious texts, few of them receive any schooling. One of four dies before the age of ten. The rest live the same overworked, underfed, ignorant, and disease-ridden lives as thirty, or three hundred, or three thousand years ago. Often they borrow (at 40 percent or more yearly interest) from the same moneylender families as their ancestors, and surrender half their crops to the same families of landlords.

Yet the last thirty years have been the age of unprecedented, accelerating growth and development! Naturally men of goodwill are puzzled and alarmed.

How can accelerated growth and development, in an era of rapidly improving communications and of "mass politics," produce so little for poor people? It is too simple to blame familiar scapegoats—foreign exploiters and domestic capitalists. Poor countries where they are relatively unimportant have experienced the paradox just as much as others. Nor, apparently, do the poorest families cause their own difficulties, whether by rapid population growth or by lack of drive. Poor families do tend to have more children than rich families, but principally because their higher death rates require it, if the aging parents are to be reasonably sure that a son will grow up, to support them if need be. And it is the structure of rewards and opportunities within poor countries that extracts, as if by force, the young man of ability and energy from his chronically stagnant rural background and lures him to serve, or even to join, the booming urban elite.

The disparity between urban and rural welfare is much greater in poor countries now than it was in rich countries during their early development. This huge welfare gap is demonstrably inefficient, as well as inequitable. It persists mainly because less than 20 percent of investment for development has gone to the agricultural sector (the situation has not changed much since 1965), although over 65 percent of the people of less-developed countries (LDCs), and over 80 percent of the really poor who live on $1 per week each or less, depend for a living on agriculture. The proportion of skilled people who support development—doctors, bankers, engineers—going to rural areas has been lower still; and the rural-urban imbalances have in general been even greater than those between agriculture and industry. Moreover, in most LDCs, governments have taken numerous measures with the unhappy side-effect of accentuating rural-urban disparities: their own allocation of public expenditure and taxation; measures raising the price of industrial production relative to farm production, thus encouraging private rural saving to flow into industrial investment because the value of industrial output has been artificially boosted; and educational facilities encouraging bright villagers to train in cities for urban jobs.

Such processes have been extremely inefficient. For instance, the impact on output of $1 of carefully selected investment is in most countries two to three times as high in agriculture as elsewhere, yet public policy and private market power have combined to push domestic savings and foreign aid into nonagricultural uses. The process has also been inequitable. Agriculture starts with about one-third the income per head as the rest of the economy, so that the people who depend on it should in equity receive special attention not special mulcting. Finally, the misallocation between sectors has created a needless and acute conflict between efficiency and equity. In agriculture the poor farmer with little land is usually efficient in his use of both land and capital, whereas power, construction, and industry often do best in big, capital-intensive units; and rural income and power, while far from equal, are less unequal than in the cities. So concentration on urban development and neglect of agriculture have pushed resources away from activities where they can help growth and benefit the poor, *and* toward activities where they do either of these, if at all, at the expense of the other.

Urban bias also increases inefficiency and inequity within the sectors. Poor farmers have little land and much underused family labor. Hence they tend to complement any extra developmental resources received—pumpsets, fertilizers, virgin land—with much more extra labor than do large farmers. Poor farmers thus tend to get most output from such extra resources (as well as needing the extra income most). But rich farmers (because they sell their extra output to the cities instead of eating it themselves, and because they are likely to use much of their extra income to support urban investment) are naturally favored by urban-biased policies; it is they, not the efficient small farmers, who get the cheap loans and the fertilizer subsidies. The patterns of allocation and distribution within the cities are damaged too. Farm inputs are produced inefficiently, instead of imported, and the farmer has to pay, even if the price is nominally "subsidized." The processing of farm outputs, notably grain milling, is shifted into big urban units and the profits are no longer reinvested in agriculture. And equalization between classes inside the cities becomes more risky, because the investment-starved farm sector might prove unable to deliver the food that a better-off urban mass would seek to buy.

Moreover, income in poor countries is usually more equally distributed within the rural sector than within the urban sector.[5] Since income creates the power to distribute extra income, therefore, a policy that concentrates on raising income in the urban sector will worsen inequalities in two ways: by transferring not only from poor to rich, but also from more equal to less equal. Concentration on urban enrichment is triply inequitable: because countryfolk start poorer; because such concentration allots rural resources largely to the rural rich (who sell food to the cities); and because the great inequality of power *within* the towns renders urban resources especially likely to go to the resident elites.

But am I not hammering at an open door? Certainly the persiflage of allocation has changed recently, under the impact of patently damaging deficiencies in rural output. Development plans are nowadays full of "top priority for agriculture."[6] This is reminiscent of the pseudo-egalitarian school where, at mealtimes, Class B children get priority, while Class A children get food.[7] We can see that the new agricultural priority is dubious from the abuse of the "green revolution" and of the oil crisis (despite its much greater impact on *industrial* costs) as pretexts for lack of emphasis on agriculture: "We don't need it," and "We can't afford it," respectively. And the 60 to 80 percent of people dependent on agriculture are still allocated barely 20 percent of public resources; even these small shares are seldom achieved; and they have, if anything, tended to diminish. So long as the elite's interests, background and sympathies remain predominantly urban, the countryside may get the "priority" but the city will get the resources. The farm sector will continue to be squeezed, both by transfers of resources from it by prices that are turned against it. Bogus justifications of urban bias will continue to earn the sincere, prestige-conferring, but misguided support of visiting "experts" from industrialized countries and international agencies. And development will be needlessly painful, inequitable and slow.

Notes

1. The UN target was a 5 percent yearly rate of "real" growth (that is, allowing for inflation) of total output. The actual rate was slightly higher.

2. Net aid from the donor countries comprising the Development Assistance Committee (DAC) of the Organization for Economic Cooperation and Development (OECD) comprises over 95 percent of all net aid to less-developing countries (LDCs). It fell steadily from 0.54 percent of donors' GNP in 1961 to 0.30 percent in 1973. The real value of aid per person in recipient countries fell by over 20 percent over the period. M. Lipton, "Aid Allocation When Aid is Inadequate," in T. Byres, ed., *Foreign Resources and Economic Development,* Cass, 1972, p. 158; OECD (DAC), *Development Cooperation* (1974 Review), p. 116.

3. L. Cooper, *Radical Jack,* Cresset, 1969, esp. pp. 183–97; C. New, *Life of Henry Brougham to 1830,* Clarendon, 1961, Preface.

4. See the mounting emphasis in his *Addresses to the Board of Governors,* all published by the International Bank for Reconstruction and Development, Washington; at Copenhagen in 1970, p. 20; at Washington in 1971, pp. 6–19, and 1972, pp. 8–15; and at Nairobi in 1973, pp. 10–14, 19.

5. M. Ahluwalia, "The Dimensions of the Problem," in H. Chenery et al., *Redistribution with Growth,* Oxford, 1974.

6. See K. Rafferty, *Financial Times,* 10 April 1974, p. 35, col. 5; M. Lipton, "Urban Bias and Rural Planning," in P. Streeten and M. Lipton, eds., *The Crisis of Indian Planning,* Oxford, 1968, p. 85.

7. F. Muir and D. Norden, "Common Entrance," in P. Sellers, *Songs for Swinging Sellers,* Parlophone PMC 111, 1958.

28

Political Regimes
and Economic Growth

Adam Przeworski and Fernando Limongi

In this chapter, Adam Przeworski and Fernando Limongi review the findings of eighteen articles that assess the relationship between regime type and economic growth. The authors show that the results have been inconclusive. According to Przeworski and Limongi, the confusion stems from the need for a more complex research design. Whereas the authors demonstrate that previous studies mistakenly attribute regime type as a cause of growth, they do not attempt to resolve the debate empirically. They state that ample evidence suggests that politics does affect growth, but they do not believe the debate over regime types captures the relevant differences between regimes that may be under investigation.

Arguments: How Democracy Might Affect Growth

Arguments that relate regimes to growth focus on property rights, pressures for immediate consumption, and the autonomy of dictators. While everyone seems to agree that secure property rights foster growth, it is controversial whether democracies or dictatorships better secure these rights. The main mechanism by which democracy is thought to hinder growth is pressures for immediate consumption, which reduce investment. Only states that are institutionally insulated from such pressures can resist them, and democratic states

Reprinted with permission of the American Economic Association from *Journal of Economic Perspectives* 7, no. 3 (Summer 1993).

are not. The main argument against dictatorships is that authoritarian rulers have no interest in maximizing total output. . . .

The Statistical Evidence

In one way, the critics and defenders of democracy talk past each other. The critics argue that dictatorships are better at mobilizing savings; the defenders that democracies are better at allocating investment. Both arguments can be true but, as we shall see, the statistical evidence is inconclusive and the studies that produced it are all seriously flawed.

Table 28.1 summarizes the 18 studies we examined. These generated 21 findings, since some distinguished areas or periods. Among them, eight found in favor of democracy, eight in favor of authoritarianism, and five discovered no difference. What is even more puzzling is that among the 11 results published before 1988, eight found that authoritarian regimes grew faster, while none of the nine results published after 1987 supported this finding. And since this difference does not seem attributable to samples or periods, one can only wonder about the relation between statistics and ideology.[1]

For reasons discussed below, we hesitate to attach much significance to these results one way or another. Hence, we still do not know what the facts are.

Inferences Based on
Standard Regression Models Are Invalid

The reason social scientists have little robust statistical knowledge about the impact of regimes on growth is that the research design required to generate such knowledge is complex. This complexity is due to three sources: simultaneity, attrition, and selection.

Following the seminal work of Lipset (1960), there is an enormous body of theoretical and statistical literature to the effect that democracy is a product of economic development. This literature suffers from ambiguities of its own. While the belief is widespread that democracy requires as a "prerequisite" some level of economic development, there is much less agreement which aspects of development matter and why. Some think that a certain level of development is required for a stable democracy because affluence reduces the intensity of distributional conflicts; others because development generates the education or the communication networks required to support democratic institutions; still others because it swells the ranks of the middle class, facilitates the formation of a competent bureaucracy, and so on. Statistical results are somewhat mixed (Lipset 1960; Cutright 1963; Neubauer 1967; Smith 1969;

Table 28.1   Studies of Democracy, Autocracy, Bureaucracy, and Growth

Author	Sample	Time Frame	Finding
Przeworksi (1966)	57 countries	1949–1963	dictatorships at medium development level grew fastest
Adelman and Morris (1967)	74 underdeveloped countries (including communist bloc)	1950–1968	authoritarianism helped less and medium developed countries
Dick (1974)	59 underdeveloped countries	1959–1968	democracies develop slightly faster
Huntington and Dominguez (1975)	35 poor nations	the 1950s	authoritarian grew faster
Marsh (1979)	98 countries	1955–1970	authoritarian grew faster
Weede (1983)	124 countries	1960–1974	authoritarian grew faster
Kormendi and Meguire (1985)	47 countries	1950–1977	democracies grew faster
Kohli (1986)	10 underdeveloped countries	1960–1982	no difference in 1960s; authoritarian slightly better in 1970s
Landau (1986)	65 countries	1960–1980	authoritarian grew faster
Sloan and Tedin (1987)	20 Latin American countries	1960–1979	bureaucratic-authoritarian regimes do better than democracy; traditional dictatorships do worse
Marsh (1988)	47 countries	1965–1984	no difference between regimes
Pourgerami (1988)	92 countries	1965–1984	democracies grew faster
Scully (1988, 1992)	115 countries	1960–1980	democracies grew faster
Barro (1989)	72 countries	1960–1985	democracies grew faster
Grier and Tullock (1989)	59 countries	1961–1980	democracy better in Africa and Latin America; no regime difference in Asia
Remmer (1990)	11 Latin American countries	1982–1988 1982 and 1988	democracy grew faster, but result statistically insignificant
Pourgerami (1991)	106 less developed countries	1986	democracies grew slower
Helliwell (1992)	90 countries	1960–1985	democracy has a negative, but statistically insignificant effect on growth

Hannan and Carroll 1981; Bollen and Jackman 1985; Soares 1987; Arat 1988; Helliwell 1992). They suggest that the level of development, measured by a variety of indicators, is positively related to the incidence of democratic regimes in the population of world countries, but not necessarily within particular regions. Moreover, the exact form of the relationship and its relation to regime stability are left open to debate. Yet the prima facie evidence in support of this hypothesis is overwhelming: all developed countries in the world constitute stable democracies while stable democracies in the less developed countries remain exceptional.

Attrition is a more complicated issue. Following Lipset again, everyone seems to believe that durability of any regime depends on its economic performance. Economic crises are a threat to democracies as well as to dictatorships. The probability that a regime survives a crisis need not be the same, however, for democracies and dictatorships: one reason is that under democracy it is easier to change a government without changing the regime, another is that democracies derive legitimacy from more than their economic performance. We also have the argument by Olson (1963; also Huntington 1968) that rapid growth is destabilizing for democracies but not for dictatorships.

This evidence suffices to render suspect any study that does not treat regimes as endogenous. If democratic regimes are more likely to occur at a higher level of development or if democracies and dictatorships have a different chance of survival under various economic conditions, then regimes are endogenously selected. Since this is the heart of the statistical difficulties, we spell out the nature of this problem in some detail. (The following discussion draws on Przeworski and Limongi 1992.)

We want to know the impact of regimes on growth. Observing Brazil in 1988, we discover that it was a democracy which declined at the rate of 2.06 percent. Would it have grown had it been a dictatorship? The information we have, the observation of Brazil in 1988, does not answer this question. But unless we know what would have been the growth of Brazil in 1988 had it been a dictatorship, how can we tell if it would have grown faster or slower than under democracy?

Had we observed in 1988 a Brazil that was simultaneously a democracy and a dictatorship, we would have the answer. But this is not possible. There is still a way out: if the fact that Brazil was a democracy in 1988 had nothing to do with economic growth, we could look for some country that was exactly like Brazil in all respects other than its regime and, perhaps, its rate of growth, and we could match this country with Brazil. But if the selection of regimes shares some determinants with economic growth, an observation that matches Brazil in all respects other than the regime and the rate of growth will be hard to find. And then the comparative inferences will be biased: Whenever observations are not generated randomly, quasi-experimental approaches yield inconsistent and biased estimates of the effect of being in a particular state on outcomes. Indeed, this much is now standard statistical wisdom, as evidenced in the vast literature reviewed by Heckman (1990), Maddala (1983), and Greene (1990). Yet the implications of this failure are profound: we can no longer use the standard regression models to make valid inferences from the observed to the unobserved cases. Hence, we cannot compare.

The pitfalls involved in the studies summarized above can be demonstrated as follows. Averaging the rates of growth of ten South American countries between 1946 and 1988, one discovers that authoritarian regimes grew at the average rate of 2.15 percent per annum while democratic regimes grew at 1.31

percent. Hence, one is inclined to conclude that authoritarianism is better for growth than democracy. But suppose that in fact regimes have no effect on growth. However, regimes do differ in their probabilities of surviving various economic conditions: authoritarian regimes are less likely than democracies to survive when they perform badly. In addition, suppose that the probability of survival of both regimes depends on the number of other democracies in the region at each moment. These probabilities jointly describe how regimes are selected: the dependence of survival on growth constitutes endogenous selection, the diffusion effect represents exogenous selection.

In Przeworski and Limongi (1992), we used the observed regime-specific conditional survival probabilities to generate 5,000 (500 per country) 43-year histories obeying these assumptions, each beginning with the level and the regime observed in 1945. As one would expect, authoritarian regimes grew faster than democracies—indeed, we reproduced exactly the observed difference in growth rates—despite the fact that these data were generated under the assumption that regimes have no effect on growth. It is the difference in the way regimes are selected—the probabilities of survival conditional on growth—that generate the observed difference in growth rates. Hence, this difference is due entirely to selection bias.[2]

If one applies ordinary least squares to data generated in this way, with a dummy variable set to 1 for Authoritarianism and 0 for Democracy, the regime coefficient turns out to be positive and highly significant. Thus standard regression fails the same way as the comparison of means, even with controls. To correct for the effect of selection, we followed the procedure developed by Heckman (1978) and Lee (1978). Once we corrected the effects of selection, we generated the unbiased means for the two regimes and these, not surprisingly, reproduced the assumptions under which the data were generated: no difference in growth between the two regimes.

These methodological comments should end with a warning. Selection models turn out to be exceedingly sensitive: minor modifications of the equation that specifies how regimes survive can affect the signs in the equations that explain growth. Standard regression techniques yield biased (and inconsistent) inferences, but selection models are not robust (Greene 1990, 750; Stolzenberg and Relles 1990). While reverting to simulation provides at least the assurance that one does not attribute to regimes the effects they do not have, it may still fail to capture the effects they do exert.

Conclusions

The simple answer to the question with which we began is that we do not know whether democracy fosters or hinders economic growth.[3] All we can offer at this moment are some educated guesses.

First, it is worth noting that we know little about determinants of growth in general. The standard neoclassical theory of growth was intuitively unpersuasive and it implied that levels of development should converge: a prediction not borne by the facts. The endogenous growth models are intuitively more appealing but empirically difficult to test since the "engine of growth" in these models consists, in Romer's (1992, 100) own words, of "ephemeral externalities." Statistical studies of growth notoriously explain little variance and are very sensitive to specification (Levine and Renelt 1991). And without a good economic model of growth, it is not surprising that the partial effect of politics is difficult to assess.

Secondly, there are lots of bits and pieces of evidence to the effect that politics in general does affect growth. At least everyone, governments and international lending institutions included, believes that policies affect growth and, in turn, scholars tend to think that politics affect policies. Reynolds (1983), having reviewed the historical experience of several countries, concluded that spurts of growth are often associated with major political transformations. Studies examining the impact of government spending on growth tend to find that the size of government is negatively related to growth, but the increase of government expenditures has a positive effect (Ram 1986; Lindauer and Velenchik 1992). Studies comparing the Far East with Latin America argue that there is something about the political institutions of the Asian countries which makes them propitious for growth. But while suggestive stories abound, there is little hard evidence.

Our own hunch is that politics does matter, but "regimes" do not capture the relevant differences. Postwar economic miracles include countries that had parliaments, parties, unions, and competitive elections, as well as countries run by military dictatorships. In turn, while Latin American democracies suffered economic disasters during the 1980s, the world is replete with authoritarian regimes that are dismal failures from the economic point of view.[4] Hence, it does not seem to be democracy or authoritarianism per se that makes the difference but something else.

What that something else might be is far from clear. "State autonomy" is one candidate, if we think that the state can be autonomous under democracy as well as under authoritarianism, as do Bardhan (1988, 1990) and Rodrik (1992). But this solution meets the horns of a dilemma: an autonomous state must be both effective at what it wants to do and insulated from pressures to do what it does not want to do. The heart of the neo-liberal research program is to find institutions that enable the state to do what it should but disable it from doing what it should not.

In our view, there are no such institutions to be found. In a Walrasian economy, the state has no positive role to play, so that the constitutional rule is simple: the less state, the better. But if the state has something to do, we would need institutions which enable the state to respond optimally to all contingent states of nature and yet prevent it from exercising discretion in the face of group pressures. Moreover, as Cui (1992) has argued, if markets are incomplete and information imperfect, the economy can function only if the state insures investors (limited liability), firms (bankruptcy), and depositors (two-tier banking system). But this kind of state involvement inevitably induces a soft-budget constraint. The state cannot simultaneously insure private agents and not pay the claims, even if they result from moral hazard.

Even if optimal rules do exist, pre-commitment is not a logically coherent solution. The reason is that just any commitment is not good enough: it must be a commitment to an optimal program. And advocates of commitment (like Shepsle 1989) do not consider the political process by which such commitments are established. After all, the same forces that push the state to suboptimal discretionary interventions also push the state to a suboptimal commitment. Assume that the government wants to follow an optimal program and it self-commits itself. At the present it does not want to respond to private pressures but it knows that in the future it would want to do so; hence, it disables its capacity to do it. The model underlying this argument is Elster's (1979) Ulysses.[5] But the analogy does not hold since Ulysses makes his decision *before* he hears the Sirens. Suppose that he has already heard them: why does he not respond to their song now and is afraid that he would respond later? If governments do bind themselves, it is already in response to the song of the Sirens and their pre-commitment will not be optimal.

Clearly, the impact of political regimes on growth is wide open for reflection and research.

Notes

1. Indeed, it is sufficient to read Scully (1992, xiii–xiv) to stop wondering: "The Anglo-American paradigm of free men and free markets unleashed human potential to an extent unparalled in history. . . . One needs evidence to persuade those who see promise in extensive government intervention in the economy. I have found such evidence, and the evidence is overwhelmingly in favor of the paradigm of classical liberalism." The evidence on the effect of democracy on growth consists of cross-sectional OLS regressions in which investment is controlled for, so that political effects measure efficiency but not the capacity to mobilize savings.

2. We could have gotten the same result in a different way. Suppose that (1) levels converge, that is, growth is a negative function of income, and (2) dictatorships occur at low levels while democracies are more frequent at high levels. Then we will observe fast growing dictatorships (at low levels) and slowly growing democracies (at high levels).

3. Note that we considered only indirect impacts of regimes on growth via investment and the size of the public sector, but we did not consider the impacts via income equality, technological change, human capital, or population growth.

4. As Sah (1991) has argued, authoritarian regimes exhibit a higher variance in economic performance than democracies: President Park of South Korea is now seen

as a developmentalist leader, while President Mobutu of Zaire is seen as nothing but a thief (Evans 1989). But we have no theory that would tell us in advance which we are going to get. We do know, in turn, that until the early 1980s the democratic regimes which had encompassing, centralized unions combined with left-wing partisan control performed better on most economic variables than systems with either decentralized unions or right-wing partisan dominance.

5. Note that Elster (1989, 196) himself argues against the analogy of individual and collective commitment.

References

Adelman, Irma, and Cynthia Morris. 1967. *Society, Politics and Economic Development*. Baltimore: Johns Hopkins University Press.

Alesina, Alberto, and Dani Rodrik. 1991. "Distributive Politics and Economic Growth," National Bureau of Economic Research, Working Paper No. 3668.

Amsden, Alice H. 1989. *Asia's Next Giant: South Korea and Late Industrialization*. New York: Oxford University Press.

Arat, Zehra F. 1988. "Democracy and Economic Development: Modernization Theory Revisited," *Comparative Politics,* October, 21:1, 21–36.

Bardhan, Pranab. 1988. "Comment on Gustav Ranis' and John C. H. Fei's 'Development Economics: What Next?'" In Ranis, Gustav, and T. Paul Schultz, eds., *The State of Development Economics: Progress and Perspectives*. Oxford: Basil Blackwell, pp. 137–38.

Bardhan, Pranab. 1990. "Symposium on the State and Economic Development," *Journal of Economic Perspectives,* Summer, 4:3, 3–9.

Barro, Robert J. 1989. "A Cross-country Study of Growth, Saving, and Government," NBER Working Paper No. 2855.

Barro, Robert J. 1990. "Government Spending in a Simple Model of Endogenous Growth," *Journal of Political Economy,* October, 98:5, S103–S125.

Becker, Gary S. 1983. "A Theory of Competition Among Pressure Groups for Political Influence," *Quarterly Journal of Economics,* August, 98:3, 371–400.

Bollen, K. A., and R. W. Jackman. 1985. "Economic and Noneconomic Determinants of Political Democracy in the 1960s," *Research in Political Sociology,* 1, 27–48.

Collini, Stefan, Donald Winch, and John Burrow. 1983. *That Noble Science of Politics*. Cambridge: Cambridge University Press.

Crain, W. Mark. 1977. "On the Structure and Stability of Political Markets," *Journal of Political Economy,* August, 85:4, 829–42.

Cui, Zhiyuan. 1992. "Incomplete Markets and Constitutional Democracy," manuscript, University of Chicago.

Cutright, Philips. 1963. "National Political Development: Measurement and Analysis," *American Sociological Review,* 28, 253–64.

de Schweinitz, Karl Jr. 1959. "Industrialization, Labor Controls and Democracy," *Economic Development and Cultural Change,* July, 385–404.

de Schweinitz, Karl Jr. 1964. *Industrialization and Democracy*. New York: Free Press.

Dick, William G. 1974. "Authoritarian Versus Nonauthoritarian Approaches to Economic Development," *Journal of Political Economy,* July/August, 82:4, 817–27.

Dore, Ronald. 1978. "Scholars and Preachers." *IDS Bulletin*. Sussex, U.K.: International Development Studies, June.

Downs, Anthony. 1957. *An Economic Theory of Democracy.* New York: Harper and Row.

Elster, Jon. 1979. *Ulysses and the Sirens: Studies in Rationality and Irrationality.* Cambridge: Cambridge University Press.

Elster, Jon. 1989. *Solomonic Judgements. Studies in the Limitations of Rationality.* Cambridge: Cambridge University Press.

Elster, Jon, and Karl Ove Moene, eds. 1989. "Introduction." In *Alternatives to Capitalism.* Cambridge: Cambridge University Press, 1–38.

Evans, Peter B. 1989. "Predatory, Developmental, and Other Apparatuses: A Comparative Political Economy Perspective on the Third World State," *Sociological Forum,* December, 4:4, 561–87.

Fernandez, Raquel, and Dani Rodrick. 1991, "Resistance to Reform; Status Quo Bias in the Presence of Individual-Specific Uncertainty," *American Economic Review,* December, 81:5, 1146–55.

Findlay, Ronald. 1990. "The New Political Economy: Its Explanatory Power for the LDCS," *Economics and Politics,* July, 2:2, 193–221.

Galenson, Walter. 1959. "Introduction" to Galenson, W., ed. *Labor and Economic Development.* New York: Wiley.

Galenson, Walter, and Harvey Leibenstein. 1955. "Investment Criteria, Productivity and Economic Development," *Quarterly Journal of Economics,* August, 69, 343–70.

Gereffi, Gary, and Donald L. Wyman, eds. 1990. *Manufacturing Miracles: Paths of Industrialization in Africa and East Asia.* Princeton: Princeton University Press.

Greene, William H. 1990. *Econometric Analysis.* New York: Macmillan.

Grier, Kevin B., and Gordon Tullock. 1989. "An Empirical Analysis of Cross-national Economic Growth, 1951–80," *Journal of Monetary Economics,* September, 24:2, 259–76.

Haggard, Stephan. 1990. *Pathways from Periphery: The Politics of Growth in the Newly Industrializing Countries.* Ithaca: Cornell University Press.

Hannan, M. T., and G. R. Carroll. 1981. "Dynamics of Formal Political Structure: An Event-History Analysis," *American Sociological Review,* February, 46:1, 19–35.

Heckman, James J. 1978. "Dummy Endogenous Variables in a Simultaneous Equation System," *Econometrica,* July, 46:4, 931–59.

Heckman, James J. 1990. "Selection Bias and Self-selection." In Eatwell, John, Murray Milgate, and Peter Newman, eds., *The New Palgrave Econometrics.* New York: W. W. Norton, 287–97.

Helliwell, John F. 1992. "Empirical Linkages Between Democracy and Economic Growth," NBER Working Paper #4066. Cambridge: National Bureau of Economic Research.

Huntington, Samuel P. 1968. *Political Order in Changing Societies.* New Haven: Yale University Press.

Huntington, Samuel P., and Jorge I. Dominguez. 1975. "Political Development." In Greenstein, F. I., and N. W. Polsby, eds., *Handbook of Political Science,* 3. Reading: Addison-Wesley, 1–114.

Kaldor, Nicolas. 1956. "Alternative Theories of Distribution," *Review of Economic Studies,* 23:2, 83–100.

Kohli, Atul. 1986. "Democracy and Development." In Lewis, John P., and Valeriana Kallab, eds., *Development Strategies Reconsidered.* New Brunswick: Transaction Books, 153–82.

Kormendi, Roger C., and Philip G. Meguire. 1983. "Macroeconomic Determinants of Growth: Cross-Country Evidence," *Journal of Monetary Economics,* September, 162: 141–63.

Landau, Daniel. 1986. "Government and Economic Growth in the Less Developed Countries: An Empirical Study for 1960–1980," *Economic Development and Cultural Change,* October, 35:1, 35–75.

Lee, L. F. 1978. "Unionism and Wage Rates: A Simultaneous Equations Model with Qualitative and Limited Dependent Variables," *International Economic Review,* June, 19:2, 415–33.

Levine, Ross, and David Renelt. 1991. "A Sensitivity Analysis of Cross-country Growth Regressions," World Bank Working Paper WPS 609.

Lindauer, David L., and Ann D. Velenchik. 1992. "Government Spending in Developing Countries: Trends, Causes, and Consequences," *World Bank Research Observer,* January, 7:1. Washington, D.C.: The World Bank, 59–78.

Lipset, Seymour M. 1960. *Political Man.* Garden City: Doubleday, 1960.

Macaulay, Thomas B. 1900. *Complete Writings,* 17. Boston and New York: Houghton-Mifflin.

Maddala, G. S. 1983. *Limited-Dependent and Qualitative Variables in Econometrics.* Cambridge: Cambridge University Press.

Marsh, Robert M. 1979. "Does Democracy Hinder Economic Development in the Latecomer Developing Nations?" *Comparative Social Research,* 2:2, 215–48.

Marsh, Robert M. 1988. "Sociological Explanations of Economic Growth," *Studies in Comparative International Development,* Winter, 23:4, 41–76.

Marx, Karl. 1934. *The Eighteenth Brumaire of Louis Bonaparte.* Moscow: Progress Publishers.

Marx, Karl. 1952. *The Class Struggle in France, 1848 to 1850.* Moscow: Progress Publishers.

Marx, Karl. 1971. *Writings on the Paris Commune.* Edited by H. Draper. New York: International Publishers.

Neubauer, Deane E. 1967. "Some Conditions of Democracy," *American Political Science Review,* December, 61:4, 1002–9.

North, Douglass C. 1990. *Institutions, Institutional Change and Economic Performance.* Cambridge, U.K.: Cambridge University Press.

North, Douglass C., and Robert Paul Thomas. 1973. *The Rise of the Western World: A New Economic History.* Cambridge, U.K.: Cambridge University Press.

North, Douglass C., and Barry R. Weingast. 1989. "Constitutions and Commitment: The Evolution of Institutions Governing Public Choice in Seventeenth-Century England," *Journal of Economic History,* December, 49:4, 803–32.

O'Donnell, Guillermo. 1973. *Modernization and Bureaucratic-Authoritarianism.* Berkeley: UC Berkeley Press.

Olson, Mancur, Jr. 1963. "Rapid Growth as a Destabilizing Force," *Journal of Economic History,* December, 23, 529–52.

Olson, Mancur, Jr. 1991. "Autocracy, Democracy and Prosperity." In Zeckhauser, Richard J., ed., *Strategy and Choice.* Cambridge: MIT Press, 131–57.

Pasinetti, Luigi. 1961-62. "Rate of Profit and Income Distribution in Relation to the Race of Economic Growth," *Review of Economic Studies,* October, 29:81, 267–79.

Persson, Torsten, and Guido Tabellini. 1991. "Is Inequality Harmful for Growth? Theory and Evidence." Working paper No. 91-155, Department of Economics, University of California, Berkeley.

Pourgerami, Abbas. 1988. "The Political Economy of Development: A Cross-national Causality Test of Development-Democracy-Growth Hypothesis," *Public Choice,* August, 58:2, 123–41.

Pourgerami, Abbas. 1991. "The Political Economy of Development: An Empirical Investigation of the Wealth Theory of Democracy," *Journal of Theoretical Politics,* April, 3:2, 189–211.

Przeworski, Adam. 1966. *Party Systems and Economic Development*. Ph.D. dissertation. Northwestern University.

Przeworski, Adam. 1990. *The State and the Economy Under Capitalism: Fundamentals of Pure and Applied Economics*, 40. Chur, Switzerland: Harwood Academic Publishers.

Przeworski, Adam, and Fernando Limongi. 1992. "Selection, Counterfactuals and Comparisons," manuscript, Department of Political Science, University of Chicago.

Przeworski, Adam, and Michael Wallerstein. 1988. "Structural Dependence of the State on Capital," *American Political Science Review*, March, 82:1, 11–29.

Ram, Rati. 1986. "Government Size and Economic Growth: A New Framework and Some Evidence from Cross-Section and Time-Series Data," *American Economic Review*, March, 76:1, 191–203.

Rao, Vaman. 1984. "Democracy and Economic Development," *Studies in Comparative International Development*, Winter, 19:4, 67–81.

Remmer, Karen. 1990. "Democracy and Economic Crisis: The Latin American Experience," *World Politics*, April, 42:3, 315–35.

Reynolds, Lloyd G. 1983. "The Spread of Economic Growth to the Third World: 1850-1980," *Journal of Economic Literature*, September, 21:3, 941–80.

Rodrik, Dani. 1992. "Political Economy and Development Policy," *European Economic Review*, April, 36:2/3, 329–36.

Romer, Paul. 1992. "Increasing Returns and New Developments in the Theory of Growth." In Barnett, W. A., ed., *Equilibrium Theory and Applications*. New York: Cambridge University Press, 83–110.

Sah, Raaj K. 1991. "Fallibility in Human Organizations and Political Systems," *Journal of Economic Perspectives*, Spring, 5:2, 67–88.

Schepsle, Kenneth. 1989. "Studying Institutions: Some Lessons from the Rational Choice Approach," *Journal of Theoretical Politics*, April, 1:2, 131–49.

Scully, Gerald W. 1988. "The Institutional Framework and Economic Development," *Journal of Political Economy*, June, 96:3, 652–62.

Scully, Gerald W. 1992. *Constitutional Environments and Economic Growth*. Princeton: Princeton University Press.

Sloan, John, and Kent L. Tedin. 1987. "The Consequences of Regimes Type for Public-Policy Outputs," *Comparative Political Studies*, April, 20:1, 98–124.

Smith, Arthur K. Jr. 1969. "Socio-economic Development and Political Democracy: A Causal Analysis," *Midwest Journal of Political Science*, 13: 95–125.

Soares, G. A. D. 1987. "Desenvolvimento Economico e Democracia na America Latina," *Dados*, 30:3, 253–74.

Stolzenberg, Ross M., and Daniel A. Relles. 1990. "Theory Testing in a World of Constrained Research Design," *Sociological Methods and Research*, May, 18:4, 395–415.

Wade, Robert. 1990. *Governing the Market: Economic Theory and the Role of Government in West Asian Industrialization*. Princeton: Princeton University Press, 1990.

Weede, Erich. 1983. "The Impact of Democracy on Economic Growth: Some Evidence from Cross-National Analysis," *Kyklos*, 36:1, 21–39.

Westphal, Larry E. 1990. "Industrial Policy in an Export-Propelled Economy: Lessons from South Korea's Experience," *Journal of Economic Perspectives*, Summer, 4:3, 41–60.

Wittman, Donald. 1989. "Why Democracies Produce Efficient Results," *Journal of Political Economy*, December, 97:6, 1395–1424.

World Bank. 1987. *World Development Report*. Washington, DC: The World Bank.

29

Inequality as a Constraint on Growth in Latin America

Nancy Birdsall and Richard Sabot

This chapter presents strong evidence that inequality and slow growth in the Third World are not inevitable but are the direct outcome of choices made by governments. The chapter contrasts Latin America, where growth has been slow and inequality high, with East Asia, where growth has been extremely rapid and inequality very low. The empirical research on which the chapter is based demonstrates that large investments in education in East Asia help to explain a "virtuous circle" that leads to both higher growth and greater equality, whereas the low and stagnating investment in education in Latin America creates an opposite "vicious circle." Human capital investment is what sets East Asia apart from Latin America, a lesson many developing countries need to learn.

THE CONVENTIONAL WISDOM HAS BEEN THAT THERE IS A TRADEOFF BE-tween augmenting growth and reducing inequality, so that an unequal distribution of income is necessary for, or the likely consequence of, rapid economic growth. If this is so, however, why do we find in Latin America relatively low rates of economic growth and high inequality, and in East Asia low inequality and rapid growth? Figure 29.1 shows rates of GNP growth for the period 1965 to 1989 and levels of income inequality in the mid-1980s (measured by the

Reprinted with permission from David Turnham, Colm Foy, and Guillermo Larrain, eds., *Social Tensions, Job Creation and Economic Policy in Latin America* (Washington, DC: OECD, 1995).

Figure 29.1   Income Inequality and Growth of GDP, 1965–1989

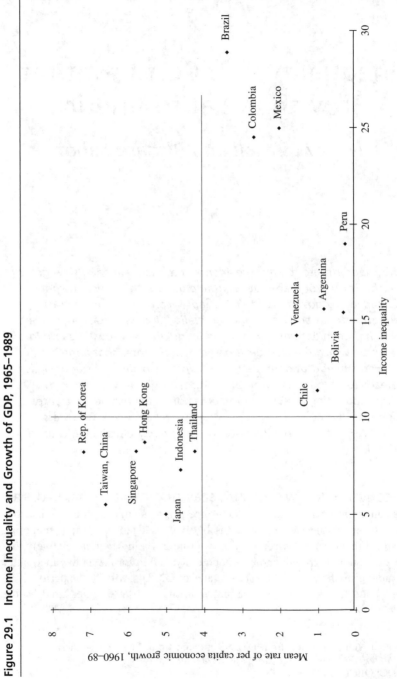

Source: World Bank, 1993. *The East Asian Miracle: Economic Growth and Public Policy.*

ratio of the income shares of the top and bottom quintiles) for Latin American and East Asian countries. The difference between the two regions is striking: Latin American countries, concentrated in the southeast corner, experienced slow or negative growth with high inequality, while East Asian countries, concentrated in the northwest corner, achieved rapid growth with low inequality.

Differences in the political economy of the two regions may be part of the explanation. In the postwar period, governing elites in East Asia, their legitimacy threatened by domestic communist insurgents, sought to widen the base of their political support via policies such as land reform, public housing, investment in rural infrastructure, and, most common, widespread high-quality basic education. In Latin America governing elites appear to have believed they could thrive irrespective of what happened to those with the lowest incomes since tax, expenditure, and trade policies benefitted the poor relatively little. For example, East Asia's export oriented, labor-demanding development strategy contributed to rapid growth of output and, by increasing employment opportunities and wages, ensured that the benefits of that growth were widely shared. In contrast, Latin America's strategy tended to be biased against both agriculture and exports, resulting in relatively slow growth in the demand for labor. . . .

The association of slow growth and high inequality in Latin America could in part be due to the fact that high inequality itself may be a constraint on growth. Conversely, East Asia's low level of inequality may have been a significant stimulus to economic growth. If so, investment in education is a key to a sustained growth not only because it contributes directly through productivity effects, but also because it reduces income inequality.

Econometric Results

To assess the impact of the distribution of income on subsequent economic growth we regressed the growth rate of real per capita income of 74 developing countries over the period 1960–85 on determinants of growth such as per capita GDP and education enrollments at the start of the period and on a measure of income inequality, the ratio of the income shares of the top 40 percent and the bottom 20 percent. We found that inequality and growth are in fact inversely related: countries with higher inequality tend to have lower growth.

How big a constraint on growth is high inequality? It is substantial. The results suggest that ceteris paribus, after 25 years, GDP per capita would be 8.2 percent higher in a country with low inequality than in a country with inequality one standard deviation higher. How big was the constraint of high inequality in Latin America? The ratio of the income shares of the top 20 percent to the bottom 20 percent is 26 in Brazil and 8 in Korea. Simulations suggest that if, in 1960, Brazil had had Korea's lower level of inequality Brazil's predicted growth rate over the following 25 years would have been 0.66 percentage points higher each year. This implies that after 25 years GDP per capita in Brazil would have been 17.2 percent higher.

Poor Educational Performance, Slow Growth, and High Inequality in Latin America

Differences in educational performance help to explain why Latin America experienced relatively low rates of growth and high inequality while East Asia experienced high rates of growth and low inequality. Most countries in East Asia have significantly higher primary and secondary enrollment rates than predicted based on their per capita income; most Latin American countries have rates at or below those predicted. Moreover, where enrollment rates are low, as in Brazil and Guatemala, children of the poor are the least likely to be enrolled, perpetuating high income inequality.

Furthermore, in contrast to East Asia, where increases in quantity were associated with improvements in the quality of education, expansion of enrollments in many Latin American countries has resulted in the erosion of quality. In Brazil, the expansion of primary school coverage has been associated with declines in completion rates—probably a sign of failure to raise quality. By contrast, in East Asian countries, as quantity increased completion rates remained high. Declines in quality also tend to hurt the poor most, since they are least able to use private schools or change residence.

Education and Growth

Human capital theory says that education augments cognitive and other skills of individuals which, in turn, augment their productivity as workers. Our growth rate functions show that this accumulation of skills at the individual level translates into higher economic growth at the country level. Our statistical work also shows that increasing primary-school enrollments for girls, though they are less likely to become formal workers, is just as effective in stimulating growth as increasing primary enrollments for boys.

The reason: the economic payoff to educating girls is not confined to increases in the productivity of wage labor. It works through changes in behavior within households. For example, educated mothers have fewer children. Closing a virtuous circle, the fertility decline in East Asia that started in the mid-1960s resulted in a marked slowing of the growth of the school-age population in the 1970s. This made it easier to increase public expenditures on basic education per child, permitting rapid increases in the quantity of schooling as well as improvements in the quality of schools. . . .

Although fertility rates in Latin America have declined during the past two decades, they remain high relative to East Asian rates, particularly in the

poorer countries. High fertility has placed added stress on already strained resources for education; per child spending on books, equipment, and teacher
training in Latin America has declined. Declines in per-child spending in the
region (from an estimated $164 per primary school child in 1980 to $118 in
1989) have probably contributed to declines in school quality and continued
high repetition—the highest in the world—and high dropout rates. Between
1970 and 1990 expenditure on basic education per eligible child increased by
350 percent in Korea and 64 percent in Mexico. During the same period, the
number of eligible children increased by 59 percent in Mexico, in Korea the
number of eligible children actually declined by 27 percent. . . .

In addition, Latin America missed out on the positive feedback between
rapid growth and household behavior with respect to human-capital accumulation. Investment in human capital by households is greater in East Asia than
in Latin America in part because the demand for educated workers is greater,
and consequently the returns to the household of investment in schooling are
higher. In other words, stronger demand for educated workers elicits a greater
supply. Furthermore, rapid economic growth in East Asia increased the numer-
ator, while declining fertility reduced the denominator, of the ratio of public
expenditures on basic education per school-age child. Neither in 1960 nor in
1989 was public expenditure on education as a percentage of GNP much
higher in East Asia than in Latin America. However, it is obvious that the more
rapid the growth of aggregate output, the more rapid the growth of the constant
share of GDP that goes to education.

Education and Inequality

In Korea the proportion of high school and postsecondary graduates in the
wage-labor force sharply increased between the mid-1970s and the mid-1980s,
and the proportion of workers with elementary schooling or less declined to
just 8 percent. As a consequence, the wage premium earned by educated workers in Korea declined. In Brazil the increment to the labor force of relatively
well-educated workers was so small that it did not take much of an increase in
the demand for educated workers to offset any wage compression effect of the
increase in supply. As a result, the educational structure of wages barely
changed in Brazil. What would the inequality of pay in Brazil have been had
educational policy resulted in educational attainment comparable to that in
Korea in the mid-1980s? Simulations indicate that Brazil would have had a log
variance of wages in the mid-1980s some 17 percent lower than the actual.
This 17 percent reduction represents over one-quarter of the gap between
Brazil and Korea in the log variance of wages.

In Latin America there has also been a feedback effect, one that closed a vicious circle from high inequality to low enrollment rates. High income inequality limits household demand for education among the poor. Poor families may

want to keep children in school, but they cannot afford to do so because they do not have money for school clothes or books or because they need children to work. Unable to borrow, poor households thus do not invest in their children's education even if they know that the benefits would be great. The pressing need to use income simply to subsist crowds out this high-return investment and reduces society's demand for education. High inequality makes this problem worse. For example, while the per capita income of Brazil (in 1983) slightly exceeded average income in Malaysia (in 1987) the bottom quintile received 4.6 percent of total income in Malaysia but only 2.4 percent of total income in Brazil. The per capita income of the poorest households in Brazil was thus only half the income of the poorest in Malaysia. Given an income elasticity of demand for basic education of 0.50 if the distribution of income were as equal in Brazil as in Malaysia, enrollments among poor Brazilian children would be more than 40 percent higher.

The Direct Effect of Inequality on Growth

Our results indicate that low inequality stimulates growth independent of its effects through education. However, using income transfers to reduce income inequality is unlikely to be good for growth: transfers often result in the diversion of scarce savings from investment to the subsidization of consumption; the targeted group is often not the one to benefit from transfers, reducing their effectiveness as a means of raising the standard of living, and hence the savings and investment rates, of the poor; transfers tend to distort incentives and reduce both allocative efficiency and X efficiency. But policies that increase the productivity and earning capacity of the poor may be quite a different matter.

Consider four ways in which low inequality can be a stimulus to growth:

- by inducing large increases in the savings and investments of the poor
- by contributing to political and macroeconomic stability—for example by reducing the tendency for fiscal prudence to be sacrificed to political expediency, by discouraging inappropriate exchange rate valuation, and by accelerating the adjustment to macroeconomic
- by increasing the "X-efficiency" of low-income workers, and
- by raising rural incomes, which limits intersectoral income gaps and the rent seeking associated with them, while increasing the domestic multiplier effects of a given increase in per capita income.

Conclusion

The contrasting experiences of Latin America and East Asia suggest that, contrary to conventional wisdom, inequalities in the distribution of both education and income may have a significant and negative impact on the rate of economic growth. The unequal distribution of education in Latin America, in terms of both quantity and quality, constrained economic growth in the region by forestalling opportunities to increase labor productivity and change household behavior. At the same time, the relatively small size of the educated labor force and high scarcity rents of the more educated contributed to high inequality in the distribution of income. Closing a vicious circle, slower growth and high income inequality, in turn, further limited the supply of, and demand for, education.

Education policy alone, however, does not explain the marked differences in equity and growth between Latin America and East Asia. Macroeconomic and sectoral policies in the former, which favored capital-intensive production and were biased against the agricultural sector, almost certainly exacerbated the inequality problem and have hindered growth as well. The East Asian development strategy promoted instead a dynamic agricultural sector and a labor-demanding, export-oriented growth path, thereby reducing inequality and stimulating growth. In East Asia low inequality not only contributes to growth indirectly, for example, by increasing investment in education, but appears to have had a direct positive effect on the growth rate.

The experience of the two regions is sufficient to reject the conventional wisdom of a necessary link between high income inequality and rapid growth. While our analysis has not been sufficient to confirm the opposite, we hope others will now seriously consider the hypothesis that high inequality, and policies that ignore or even exacerbate inequality, constrain growth in the long run. The challenge in Latin America is to find ways to reduce inequality, not by transfers, but by eliminating consumption subsidies for the rich and increasing the productivity of the poor.

30

What Makes Countries Rich or Poor?

Jared Diamond

*D*o institutions really determine growth? The chapters in this section
have made a strong case that they do. Yet earlier in this volume,
*Jared Diamond (Chapter 8) presented his theory of very long-term
growth, starting with the evolution of human settlement in the Neolithic
age, when geography made a huge difference in determining which
nations emerged rich and which poor. In this chapter, Diamond, whose
earlier work made him an internationally renowned figure, moves the
clock up to the contemporary period and reviews the work of Acemoglu,
Johnson, and Robinson (Chapter 10), who made a strong case that
colonial institutions determine contemporary outcomes. In this chapter,
Diamond looks at the "resource curse" (see Chapter 31 by Collier and
Goderis). He argues that institutions are actually only part of the story.
Diamond makes a strong case that geography also matters. He takes note
of the low agricultural productivity and high disease level in tropical
lands. In addition, geography matters when it comes to access to the
seacoast, with landlocked countries far more likely to be poor (e.g.,
Bolivia and Paraguay) than rich. Argentina, for example, is seen by
Diamond as a country with poor institutions, yet its temperate climate
has resulted in a high GNP and extensive agricultural exports.*

THE FENCE THAT DIVIDES THE CITY OF NOGALES IS PART OF A NATURAL
experiment in organizing human societies. North of the fence lies the American
city of Nogales, Arizona; south of it lies the Mexican city of Nogales, Sonora.
On the American side, average income and life expectancy are higher, crime

and corruption are lower, health and roads are better, and elections are more democratic. Yet the geographic environment is identical on both sides of the fence, and the ethnic makeup of the human population is similar. The reasons for those differences between the two Nogaleses are the differences between the current political and economic institutions of the US and Mexico.

This example, which introduces *Why Nations Fail* by Daron Acemoglu and James Robinson, illustrates on a small scale the book's subject. Power, prosperity, and poverty vary greatly around the world. Norway, the world's richest country, is 496 times richer than Burundi, the world's poorest country (average per capita incomes $84,290 and $170 respectively, according to the World Bank). Why? That's a central question of economics.

Different economists have different views about the relative importance of the conditions and factors that make countries richer or poorer. The factors they most discuss are so-called "good institutions," which may be defined as laws and practices that motivate people to work hard, become economically productive, and thereby enrich both themselves and their countries. They are the basis of the Nogales anecdote, and the focus of *Why Nations Fail*. In the authors' words:

> The reason that Nogales, Arizona, is much richer than Nogales, Sonora, is simple: it is because of the very different institutions on the two sides of the border, which create very different incentives for the inhabitants of Nogales, Arizona, versus Nogales, Sonora.
>
> Among the good economic institutions that motivate people to become productive are the protection of their private property rights, predictable enforcement of their contracts, opportunities to invest and retain control of their money, control of inflation, and open exchange of currency. For instance, people are motivated to work hard if they have opportunities to invest their earnings profitably, but not if they have few such opportunities or if their earnings or profits are likely to be confiscated.

The strongest evidence supporting this view comes from natural experiments involving borders: i.e., division of a uniform environment and initially uniform human population by a political border that eventually comes to separate different economic and political institutions, which create differences in wealth. Besides Nogales, examples include the contrasts between North and South Korea and between the former East and West Germany. Many or most economists, including Acemoglu and Robinson, generalize from these examples of bordering countries and deduce that good institutions also explain the differences in wealth between nations that aren't neighbors and that differ greatly in their geographic environments and human populations.

There is no doubt that good institutions are important in determining a country's wealth. But why have some countries ended up with good institutions, while others haven't? The most important factor behind their emergence is the historical duration of centralized government. Until the rise of the world's first states, beginning around 3400 BC, all human societies were bands or tribes or chiefdoms, without any of the complex economic institutions of governments. A long history of government doesn't guarantee good institutions but at least permits them; a short history makes them very unlikely. One can't just suddenly introduce government institutions and expect people to adopt them and to unlearn their long history of tribal organization.

That cruel reality underlies the tragedy of modern nations, such as Papua New Guinea, whose societies were until recently tribal. Oil and mining companies there pay royalties intended for local landowners through village leaders, but the leaders often keep the royalties for themselves. That's because they have internalized their society's practice by which clan leaders pursue their personal interests and their own clan's interests, rather than representing everyone's interests.

The various durations of government around the world are linked to the various durations and productivities of farming that was the prerequisite for the rise of governments. For example, Europe began to acquire highly productive agriculture 9,000 years ago and state government by at least 4,000 years ago, but subequatorial Africa acquired less productive agriculture only between 2,000 and 1,800 years ago and state government even more recently. Those historical differences prove to have huge effects on the modern distribution of wealth. Ola Olsson and Douglas Hibbs showed that, on average, nations in which agriculture arose many millennia ago—e.g., European nations—tend to be richer today than nations with a shorter history of agriculture (e.g., subequatorial African nations), and that this factor explains about half of all the modern national variation in wealth. Valerie Bockstette, Areendam Chanda, and Louis Putterman showed further that, if one compares countries that were equally poor fifty years ago (e.g., South Korea and Ghana), the countries with a long history of state government (e.g., South Korea) have on the average been getting rich faster than those with a short history (e.g., Ghana).

An additional factor behind the origin of the good institutions that I discussed above is termed "the reversal of fortune." . . . Among non-European countries colonized by Europeans during the last five hundred years, those that were initially richer and more advanced tend paradoxically to be poorer today. That's because, in formerly rich countries with dense native populations, such as Peru, Indonesia, and India, Europeans introduced corrupt "extractive" economic institutions, such as forced labor and confiscation of produce, to drain wealth and labor from the natives. (By extractive economic institutions, Acemoglu and Robinson mean practices and policies "designed to extract incomes and wealth from one subset of society [the masses] to benefit a different subset [the governing elite].")

But in formerly poor countries with sparse native populations, such as Costa Rica and Australia, European settlers had to work themselves and developed institutional incentives rewarding work. When the former colonies achieved independence, they variously inherited either the extractive institutions that coerced the masses to produce wealth for dictators and the elite, or else institutions by which the government shared power and gave people incentives to pursue. The extractive institutions retarded economic development, but incentivizing institutions promoted it.

The remaining factor contributing to good institutions, of which Acemoglu and Robinson mention some examples, involves another paradox, termed "the curse of natural resources." One might naively expect countries generously endowed with natural resources (such as minerals, oil, and tropical hardwoods) to be richer than countries poorer in natural resources. In fact, the trend is opposite, the result of the many ways in which national dependence on certain types of natural resources (like diamonds and oil) tends to promote bad institutions, such as corruption, civil wars, inflation, and neglect of education.

An example . . . is the diamond boom in Sierra Leone, which contributed to that nation's impoverishment. Other examples are Nigeria's and the Congo's poverty despite their wealth in oil and minerals respectively. In all three of those cases, selfish dictators or elites found that they themselves could become richer by taking the profits from natural resources for their personal gain, rather than investing the profits for the good of their nation. But some countries with prescient leaders or citizens avoided the curse of natural resources by investing the proceeds in economic development and education. As a result, oil-producing Norway is now the world's richest country, and oil-producing Trinidad and Tobago now enjoys an income approaching that of Britain, its former colonial ruler.

Those are the main sets of institutional factors promoting power, prosperity, or poverty, and their roots. The other large set consists of geographic factors with direct economic consequences not mediated by institutions. One of those geographic factors leaps out of a map of the world in *Why Nations Fail* that depicts national incomes. On that map, both Africa and the Americas resemble peanut butter sandwiches, with thick cores of poor tropical countries squeezed between two thin slices of richer countries in the north and south temperate zones.

In the New World the two north temperate countries (the US and Canada, average incomes respectively $47,390 and $43,270) and the three south temperate countries (Uruguay, Chile, and Argentina, respectively $10,590, $10,120, and $8,620) are all richer—on the average five times richer—than almost all of the intervening seventeen tropical countries of mainland Central and South America (incomes mostly between $1,110 and $6,970). Similarly, mainland Africa is a sandwich of thirty-seven mostly desperately poor tropical countries, flanked by two thin slices each consisting of five modestly affluent or less desperately poor countries in Africa's north and south temperate zones. . . . All temperate mainland African countries except landlocked Lesotho in the south have average annual incomes above $2,400, ranging up to over $12,000. All except three tropical mainland African countries—Equatorial Guinea, Gabon, and Angola—have average incomes below $2,200, ranging down to as low as $170 (Burundi).

While institutions are undoubtedly part of the explanation, they leave much unexplained: some of those richer temperate countries are notorious for their histories of bad institutions (think of Algeria, Argentina, Egypt, and Libya), while some of the tropical countries (e.g., Costa Rica and Tanzania) have had relatively more honest governments. What are the economic disadvantages of a tropical location?

Two major factors contribute to the poverty of tropical countries compared to temperate countries: diseases and agricultural productivity. The tropics are notoriously unhealthy. Tropical diseases differ on average from temperate diseases, in several respects. First, there are far more parasitic diseases (such as elephantiasis and schistosomiasis) in tropical areas, because cold temperate winters kill parasite stages outside our bodies, but tropical parasites can thrive outside our bodies all year long. Second, disease vectors, such as mosquitoes and ticks, are far more diverse in tropical than in temperate areas.

Finally, biological characteristics of the responsible microbes have made it easier to develop vaccines against major infectious diseases of temperate areas than against tropical diseases; we still aren't close to a vaccine against malaria, despite billions of dollars invested. Hence tropical diseases impose a huge burden on economies of tropical countries. At any given moment, much of the population is sick and unable to work efficiently. Many women in tropical areas can't join the workforce because they are constantly nursing and caring for babies conceived as insurance against the expected deaths of some of their older children from malaria.

As for agricultural productivity, it averages lower in tropical than in temperate areas, again for several reasons. First, temperate plants store more energy in parts edible to us humans (such as seeds and tubers) than do tropical plants. Second, diseases borne by insects and other pests reduce crop yields more in the tropics than in the temperate zones, because the pests are more diverse and survive better year-round in tropical than in temperate areas. Third, glaciers repeatedly advanced and retreated over temperate areas, creating young nutrient-rich soils. Tropical lowland areas haven't been glaciated and hence tend to have older soils, leached of their nutrients by rain for thousands of years. (Young fertile volcanic and alluvial soils are exceptions.) Fourth, the higher average rainfall of tropical than of temperate areas results in more nutrients being leached out of the soil by rain.

Finally, higher tropical temperatures cause dead leaves and other organic matter falling to the ground to be broken down quickly by microbes and other organisms, releasing their nutrients to be leached away. Hence in temperate areas soil fertility is on average higher, crop losses to pests lower, and agricultural productivity higher than in tropical areas. That's why Argentina in South America's south temperate zone, despite its conspicuous lack (for most of its history) of the good institutions praised by economists, is the leading food exporter in Latin America, and one of the leading ones in the world.

Thus, geographical latitude acting independently of institutions is an important geographic factor affecting power, prosperity, and poverty. The other important geographic factor is whether an area is accessible to ocean-going ships because it lies either on the sea coast or on a navigable river. It costs roughly seven times more to ship a ton of cargo by land than by sea. That puts landlocked countries at an economic disadvantage, and helps explain why landlocked Bolivia and semilandlocked Paraguay are the poorest countries of South America. It also helps explain why Africa, with no river navigable to the sea for hundreds of miles except the Nile, and with fifteen landlocked nations, is the poorest continent. Eleven of those fifteen landlocked African nations have average incomes of $600 or less; only two countries outside Africa (Afghanistan and Nepal, both also landlocked) are as poor.

The remaining major factor underlying wealth and poverty is the state of the natural environment. All human populations depend to varying degrees on renewable natural resources—especially on forests, water, soils, and seafood. It's tricky to manage such resources sustainably. Countries that excessively deplete their resources—whether inadvertently or intentionally—tend to impoverish themselves, although the difficulty of estimating accurately the costs of resource destruction causes economists to ignore it. It helps explain why notoriously deforested countries—such as Haiti, Rwanda, Burundi, Madagascar, and Nepal—tend to be notoriously poor and politically unstable.

These, then, are the main factors invoked to understand why nations differ in wealth. The factors are multiple and diverse. We all know, from our personal experience, that there isn't one simple answer to the question why each of us becomes richer or poorer: it depends on inheritance, education, ambition, talent, health, personal connections, opportunities, and luck, just to mention some factors. Hence we shouldn't be surprised that the question of why whole societies become richer or poorer also cannot be given one simple answer.

Within this frame, Acemoglu and Robinson focus on institutional factors: initially on economic institutions, and then on the political institutions that create them. In their words, "while economic institutions are critical for determining whether a country is poor or prosperous, it is politics and political institutions that determine what economic institutions a country has." In particular, they stress what they term inclusive economic and political institutions: "Inclusive economic institutions . . . are those that allow and encourage participation by the great mass of people in economic activities that make best use of their talents and skills and that enable individuals to make the choices they wish." For example, in South Korea but not in North Korea people can get a good education, own property, start a business, sell products and services, accumulate and invest capital, spend money in open markets, take out a mortgage to buy a house, and thereby expect that by working harder they may enjoy a good life.

Such inclusive economic institutions in turn arise from "political institutions that distribute power broadly in society and subject it to constraints. . . . Instead of being vested in a single individual or a narrow group, [inclusive] political power rests with a broad coalition or a plurality of groups." South Korea recently, and Britain and the US beginning much earlier, do have broad participation of citizens in political decisions; North Korea does not. Inclusive economic and political institutions provide individuals with incentives to increase their economic productivity as they think best. Such inclusive institutions are to be contrasted with absolutist political institutions that narrowly concentrate political power, and with extractive economic institutions that force people to work largely for the benefit of dictators. The ultimate development of inclusive political institutions to date is in modern Scandinavian democracies with universal suffrage and relatively egalitarian societies. However, compared to modern dictatorships (like North Korea) and the absolute monarchies widespread in the past, societies (such as eighteenth-century Britain) in which only a minority of citizens could vote or participate in political decisions still represented a big advance toward inclusiveness.

From this striking dichotomy, the authors draw thought-provoking conclusions. While absolutist regimes with extractive economic institutions can sometimes achieve economic growth, that growth is based on existing technology, and is nonsustainable and prone to collapse; whereas inclusive institutions are required for sustained growth based on technological change. One might naively expect dictators to promote long-term economic growth, because such growth would generate more wealth for them to extract. But their efforts are warped, because what's economically good for individual citizens may be bad for the political elite, and because economic growth may be best promoted by political institutions that would shake the elite's hegemony.

Why Nations Fail offers case studies to illustrate these points: the economic rises and subsequent declines of the Soviet Union and the Ottoman Empire; the resistance of tsarist Russia and the Habsburg Empire to building railroads, out of fear that they would undermine the landed aristocracy's power and foster revolution; and, especially relevant today, the likely future trajectory of Communist China, whose growth prospects appear unlimited to many Western observers—but not to Acemoglu and Robinson, who write that China's growth "is likely to run out of steam."

In their narrow focus on inclusive institutions, however, the authors ignore or dismiss other factors. I mentioned earlier the effects of an area's being landlocked or of environmental damage, factors that they don't discuss. Even within the focus on institutions, the concentration specifically on inclusive institutions causes the authors to give inadequate accounts of the ways that natural resources can be a curse. True, the book provides anecdotes of the resource curse (Sierra Leone cursed by diamonds), and of how the curse was successfully avoided (in Botswana). But the book doesn't explain which resources especially lend themselves to the curse (diamonds yes, iron no) and why. Nor does the book show how some big resource producers like the US and Australia avoid the curse (they are democracies whose economies depend on much else besides resource exports), nor which other resource-dependent countries besides Sierra Leone and Botswana respectively succumbed to or overcame the curse. The chapter on reversal of fortune surprisingly doesn't mention the authors' own interesting findings about how the degree of reversal depends on prior wealth and on health threats to Europeans.

Two major factors that Acemoglu and Robinson do mention, only to dismiss them in a few sentences, are tropical diseases and tropical agricultural productivity: Tropical diseases obviously cause much suffering and high rates of infant mortality in Africa, but they are not the reason Africa is poor. Disease is largely a consequence of poverty and of governments being unable or unwilling to undertake the public health measures necessary to eradicate them. . . . The prime determinant of why agricultural productivity—agricultural output per acre—is so low in many poor countries, particularly in sub-Saharan Africa, has little to do with soil quality. Rather, it is a consequence of the ownership structure of the land and the incentives that are created for farmers by the governments and institutions under which they live.

These sweeping statements, which will astonish anyone knowledgeable about the subjects, brush off two entire fields of science, tropical medicine and agricultural science. As I summarized above, the well-known facts of tropical biology, geology, and climatology saddle tropical countries with much bigger problems than temperate countries.

A second weakness involves the historical origins of what Acemoglu and Robinson identify as inclusive economic and political institutions, with their consequences for wealth. Some countries, such as Britain and Japan, have such institutions, while other countries, such as Ethiopia and the Congo, don't. To explain why, the authors give a just-so story of each country's history, which ends by concluding that that story explains why that country either did or didn't develop good institutions. For instance, Britain adopted inclusive institutions, we are told, as a result of the Glorious Revolution of 1688 and preceding events; and Japan reformed its institutions after 1868; but Ethiopia remained absolutist. Acemoglu and Robinson's view of history is that small effects at critical junctures have long-lasting effects, so it's hard to make predictions. While they don't say so explicitly, this view suggests that good institutions should have cropped up randomly around the world, depending on who happened to decide what at some particular place and time.

But it's obvious that good institutions, and the wealth and power that they spawned, did not crop up randomly. For instance, all Western European countries ended up richer and with better institutions than any tropical African country. Big underlying differences led to this divergence of outcomes. Europe has had a long history (of up to nine thousand years) of agriculture based on the world's most productive crops and domestic animals, both of which were domesticated in and introduced to Europe from the Fertile Crescent, the crescent-shaped region running from the Persian Gulf through southeastern Turkey to Upper Egypt. Agriculture in tropical Africa is only between 1,800 and 5,000 years old and based on less productive domesticated crops and imported animals.

As a result, Europe has had up to four thousand years' experience of government, complex institutions, and growing national identities, compared to a few centuries or less for all of sub-Saharan Africa. Europe has glaciated fertile soils, reliable summer rainfall, and few tropical diseases; tropical Africa has unglaciated and extensively infertile soils, less reliable rainfall, and many tropical diseases. Within Europe, Britain had the further advantages of being an island rarely at risk from foreign armies, and of fronting on the Atlantic Ocean, which became open after 1492 to overseas trade. It should be no surprise that countries with those advantages ended up rich and with good institutions, while countries with those disadvantages didn't. The chain of causation leading slowly from productive agriculture to government, state formation, complex institutions, and wealth involved agriculturally driven population explosions and accumulations of food surpluses, leading in turn to the need for centralized decision-making in societies much too populous for decision-making by face-to-face discussions involving all citizens, and the possibility of using the food surpluses to support kings and their bureaucrats. This process unfolded independently, beginning around 3400 BC, in many different parts of the ancient world with productive agriculture, including the Fertile Crescent, Egypt, China, the Indus Valley, Crete, the Valley of Mexico, the Andes, and Polynesian Hawaii.

The remaining weakness is the authors' resort to assertion unsupported or contradicted by facts. An example is their attempt to expand their focus on institutions in order to explain the origins of agriculture. All humans were originally hunter/gatherers who independently became farmers in only about nine small areas scattered around the world. A century of research by botanists and archaeologists has shown that what made those areas exceptional was their wealth of wild plant and animal species suitable for domestication (such as wild wheats and corn).

While the usual pattern was for nomadic hunter/gatherers to become sedentary farmers, there were exceptions: some nomadic hunter/gatherers initially became nomadic farmers (Mexico and lowland New Guinea) while others never became farmers (Aboriginal Australia); some sedentary hunter/gatherers became sedentary farmers (the Fertile Crescent) while others never became farmers (Pacific Northwest Indians); and some sedentary farmers reverted to being nomadic hunter/gatherers (southern Sweden about four thousand years ago).

In their Chapter 5, Acemoglu and Robinson use one of those exceptional patterns (that for the Fertile Crescent) to assert, in the complete absence of evidence, that those particular hunter/gatherers had become sedentary because, for unknown reasons, they happened to develop innovative institutions through a hypothesized political revolution. They assert further that the origins of farming depended on their preferred explanation of institutional innovation, rather than on the local availability of domesticable wild species identified by botanists and archaeologists.

Among arguments to refute that widely shared interpretation, Acemoglu and Robinson redraw in their Map 5 on page 56 the maps on pages 56 and 66 of archaeobotanists Daniel Zohary and Maria Hopf's book *Domestication of Plants in the Old World,* depicting the distributions of wild barley and of one of the two hybrid ancestors of one of the three wheats (which Acemoglu and Robinson misleadingly identify just as "wheat"). They take these maps to mean that "the ancestors of barley and wheat were distributed along a long arc" beyond the Fertile Crescent, hence that the Fertile Crescent's unique role in agriculture's origins "was not determined by the availability of plant and animal species."

What Zohary and Hopf actually showed was that wild emmer wheat is confined to the Fertile Crescent, and that the areas of extensive spread of wild barley and wild einkorn wheat are also confined to the Fertile Crescent, and that the wild ancestors of all the other original Fertile Crescent crops are also confined to or centered on the Fertile Crescent, and hence that the Fertile Crescent was the only area in which local agriculture could have arisen. Acemoglu and Robinson do themselves a disservice by misstating these findings.

My overall assessment of the authors' argument is that inclusive institutions, while not the overwhelming determinant of prosperity that they claim, are an important factor. Perhaps they provide 50 percent of the explanation for national differences in prosperity. That's enough to establish such institutions as one of the major forces in the modern world. *Why Nations Fail* offers an excellent way for any interested reader to learn about them and their consequences. Whereas most writing by academic economists is incomprehensible to the lay public, Acemoglu and Robinson have written this book so that it can be understood and enjoyed by all of us who aren't economists.

Why Nations Fail should be required reading for politicians and anyone concerned with economic development. The authors' discussions of what can and can't be done today to improve conditions in poor countries are thought-provoking and will stimulate debate. Donors and international agencies try to "engineer prosperity" either by foreign aid or by urging poor countries to adopt good economic policies. But there is widespread disappointment with the results of these well-intentioned efforts. Acemoglu and Robinson pithily diagnose the cause of these disappointing outcomes in their final chapter: "Attempting to engineer prosperity without confronting the root cause of the problems—extractive institutions and the politics that keeps them in place—is unlikely to bear fruit."

Part 8

Natural Resources, Climate Change, and the Gap

31

Commodity Prices, Growth, and the Natural Resource Curse: Reconciling a Conundrum

Paul Collier and Benedikt Goderis

*I*t is a common assumption that countries that are well endowed with natural resources are the ones most likely to become rich. Yet can there be too much of a good thing? The literature on the so-called resource curse has found that commodity booms in such extractive reserves as oil, diamonds, and other highly priced commodities can lead to slowed growth over the long term, even while they can produce growth spurts in the short term. In this chapter, well-known development economist Paul Collier and his University of Oxford coauthor, Benedikt Goderis, find that the resource curse emerges because of overconsumption, low levels of investment, and an overvalued exchange rate, yet find that those factors can be avoided if countries have good-quality institutions. Sadly, few resource-rich nations today are successful in avoiding the resource curse.

THE LITERATURE OFFERS SIX CANDIDATE EXPLANATIONS FOR THE RE-source curse effect: Dutch disease, governance, conflict, excessive borrowing, inequality and volatility. Since the responses appropriate for overcoming the resource curse differ radically as between these routes, their relative magnitude is evidently of importance. In this section we test for the importance of these explanations.

Reprinted from Paul Collier and Benedikt Goderis, "Commodity Prices and Growth: An Empirical Investigation," *European Economic Review* 56, no. 6: 1241–1260. Copyright © 2012, with permission from Elsevier, Ltd.

We first explore the possibility that the long-run negative effect reflects the occurrence of Dutch Disease effects. An increase in commodity prices appreciates the real exchange rate, lowering the competitiveness of the non-resource exports sector, and potentially harming long-run output if there are positive externalities to production in this sector (Corden and Neary, 1982; Van Wijnbergen, 1984; Sachs and Warner, 1995, 1999; Torvik, 2001). This argument is related to recent literature that shows how specialization in natural resources can divert economies away from manufacturing or other skill-intensive activities, thereby slowing down learning-by-doing and reducing incentives for people to educate themselves (Matsuyama, 1992; Michaels, 2006). To test for the importance of this channel, we add an index of real exchange rate overvaluation to the specifications. . . . As an overvalued exchange rate could potentially affect GDP both in the short run and in the long run, we include both the level and the first difference of the index. Further, to allow for the possibility that the effect of exchange rate overvaluation is different for resource-abundant countries, we also include interaction terms of the level and differenced overvaluation index with the share of non-agricultural exports in GDP. If the negative long-run effect of non-agricultural commodity export prices works through their impact on the real exchange rate, then the effect of the export price indices should disappear once we control for exchange rate overvaluation. The results are reported in the two columns in the top left corner of Table 31.1. In the first column, the level of the overvaluation index enters negative, although not significant, suggesting that, consistent with Dutch disease, an overvalued exchange rate indeed has a negative effect on long-run GDP per capita. The interaction of the index with the share of exports in GDP also enters negative, suggesting that the effect of an overvalued exchange rate is more severe in resource-abundant countries. The differenced index enters positive, but for resource-abundant countries this effect is smaller or even negative as the interaction term enters negative. All in all, these results seem to suggest that, at least in the long run, an overvalued exchange rate lowers GDP. In addition, adding the overvaluation index leads to a slightly smaller coefficient of the non-agricultural export price index, as can be seen from the results in the second column for the same sample without the overvaluation index. More specifically, the long-run coefficient changes from -1.25 to -1.11, which suggests that Dutch Disease explains around 11 percent of the long-run resource curse effect. Although countries with good governance do not suffer from a resource curse, their long-term gain from higher commodity export prices might be negatively affected by Dutch Disease. This long-term gain is captured by the linear combination of the coefficients of the non-agricultural export price index and its interaction with the good governance dummy. This combination changes from 0.75 for the sample without the overvaluation index to 0.83 in the sample with the overvaluation index, indicating that Dutch Disease also harms long-run GDP in good governance countries.

Table 31.1 Testing the Channels of the Resource Curse

	Dutch Disease		Governance		Conflict		Excessive Borrowing		Inequality		Volatility	
Indicator	-0.10		-0.12***		0.01		-0.18**		-0.72		0.93	
	(0.07)		(0.04)		(0.02)		(0.08)		(1.01)		(1.43)	
Indicator* Non-agri exports/GDP	-0.46		0.61**		0.02		0.46		5.22		-0.99	
	(0.43)		(0.24)		(0.17)		(0.32)		(9.03)		(6.28)	
Δ Indicator		0.01		-0.01**		-0.02***		-0.07***		-0.12		-0.27**
		(0.02)		(0.00)		(0.01)		(0.02)		(0.09)		(0.13)
Δ Indicator Indicator* Non-agri exports/GDP		-0.04		0.03		-0.06		0.17*		1.97**		0.37
		(0.10)		(0.03)		(0.04)		(0.08)		(0.87)		(0.87)
Non-agri export price index	-1.11**	-1.25***	-1.16***	-1.05***	-1.36***	-1.29***	-1.66***	-1.46***	-1.14**	-0.99*	-1.30***	-1.29***
	(0.46)	(0.42)	(0.30)	(0.27)	(0.37)	(0.35)	(0.47)	(0.40)	(0.50)	(0.52)	(0.36)	(0.35)
Non-agri export price index* good governance	1.94***	2.00***	2.07***	2.03***	2.14***	2.12***	-0.72	1.14	1.64***	1.69***	2.14***	2.12***
	(0.63)	(0.63)	(0.57)	(0.53)	(0.63)	(0.61)	(4.72)	(4.36)	(0.60)	(0.61)	(0.61)	(0.61)
Observations	2689	2689	2317	2317	3087	3087	1872	1872	1752	1752	3087	3087
R-squared within	0.31	0.31	0.33	0.32	0.28	0.28	0.32	0.29	0.37	0.37	0.28	0.28

(continues)

Table 31.1 continued

	Manufacturing		Services		De jure openness		Public Consumption		Private Consumption		Total Investment	
Indicator	1.34		0.05		0.00		−0.60		−1.14***		2.60***	
	(0.95)		(0.50)		(0.08)		(0.74)		(0.40)		(0.58)	
Indicator* Non-agri exports/GDP	−7.58*		2.55		0.95		−5.08		6.23***		−7.54***	
	(3.98)		(2.60)		(0.70)		(6.75)		(2.17)		(2.57)	
Δ Indicator	0.07		−0.13		0.01		−0.22		−0.18***		0.42***	
	(0.15)		(0.09)		(0.01)		(0.15)		(0.05)		(0.07)	
Δ Indicator* Non-agri exports/GDP	−0.46		−0.19		0.11		−1.14		−0.11		−0.16	
	(1.45)		(0.56)		(0.07)		(0.84)		(0.47)		(0.73)	
Non-agri export price index	−1.41***	−1.45***	−1.30***	−1.36***	−0.71**	−0.72***	−0.99**	−1.27***	−1.15***	−1.39***	−1.18***	−1.37***
	(0.36)	(0.37)	(0.37)	(0.38)	(0.33)	(0.31)	(0.43)	(0.36)	(0.38)	(0.37)	(0.35)	(0.37)
Non-agri export price index* good governance	0.65	0.81	1.44**	1.32*	1.52***	1.51***	1.89***	2.03***	1.97***	2.26***	2.10***	2.34***
	(0.61)	(0.62)	(0.71)	(0.68)	(0.49)	(0.48)	(0.61)	(0.61)	(0.52)	(0.58)	(0.78)	(0.58)
Observations	2396	2396	2742	2742	1956	1956	3046	3046	2972	2972	2989	2989
R-squared within	0.31	0.30	0.29	0.29	0.35	0.34	0.30	0.28	0.30	0.28	0.35	0.28

Notes: The dependent variable is the first-differenced log of real GDP per capita. All regressions are based on the specification in Table 5, column (3) [of original text], and include country-specific fixed effects and regional time dummies. ***, **, and * denote significance at the 1%, 5%, and 10% levels, respectively. We only report the coefficients and standard errors of the variables of interest. See section 5 [of original text] for an explanation of the indicators.

We next explore whether the resource curse induces weak institutions of governance. The literature has proposed several such routes. Resource rents may invite non-productive lobbying and rent seeking, as in Lane and Tornell (1996), Tornell and Lane (1999), Baland and Francois (2000), Torvik (2002), and Wick and Bulte (2006). Mehlum et al. (2006) argue that this problem only occurs in countries with grabber-friendly institutions, while countries with producer-friendly institutions do not suffer from a curse. A related literature emphasizes the role of government in the misallocation of resource revenues. Acemoglu et al. (2004) and Robinson et al. (2006) argue that resource booms have adverse effects because they provide incentives for politicians to engage in inefficient redistribution in return for political support. Again, existing institutions are crucial, as they determine the extent to which politicians can respond to these perverse incentives. The inefficient redistribution can take various forms such as public employment provision (Robinson et al., 2006), subsidies to farmers, labor market regulation, and protection of domestic industries from international competition (Acemoglu and Robinson, 2001). The protection of domestic industries as a possible explanation of the resource curse is also emphasized by Arezki and Van der Ploeg (2007). We investigate governance using the same approach as for Dutch disease. There is no agreed composite measure of the quality of governance and so we have investigated a range of commonly used proxies: the parallel market exchange rate premium, civil liberties and political rights (Freedom House), two measures of political constraints (Henisz, 2000, 2002), democracy, autocracy, and a combined measure of democracy and autocracy (Polity IV), checks and balances (Database of Political Institutions, 2004), and the Composite International Country Risk Guide (ICRG) risk rating (PRS Group). . . . The parallel market premium enters negative and is significant at 1 percent. This indicates that countries with high premiums on the parallel market exchange rate grow more slowly. For resource abundant countries, this effect is smaller, as the interaction term of the parallel market premium with the share of exports in GDP enters positive and is significant at 5 percent. The short-run effect of the parallel market premium is also negative and is significant at 5 percent, while not significantly different for resource-abundant countries. Although these results indicate that this governance indicator is an important GDP determinant, it does not lead to a smaller resource curse effect. In fact, the long-run coefficient of commodity prices even increases in absolute size. This suggests that the deterioration of governance is not the central explanation of the resource curse. So even though the resource curse only occurs in countries with weak governance, it is not explained by a deterioration of governance in those countries.

We next turn more briefly to four other proposed channels for the resource curse. Resource abundance can increase the incidence of violence (Collier and Hoeffler, 2004). This can occur through a weakening of the state, easy finance for rebels and warlords (Skaperdas, 2002), or quasi-criminal activities and gang rivalries (Mehlum et al., 2006; Hodler, 2006). Resource abundance can also tempt a government into excessive external borrowing, as in Mansoorian (1991), Manzano and Rigobon (2006), and Kuralbayeva and Vines (2006). It also exposes countries to commodity price volatility which could, for example, discourage investment (Sala-i-Martin and Subramanian, 2003). Finally, as suggested by Sokoloff and Engerman (2000), resource abundance can lead to increased inequality and this could harm growth through lower savings or investment rates, lower quality of institutions, credit market imperfections, distorting redistribution, or socio-political unrest (Barro, 2000).

We investigate the importance of these channels through the same approach. Controlling for these possible channels does not lead to smaller coefficients for our export price index, suggesting that individually these channels do not explain our resource curse finding.

Testing the Routes Through Which Governance Drives the Resource Curse

Even though the resource curse does not work through governance, we have found strong evidence that it works conditional on governance. The recent theoretical literature proposes two explanations, each of which implies additional channels of the resource curse. Mehlum et al. (2006) argue that resource rents invite non-productive lobbying and rent seeking, and that the pay-offs from these activities are high in countries with grabber-friendly ("bad") institutions but low in countries with producer-friendly ("good") institutions. This leads entrepreneurs in countries with bad institutions away from productive activities into non-productive rent-seeking activities, which in the long run slows down industrial development. We empirically test this theory by adding a measure of industrial development, the share of manufacturing in GDP, to our specification. If the resource curse works through the underdevelopment of the manufacturing sector, then the effect of the export price index should disappear once we control for the size of this sector. We also investigate the importance of the high-productivity services sector. The results for manufacturing are reported in the two columns in the bottom left corner of Table 31.1. The level of manufacturing enters with a positive sign, indicating that a larger manufacturing sector leads to a higher level of long-run GDP. However, this effect is not statistically significant. Also, the negative coefficient on the interaction term with the share of exports suggests that the effect of manufacturing is smaller for resource rich economies. Although we find some evidence that a larger manufacturing sector is good for long-run growth, this does not seem to explain much of the resource curse effect. The absolute size of the coefficient is only around 3 percent smaller when controlling for the share of manufacturing in GDP. We can therefore conclude that the resource curse does not seem to work through a slower speed of industrial development. It also does not work through lower growth in the services sector, as can be seen from the results in the third and fourth column of the bottom part of Table 31.1.

The other recently proposed explanation points at inefficient redistribution by the government. Robinson et al. (2006) argue that permanent commodity booms increase incentives for politicians to stay in power. In countries where government accountability is lacking, politicians will use the resource windfall revenues to bias the outcome of elections or in non-democratic regimes' political contests. This bias can be induced in many ways but Robinson et al. refer to informal literature that "points to the centrality of public sector employment as a tool for influencing people's voting behaviour" (Robinson et al., 2006). Hence, resource rents create inefficiencies by facilitating public employment provision by politicians in return for political support, but only in countries with weak institutions. In countries with strong institutions, the extent to which politicians can use public money to bias elections is limited and therefore the resource curse does not occur. In addition to public employment provision, inefficient redistribution can take place through protection of domestic industries from international competition, subsidies to farmers, and labor market regulation (Acemoglu and Robinson, 2001). We empirically test this theory by adding measures of public consumption and de jure trade openness to our specification. If the resource curse works through the provision of public sector jobs, then the effect of the export price index should disappear once we control for public consumption, which amongst other things includes civil servant salaries. Similarly, if the curse works through trade protection, then controlling for trade openness should make the resource curse effect disappear. The results for openness are reported in the fifth and sixth columns of the bottom part of Table 31.1 and indicate that more open countries grow faster, although the effects are not significant. However, the long-run resource curse effect hardly changes when controlling for this possible channel, suggesting that trade protection is not an important driver of the resource curse. The results for public consumption are reported in the next two columns of the bottom part of Table 31.1. The long-run and short-run coefficients are all negative, although not significant, suggesting that higher levels of public consumption negatively affect growth, both in the short run and in the long run. The negative effect of public consumption also seems to explain part of the resource curse effect. When controlling for government consumption, the absolute size of the coefficient falls by 22 percent. These results support the argument of Robinson et al. (2006) that commodity booms lead to inefficient public sector employment provision which then slows down economic development.

In both explanations of why governance is crucial for the occurrence of the curse, commodity booms lead workers or entrepreneurs away from productive activities into less productive rent-seeking or public sector activities. With this shift away from productive activities, one might expect to see a shift in the pattern of a country's aggregate expenditures as well. As more people secure their income through rent-seeking or public employment and the government allocates more of its revenue to public employment provision, aggregate investment levels will fall and public and private consumption will increase. In addition to lowering investment levels, commodity booms may also lead to a lower quality of investment projects. Robinson and Torvik (2005) provide a theory in which "white elephants," investment projects with negative social surplus, are used as a means of inefficient redistribution aimed at influencing the outcomes of elections. This suggests yet another channel of the resource curse. In addition to public sector employment, trade protection, subsidies, and regulation, inefficient redistribution during and after commodity booms can also occur through inefficient investment projects.

We test the importance of these shifts in expenditure by adding measures of private consumption and total investment to our specification. The results are reported in the last four columns of the bottom part of Table 31.1. We find that the share of private consumption in GDP has a negative effect on GDP growth, both in the short run and in the long run. Both effects are statistically significant at 1 percent. However, we also find that the long-run effect is significantly smaller for resource-rich economies, as the interaction term enters with a positive sign and is significant at 1 percent. Just as in the case of public consumption, controlling for private consumption takes away part of the long-run resource curse effect. The absolute size of the coefficient falls by 17 percent.

We next turn to the results for total investment. The long-run and short-run coefficients are positive and statistically significant at 1 percent. This indicates that higher levels of total (public and private) investment lead to higher GDP levels, as one would expect. The positive long-run effect of investment is significantly smaller in resource-rich economies. This is clearly consistent with the theory of inefficient redistribution through inefficient investment projects in Robinson and Torvik (2005). Controlling for the level of total investment and the lower long-run return on investment in resource-rich economies also explains part of the resource curse effect, as the absolute size of the long-run coefficient falls by 14 percent.

So far we have only considered indicators individually. We next investigate whether combinations of indicators can explain the resource curse effect in our estimations. We start by combining the four variables that are individually important in explaining the resource curse: exchange rate overvaluation, public consumption, private consumption, and total investment. The results are reported in the first two columns of Table 31.2. We again find that exchange rate overvaluation negatively affects GDP in the long run, while public consumption and private consumption negatively affect GDP both in the short run and in the long run. However, of these effects only the long-run effect of public consumption is statistically significant at 10 percent. In addition, we again find a positive and highly significant long-run effect of total investment on GDP, both in the short and in the long run. The interaction term of the level of total investment with the share of exports in GDP again enters negative, although the coefficient is now statistically insignificant. The combination of the four variables explains a substantial part of the resource curse effect. Once we control for these variables, the absolute size of the long-run resource curse coefficient falls by 47 percent, while its statistical significance disappears.

We next test whether the four variables all contribute to the lower long-run resource curse effect by eliminating each of them individually and observing the change in the long-run coefficient, while keeping the sample constant. We find that indeed all four variables are important in explaining the curse. As a robustness check we again considered all of the other channels by adding each of the indicators individually to the specification in Table 31.2, column (1), and observing the long-run coefficient, while again keeping the sample constant. The results support our earlier finding that these other channels cannot account for the curse: controlling for them does not lead to smaller coefficients for our export price index. The only two exceptions are volatility and the share of services in GDP. If we control for each of these two additional variables, the absolute size of the long-run resource curse coefficient further decreases. Table 31.2, columns (3) and (4), report the results when we add both of these variables to the four variables that were included in the specifications of columns (1) and (2). While volatility has a positive but highly insignificant long-run effect on GDP, the large negative coefficient of the interaction of volatility with the share of exports in GDP suggests that the long-run effect of volatility is negative for countries with substantial commodity exports. The long-run effect of a growing services sector is positive, although insignificant. Its short-run effect is negative, but the positive and significant interaction with the share of exports in GDP suggests that this effect is positive for countries with substantial commodity exports. These results provide some evidence that volatility and growth in the services sector affect GDP in resource-rich economies. The combination of the six variables explains almost the entire long-run resource curse effect. Once we control for these variables, the absolute size of the long-run resource curse coefficient falls by 95 percent and becomes highly insignificant. We conclude that a substantial part of the resource curse effect can be explained by exchange rate overvaluation, public and private consumption, total investment, and to a lesser extent volatility and services. This supports recent theory that points at the importance of inefficient redistribution through public sector employment provision or inefficient investment projects (white elephants). It also supports the more general idea that commodity booms lead the entrepreneurs in an economy away from productive activities and into non-productive rent-seeking, lobbying, or public sector activities. Finally, it lends some support to the large literature that stresses the importance of Dutch disease in resource-rich economies.

Table 31.2   Testing the Channels of the Resource Curse

	(1)	(2)	(3)	(4)
		Estimates of long-run coefficients		
Real exchange rate overvaluation	−0.07		−0.01	
	(0.06)		(0.07)	
Real exchange rate overvaluation* Non-agri exports/GDP	−0.46		−1.35**	
	(0.49)		(0.57)	
Public consumption	−1.75*		−1.69*	
	(0.91)		(0.90)	
Public consumption* Non-agri exports/GDP	5.81		4.46	
	(8.76)		(8.49)	
Private consumption	−0.89		−0.99*	
	(0.58)		(0.57)	
Private consumption* Non-agri exports/GDP	3.86		4.60	
	(3.12)		(3.03)	
Total investment	2.20***		2.23***	
	(0.71)		(0.68)	
Total investment* Non-agri exports/GDP	−5.15		−5.34	
	(3.94)		(3.82)	
Volatility			0.96	
			(1.24)	
Volatility* Non-agri exports/GDP			−10.35	
			(7.16)	
Services			0.37	
			(0.41)	
Services * Non-agri exports/GDP			−0.40	
			(2.56)	
Non-agricultural export price index	−0.78	−1.46***	−0.07	−1.32***
	(0.48)	(0.45)	(0.45)	(0.42)
Non-agricultural export price index* good governance	1.75**	2.23***	0.18	1.26*
	(0.73)	(0.63)	(1.05)	(0.66)
		Estimates of short-run coefficients		
Δ Real exchange rate overvaluation	0.01		0.02	
	(0.02)		(0.02)	
Δ Real exchange rate overvaluation* Non-agri exports/GDP	0.04		0.01	
	(0.07)		(0.07)	
Δ Public consumption	−0.26		−0.22	
	(0.16)		(0.16)	
Δ Public consumption* Non-agri exports/GDP	−0.70		−1.01	
	(0.85)		(0.98)	
Δ Private consumption	−0.06		−0.04	
	(0.05)		(0.05)	
Δ Private consumption* Non-agri exports/GDP	−0.66*		−0.70*	
	(0.34)		(0.39)	
Δ Total investment	0.38***		0.40***	
	(0.08)		(0.08	
Δ Total investment* Non-agri exports/GDP	0.21		0.22	
	(0.53)		(0.49)	

(continues)

Table 31.2   continued

	(1)	(2)	(3)	(4)
		Estimates of short-run coefficients		
Δ Volatility			−0.19	
			(0.13)	
Δ Volatility*			1.11	
Non-agri exports/GDP			(0.79)	
Δ Services			−0.12	
			(0.09)	
Δ Services *			0.73*	
Non-agri exports/GDP			(0.41)	
Observations	2577	2577	2367	2367
R-squared within	0.42	0.31	0.43	0.31

Notes: The dependent variable is the first-differenced log of real GDP per capita. All regressions are based on the specification in Table 5, column (3) [of original text], and include country-specific fixed effects and regional time dummies. We only report the coefficients and standard errors of the variables of interest. ***, **, and * denote significance at the 1%, 5%, and 10% levels, respectively.

Explaining the Results in the Empirical Literature

Finally, we investigate to what extent our empirical findings can explain the cross section results in the empirical resource curse literature. We first collect the data from the seminal paper by Sachs and Warner (1995) (S&W hereafter) and replicate their main results. Table 31.3, columns (1) to (5), report the results of the specifications in Table 1 of the revised 1997 version of S&W. The dependent variable is the 1970–1990 average annual growth in real GDP divided by the economically active population. The regressors are the 1970 share of primary exports in GNP (sxp), the 1970 log of real GDP divided by the economically-active population (lgdpea70), the fraction of years between 1970 and 1990 in which the country is rated as an open economy (sopen), the average 1970–1989 log of the ratio of real gross domestic investment to real GDP (linv7089), a rule of law index (rl), and the 1970–1990 average annual growth in the log of the external terms of trade. The results in Table 31.3, columns (1) to (5), are very similar to the results in S&W. In particular, the coefficients of the share of primary exports in GNP (sxp) are always negative and statistically significant at 1 percent, as in S&W. This is the familiar resource curse effect. To explore how much of this effect can be explained by the long-run adverse effect of commodity prices in our estimations, we ran two regressions. The only difference between the two regressions is that the first does not control for our long-run resource curse effect, while the second does. We collect the country-specific fixed effects from both regressions and use each set of fixed effects as a dependent variable in the S&W regressions. Table 31.3,

Table 31.3 Explaining the Results in Sachs and Warner (1995)

	Dependent variable: average GDP growth 1970–1990 (Sachs and Warner, 1995)					Dependent variable: fixed effects from Table 5,[a] column (1), excluding the long-run effect of commodity prices					Dependent variable: fixed effects from Table 5,[a] column (1), including the long-run effect of commodity prices				
	(1)	(2)	(3)	(4)	(5)	(6)	(7)	(8)	(9)	(10)	(11)	(12)	(13)	(14)	(15)
sxp	-6.71***	-5.90***	-6.99***	-8.48***	-8.24***	-0.17***	-0.16***	-0.17***	-0.18***	-0.18***	-0.00	-0.00	-0.02	0.00	0.01
	(1.93)	(1.41)	(1.43)	(1.59)	(1.46)	(0.04)	(0.03)	(0.03)	(0.03)	(0.03)	(0.06)	(0.06)	(0.05)	(0.06)	(0.06)
lgdpea70	0.09	-0.84***	-1.32***	-1.71***	-1.75***	0.06***	0.05***	0.04***	0.04***	0.04***	0.06***	0.05***	0.04***	0.04***	0.04***
	(0.18)	(0.18)	(0.16)	(0.26)	(0.27)	(0.00)	(0.00)	(0.00)	(0.01)	(0.00)	(0.00)	(0.01)	(0.00)	(0.01)	(0.01)
Sopen		3.10***	2.43***	1.54***	1.59***		0.04***	0.03***	0.02*	0.02**		0.02*	-0.00	-0.00	-0.00
		(0.40)	(0.40)	(0.39)	(0.37)		(0.01)	(0.01)	(0.01)	(0.01)		(0.01)	(0.01)	(0.01)	(0.01)
linv7089			1.35***	1.12***	0.82***			0.02***	0.01	0.02**			0.03***	0.03***	0.03***
			(0.20)	(0.27)	(0.29)			(0.01)	(0.01)	(0.01)			(0.01)	(0.01)	(0.01)
RI				0.33**	0.39***				0.01**	0.00				0.00	0.00
				(0.13)	(0.13)				(0.00)	(0.00)				(0.00)	(0.00)
dtt7090					0.11**					-0.00***					0.00
					(0.06)					(0.00)					(0.00)
Obs.	93	89	89	72	72	85	83	83	71	71	85	83	83	71	71
R–sq.	0.16	0.52	0.67	0.71	0.74	0.77	0.83	0.85	0.87	0.90	0.68	0.69	0.77	0.75	0.77

	(16)	(17)	(18)	(19)	(20)	(21)	(22)	(23)	(24)	(25)	(26)	(27)	(28)	(29)	(30)
snr	-6.02***	-2.81*	-3.55**	4.29*	6.44***	-0.16***	-0.12***	-0.12***	-0.15***	-0.13***	0.09	0.11*	0.11**	0.12***	0.11**
	(1.49)	(1.49)	(1.44)	(2.42)	(1.92)	(0.03)	(0.03)	(0.03)	(0.04)	(0.05)	(0.06)	(0.06)	(0.04)	(0.04)	(0.05)
lgdpea70	0.21	-0.68***	-1.08***	-1.45***	-1.51***	0.06***	0.05***	0.05***	0.04***	0.04***	0.06***	0.05***	0.04***	0.04***	0.04***
	(0.16)	(0.19)	(0.18)	(0.31)	(0.31)	(0.00)	(0.00)	(0.00)	(0.01)	(0.01)	(0.00)	(0.00)	(0.00)	(0.01)	(0.01)
Sopen		3.20***	2.51***	1.66***	1.54***		0.04***	0.03***	0.02	0.02		0.03***	0.01	0.01	0.01
		(0.45)	(0.42)	(0.39)	(0.36)		(0.01)	(0.01)	(0.01)	(0.01)		(0.01)	(0.01)	(0.01)	(0.01)
linv7089			1.25***	1.11***	0.72			0.01**	0.01	0.02**			0.02***	0.03***	0.03***
			(0.26)	(0.41)	(0.41)			(0.01)	(0.01)	(0.01)			(0.01)	(0.01)	(0.01)
RI				0.33*	0.42**				0.01*	0.00				0.00	0.00
				(0.18)	(0.16)				(0.00)	(0.00)				(0.00)	(0.00)
dtt7090					0.22***					-0.00					0.00
					(0.08)					(0.00)					(0.00)
Obs.	93	93	93	72	72	90	88	88	71	71	90	88	88	71	71
R–sq.	0.45	0.58	0.57	0.57	0.64	0.77	0.81	0.82	0.86	0.86	0.68	0.70	0.74	0.79	0.80

Notes: All estimations by OLS. See section 7 [of original text] and the revised 1997 version of Sachs and Warner (1995) for explanation of variables. Robust standard columns (6) to (10), reports the results of the S&W regressions when replacing the dependent variable of S&W by the fixed effects from the regression without the level of the nonagricultural commodity export price index. Our results are very similar to the S&W results. In particular, the coefficients of the share of primary exports in GNP (sxp) are again always negative and statistically significant at 1 percent. In other words, when we use the fixed effects from the regression in which we do not control for the negative long-run effect of nonagricultural commodity prices, the S&W resource curse effect remains.

We next repeat the same procedure but now using the fixed effects from the regression with the level of the commodity export price index. The results are reported in Table 31.3, columns (11) to (15). The coefficients of the share of primary exports in GNP (sxp) are now positive in two out of the five specifications and equal to zero or very close to zero in the three other specifications. All five coefficients are highly insignificant. These results indicate that the S&W resource curse effect disappears once we control for our long-run negative effect of commodity prices.

We test the robustness of these results by replacing the share of primary exports in GNP (sxp) by the 1971 share of mineral production in GNP (snr), an alternative measure of resource intensity also taken from S&W. This measure is particularly suited as it nicely squares with our finding that the resource curse is confined to non-agricultural commodities (minerals). The estimation results are reported in Table 31.3, columns (16) to (30). Again, our long-run negative effect of nonagricultural commodity prices fully explains the resource curse effect in S&W. In fact, the coefficients of the share of mineral production in GNP (snr) in the specifications of Table 31.3, columns (26) to (30), are positive and statistically significant in four out of the five specifications. So once we control for the adverse long-run effects of higher mineral prices, minerals are a blessing, not a curse.

These results provide robust evidence that the S&W cross-sectional resource curse effect disappears once we control for the long-run negative effect of nonagricultural commodity prices. We therefore believe that our panel data analysis on the short- and long-run effects of commodity booms within countries also provides a comprehensive explanation of why the empirical resource curse literature so often finds a negative effect of resource abundance on growth in cross-section regressions.

Conclusions

We find strong evidence of a resource curse. Commodity booms have positive short-term effects on output, but adverse long-term effects. The long-term effects are confined to "high-rent," non-agricultural commodities. Within this group, we find that the resource curse is avoided by countries with sufficiently good institutions. We investigate possible transmission channels and find that an overvalued exchange rate, high public and private consumption, low or inefficient investment, and to a lesser extent commodity price volatility and slow growth in the services sector explain a substantial part of the curse. These findings are consistent with recent theory that points at inefficient redistribution in return for political support as the root of the curse but also lend some support to the large Dutch disease literature. In addition, the results support the more general idea that commodity booms lead countries away from productive activities and provide incentives for non-productive activities, such as rent-seeking, lobbying, or public sector employment. We find that the negative long-run effects of commodity booms that we identify in our estimations fully account for the cross-section results in the seminal paper by Sachs and Warner (1995). Once we control for these long-run adverse effects, non-agricultural resource abundance has a positive effect on average cross-country growth rates.

References

Acemoglu, Daron and James A. Robinson, "Inefficient Redistribution," *American Political Science Review* 95 (2001), 649–661.

Acemoglu, Daron, James A. Robinson and Simon Johnson, "The Colonial Origins of Comparative Development: An Empirical Investigation," *American Economic Review* 91 (2001), 1369–1401.

Acemoglu, Daron, James A. Robinson and Thierry Verdier, "Kleptocracy and Divide-and-Rule: A Model of Personal Rule (The Alfred Marshall Lecture)," *Journal of the European Economic Association Papers and Proceedings* 2 (2004), 162–192.

Arezki, Rabah and Frederick van der Ploeg, "Can the Natural Resource Curse Be Turned into a Blessing? The Role of Trade Policies and Institutions," CEPR Discussion Paper no. 6225 (2007).

Baland, Jean-Marie and Patrick Francois, "Rent-Seeking and Resource Booms," *Journal of Development Economics* 61 (2000), 527–542.

Barro, Robert J., "Inequality and Growth in a Panel of Countries," *Journal of Economic Growth* 5 (2000), 5–32.

Collier, Paul and Anke Hoeffler, "Greed and Grievance in Civil Wars," *Oxford Economic Papers* 56 (2004), 563–595.

Corden, W. Max and J. Peter Neary, "Booming Sector and De-Industrialization in a Small Open Economy," *The Economic Journal* 92 (1982), 825–848.

Henisz, Witold J., "The Institutional Environment for Economic Growth," *Economics and Politics* 12 (2000), 1–31.

Henisz, Witold J., "The Institutional Environment for Infrastructure Investment," *Industrial and Corporate Change* 11 (2002), 355–389.

Hodler, Roland, "The Curse of Natural Resources in Fractionalized Countries," *European Economic Review* 50 (2006), 1367–1386.

Kuralbayeva, Karlygash and David Vines, "Terms of Trade Shocks in an Intertemporal Model: Should We Worry about the Dutch Disease or Excessive Borrowing?," CEPR Discussion Paper no. 5857 (2006).

Lane, Philip. R. and Aaron Tornell, "Power, Growth and the Voracity Effect," *Journal of Economic Growth* 1 (1996), 213–241.

Matsuyama, Kiminori, "Agricultural Productivity, Comparative Advantage, and Economic Growth," *Journal of Economic Theory* 58 (1992), 317–334.

Mehlum, Halvor, Karl Moene and Ragnar Torvik, "Institutions and the Resource Curse," *The Economic Journal* 116 (2006), 1–20.

Michaels, Guy, "The Long-Term Consequences of Regional Specialization," CEPR Discussion Paper no. 6028 (2006).

Robinson, James A. and Ragnar Torvik, "White Elephants," *Journal of Public Economics* 89 (2005), 197–210.

Robinson, James A., Ragnar Torvik and Thierry Verdier, "The Political Foundations of the Resource Curse," *Journal of Development Economics* 79 (2006), 447–468.

Sachs, Jeffrey D. and Andrew M. Warner, "Natural Resource Abundance and Economic Growth," NBER Working Paper no. 5398 (1995, revised 1997, 1999).

Sachs, Jeffrey D. and Andrew M. Warner, "The Big Push, Natural Resource Booms and Growth," *Journal of Development Economics* 59 (1999), 43–76.

Sachs, Jeffrey D. and Andrew M. Warner, "The Curse of Natural Resources," *European Economic Review* 45 (2001), 827–838.

Sala-i-Martin, Xavier and Arvind Subramanian, "Addressing the Natural Resource Curse: An Illustration from Nigeria," NBER Working Paper no. 9804 (2003).

Skaperdas, Stergios, "Warlord Competition," *Journal of Peace Research* 39 (2002), 435–446.

Sokoloff, Kenneth L. and Stanley L. Engerman, "Institutions, Factor Endowments, and Paths of Development in the New World," *Journal of Economic Perspectives* 14 (2000), 217–232.

Tornell, Aaron and Philip R. Lane, "The Voracity Effect," *American Economic Review* 89 (1999), 22–46.

Torvik, Ragnar, "Learning By Doing and the Dutch Disease," *European Economic Review* 45 (2001), 85–306.

Torvik, Ragnar, "Natural Resources, Rent Seeking and Welfare," *Journal of Development Economics* 67 (2002), 455–470.

Van Wijnbergen, Sweder J. G., "The Dutch Disease: a Disease after All?," *Economic Journal* 94 (1984), 41–55.

Wick, Katharina and Erwin H. Bulte, "Contesting Resources—Rent Seeking, Conflict and the Natural Resource Curse," *Public Choice* 128 (2006), 457–476.

32

Parasite Prevalence and the Worldwide Distribution of Cognitive Ability

Christopher Eppig, Corey Fincher, and Randy Thornhill

While Diamond makes the case in Chapter 8 that geography is the most important factor in economic development, in this chapter attention moves from geography to health. Christopher Eppig, Corey Fincher, and Randy Thornhill find that the higher the prevalence of infectious disease in a given country, the lower the average intelligence of the population, as measured by IQ tests. Carefully controlling for the effects of confounding variables, such as winter temperatures, distance from sub-Saharan Africa, and average education, the authors find infectious disease to be the strongest predictor of IQ. This leads them to conclude that parasites cause reduced national averages of intelligence, which in turn goes a long way to restricting economic growth.

HERE, WE OFFER A NEW HYPOTHESIS—THE PARASITE-STRESS HYPOTHE-sis—to explain the worldwide distribution of intelligence. The brain is the most complex and costly organ in the human body. In human newborns, the brain demands 87 per cent of the body's metabolic budget, 44 per cent at age five, 34 per cent at age ten, and 23 per cent and 27 per cent for adult males and females, respectively (Holliday 1986). Presumably, if an individual cannot meet these energetic demands while the brain is growing and developing, the brain's growth and developmental stability will suffer. Lynn (1990, 1993) has

Reprinted by permission of The Royal Society from Christopher Eppig, Corey L. Fincher, and Randy Thornhill, "Parasite Prevalence and the Worldwide Distribution of Cognitive Ability," *The Royal Society* 277, no. 1701 (2010).

argued that nutrition is vital to high degrees of mental development. Lynn (1990) suggested that nutrition may account for the Flynn effect (large increases in IQ over short periods of time as nations develop; Flynn 1987), and later (Lynn 1993) reviewed evidence showing that undernourished children have smaller heads, smaller brains and lower psychometric intelligence than sufficiently nourished children.

Parasitic infection affects the body, and hence the brain, energetically in four ways. (i) Some parasitic organisms feed on the host's tissues: the loss must be replaced at energetic cost to the host. Such organisms notably include flukes and many kinds of bacteria. (ii) Some parasites inhabit the intestinal tract or cause diarrhoea, limiting the host's intake of otherwise available nutrients. These notably include tapeworms, bacteria, giardia and amoebae. (iii) Viruses use the host's cellular machinery and macromolecules to reproduce themselves, at the energetic expense of the host. (iv) The host must activate its immune system to fight off the infection, at energetic expense. Of these, diarrhoeal diseases may impose the most serious cost on their hosts' energy budget. First, diarrhoeal diseases are the most common category of disease on every continent, and are one of the two top killers of children under five, accounting for 16 to 17 per cent of all of these deaths worldwide (WHO 2004a). Second, diarrhoea can prevent the body from accessing any nutrients at all. If exposed to diarrhoeal diseases during their first five years, individuals may experience lifelong detrimental effects to their brain development, and thus intelligence. Parasites may negatively affect cognitive function in other ways, such as by infecting the brain directly, but we focus only on energetic costs.

The worldwide distribution of parasites is well known. Disease-causing organisms of humans are more prevalent in equatorial regions of the world and become less prevalent as latitude increases. Ecological factors contributing to this distribution include mean annual temperature, monthly temperature range and precipitation (e.g. Guernier et al. 2004). Similar trends of parasite distribution have been shown in other host species (e.g. Møller 1998).

Many studies have shown a negative relationship between intestinal helminth infection and cognitive ability (reviewed in Watkins & Pollitt 1997; see also Dickson et al. 2000). Although several hypotheses have been proposed to explain this phenomenon, none have considered intestinal worms in the larger context of all parasitic infection, nor have they considered fully the energetic cost of infection and its consequences on the brain. Other studies have shown relationships between helminth infection and economic and educational factors that are related to intelligence. For example, Bleakley (2007) studied the effects of eradication of hookworm in the southern US during the early twentieth century, and found that areas where hookworm infections had been greatly reduced had higher average incomes after treatment than areas that had not received treatment. Jardin-Botelho et al. (2008) found that Brazilian children infected with hookworm performed more poorly on cognitive tests than uninfected children, and that children infected with more than one type of intestinal helminth performed more poorly than children infected with only one.

Thus, from the parasite-stress hypothesis, we predict that average national intelligence will correlate significantly and negatively with rates of infectious disease, and that infectious disease will remain an important predictor of average national intelligence when other variables are controlled for. It is the purpose of this study to introduce this hypothesis to describe the worldwide variation in intelligence, and to provide some supportive evidence using correlations and linear modelling techniques. . . .

Discussion

The negative relationship between infectious disease and IQ was statistically significant at the national level both worldwide and within five of Murdock's (1949) six world regions. All analyses showed that infectious disease was a significant predictor of average national IQ, whether using either of Lynn & Vanhanen's (2006) two datasets or Wicherts et al.'s (2010b) data. The zero-order correlation between DALY owing to infectious disease and average national IQ was higher than that of any other variable for which there is a previously proposed causal explanation. The world regions analysis showed that the international pattern is repeated within five of the six regions despite a region's generally similar cultural history. The only world region in which this relationship was not significant was South America. This exception may be owing to the presence of several outliers. The group of conspicuous outliers in which IQ was much lower than expected in the worldwide trend are all Caribbean countries (St Lucia, Dominica, St Kitts and Nevis, Antigua and Barbuda, Grenada, St Vincent and Grenadines, and Jamaica), which represent 4 of 23 nations in the South America analysis (St Lucia, Dominica, Grenada, and St Vincent and the Grenadines). Because these outliers are in the same geographical location, it is possible that local parasites that are not included in the DALY owing to infectious disease variable are causing these outliers. HLM analysis shows that, despite the nonsignificance of the correlation between IQ and infectious disease within South American nations, this trend is significant overall across Murdock's (1949) six world areas.

Nutritional stress correlated with average national IQ ($r \frac{1}{4} 20.72$), but this relationship was not significant when the effects of infectious disease were removed. This supports the suggested link between intelligence and nutrition. Given the energetic cost of infectious disease, individuals who are burdened with parasites may be more likely to be affected by nutritional deficiencies. Likewise, individuals who are suffering from nutritional deficiencies may be less able to mount an effective immune response.

Multiple regression shows that, of infectious disease, temperature, evolutionary novelty and AVED, infectious disease is the best predictor of intelligence by a large margin. The effects of years of education are not significant, while temperature and evolutionary novelty seem to have distinct predictive power beyond infectious disease. Although this model cannot rule out the independent effect of distance from central Africa, this effect is difficult to interpret because of the doubt cast on the theory underlying this variable (Wicherts et al. 2010a). Although the effects of education and GDP per capita are not statistically significant when other factors are controlled for, this is not to say that these factors are not involved. A nation of more intelligent individuals is likely to produce a higher GDP, but a wealthier nation is also more able to pay for public education, as well as public medical and sanitation services. An indirect link between education and intelligence may also exist, as a better-educated population may be more interested in public health measures—leading to increased IQ by reducing parasite stress—provided that education includes information about germ theory and hygiene. These sources of endogeneity must be considered when interpreting our findings (and see below). It should also be mentioned that we are not arguing that global variation in intelligence is only caused by parasite stress. Rather, variation in intelligence is probably caused by a variety of factors, including those we have mentioned here as well as factors that are yet unknown.

If the general pathway we propose is correct, there are two plausible mechanisms by which a trade-off in allocation of energy to immune function versus brain development and maintenance may occur. First, parasitic infection may intermittently cause the redirection of energy away from brain development. In this case, during periods of infection, the brain receives fewer energetic resources, but this allocation to brain function will return to pre-infection levels during healthy periods. During periods of infection, whatever aspects of the brain that are growing and developing will suffer reduced phenotypic quality. Second, exposure to infectious agents may cause a developmental pathway that permanently invests more energy into immune function at the expense of brain growth. In this scenario, large amounts of energy would be allocated into immune function during periods of health, as opposed to only redirecting energy during periods of infection. This could operate through a variety of mechanisms. A plausible mechanism is that higher investment in immune system is triggered by individual exposure to infectious disease at some point during ontogeny. This may include triggering from exposure to maternal antibodies while in utero.

We also propose a complementary hypothesis that may explain some of the effects of infectious disease on intelligence. As we mentioned, it is possible that a conditional developmental pathway exists that invests more energy into the immune system at the expense of brain development. In an environment where there has consistently been a high metabolic cost associated with parasitic infection, selection would not favour the maintenance of a phenotypically plastic trait. That is, the conditional strategy of allocating more energy into brain development during periods of health would be lost, evolutionarily, if periods of health were rare. Peoples living in areas of consistently high prevalence of infectious disease over evolutionary time thus may possess adaptations that favour high obligatory investment in immune function at the expense of other metabolically expensive traits such as intelligence. Data do not currently exist on temporal variation of the severity of infectious disease across the world over human history. For genetically distinct adaptations in intelligence to exist based on this principle, parasite levels must be quite consistent over evolutionary time. If this is not the case, then selection would maintain investment in the immune system and in the brain as a plastic (as opposed to static) trait. The Flynn effect (Flynn 1987) indicates that conditional developmental causes must be at work at least in part. Large increases in intelligence across a few generations cannot be attributed to genetic differences caused by evolutionary processes. Hence, it does not seem probable that region-specific genetic adaptations are the primary cause of the worldwide variation in intelligence.

Our findings suggest that the heritable variation in intelligence may come from two sources: brain structure and immune system quality. Thus, two individuals may possess identical genes for brain structure, but have different IQ owing to differences in immune system quality reflecting their personal allocation of energy into brain development versus immunity.

Our findings are consistent with a number of other findings in the literature. In particular, the Flynn effect (Flynn 1987) demands that any hypothesis regarding the worldwide variation and distribution of intelligence must be able to account for some factor that allows for large IQ gains over time spans seemingly too short to be attributed to evolution by natural selection. The parasite-stress hypothesis allows for such a factor in the form of reduced parasitic infection. As societies become modernized, decreased parasite stress may occur through multiple pathways. As national wealth increases, medicine, vaccinations and potable water can be purchased by both the government and by individuals. Moreover, there is cross-national evidence that, as democratization increases, there are corresponding increases in public health legislation and infrastructure. Democratization also increases levels of education, better allowing individuals to seek out and understand information that reduces parasitic infection (Thornhill et al. 2009). This source of endogeneity is not a flaw, but a prediction of our hypothesis.

Mackintosh (2001) presented comprehensive evidence that skin darkness and the associated cellular components (e.g. melanocytes) have an important role in defending against infectious disease. Moreover, Manning et al. (2003) found that, in sub-Saharan Africa, rates of HIV infection were negatively associated with skin darkness. Manning et al. (2003) attributed this relationship in part to lower infection rates of other parasites, especially bacteria and fungi, that lead to tissue damage in the genital tract and hence increased opportunity for contracting HIV. Templer & Arikawa (2006) concluded that, despite the strong negative correlation between skin colour and average national IQ, there must be an unknown mediating factor accounting for both because there is no obvious reason for skin darkness to reduce IQ. Given the previous research linking skin colour to infectious disease (Mackintosh 2001; Manning et al. 2003), the unknown factor linking skin colour and IQ may be infectious disease.

Several studies have shown a positive relationship between IQ and body symmetry (e.g. Furlow et al. 1997; Prokosch et al. 2005; Bates 2007; Penke et al. 2009; but see also Johnson et al. 2008). There is evidence that body symmetry is a measure of developmental stability, an important component of which is owing to reduced contact with infectious disease (Thornhill & Møller 1997). Our study suggests that IQ and body symmetry correlate because they are both affected negatively by exposure to high infectious disease. Individuals who are exposed to infectious disease may have many aspects of their body develop imperfectly, including the brain, negatively affecting both their body symmetry and cognitive ability. Indeed, recent research indicates that there is a positive relationship between body asymmetry and atypical brain asymmetries (Yeo et al. 2007).

The hygiene hypothesis proposes that some autoimmune diseases may be caused by low exposure to pathogens during ontogeny (e.g. Strachan 1989). Previous studies of individual differences have shown that intelligence correlated positively with the frequency of asthma and allergies (reviewed in Jensen & Sinha 1993). According to the parasite-stress hypothesis, high intelligence is allowed in part by low exposure to infectious disease. Thus the relationship between intelligence and autoimmune diseases, such as asthma and allergies (reviewed in Gangal & Chowgule 2009), is probably mediated through exposure to infectious disease. We predict that this positive relationship between IQ and autoimmune diseases will also be robust across nations, and that it will be mediated by infectious disease.

Although our results support our predictions, further studies must be done to establish causation. Longitudinal methods could be used to test this hypothesis on the individual level. Children's IQ could be measured at an early age and remeasured later in life, while monitoring for infectious diseases throughout childhood. This would not only provide another test of our hypothesis, but may be able to determine the effects of individual infectious diseases on cognitive development. Additionally, it could be determined which, if either, trade-off mechanism we discussed is responsible for the detrimental effects of infectious disease on intelligence. Both may operate but with geographical differences based on the consistency of infectious disease over time. As nations develop, they would be monitored for declining rates of parasitic infection to determine (i) whether this corresponds with elevated IQ and (ii) whether any IQ gain is sufficient to account for the Flynn effect.

References

Bates, T. C. 2007 Fluctuating asymmetry and intelligence. Intelligence 35, 41–46. (doi:10.1016/j.intell.2006.03.013)

Bleakley, H. 2007 Disease and development: evidence from hookworm eradication in the American south. Q. J. Econ. 122, 73–117.

Dickson, R., Awasthi, S., Williamson, P., Demellweek, C. & Garner, P. 2000 Effects of treatment for intestinal helminth infection on growth and cognitive performance in children: systematic review of randomized trials. Br. Med. J. 320, 1697–1701. (doi:10.1136/bmj.320. 7251.1697)

Flynn, J. R. 1987 Massive IQ gains in 14 nations: what IQ tests really measure. Psychol. Bull. 101, 171–191. (doi:10.1037/0033-2909.101.2.171)

Furlow, F. B., Armijo-Prewitt, T., Gangestad, S. W. & Thornhill, R. 1997 Fluctuating asymmetry and psychometric intelligence. Proc. R. Soc. Lond. B 264, 823–829. (doi:10.1098/rspb.1997.0115)

Gangal, S. V. & Chowgule, R. 2009 Infections in early life and susceptibility to allergic diseases: relevance of hygiene hypothesis. Curr. Sci. India 96, 784–793.

Guernier, V., Hochberg, M. E. & Gue'gan, J. 2004 Ecology drives the worldwide distribution of human diseases. PLOS Biol. 2, 740–746.

Holliday, M. A. 1986 Body composition and energy needs during growth. In Human growth: a comprehensive treatise, vol. 2 (eds F. Falkner & J. M. Tanner), pp. 101–117. New York, NY: Plenum.

Jardin-Botelho, A., Raff, S., Rodrigues, R. A., Hoffman, H. J., Diemert, J. H., Correa-Oliviera, R., Bethony, J. M. & Gazzinelli, M. F. 2008 Hookworm, Ascaris lumbricoides infection and polyparasitism associated with poor cognitive performance in Brazilia.

Jensen, A. R. & Sinha, S. N. 1993 Physical correlates of human intelligence. In Biological approaches to the study of human intelligence (ed. P. A. Vernon), pp. 139–242. Norwood, NJ: Ablex.

Johnson, W., Segal, N. L. & Bouchard Jr, T. J. 2008 Fluctuating asymmetry and general intelligence: no genetic or phenotypic association. Intelligence 36, 279–288. (doi: 10.1016/j.intell.2007.07.001)

Lynn, R. 1990 The role of nutrition in secular increases in intelligence. Person. Indiv. Differ. 11, 263–285.

Lynn, R. 1991 The evolution of racial differences in intelligence. Mankind Quart. 32, 99–121.

Lynn, R. 1993 Nutrition and intelligence. In Biological approaches to the study of human intelligence (ed. P. A. Vernon), pp. 243–258. Norwood, NJ: Ablex.

Lynn, R. & Meisenberg, G. 2010 The average IQ of sub-Saharan Africans: comments of Wicherts, Dolan, and van der Maas. Intelligence 38, 21–29. (doi:10.1016/j. intell.2009.09.009)

Lynn, R. & Mikk, J. 2007 National differences in intelligence and educational attainment. Intelligence 35, 115–121. (doi:10.1016/j.intell.2006.06.001)

Lynn, R. & Vanhanen, T. 2001 National IQ and economic development: a study of eighty-one nations. Mankind Quart. 41, 415–435.

Lynn, R. & Vanhanen, T. 2002 IQ and the wealth of nations. Westport, CT: Praeger.

Lynn, R. & Vanhanen, T. 2006 IQ and global inequality. Augusta, GA: Washington Summit.

Mackintosh, J. A. 2001 The antimicrobial properties of malanocytes, melanosomes and melanin and the evolution of black skin. J. Theor. Biol. 211, 101–113. (doi:10 .1006/jtbi.2001.2331)

Manning, J. T., Bundred, P. E. & Henzi, P. 2003 Melanin and HIV in sub-Saharan Africa. J. Theor. Biol. 223, 131–133. (doi:10.1016/S0022-5193(03)00070-5)

Møller, A. P. 1998 Evidence of larger impact of parasites on hosts in the tropics: investment in immune function within and outside the tropics. Oikos 82, 265–270. (doi:10.2307/3546966)

Murdock, G. P. 1949 Social structure. New York, NY: Macmillan.

Penke, L., Bates, T. C., Gow, A. J., Pattie, A., Starr, J. M., Jones, B. C., Perrett, D. I. & Deary, I. J. 2009 Symmetric faces are a sign of successful cognitive aging. Evol. Hum. Behav. 30, 429–437. (doi:10.1016/j.evolhumbehav. 2009.06.001)

Prokosch, M. D., Yeo, R. A. & Miller, G. F. 2005 Intelligence tests with higher g-loadings show higher correlations with body symmetry: evidence for a general fitness factor mediated by developmental stability. Intelligence 33, 203–213. (doi:10.1016/j .intell.2004.07.007)

Strachan, D. P. 1989 Hay-fever, hygiene, and household size. Brit. Med. J. 299, 1259–1260. (doi:10.1136/bmj.299. 6710.1259)

Templer, D. I. & Arikawa, H. 2006 Temperature, skin color, per capita income, and IQ: an international perspective. Intelligence 34, 121–139. (doi:10.1016/j. intell.2005 .04.002)

Thornhill, R., Fincher, C. L. & Aran, D. 2009 Parasites, democratization, and the liberalization of values across contemporary countries. Biol. Rev. 84, 113–131. (doi:10.1111/j.1469-185X.2008.00062.x)

Thornhill, R. & Møller, A. P. 1997 Developmental stability, disease and medicine. Biol. Rev. 72, 497–548. (doi:10. 1017/S0006323197005082)

Watkins, W. E. & Pollitt, E. 1997 'Stupidity or worms': do intestinal worms impair mental performance? Psychol. Bull. 121, 171–191. (doi:10.1037/0033-2909.121 .2.171)

WHO 2004a Global burden of disease: 2004 update. Geneva, Switzerland: World Health Organization.

WHO 2004b World health report 2004. Geneva, Switzerland: World Health Organization.

Wicherts, J. M., Borsboom, D. & Dolan, C. V. 2010a Why national IQs do not support volutionary theories of intelligence. Person. Indiv. Differ. 48, 91–96. (doi:10.1016 /j. paid.2009.05.028)

Wicherts, J. M., Dolan, C. V. & van der Maas, H. L. J. 2010b A systematic literature review of the average IQ of sub-Saharan Africans. Intelligence 38, 1–20. (doi:10. 1016/j.intell.2009.05.002)

Yeo, R. A., Gangestad, S. W. & Thoma, R. J. 2007 Developmental instability and individual variation in brain development: implications for the origin of neuro-developmental disorders. Curr. Dir. Psychol. Sci. 16, 245–249. (doi:10.1111/j. 1467-8721.2007. 00513.x)

33

Climate Change and Economic Growth: Evidence from the Last Century

Melissa Dell, Benjamin F. Jones, and Benjamin A. Olken

In this section of the book we have included chapters covering the ongoing debate over the potential consequences of natural resources on economic growth and the gap as well as the impact of diseases. In this chapter, Melissa Dell, Benjamin Jones, and Benjamin Olken examine the impact of climate change on economic growth. They ask whether changes in temperature have differentially affected rich and poor countries. The authors find that climate change has slowed growth in poor countries, but not in wealthier countries. Their results suggest that the slowing of growth is the result not simply of lower agricultural output, but of lower industrial output as well. There is also some evidence that lower growth rates could trigger political instability, which in turn further slows growth.

CLIMATE CHANGE MAY—OR MAY NOT—BE A CENTRAL ISSUE FOR THE world economy. Yet assessing the economic impact of climate change faces a fundamental challenge of complexity: the set of mechanisms through which climate may influence economic outcomes, positively or negatively, is extremely large and difficult to investigate comprehensively. Even if the effect of climate on each relevant mechanism were known, one would still be faced with the challenge of how various mechanisms interact to shape macroeconomic outcomes.

Reprinted with permission of the American Economic Association from *American Economic Journal* 4, no. 3 (2012).

The complexity of the climate-economy relationship is apparent in a brief survey of the literature. Much research focuses on agriculture (e.g., Adams et al. 1990; Mendelsohn et al. 2001; Deschenes and Greenstone 2007; Guiteras 2007). Other research examines ocean fisheries, fresh water access, storm frequency, migration, tourism and many other potential issues, as reviewed extensively in the recent Intergovernmental Panel on Climate Change 4th Assessment Report (IPCC 2007). Less discussed, but perhaps critical, are classic ideas in economic development that link productivity to temperature (e.g., Montesquieu 1750; Marshall 1890; Huntington 1915). Meanwhile, there are well-established, substantial effects of temperature on mortality (e.g., Curriero et al., 2002; Deschenes and Moretti 2007; Deschenes and Greenstone 2007), temperature on crime (e.g., Field 1992; Jacob et al. 2007), and drought on conflict (Miguel et al. 2004), all of which have direct and indirect effects on economic activity. Faced with these different channels, the traditional approach to estimating the overall economic impact of climate change is to use "Integrated Assessment Models" (IAM), which take some subset of mechanisms, specify their effects, and then add them up (e.g., Mendelsohn et al. 2000, Nordhaus and Boyer 2000, Tol 2002). Implementations of the IAM approach require many assumptions about which effects to include, how each operates, and how they aggregate.

This paper takes a different approach. Rather than identifying mechanisms one-by-one and summing up, we examine the effects of temperature and precipitation on a single aggregate measure: economic growth. Specifically, we construct historical temperature and precipitation data for each country and year in the world from 1950 to 2003 and combine this dataset with historical growth data. The main identification strategy uses year-to-year fluctuations in temperature and precipitation within countries to estimate the impact of temperature and precipitation on economic growth. This approach estimates the effect of short-run climate fluctuations using relatively few assumptions. It examines aggregated outcomes directly, rather than relying on a priori assumptions about what mechanisms to include and how they might operate, interact, and aggregate.

Our main results show large, negative effects of higher temperatures on growth, but only in poor countries. In poorer countries, we estimate that a 1°C rise in temperature in a given year reduces economic growth in that year by about 1.1 percentage points. In rich countries, changes in temperature have no discernable effect on growth. Changes in precipitation also have no substantial effects on growth in either poor or rich countries. We find broadly consistent results across a wide range of alternative specifications.

To interpret these effects, one can distinguish two potential ways temperature could affect economic activity: 1) influencing the level of output, for example by affecting agricultural yields, or 2) influencing an economy's ability to grow, for example by affecting investments or institutions that influence productivity growth. By looking at multiple lags of temperature, we can examine whether temperature shocks appear to have temporary or persistent impacts on economic output—and thus whether temperature has level or growth effects (or both). Our results suggest that higher temperatures may reduce the growth rate in poor countries, not simply the level of output. Since even small growth effects have large consequences over time, these growth effects—if they persist in the medium run—would imply large impacts of temperature increases.

We also find evidence for a broad set of mechanisms through which temperature might affect growth in poor countries. While agricultural output contractions are part of the story, we also find adverse effects of hot years on industrial output and aggregate investment. Further, higher temperatures lead to political instability in poor countries, as evidenced by irregular changes in the national leadership. These industry, investment, and institutional effects sit outside the primarily agricultural focus of most economic research on climate change and underscore the importance of an inclusive approach to understanding climate change implications. These broader mechanisms also help explain how temperature might affect growth rates in poor countries, not simply the level of output.

These results are identified using short-run fluctuations in temperature and precipitation. A fundamental issue, however, is that the long-run effects of climate change may be quite different from the effects of short-run fluctuations. For example, in the long run, adaptation mechanisms might mitigate the short-run economic impacts that we observe. Alternatively, climate change may have additional long-run effects, including changes in water tables, soil quality, and sea level, producing larger impacts (IPCC, 2007; Meehl et al., 2004; Nicholls and Leatherman, 1995). . . . .

Models with Lags

The above results, using the simple model with no lags, reject the null hypothesis that temperature has no effect on growth in poor countries. This section considers more flexible models with up to 10 lags of temperature to better understand the dynamics of these temperature effects, nesting both the level and growth effects of temperature.

Table 33.1 presents results from estimating equation (4) with no lags, one lag, three lags, five lags, or ten lags of the climate variables. In columns (1)–(5), temperature and its lags are the only climate variables included. Columns (6)–(10) present results where precipitation and its lags are also included. All climate variables are interacted with poor and rich country dummies. The bottom two rows of each column present, separately, the cumulated effect of temperature for poor and rich countries, calculated by summing the respective temperature

Table 33.1 Models with Lags

	(1) No lags	(2) 1 lag	(3) 3 lags	(4) 5 lags	(5) 10 lags	(6) No lags	(7) 1 lag	(8) 3 lags	(9) 5 lags	(10) 10 lags
Temperature × Poor	-1.087**	-0.954*	-0.932*	-0.933*	-1.112*	-1.074**	-0.945*	-0.925*	-0.925	-1.071*
	(0.442)	(0.559)	(0.560)	(0.562)	(0.586)	(0.446)	(0.558)	(0.557)	(0.559)	(0.585)
L1: Temperature × Poor		-0.351	-0.247	-0.328	-0.216		-0.33	-0.213	-0.333	-0.217
		(0.854)	(0.919)	(0.909)	(0.958)		(0.852)	(0.921)	(0.909)	(0.954)
L2: Temperature × Poor			-0.210	-0.183	-0.120			-0.249	-0.226	-0.140
			(0.441)	(0.459)	(0.485)			(0.443)	(0.458)	(0.484)
L3: Temperature × Poor			-0.216	-0.096	-0.231			-0.189	-0.075	-0.262
			(0.519)	(0.559)	(0.606)			(0.511)	(0.549)	(0.594)
Temperature × Rich	0.219	0.202	0.243	0.293	0.392	0.208	0.197	0.237	0.272	0.383
	(0.210)	(0.232)	(0.241)	(0.238)	(0.255)	(0.212)	(0.234)	(0.243)	(0.240)	(0.260)
L1: Temperature × Rich		0.047	0.074	0.094	0.093		0.038	0.067	0.083	0.056
		(0.268)	(0.251)	(0.252)	(0.268)		(0.269)	(0.250)	(0.252)	(0.266)
L2: Temperature × Rich			0.062	0.115	0.043			0.064	0.143	0.098
			(0.190)	(0.195)	(0.209)			(0.190)	(0.194)	(0.209)
L3: Temperature × Rich			-0.019	0.120	0.203			-0.045	0.097	0.211
			(0.197)	(0.186)	(0.198)			(0.197)	(0.185)	(0.197)
Includes precipitation vars.	NO	NO	NO	NO	NO	YES	YES	YES	YES	YES
Observations	6014	6014	5905	5785	5449	6014	6014	5905	5785	5449
R-squared	0.14	0.14	0.15	0.15	0.15	0.15	0.15	0.15	0.15	0.15
Sum of all temp. coeff. in poor countries	-1.087**	-1.304*	-1.605**	-1.718**	-2.006**	-1.074**	-1.275*	-1.576**	-1.662**	-1.946**
	(0.442)	(0.677)	(0.641)	(0.720)	(0.866)	(0.446)	(0.689)	(0.651)	(0.737)	(0.881)
Sum of all temp. coeff. in rich countries	-0.102	0.219	0.249	0.361	0.184	0.208	0.235	0.324	0.155	-0.147
	(0.647)	(0.210)	(0.268)	(0.331)	(0.455)	(0.212)	(0.271)	(0.332)	(0.460)	(0.654)

Notes: All specifications use PWT data and include country FE, region × year FE, and poor × year FE. Robust standard errors in parentheses, adjusted for clustering at parent-country level. Sample includes all countries with at least 20 years of growth observations. Columns (6) – (10) also include Precipitation × Poor and Precipitation × Rich, with the same number of lags as the temperature variables shown in the table. Columns (4) and (9) also include the 4th and 5th lags of Temperature × Poor, Temperature × Rich, Precipitation × Poor and Precipitation × Rich. Similarly columns (5) and (10) also include the 4th through 10th lags of Temperature × Poor, Temperature × Rich, Precipitation × Poor and Precipitation × Rich; those coefficients are suppressed in the table to save space. Sum of all temperature coefficients in poor countries shows the sum (and calculated standard error) of Temperature × Poor and all of the lags of Temperature × Poor included in the regression; sum of all temperature coefficients in rich countries is calculated analogously.

* significant at 10%; ** significant at 5%; *** significant at 1%

variable and its lags. In models with more than three lags, given space constraints, the table reports only the first three lags and the sum of all the lags.

Table 33.1 shows that the cumulative effect of temperature in poor countries becomes more negative as more lags are included. With no lags, in columns (1) and (6), a one-time 1°C temperature increase in a poor country reduces growth by 1.07–1.09 percentage points. With one lag included, the cumulative effect is a reduction of 1.28–1.30 percentage points. Including three, five, or ten lags increases the magnitude and statistical significance of these cumulative effects, with a 1°C temperature increase producing a 1.58–2.01 percentage point reduction in growth.

The individual lag coefficients show little evidence of a level effect of temperature on output. That is, the effects of above average temperature appear to persist in the medium-run, rather than being reversed. Recalling the empirical framework, level effects are reversed when the climate shock is reversed. In the model with one lag—i.e., columns (2) and (6)—a level effect would appear as equal and opposite coefficients on the immediate effect and the first lag. More generally, even if level effects occur with lags—i.e., if last year's temperature affects this year's harvest—level effects are eventually reversed once the shock disappears. Therefore, to the extent temperature effects are level effects, the cumulated sum of the temperature effect and all its lags should be zero. That the lags in Table 33.1 do not sum to zero—and, in fact, the cumulated effect of temperature becomes stronger as more lags are added—suggests that the effects of temperature persist in the medium run; i.e., they look more like growth effects than level effects.

Of course, temperature effects may be mitigated beyond the 10-year horizon examined here. However, the increasing cumulative impact of temperature as longer lags are considered suggests that, if anything, the effects of temperature shocks strengthen over time rather than diminish. . . .

Channels

The climate change literature suggests a wide array of channels through which climate may affect economic outcomes, from agriculture to political instability to health. In this section, we apply the panel methodology developed above to investigate several such mechanisms.

It is important to note that these analyses are reduced-form, and therefore do not identify the possibly complex structural relationships between climate, growth, and other outcomes. For example, higher temperature could lead directly to political instability by making a population more prone to riot, with possible effects on growth. Conversely higher temperature could cause lower agriculture yields, with the resulting GDP reduction leading to political instability. Teasing out structural relationships between these many variables would require a large number of identifying assumptions. Instead, we focus on net climate effects, documenting several plausible channels through which climate may affect aggregate output.

Decomposing the Impacts of Climate

Table 33.2 examines the impact of temperature and precipitation on several components of GDP. Panel A begins with zero-lag models to test the null hypotheses of no effects of temperature and precipitation. Column (1) examines growth in agricultural value-added, and column (2) investigates growth in industrial value-added. These variables are taken from the World Development Indicators. (Note that the WDI sample is more limited than the PWT sample.) Column (3) examines growth in investment, using data from the Penn World Tables.

The results in Panel A show substantial, negative effects of temperature in poor countries on all three of these components of GDP. Column (1) shows that a 1°C higher temperature in poor countries is associated with 2.37 percentage points lower growth in agricultural output. For wealthier countries, the point estimate is substantially smaller and not statistically significant, showing 0.34 percentage points lower growth in agricultural output for each additional 1°C of temperature. As might be expected, precipitation positively impacts agriculture—each additional 100mm of annual rainfall is associated with 0.24 percentage points higher growth in agricultural output in poor countries and 0.14 percentage points higher growth in agricultural output in richer countries.

Column (2) of Panel A shows negative temperature impacts on the growth of industrial value-added in poor countries. Specifically, a 1°C higher temperature in poor countries is associated with 2.44 percentage points lower growth in industrial output. This effect may reflect labor productivity losses, consistent with a long literature documenting the impact of temperature on output in factory settings. Alternatively, this effect could represent a demand-side spillover from the negative effect of temperature on agricultural output.

The results on investment in column (3) also show substantial negative impacts of temperature in poor countries. Specifically, a 1°C higher temperature in poor countries reduces the growth rate of investment by 3 percentage points. We find no temperature effects in rich countries.

Panel B examines the lag structure of these effects. For each dependent variable (growth in agriculture, growth in industry, and growth in investment), we present results with 1, 5, and 10 lags. For all three dependent variables, the impact effect—i.e., the coefficient on contemporaneous temperature—is negative, large, and statistically significant. For agriculture and investment, the point estimates of the cumulative effects, while imprecise, are somewhat

Table 33.2 Components of Output Growth

Panel A: Models with no lags

| | Dependent Variable is: | | |
	(1) Growth in Agriculture Value-Added	(2) Growth in Industrial Value-Added	(3) Growth in Investment
	No lags	No lags	No lags
Temperature			
Immediate effect – Poor	-2.367***	-2.443**	-2.991**
	(0.816)	(0.958)	(1.189)
Immediate effect – Rich	-0.340	0.410	-0.103
	(0.512)	(0.376)	(0.470)
Precipitation			
Immediate effect – Poor	0.242**	0.295**	0.040
	(0.117)	(0.133)	(0.170)
Immediate effect – Rich	0.138*	-0.050	-0.425***
	(0.077)	(0.071)	(0.109)
Observations	3812	3812	6014

Panel B: Models with lags

| | Dependent Variable is: | | | | | | | | |
| | (1) | (2) | (3) | (4) | (5) | (6) | (7) | (8) | (9) |
	Growth in Agriculture Value-Added			Growth in Industrial Value-Added			Growth in Investment		
	1 Lag	5 Lags	10 Lags	1 Lag	5 Lags	10 Lags	1 Lag	5 Lags	10 Lags
Temperature									
Cumulative effect – Poor	-1.078	-1.440	-1.800*	-2.842**	-2.076	-2.410	-2.078	-2.071	-2.118
	(0.777)	(0.880)	(1.044)	(1.235)	(1.672)	(2.129)	(1.325)	(2.070)	(2.896)
Cumulative effect – Rich	0.419	0.346	0.662	0.517	0.473	0.852	-0.401	-1.194	-1.312
	(0.538)	(0.588)	(0.717)	(0.455)	(0.565)	(0.762)	(0.534)	(0.817)	(1.112)
Immediate effect – Poor	-3.081***	-2.947***	-3.044***	-2.182**	-2.350**	-2.532**	-3.512**	-3.943***	-3.930***
	(1.056)	(1.008)	(1.019)	(0.930)	(0.999)	(1.000)	(1.417)	(1.338)	(1.386)
Immediate effect – Rich	0.791	-0.731	-0.861	0.369	0.323	0.292	0.091	0.316	0.303
	(0.640)	(0.625)	(0.641)	(0.372)	(0.381)	(0.389)	(0.600)	(0.638)	(0.719)

(continues)

Table 33.2 continued

Panel B: Models with lags	(1)	(2)	(3)	(4)	(5)	(6)	(7)	(8)	(9)
					Dependent Variable is:				
	Growth in Agriculture Value-Added			Growth in Industrial Value-Added			Growth in Investment		
Precipitation									
Cumulative effect – Poor	0.153	0.118	0.087	0.416***	0.407**	0.390	0.196	-0.076	-0.030
	(0.105)	(0.129)	(0.169)	(0.132)	(0.166)	(0.301)	(0.192)	(0.269)	(0.305)
Cumulative effect – Rich	0.174**	0.392***	0.495**	-0.118	-0.259	-0.147	-0.456***	-0.236	-0.512*
	(0.078)	(0.095)	(0.197)	(0.108)	(0.197)	(0.252)	(0.128)	(0.211)	(0.297)
Immediate effect – Poor	0.270**	0.309**	0.331**	0.238	0.138	0.098	-0.037	0.032	0.000
	(0.127)	(0.130)	(0.132)	(0.145)	(0.125)	(0.117)	(0.209)	(0.209)	(0.209)
Immediate effect – Rich	0.136	0.137	0.149	-0.030	-0.038	-0.027	-0.405***	-0.454***	-0.445***
	(0.091)	(0.093)	(0.093)	(0.068)	(0.071)	(0.072)	(0.123)	(0.135)	(0.146)
Observations	3812	3804	3794	3812	3804	3794	6014	5785	5449

Notes: Growth in agriculture value-added and industrial value-added are from the World Development Indicators; growth in investment is from the Penn World Tables. All specifications include country FE, region × year FE, and poor × year FE. Robust standard errors in parentheses, adjusted for clustering at parent-country level. Sample includes all countries with at least 20 years of PWT growth observations (i.e., the same set of countries considered in the previous tables.)

smaller than the immediate effects, suggesting the presence of some combination of growth and level effects for these variables. By contrast, for industrial value-added, the point estimates of the cumulative effects are virtually identical to the immediate effect.

Overall, the findings in Table 33.2 demonstrate broad negative effects of increased temperature. We find effects not only on agriculture, but also on industrial output and investment. The fact that temperature has such broad effects may help explain both the magnitude of the overall effect of temperature on output as well as its persistence.

Political Economy Effects

Temperature may also impact growth if increased temperature leads to political instability, which in turn impedes investment and productivity growth. The idea that riots and protests are more likely in warmer weather is an old idea that has found substantial empirical support (e.g., United States Riot Commission, 1968; Carlsmith and Anderson, 1979; Boyanowsky, 1999). If warm weather causes riots, in some fraction of cases these riots could spill over into political change and instability. Alternatively, economic shocks from climate might provoke dissatisfied citizens to seek institutional change.

We examine the impact of temperature on several measures of political instability. First, the Polity IV dataset (Marshall and Jaggers 2004) rates the political system in each country annually from −10 (fully autocratic) to +10 (fully democratic). This POLITY variable further designates "interregnum periods," which are years when the political system is in flux and no clear political regime has emerged. We consider two dummy variables: one for any change in the POLITY variable, indicating a political change, and one for a POLITY interregnum period, indicating a period of political turmoil.

The second set of measures comes from the Archigos dataset on political leaders (Goemans et al. 2006). This dataset classifies the primary national political leader for each country and year and codes all leader transitions into two categories: "regular" transitions, which take place according to the prevailing institutional rules of the country, and "irregular" transitions (such as coups), which do not follow the prevailing institutional rules. We consider a dummy variable for years with leadership transitions, as well as separate dummy variables for regular and irregular transitions.

The results are presented in Table 33.3. Looking first at POLITY, an additional 1°C in poor countries is associated with a (statistically insignificant) 2.3 percentage point increase in the probability of any change in POLITY. Column (2) shows that a 1°C increase in temperature leads to a 2.3 percentage point increase in the probability of a POLITY interregnum period, which suggests that all of the changes in POLITY induced by temperature occur through increases

Table 33.3 Political Economy Effects

	(1)	(2)	(3)	(4)	(5)	(6)	(7)
						Conflict	
	Any change in POLITY score	POLITY interregnum period	Political Stability leader transition	Regular leader transition	Irregular leader transition	Start of new conflicts (conditional on conflict = 0 in t–1)	End of conflicts (conditional on conflict > 0 in t–1)
Temperature	−0.008	−0.015**	−0.003	−0.002	−0.001	−0.005	0.019
	(0.009)	(0.007)	(0.013)	(0.013)	(0.005)	(0.005)	(0.051)
Temperature X Poor	0.031*	0.037**	0.040*	0.001	0.041***	0.014	0.017
	(0.018)	(0.018)	(0.022)	(0.001)	(0.013)	(0.012)	(0.056)
Precipitation	0.000	0.001	0.002	0.002	0.000	0.001	0.009
	(0.003)	(0.001)	(0.002)	(0.002)	(0.001)	(0.001)	(0.015)
Precipitation X Poor	−0.010**	−0.010*	−0.006*	−0.006*	0.000	−0.003	−0.015
	(0.004)	(0.005)	(0.004)	(0.003)	(0.002)	(0.002)	(0.016)
Obs.	5804	5804	7143	7143	7143	6087	966
R–squared	0.14	0.21	0.18	0.2	0.11	0.09	0.43
Temperature effect in poor countries	0.023	0.023	0.037**	−0.002	0.039***	0.009	0.002
	(0.016)	(0.018)	(0.018)	(0.010)	(0.012)	(0.011)	(0.032)
Precipitation effect in poor countries	−0.010***	−0.005	−0.004	−0.004	0.000	−0.001	−0.006
	(0.004)	(0.003)	(0.003)	(0.002)	(0.001)	(0.001)	(0.006)

Notes: Columns (1) and (2) use data from the POLITY IV dataset; columns (3), (4), and (5) use data from the Archigos dataset; and columns (6) and (7) use data from the PRIO dataset. Columns (1) – (5) include country FE, region × year FE, and poor × year FE; columns (6) and (7) include country FE and year FE. Robust standard errors in parentheses, adjusted for clustering at parent-country level. Sample includes all countries with at least 20 years of PWT growth observations (i.e., the same set of countries considered in the previous tables.)

*significant at 10%; **significant at 5%; ***significant at 1%

in political instability. Though these effects are statistically insignificant (p-values of 0.16 and 0.20 respectively), the estimated magnitudes are substantial, given that the baseline probability of a POLITY change in poor countries is 13.1 percent and the baseline probability of an interregnum period in poor countries is only 5.7 percent. The results on precipitation are somewhat weaker, but suggest that political change in poor countries is more likely in years with lower rainfall.

The Archigos results show a similar pattern and are stronger statistically. A one degree rise of temperature raises the probability of leader transitions by 3.7 percentage points in poor countries (column 3). Moreover, this effect comes not from regular leadership transitions (column 4) but from irregular leader transitions—i.e., coups (column 5). This effect of 3.9 percentage points is large, as the baseline probability of an irregular leader transition is only 4.5 percent per year in poor countries. By contrast, we see no effects on leader transitions in rich countries.

Combined, the POLITY and Archigos data tell a consistent story: higher temperatures are associated with political instability in poor countries. Whether temperature has direct effects on political instability, which in turn affects economic growth, or whether temperature has direct effects on economic growth, which in turn affects political instability—or both—is difficult to distinguish, since poor economic performance and political instability are likely mutually reinforcing. Nevertheless, the impact of temperature on political instability in poor countries is suggestive of an institutional mechanism through which temperature might affect productivity growth, rather than just the level of income.

The final columns of Table 33.3 consider the impact of temperature and precipitation on conflict. We use the PRIO conflict data (PRIO 2006), which indicates for every country-year whether the country was involved in a high-intensity conflict (defined as = 1,000 conflict deaths/year) or a low-intensity conflict (defined as 25 to 1000 conflict deaths/year). Column (6) examines the start of conflicts (i.e., the probability a conflict begins given no conflict in the previous period), and column (7) examines the end of conflicts (i.e., the probability a conflict ends given conflict in the previous period). We find no significant effect of temperature or precipitation on either the start or conclusion of conflicts. The political impacts of temperature and precipitation thus appear more concentrated in political instability rather than outright civil or interstate wars.

Part 9
Conclusion

34

Inequality in a Global Perspective: Directions for Further Research

Mitchell A. Seligson

That there is a vast gap between the world's rich and poor is beyond dispute. The causes and dynamics of the gap, however, are the subject of considerable debate, as the reader of the preceding chapters in this volume will now know. Fortunately, debate over the gap between rich and poor has led to a vast increase in our understanding of the origins and persistence of both the domestic and the international gaps between rich and poor. Indeed, it can be said that research in this area represents one of the best illustrations of a cumulative social science continually deepening its understanding of an important, multifaceted problem. This concluding chapter suggests some directions for future research so that continued rapid progress can be made in our understanding of the gaps.

Evolution of Research on the Gaps

The enormous success of the Marshall Plan in helping to rapidly rebuild war-devastated economies in Europe in the 1940s and early 1950s was not met with similar success in other parts of the world as the US implemented its initial foreign assistance in the form of the "Point IV" program. The economies of poor countries remained surprisingly resistant to steady growth as the norm. Moreover, within poor countries, little progress was being made in reducing the gaps between rich and poor people. Once it became clear that the post–World War II hopes for rapid, universal development in the third world would not be fulfilled, social scientists set their minds to determining why that was the case. It was obvious, then as now, that unless development in the third

423

world was to surge ahead, the gap between these economies and those of the increasingly prosperous developed countries would inevitably widen. The serious implications of this development for world peace have been too great to ignore.

Early thinking about the source of the problem focused on the cultural distinctiveness of the third world. The observation that these cultures were indeed different from those found in the first world with its industrial, capitalist development was enough to convince a generation of social scientists to view cultural barriers as the principal explanation for underdevelopment. Many of these explanations were fascinating, showed creative scholarship, and, moreover, seemed to make a good deal of sense. As research proceeded, however, disenchantment with this perspective began to grow. The more that was understood about the third world, the less that cultural factors seemed to be able to explain its underdevelopment. Many researchers found the explanation ethnocentric at best and insulting at worst. Studies also revealed many instances of "underdeveloped cultures" producing rapid growth. A good example is China, whose culture was seen as a barrier to growth, when that same culture, for the past few decades, seems to be producing unprecedented rates of growth. It seems that some people proved highly capable of tailoring their cultures to conform to more "modern" ways of doing things. As a result, cultures proved to be far more malleable and responsive than had been originally believed. Finally, despite putative cultural limitations, some third world nations made rapid strides in economic growth; some middle-income countries, for example, have been able to achieve higher growth rates in recent years than have many industrialized countries. Yet in recent years the debate on the impact of culture on development has again become quite lively, and the empirical research reported in this volume shows that values might indeed matter. This entire paradigm of thinking is reflected by Francis Fukuyama (1995a, 1995b), who has argued for the importance of trust in development. More recently, Larry Harrison and Samuel Huntington have edited a book called *Culture Matters: How Values Shape Human Progress* (2002) that collects a great deal of scholarship on this point. The debate has become more technical as a series of quantitative studies have attempted to reinvigorate the study of culture (Inglehart 1988, 1990) and as other studies have challenged this approach (Booth and Seligson 1984; Seligson and Booth 1993). One of the most recent empirical studies on the subject is included in this volume (Chapter 22). This article, written by Jim Granato, Ronald Inglehart, and David Leblang, was strongly refuted, however, by Robert Jackman and Ross Miller (1996b) in an article on the subject, and I myself have criticized the entire approach (Seligson 2002). Further research on the impact of inequality on civic participation has been published by Eric Uslaner and Mitchell Brown (2005) as well as Frederick Solt (2008, 2010). Most recently, as shown by Gregory Clark (2007), cultural values related to education and hard work may be concentrated in certain populations and not others. According to Clark, the industrial revolution is the outcome, a revolution that dramatically widened the gap between rich and poor nations.

Whatever their explanatory power, cultural explanations no longer dominate the field, and as a result, other theories have emerged. Increasingly, the thinking about development has become "globalized." The very nature of the gap problem probably forced such thinking to emerge. After all, in order to study the gap, one must first specify the frame of reference in some sort of comparative perspective. Studies can focus on the "absolute" or the "relative" gap, but these terms have no meaning unless they are situated within a comparative framework; poor people are poor only with respect to rich people.

In this book, extensive consideration has been given to the "inverted U-curve" of development. In global terms, according to Simon Kuznets (see Chapter 12) and other proponents of this thesis, developing nations are likely to experience a widening internal gap before they see the gap narrow in the later phases of industrialization. Dependency and world-systems thinkers agree that the gaps are widening, but do not believe that they will ultimately narrow as industrialization matures, because both the widening internal and the widening external gaps between rich and poor are seen as a function of the world capitalist economic system.

The studies by John Passé-Smith (Chapters 2 and 5) suggest strongly that the gaps are very wide, and are continuing to widen with each passing decade. Yet the controversy presented in Part 4 of this book, between those who argue that the economies of the world are on a path toward convergence and those who argue that the gaps are widening, shows that the issue has still not been resolved.

This disagreement has led some to examine more closely the key cases of dependency and development. Heather-Jo Hammer and John Gartrell (Chapter 24) show that dependency is not confined to poor nations, but seems to affect Canada as well. Yet Glenn Firebaugh (Chapter 4), in a masterful analysis, shows that much of the slowed growth that is reportedly caused by dependency (as argued by Andre Gunder Frank in Chapter 23) comes from a serious misreading of the data. Jonathan Conning and James Robinson (2009) provide important empirical analysis of the so-called enclave economy, a central notion in dependency theory. Like the culture paradigm before it, dependency and world-systems thinking no longer seem to offer *the* explanation for the gaps between rich and poor.

Today, attention is focused on the role of institutions, policies, and the state, and some of the key thinking in that area is contained in the contributions in Part 7 of this volume. Mancur Olson Jr. (Chapter 26), in a careful comparison of cases, such as North Korea versus South Korea, in which culture, history, and resources are largely held constant and in which what varies is the political system and the policies made, presents a strong case that countries are not prisoners of their pasts or their environments but rather can make good or bad choices. Some states choose a capitalist route, but then engage in "rent-seeking" behavior that enables privileged groups to benefit from state policies, while producing an overall negative impact on the national level of economic development. Michael Lipton (Chapter 27) shows how rent-seeking has a pernicious impact on development. Rent-seeking states, therefore, seem bad for economic growth. At the same time, however, the democratic versus authoritarian nature of the state seems to make little difference in growth. For a long time it was thought that dictatorships do better than democracies, and this allowed such highly regarded scholars as Samuel Huntington to suggest that in order to get development, a state needed to pass through a protected period of strong-man rule. Yet as Adam Przeworski and Fernando Limongi (Chapter 28) show, dictatorships seem no better at stimulating economic development than do democracies. Indeed, in other work by this team, it has been shown that democracies do better on a per capita basis compared to dictatorships, and Erich Weede (1996) has found that democracies produce more stable growth than dictatorships. Moreover, even more recent research forces us to completely reexamine the role of democracy (Gerring et al. 2005; Epstein et al. 2006; Doucouliagos and Ulubaşoğlu 2008; Boix 2011). What does seem to be true, however, is that investment in human capital in the form of education and health really does spur growth and reduce inequality (as shown by Nancy Birdsall and Richard Sabot in Chapter 29). Research on this topic continues (Keun and Kim 2009; Acemoglu and Johnson 2007).

Considerable data have been brought to bear on the various theories seeking to explain these dual gaps. It is in the analysis and interpretation of these data that we see the clearest example of cumulative social science in the making. This volume presents some of the best examples of rigorous testing of theory with data. While it is too early to predict a definitive resolution of the debates, and it may even be too early to say which side seems to have the edge, it is possible to look ahead and suggest some directions for future research. A pessimistic interpretation of the present state of the debate is that each side is locked into its own respective position and thus that future research will be stalemated. The vital importance of the problem, not only to the world's poor but also to those responsible for helping to secure peace, requires that such a stalemate be avoided. It is therefore appropriate at this juncture to assess where the research has taken us and where it ought to go. The contributions in this volume trace the intellectual history of the debate over the gaps; the remainder of this chapter is devoted to outlining the directions in which fruitful further research might proceed.

The International Gap

By the early 1980s, in terms of gross national product (GNP) per capita, a small group of oil-exporting nations enjoyed incomes higher than the average found among industrial market economies. In 1981, Saudi Arabia had a GNP per capita of $12,600; the United Arab Emirates, $24,660; while the mean income of the industrial market economies was $11,120. None of the industrialized countries came even close to exceeding the income of Kuwait and the United Arab Emirates; Switzerland had a GNP per capita of $17,430, the highest of the industrial countries. The United States, traditionally the world's GNP per capita leader, was far behind, at $12,820. Oil-rich Libya was moving up rapidly, with a GNP per capita reaching $8,450, only slightly behind that of the United Kingdom, at $9,110.

Yet we now know that much of the dramatic increase in the GNP of the oil states was a short-term phenomenon owing to the sharp price rises of petroleum in the 1970s. By 2011 the World Bank was reporting on its website that Saudi Arabia had a GNP per capita of only $17,820, compared to $48,620 for the United States. Libya in 2011 had a GNP per capita of $12,230, while the tiny United Arab Emirates, with a GNP per capita of $40,600, had largely closed the gap.

The rapid growth and equally rapid decline of the oil states, however, is the exception to the rule. As John Passé-Smith (Chapter 2) has shown, there is very little movement, over the long term, from rich to poor and vice versa. While South Korea, Taiwan, and Malaysia, for example, have been rapidly growing, they have incomes that are only a fraction of those found in the industrialized countries. Consider China, which has had very strong growth for over a decade, but whose GNP per capita was only $4,940 in 2011, compared to $48,620 for the United States. In terms of GNP per capita, it seems clear that there is a near-universal widening gap between rich and poor.

This conclusion, however, is based upon a single indicator, namely per capita gross national product, recently renamed by the World Bank as gross national income (GNI). The use of a single indicator of any social phenomenon has long fallen into disrepute in the social sciences. Why then base conclusions about such an important subject entirely upon per capita income data? The response to this query from those who use it in their research as a sole indicator of income is that it is by far the most widely accepted indicator. The principal problem emerges not because of the unreliability of data collected on each nation, but because of validity problems associated with converting local currency values into dollars using exchange rates, the standard currency normally employed by those who compare such data. Broader indexes, such as the Human Development Index (HDI) of the United Nations Development Programme, constitute one promising alternative.

In order to convert the multitude of currencies used around the world into a single standard, it has long been common practice to use the exchange rate of the foreign currency in US dollars. The exchange rate appeared for a long time to be the only reasonable way to compare the value of different currencies. In fact, however, it is now known that such comparisons introduce considerable distortion in the data. The exchange rate comparisons do not accurately measure differences in the relative domestic purchasing power of currencies. The net result is that the exchange rate GNP measures can greatly exaggerate the gap between rich and poor countries. This exaggeration occurs in part because international exchange rates are susceptible to fluctuations from equilibrium value. In addition, according to the "law of one price," the costs of goods and services that are traded (among countries) tend to equalize. For a developing country in which most of the production does not enter the world trade market, the exchange rate–converted GNP figures will be an underestimate of true income.

In order to correct for this bias, the United Nations undertook the International Comparisons Project (ICP), now a larger project involving the World Bank, which has provided some revealing findings. Using purchasing power parity (PPP), Passé-Smith (Chapter 5) finds that the gap is less expansive than it is when measured with exchange rate–converted GNPs, but that this gap is still considerable. For some countries the change has been large; for example, a country like Sri Lanka, when the traditional measure is used, exhibits a gap nearly four times as large as when the new, purchasing power index is computed. Countries such as Colombia and Mexico also reveal considerable differences, although these differences are not as great as in the case of Sri Lanka. Because of these shifts, the appendix of this book provides PPP figures as well as GNI figures.

It would seem appropriate to suggest that future research on the international gap employ the purchasing power index rather than the exchange rate–based comparison, in order to obtain a truer picture of income comparisons. This is what Firebaugh does in Chapter 4 of this volume. When measured with purchasing power–converted GNPs, the gap remains, albeit slightly smaller overall. Hence, despite the dramatic narrowing of the international gap in the case of Sri Lanka, that country's income per capita in 2006, even when using the purchasing power index, was only 8 percent of that of the United States. Kenya, in which the GNP per capita is more than quadrupled with the new index, still confronts income levels that are only 3.3 percent of those of the United States according to the World Bank. The revised measure, therefore, does not eliminate the gap between rich and poor. It does, however, provide what appears to be a more appropriate standard of comparison. The mere fact that the gap narrows through the use of the new index does not necessarily imply that there is an overall trend toward a narrowing of the international gap. Fortunately, the World Bank now annually reports these purchasing power parity measures online.

Another way of looking at the gap question is to shift the focus away from per capita income measures and to look at human needs and human development instead. Using this criterion, one obtains a rather different perspective on the international gap question. According to studies conducted by the World Bank (1980: 32–45), major strides have been made in the reduction of absolute poverty since the close of World War II. These studies have found that the proportion of people around the world living in absolute poverty has declined. In addition, there has been a sharp worldwide increase in literacy levels over the past three decades. Even more dramatic improvements have been experienced in the area of health. Infant mortality rates have dropped considerably and life expectancy has been extended. For example, citizens of low-income countries in 1950 had a life expectancy of only thirty-five years, whereas by 2011 that had risen to fifty-nine years. But citizens of the advanced industrial countries have a life expectancy of eighty years.

Research on the international gap that is more consciously directed at these indicators of basic human needs may provide a clearer picture of the impact of the gap than that presented by income figures alone. But before one leaps to the conclusion that the human-needs approach can demonstrate that the gap is narrowing, some additional context needs to be added to the discussion. While it is true that the *proportion* of people who are experiencing improved education, health, and life expectancy has increased, the absolute number of poor people in the world has increased dramatically because of high birthrates in the developing world. Hence the World Bank (1980: 35) estimated that despite the increases in the levels of literacy, the number of illiterate people grew by some 100 million between 1950 and 1980. And by 1995, in the low-income countries of the world alone, the number of illiterate adults grew to 1.1 billion compared to 800 million in 1980 (World Bank 1980: 110; 1995: 214). The sharp increases in wealth in China in recent years, however, have reduced this number, as China has moved out of the low-income group of countries. Moreover, there is increasing evidence that the quality of education in much of the developing world outside East Asia lags far behind that found in the industrialized countries. The quality gap is especially acute in secondary and higher education, where technical advances are so very rapid and the cost of obtaining modern training equipment is becoming ever more expensive. It is increasingly difficult for developing countries to adequately train their young people for the skills they need to compete in the high-technology world of today.

The education gap has two particularly pernicious implications. First, the increasing frustration that the brightest young people face in developing countries as a result of antiquated equipment and poorly prepared teachers results in an increasing tendency for them to migrate to the industrialized nations. Hence, the problem of the "brain-drain" is a growing one, a process that threatens to adversely affect the ability of poor nations to develop as they steadily lose that sector of their population that has the greatest intellectual potential. Second, the high-technology nature of contemporary society seems to be creating a higher and more impenetrable barrier between rich and poor countries. The efficiency of modern manufacturing techniques, along with the requirement of exceptional precision in manufacturing, makes it more and more difficult for developing nations to compete with the industrialized nations. The price advantage that developing nations have as a result of their considerably lower labor costs remains an advantage only for those items that require relatively low technical inputs. Hence, the proliferation of in-bond industries (i.e., "maquiladoras") in Central America and the Caribbean, where consumer goods are assembled for reexport, only highlights the gap in technology, since nearly all of the machinery and a good deal of the managerial skill used in those factories are imported from the industrialized nations. Even without tariff barriers, the third world faces a growing gap in technology, which is serving to reinforce the income gap.

In sum, improved income measures and basic needs data provide important avenues of research for those who wish to study the international income gap. A look at some of these data gives reason for optimism that conditions in poor countries are improving. At the same time, however, there is little reason to believe that the international income gap is narrowing. This gap, then, seems to remain the single most serious problem confronting the family of nations, and one that cries out for the attention of policymakers.

The Internal Gap

However problematical the reliability, validity, and availability of data on the international gap, they present an even more formidable barrier to the study of the internal gap. The empirical testing of dependency/world-systems explanations for the internal gap has produced widely varying results. Any reader of the major social science journals today would be rightly confused by the varied findings reported in the ever more frequently appearing articles on this subject. In reviewing this growing body of research, Edward Muller (1993) has pointed out a number of the weaknesses of those articles and goes a long way toward correcting many of them. Nonetheless, there are at least four chronic problems that beset macrolevel empirical tests of internal gap theories and that may ultimately lead down a blind alley of inconclusive findings even after the "best" methodology has been applied.

The first difficulty plaguing these macroanalytic investigations concerns sample skewing. Inequality data are difficult to obtain because many nations do not collect them (or at least do not publicly acknowledge that they do), a problem noted in several of the articles included in this volume. Despite the availability problem, researchers have proceeded with the data that are available, following the time-honored tradition in the social sciences of making do with what one finds rather than postponing research indefinitely. While such a procedure is often justifiable in many research situations, one wonders if it is justifiable in this one. The principal reason for expressing this cautionary note is that it is probably not the case that the countries reporting income distribution data are a random sample of all nations. Rather, one suspects that there are at least two factors that tend to skew the sample. First, the poorest, least-developed nations often do not have the resources (financial and technical) to conduct such studies, and indeed there may not even arise the need for such data to be collected in some of these nations. Second, nations in which income distributions are very badly skewed are probably reluctant to authorize the collection of such data, and even if the data are collected, governments may not make them publicly available. Hence, the data we do have may reflect a sample that has fewer cases of the poorest nations and fewer cases of highly unequal distribution than one might expect if the sample were random.

The second major problem with macroanalytic investigations is a direct outgrowth of the first. I call this problem the "Mauritania effect," that is, the dramatic differences in regression results that are produced from the inclusion or exclusion of as few as one or two countries. In one investigation, for example, the inclusion of Mauritania, which at the time of the study had a population of only 2.8 million people, had a major impact on the results of a key regression equation. The findings, therefore, tend not to be robust when minor variations in sample design occur; one's confidence in the results, therefore, is shaken. An unusually frank comment by a proponent of macroanalytic investigations of this type is contained in an article coauthored by Erich Weede: "it seems impossible to predict with any confidence what would happen if inequality data on all or about twice as many countries were to become available" (Weede and Tiefenbach 1981: 238).

The third problem concerns the general lack of cross-time data. However limited the sample of countries may be for the present period, even less reliable information exists on developing countries for the pre–World War II period. This is a particularly serious problem since both dependency/world-systems analysis as well as the traditional developmental approach propose longitudinal hypotheses, whereas data limitations generally impose cross-sectional designs. While such cross-sectional designs can sometimes be a useful surrogate for longitudinal studies, the problem of skewed samples reduces the value of these studies.

One serious manifestation of the lack of longitudinal data emerges in studies that include Latin American cases. As a region, Latin America is more developed than are most third world nations, and has somewhat more income distribution data available compared to other third world regions. It is also the case that Latin American nations have been found to exhibit comparatively high levels of both dependency and income inequality. One might leap to the conclusion, as some have, that this proves that inequality is a function of dependency. However, there is another equally appealing thesis, one that suggests that inequality in Latin America is part of a corporatist bureaucratic/authoritarian political culture considered to be characteristic of the region. One does not know, therefore, if Latin America's comparatively high level of inequality is a function of its intermediate level of development (as Kuznets in

Chapter 12 would suggest), or of its dependency (as the dependency/world-systems proponents would suggest; see Part 6 of this volume), or of its culture (see Part 5). To determine which of these hypotheses is correct would require longitudinal data, in order to explore the dynamics of dependency, development, and inequality.

A final difficulty with the macroanalytic research is that there is no meeting of the minds as to suitable standards of verifiability. For example, there is a wide gulf separating many dependency/world-systems theorists on the one hand, and those researchers who seek to test their hypotheses with quantitative data on the other. Fernando Henrique Cardoso and Enzo Faletto (1979), whose book on dependency theory is among the most influential and highly respected works on the subject (see Packenham 1982: 131–132), argue that empirical tests of dependency theory have largely missed the target. Cardoso (1977: 23, n. 12) explains that this is so because the tests have been "ahistorical." In addition, although not rejecting empirical verification as useful, he questions the validity of many of these studies, even those sustaining the dependency approach. Finally, in the preface to the English edition of their book, Cardoso and Faletto argue that "statistical information and demonstrations are useful and necessary. But the crucial questions for demonstration are of a different nature" (1979: xiii). The thrust of the demonstrations proposed are ones heavily grounded in historical detail and therefore highlight all the more the problem of the lack of longitudinal income distribution data.

In the coming years, it is likely that many more macroanalytic empirical investigations will be published and will continue to add to our understanding. However, it is difficult to imagine how the four major problems enumerated here will be overcome entirely. Given the difficulties apparently inherent (to a greater or lesser degree) in the macroanalytic studies conducted to date, more attention needs to be paid to methodologies that can examine, from a microanalytic perspective, the question of the origin of domestic inequality. In concluding an extensive review of the dependency/world-systems literature, Gabriel Palma argues for microanalytic studies of "specific situations in concrete terms" (1981: 413). And Volker Bornschier, Cristopher Chase-Dunn, and Richard Rubinson conclude by arguing for microsociological studies that would "clarify the specific mechanisms by which these processes operate" (1978: 679).

Problems of data availability need not cause the abandonment of future studies of the internal gap. Rather, a series of microanalytic studies would seem like a promising alternative. Such investigations would make it possible to trace the ways in which inequality is stimulated in developing countries. The emphasis needs to be placed on drawing the explicit links, if they exist, between income distribution and factors such as culture, dependency, rent-seeking, urban bias, and the like. Indeed, it can be argued that even if the data problems were not as serious as they in fact are, and if macroanalytic empirical research were to demonstrate unequivocally the existence of a connection between, for example, culture and domestic inequality, one would still need to understand *how* one affects the other, something that cannot be known from the macroanalytic studies. Without knowing how the process works, it is not possible to recommend policy "cures."

Some research has already been published that opens the door to this type of analysis. Studies of transnational corporations in Colombia (Chudnowsky 1974) and Brazil (Evans 1979; Newfarmer 1980) reveal much about the internal dynamics of dependency. A more recent microanalytic study, however, has demonstrated that imperialist penetration into one African state, Yorubaland, at the end of the nineteenth century, produced a "vibrant and creative" reaction on the part of Yoruba traders in response to new opportunities in the international market (Laitin 1982: 702).

These microanalytic studies, helpful though they are in beginning to penetrate the "black box," reflect weaknesses that would need to be overcome by those seeking to test the various explanations of income inequality proposed in this volume. First, these detailed case studies, while providing a wealth of rich, descriptive material, betray all of the limitations of generalizability inherent in the case-study method. It is to be hoped, of course, that the accumulation of these various cases ultimately will lead to a synthesis; but given the widely divergent methods, time periods, and databases employed in these studies, it is unclear at this juncture if such optimism is warranted. What is clear is that if a cumulative social science is to continue to emerge in this field, future research will need to be not only microanalytic, but self-consciously comparative as well. Only by applying the comparative method at the outset of a study of the internal causes of inequality will the data generated allow immediate comparisons and subsequent theory-testing.

Recently, as discussed by the authors of Part 7 of this volume, policies and institutions seem to be crucial factors in explaining the gap. Over the long term, "good" institutions seem to powerfully explain high growth in some countries, while "bad" institutions explain slow growth in other countries. Among the key institutions that seem to matter are private property rights. States that guarantee such rights have citizens who invest for the long term. When those rights are in doubt, quick profits and a lack of investment for the long term are the outcome. But how do such institutions come into being, and why are some resilient while others disappear? These are the questions that require microlevel analysis.

In sum, an appropriate study ought to be (1) microanalytic, (2) comparative, and (3) capable of testing the relative merits of competing paradigms. That certainly is a tall order for any researcher, but one way to achieve this goal and still plan a project of manageable proportions is to focus on key institutions through which dependency mechanisms are thought to operate. In an effort to accomplish this task, one study analyzed exchange rate policies as the "linchpin" that helps "uncover the mechanisms through which these various [dependency] effects occur" (Moon 1982: 716). A major advance of this study over previous work is the explicit linking of dependency effects to particular policies of third world governments. Hence the analysis goes far beyond most dependency literature, which typically makes frequent reference to the so-called internal colonialist *comprador* elite without revealing precisely how such elites affect income distribution. Studies such as Moon's, which examine the impact of other such crucial "linchpins" through which dependency is thought to operate, are to be encouraged.

Two efforts, therefore, need to be made if one is to hope for the advancement of the debate beyond its present state. First, historians need to assist those working in this field to develop measures of income distribution for prior epochs. Creative use of historical records (e.g., tax rolls, property registers, census data) might permit the reconstruction of such information. This, in turn, would provide the longitudinal data that are so sadly lacking at this time. John Coatsworth (1993) has already done precisely this for Latin America, and the payoffs of his approach are evident, since he seems to have been able to refute dependency theory and make a case for the role of institutions on development and underdevelopment. William Glade (1996) has extended this argument. Second, once the historical data have been gathered, social scientists need to direct their attention to the various linchpins of the causes of growth and inequality and study them in a comparative context. Perhaps with these two efforts under way, significant advances are possible in a relatively short period of time.

Conclusions

The research presented in this volume was not written in a vacuum. Investigators study problems such as the gap between rich and poor because they are concerned; and the great majority of them hope that their findings ultimately will be translated into public policy. Even though definitive findings are still far from our grasp, as has been made clear by the debate presented here, many world leaders already have sought to implement policies to correct the problem.

As the gaps between rich and poor grow wider throughout the world, the debate grows more heated. Discussions in international forums today are characterized by increasing intolerance, and terrorism has become a way of life in many parts of the world. It is hoped that this collection of studies, along with the suggestions made in this concluding chapter, will help, in some small way, to moderate tempers and guide thinking and research toward more productive answers to the important question of the causes and consequences of the gap between the rich and poor.

References

Acemoglu, Daron, and Simon Johnson. 2007. "Disease and Development: The Effect of Life Expectancy on Economic Growth." *Journal of Political Economy* 115, no. 6: 925–985.

Boix, Carles. 2011. "Democracy, Development, and the International System." *American Political Science Review* 105, no. 4 (November): 809–828.

Booth, J. A., and M. A. Seligson. 1984. "The Political Culture of Authoritarianism in Mexico: A Reexamination." *Latin American Research Review* no. 1: 106–124.

Bornschier, V., C. Chase-Dunn, and R. Rubinson. 1978. "Cross-National Evidence of the Effects of Foreign Investment and Aid on Economic Growth and Inequality: A Survey of Findings and a Reanalysis." *American Journal of Sociology* 84 (November): 651–683.

Cardoso, F. H. 1977. "The Consumption of Dependency Theory in the United States." *Latin American Research Review* 12, no. 3: 7–24.

Cardoso, F. H., and E. Faletto. 1979. *Dependency and Development in Latin America.* Berkeley: University of California Press.

Chudnowsky, D. 1974. *Empresas multinacionales y ganancias monopolicias en una economía latinoamericana.* Buenos Aires: Siglo XXI Editores.

Clark, Gregory. 2007. *A Farewell to Alms: A Brief Economic History of the World.* Princeton: Princeton University Press.

Coatsworth, John H. 1993. "Notes on the Comparative Economic History of Latin America and the United States." In Walther L. Bernecker and Hans Werner Tobler, *Development and Underdevelopment in America: Contrasts of Economic Growth in North and Latin America in Historical Perspective.* Berlin: Walter de Gruyter.

Collier, D., ed. 1979. *The New Authoritarianism in Latin America.* Princeton: Princeton University Press.

Conning, Jonathan H., and James A. Robinson. 2009. "Enclaves and Development: An Empirical Assessment." *Studies in Comparative International Development* 44 (December): 359–385.

Doucouliagos, Hristos, and Mehmet Ali Ulubaşoğlu. 2008. "Democracy and Economic Growth: A Meta-Analysis." *American Journal of Political Science* 52, no. 1: 61–83.

Epstein, David L., Robert Bates, Jack Goldstone, Ida Kristensen, and Sharyn O'Halloran. 2006. "Democratic Transitions." *American Journal of Political Science* 50, no. 3: 551–569.

Evans, P. 1979. *Dependent Development: The Alliance of Multinational, State, and Local Capital in Brazil.* Princeton: Princeton University Press.

Fukuyama, Francis. 1995a. "Social Capital and the Global Economy." *Foreign Affairs* 74 (September–October): 89–103.

———. 1995b. *Trust: The Social Virtues and the Creation of Prosperity.* New York: Free Press.

Gerring, John, Philip Bond, William T. Barndt, and Carola Moreno. 2005. "Democracy and Economic Growth: A Historical Perspective." *World Politics* 57 (April): 323–364.

Glade, William. 1996. "Institutions and Inequality in Latin America: Text and Subtext." *Journal of Interamerican Studies and World Affairs* 38 (Summer–Fall): 159–179.

Harrison, Larry E., and Samuel P. Huntington. 2002. *Culture Matters: How Values Shape Human Progress*. New York: Basic Books.

Inglehart, R. 1988. "The Renaissance of Political Culture." *American Political Science Review* 82 (December): 1203–1230.

————. 1990. *Culture Shift in Advanced Industrial Societies*. Princeton: Princeton University Press.

Jackman, Robert W. 1982. "Dependency on Foreign Investment and Economic Growth in the Third World." *World Politics* 34 (January): 175–197.

Jackman, Robert W., and Ross A. Miller. 1996a. "The Poverty of Political Culture." *American Journal of Political Science* 40, no. 3: 697–717.

————. 1996b. "A Renaissance of Political Culture?" *American Journal of Political Science* 40, no. 3: 632–659.

Keun, Lee, and Byung-Yeon Kim. 2009. "Both Institutions and Policies Matter but Differently for Different Income Groups of Countries: Determinants of Long-Run Economic Growth Revisited." *World Development* 37, no. 3: 533–549.

Kravis, I., et al. 1975. *A System of International Comparisons of Gross Product and Purchasing Power*. Baltimore: Johns Hopkins University Press.

————. 1982. *World Product and Income: International Comparisons of Real GDP*. Baltimore: Johns Hopkins University Press.

Laitin, David D. 1982. "Capitalism and Hegemony: Yorubaland and the International Economy." *International Organization* 36 (Autumn): 687–714.

Moon, B. E. 1982. "Exchange Rate System, Policy Distortions, and the Maintenance of Trade Dependence." *International Organization* 36 (Autumn): 715–740.

Muller, Edward N. 1993. "Financial Dependence in the Capitalist World Economy and the Distribution of Income Within States." In Mitchell A. Seligson and John T Passé-Smith, eds., *Development and Underdevelopment: The Political Economy of Inequality*. Boulder: Lynne Rienner.

Newfarmer, Richard. 1980. *Transnational Conglomerates and the Economics of Dependent Development: A Case Study of the International Electrical Oligopoly and Brazil's Electrical Industry*. Greenwich, CT: JAI.

O'Donnell, Guillermo. 1973. *Modernization and Bureaucratic Authoritarianism: Studies in South American Politics*. Politics of Modernization Series, no. 9. Berkeley: Institute of International Studies, University of California.

Packenham, R. A. 1982. "*Plus ça change . . .* : The English Edition of Cardoso and Faletto's *Dependencia y desarrollo en América Latina*." *Latin American Research Review* 17, no. 1: 131–151.

Palma, Gabriel. 1981. "Dependency: A Formal Theory of Underdevelopment or a Methodology for the Analysis of Concrete Situations." In Paul Streetin and Richard Jolly, eds., *Recent Issues in World Development*. New York: Pergamon.

Ray, James L., and T. Webster. 1978. "Dependency and Economic Growth in Latin America." *International Studies Quarterly* 22 (September): 409–434.

Seligson, Mitchell A. 2002. "The Renaissance of Political Culture or the Renaissance of Ecological Fallacy?" *Comparative Politics* 34: 273–292.

Seligson, Mitchell A., and J. A. Booth. 1993. "Political Culture and Regime Type: Evidence from Nicaragua and Costa Rica." *Journal of Politics* 55 (August): 777–792.

Solt, Frederick. 2008. "Economic Inequality and Democratic Political Engagement." *American Journal of Political Science* 52, no. 1: 48–60.

————. 2010. "Does Economic Inequality Depress Electoral Participation? Testing the Schattschneider Hypothesis." *Political Behavior* 32, no. 2: 285–301.

Uslaner, Eric, and Mitchell Brown. 2005. "Inequality, Trust, and Civic Engagement." *American Politics Research* 33, no. 6: 868–894.

Weede, Erich. 1996. "Political Regime Type and Variation in Economic Growth Rates." *Constitutional Political Economy* 7, no. 3: 167–176.

Weede, Erich, and H. Tiefenbach. 1981. "Some Recent Explanations of Income Inequality." *International Studies Quarterly* 25 (June): 255–282.

World Bank. 1980. *World Development Report*. New York: Oxford University Press.

———. 1995. *World Development Report*. New York: Oxford University Press.

———. 2003. *World Development Report*. New York: Oxford University Press.

Basic Indicators of
the Gaps Between
Rich and Poor Countries

	Gross National Income (GNI) per Capita 2010 (constant 2000 US$)	PPP GNI per Capita, (constant 2005 international $)	GNI per Capita Growth 2009–2010	Life Expectancy: Female	Life Expectancy: Male	Adult Literacy (% ages 15 and above)	Gini Index
Afghanistan	—	—	—	48	48	—	—
Albania	1,893	7,563	3.22	80	74	—	—
Algeria	—	—	—	74	71	—	—
American Samoa	—	—	—	—	—	—	—
Andorra	—	—	—	—	—	—	—
Angola	—	4,551	-4.09	52	49	70.14	—
Antigua and Barbuda	—	—	—	—	—	98.95	—
Argentina	—	5,076	3.64	79	72	97.80	44.49
Armenia	1,375	—	—	77	71	99.55	—
Aruba	—	—	—	77	73	96.82	—
Australia	24,411	33,195	0.67	84	80	—	—
Austria	26,581	35,232	2.50	83	78	—	—
Azerbaijan	2,169	8,581	6.42	74	68	—	—
Bahamas, The	18,570	26,995	-4.41	78	72	—	—
Bahrain	—	—	—	76	74	91.92	—
Bangladesh	607	1,621	5.11	69	68	56.78	32.12
Barbados	—	—	—	80	73	—	—
Belarus	2,673	12,198	8.08	77	65	—	—
Belgium	25,028	33,523	4.12	83	78	—	—
Belize	—	—	—	77	74	—	—
Benin	388	1,409	-0.61	57	54	42.36	—
Bermuda	—	—	—	82	77	—	—
Bhutan	1,332	4,756	8.88	69	65	—	—
Bolivia	1,174	4,149	1.73	69	64	—	—
Bosnia and Herzegovina	2,246	7,627	-0.36	78	73	97.88	—
Botswana	4,152	12,368	4.57	52	54	84.47	—
Brazil	4,628	9,904	6.74	77	70	—	—

(continues)

	Gross National Income (GNI) per Capita 2010 (constant 2000 US$)	PPP GNI per Capita, (constant 2005 international $)	GNI per Capita Growth 2009–2010	Life Expectancy: Female	Life Expectancy: Male	Adult Literacy (% ages 15 and above)	Gini Index
Brunei Darussalam	—	—	—	80	76	95.22	—
Bulgaria	2,469	11,120	1.35	77	70	—	—
Burkina Faso	283	1,136	4.76	56	54	—	—
Burundi	—	526	1.15	51	49	67.16	—
Cambodia	530	1,869	4.66	64	61	—	—
Cameroon	645	2,017	-0.01	52	50	—	—
Canada	25,103	34,599	1.78	83	79	—	—
Cape Verde	1,856	3,312	2.10	78	70	84.29	—
Cayman Islands	—	—	—	—	—	—	—
Central African Republic	229	704	1.89	49	46	55.99	—
Chad	—	—	—	51	48	34.47	—
Channel Islands	—	—	—	82	78	—	—
Chile	6,253	13,421	4.14	82	76	94.27	—
China	2,416	6,789	9.25	75	72	93.37	—
Colombia	3,078	8,113	2.29	77	70	74.94	55.91
Comoros	—	—	—	62	59	66.80	—
Congo, Dem. Rep.	99	294	72.53	50	47	—	—
Congo, Rep.	819	2,757	0.08	58	56	96.16	—
Costa Rica	5,092	10,160	3.43	82	77	56.17	—
Cote d'Ivoire	563	1,610	0.29	56	54	98.83	—
Croatia	6,016	15,318	-0.81	80	74	99.83	—
Cuba	4,430	—	2.13	81	77	—	—
Curacao	—	—	—	—	—	—	—
Cyprus	14,929	25,291	-0.13	82	77	98.28	—
Czech Republic	—	21,903	1.39	81	74	—	—
Denmark	31,383	33,147	1.92	81	77	—	—
Djibouti	—	—	—	59	56	—	—

(continues)

	Gross National Income (GNI) per Capita 2010 (constant 2000 US$)	PPP GNI per Capita, (constant 2005 international $)	GNI per Capita Growth 2009–2010	Life Expectancy: Female	Life Expectancy: Male	Adult Literacy (% ages 15 and above)	Gini Index
Dominica	—	—	—	—	—	—	—
Dominican Republic	3,921	8,115	6.97	76	70	89.54	47.20
Ecuador	1,695	7,077	3.00	78	73	91.85	49.26
Egypt, Arab Rep.	1,940	5,441	1.34	75	71	72.05	—
El Salvador	2,492	5,830	0.97	77	67	84.49	—
Equatorial Guinea	4,861	25,319	-17.90	52	50	93.94	—
Eritrea	—	—	—	63	59	67.77	—
Estonia	—	—	—	81	71	99.80	—
Ethiopia	218	928	7.34	60	57	—	—
Faeroe Islands	—	—	—	84	79	—	—
Fiji	—	—	—	72	66	—	—
Finland	27,349	31,763	2.73	83	77	—	—
France	23,193	30,047	1.16	85	78	—	—
French Polynesia	—	—	—	78	73	—	—
Gabon	3,615	11,674	-2.36	63	61	88.38	—
Gambia, The	642	1,662	3.66	59	57	49.96	—
Georgia	—	—	—	77	70	99.73	—
Germany	25,930	34,240	3.87	83	78	—	—
Ghana	—	—	4.08	65	63	67.27	—
Greece	13,077	23,311	-5.57	83	78	97.19	—
Greenland	—	—	—	73	68	—	—
Grenada	—	—	—	77	74	—	—
Guam	—	—	—	78	74	—	—
Guatemala	1,808	4,169	0.37	74	67	75.18	—
Guinea	—	—	2.33	55	52	41.05	—
Guinea-Bissau	—	—	—	49	46	54.18	—
Guyana	—	—	—	73	66	—	—
Haiti	—	1,006	-4.96	63	61	—	—

(continues)

	Gross National Income (GNI) per Capita 2010 (constant 2000 US$)	PPP GNI per Capita, (constant 2005 international $)	GNI per Capita Growth 2009–2010	Life Expectancy: Female	Life Expectancy: Male	Adult Literacy (% ages 15 and above)	Gini Index
Honduras	1,344	3,387	0.58	75	71	84.76	—
Hong Kong SAR, China	36,951	43,474	4.86	86	80	—	—
Hungary	5,363	16,149	1.05	78	71	99.05	—
Iceland	27,969	27,006	-2.10	84	80	—	—
India	—	—	—	67	64	—	—
Indonesia	1,089	3,776	5.84	71	67	—	—
Iran, Islamic Rep.	—	—	—	75	71	—	—
Iraq	—	—	—	72	65	78.17	—
Ireland	23,421	30,417	-0.04	83	79	—	—
Isle of Man	—	—	—	—	—	—	—
Israel	21,661	25,245	2.68	84	80	98.93	—
Italy	18,856	26,956	1.32	84	79	—	—
Jamaica	—	—	—	76	70	86.62	—
Japan	40,957	31,736	4.36	86	80	—	—
Jordan	2,572	5,252	-2.29	75	72	92.55	35.43
Kazakhstan	2,152	9,439	2.96	73	64	99.69	—
Kenya	468	1,478	2.64	58	55	87.38	—
Kiribati	—	—	—	—	—	—	—
Korea, Dem. Rep.	—	—	—	72	65	—	—
Korea, Rep.	16,242	26,806	5.50	84	77	—	—
Kosovo	—	—	—	72	68	—	—
Kuwait	—	—	—	76	74	—	—
Kyrgyz Republic	352	1,898	-4.18	74	65	—	—
Lao PDR	519	2,162	2.91	68	66	—	—
Latvia	5,118	13,226	-4.87	78	69	99.78	—
Lebanon	6,649	12,445	5.48	75	70	—	—
Lesotho	650	1,816	-0.99	47	48	89.65	—
Liberia	240	396	5.48	57	55	60.78	—

(continues)

	Gross National Income (GNI) per Capita 2010 (constant 2000 US$)	PPP GNI per Capita, (constant 2005 international $)	GNI per Capita Growth 2009–2010	Life Expectancy: Female	Life Expectancy: Male	Adult Literacy (% ages 15 and above)	Gini Index
Libya	—	—	—	77	72	89.21	—
Liechtenstein	—	—	—	—	—	—	—
Lithuania	—	—	—	79	68	99.70	—
Luxembourg	33,899	44,814	1.68	84	78	—	—
Macao SAR, China	—	51,394	21.81	83	78	—	—
Macedonia, FYR	2,215	9,165	2.26	77	73	97.27	44.11
Madagascar	—	—	—	68	65	—	—
Malawi	—	761	2.27	54	53	74.77	—
Malaysia	4,981	13,244	3.88	76	72	93.12	—
Maldives	—	—	—	78	75	—	—
Mali	—	—	—	52	50	31.10	33.02
Malta	10,158	20,851	2.57	83	79	—	—
Marshall Islands	—	—	—	—	—	—	—
Mauritania	592	2,138	-2.61	60	57	58.02	—
Mauritius	5,244	12,423	5.30	77	69	88.51	—
Mexico	6,044	12,318	4.50	79	74	93.07	—
Micronesia, Fed. Sts.	—	—	—	70	68	—	—
Moldova	649	3,030	10.38	73	65	98.52	33.03
Monaco	—	—	—	—	—	—	—
Mongolia	—	3,244	-1.89	72	64	97.41	—
Montenegro	2,206	10,068	1.28	77	72	98.38	—
Morocco	1,800	4,126	2.85	74	70	56.11	—
Mozambique	389	815	6.05	51	49	—	—
Myanmar	—	—	—	66	63	92.29	—
Namibia	2,544	5,542	2.24	63	62	88.75	—
Nepal	—	1,091	2.60	69	68	60.31	32.82
Netherlands	26,085	36,339	1.95	83	79	—	—
New Caledonia	—	—	—	80	73	96.49	—
New Zealand	14,225	23,760	0.55	83	79	—	—

(continues)

	Gross National Income (GNI) per Capita 2010 (constant 2000 US$)	PPP GNI per Capita, (constant 2005 international $)	GNI per Capita Growth 2009–2010	Life Expectancy: Female	Life Expectancy: Male	Adult Literacy (% ages 15 and above)	Gini Index
Nicaragua	1,138	3,143	1.68	77	71	—	—
Niger	—	—	—	55	54	—	—
Nigeria	—	—	—	52	51	61.34	48.83
Northern Mariana Islands	—	—	—	—	—	—	—
Norway	40,436	47,486	0.09	83	79	—	—
Oman	—	—	—	76	71	—	—
Pakistan	688	2,484	2.70	66	64	—	—
Palau	—	—	—	—	—	—	—
Panama	5,686	11,813	5.21	79	73	94.09	51.92
Papua New Guinea	—	—	—	65	60	60.61	—
Paraguay	1,547	4,532	12.95	74	70	93.87	52.42
Peru	2,931	7,900	5.69	76	71	—	48.14
Philippines	1,387	3,569	6.22	72	65	—	—
Poland	6,335	16,718	4.05	81	72	99.52	—
Portugal	11,351	20,940	2.19	82	76	95.18	—
Puerto Rico	9,865	—	-3.06	83	75	90.41	—
Qatar	—	—	—	78	78	96.28	—
Romania	2,592	10,735	-1.70	77	70	97.68	—
Russian Federation	2,811	13,655	3.62	75	63	99.58	—
Rwanda	350	1,068	3.97	56	54	71.05	—
Samoa	—	—	—	75	69	98.79	—
San Marino	—	—	—	86	80	—	—
Sao Tome and Principe	—	—	—	66	63	89.19	—
Saudi Arabia	—	—	—	75	73	86.55	—
Senegal	555	1,719	1.76	60	58	—	—
Serbia	1,168	9,378	0.86	77	71	97.90	—
Seychelles	—	—	—	77	70	91.84	—

(continues)

	Gross National Income (GNI) per Capita 2010 (constant 2000 US$)	PPP GNI per Capita, (constant 2005 international $)	GNI per Capita Growth 2009–2010	Life Expectancy: Female	Life Expectancy: Male	Adult Literacy (% ages 15 and above)	Gini Index
Sierra Leone	195	946	2.81	48	47	42.12	—
Singapore	32,117	51,335	8.07	84	79	95.86	—
Sint Maarten (Dutch part)	—	—	—	—	—	—	—
Slovak Republic	7,950	18,980	3.53	79	72	—	—
Slovenia	12,545	24,685	1.56	83	76	99.69	—
Solomon Islands	—	—	—	69	66	—	—
Somalia	—	—	—	53	49	—	—
South Africa	3,673	9,299	1.73	53	51	—	—
South Sudan	—	—	—	—	—	—	—
Spain	15,220	26,558	-0.05	85	79	97.75	—
Sri Lanka	1,290	4,542	6.86	78	72	91.18	—
St. Kitts and Nevis	—	—	—	—	—	—	—
St. Lucia	—	—	—	77	72	—	—
St. Martin (French part)	—	—	—	—	—	—	—
St. Vincent and the Grenadines	—	—	—	74	70	—	—
Sudan	—	—	—	63	59	71.06	—
Suriname	—	—	—	74	67	94.68	—
Swaziland	1,696	4,994	-3.09	48	49	87.44	51.49
Sweden	33,324	34,841	5.84	84	80	—	—
Switzerland	41,176	41,401	5.64	85	80	—	—
Syrian Arab Republic	1,473	4,595	-0.18	77	74	83.44	—
Tajikistan	276	1,914	5.19	71	64	99.69	—
Tanzania	452	1,276	3.84	58	57	73.21	—
Thailand	2,604	7,332	6.80	77	71	—	—
Timor-Leste	—	—	—	63	61	58.31	—

(continues)

	Gross National Income (GNI) per Capita 2010 (constant 2000 US$)	PPP GNI per Capita, (constant 2005 international $)	GNI per Capita Growth 2009–2010	Life Expectancy: Female	Life Expectancy: Male	Adult Literacy (% ages 15 and above)	Gini ndex
Togo	264	895	1.77	58	55	—	—
Tonga	—	—	—	75	69	—	—
Trinidad and Tobago	—	—	—	73	66	98.79	—
Tunisia	2,994	8,075	2.10	77	73	—	—
Turkey	5,303	12,443	8.19	76	71	99.58	—
Turkmenistan	—	—	—	69	61	—	—
Turks and Caicos Islands	—	—	—	—	—	—	—
Tuvalu	—	—	—	—	—	—	—
Uganda	373	1,127	2.40	54	53	73.21	—
Ukraine	1,023	5,935	5.28	76	65	99.71	—
United Arab Emirates	—	42,387	-7.41	78	76	—	—
United Kingdom	28,467	33,090	0.69	82	79	—	—
United States	37,808	42,619	3.29	81	76	—	—
Uruguay	8,780	12,200	7.93	80	73	98.07	45.32
Uzbekistan	—	—	—	71	65	99.39	—
Vanuatu	—	—	—	73	69	82.57	—
Venezuela, RB	5,430	10,821	-3.75	77	71	—	—
Vietnam	691	2,747	6.28	77	73	93.18	—
Virgin Islands (U.S.)	—	—	—	82	76	—	—
West Bank and Gaza	—	—	—	74	71	94.93	—
Yemen, Rep.	571	2,227	2.82	67	64	63.91	—
Zambia	361	1,227	-9.28	49	48	71.21	—
Zimbabwe	304	—	10.13	49	51	92.24	—

Source: World Bank, *World Development Indicators Online*, http://databank.worldbank.org/data/home.aspx.

Index

Abramovitz, Moses, 56, 213, 215, 218, 219, 233
Abramson, Paul, 273, 277
absolute gap, 1, 11, 17–23, 25, 29, 69, 341
Afghanistan, 376
Africa, 2, 80, 98, 99–100, 104, 108–109, 113, 131, 353, 433; agriculture in, 373; climate zones, 374–375; economic performance, 15, 28, 30, 72, 108–109, 152, 268; and government capacity 37; and income inequality, 155 (n4), 187; infectious diseases, 125–126, 378, 379, 404, 405; and land inequality, 163; mortality rates, 121; and political culture, 271; navigable rivers, 374–376; North, 25; the relative gap, 25; slavery and the slave trade, 122, 124, 133, 134; sub-Saharan 15, 103, 104, 108–109, 401; southern, 106; tax collection, 123
agriculture, 87–88, 89, 143, 147, 410; and climate change, 413–414, 417; corn, 107, 379; dependence, 310, 380; development of, 104, 109; and Dutch Disease, 136; for export, 124, 228, 291, 386; and globalization, 316–317; hacienda, 291–293 (n9, n10); and income inequality, 146, 369; innovations in, 108, 205, 207; labor, 297, 298; and land inequality, 158,

164–167; and population density, 332; productivity, 112, 204, 371, 373, 375–376, 378–379, 409, 410, 411; plantation, 134; policy, 259, 365, 369; rice, 83, 86, 133, 137, 221, 346, 390, 391, 393, 397; sugar, 83, 133, 134, 291, 292; urban bias, 346–349; wheat, 83, 107, 109, 292, 298, 346, 380
Algeria, 247, 331, 375
Americans. *See* United States
Americas, 2, 96, 104, 106, 107, 108, 109, 163, 374
Angola, 331, 375
Antigua and Barbuda, 403
Argentina, 223, 247, 310, 332, 364; and convergence, 227–228, 230, 232, 233, 234; globalization, 316, 320; industrial development, 288, 289; investment rate, 207; latifundium, 291; need for affiliation, 248; political violence in, 164; populism in, 313; temperate climate, 371, 374–376; underdevelopment, 290
Asia, xiii, 2, 13, 27, 80, 96, 97, 98, 100, 104, 105, 122, 353, 369, 429; authoritarianism, 271; Confucianism, 268; crop domestication, 107; education, 363, 366; growth rates in, 15, 37, 72, 99, 187, 356; Hinduism, 262; human capital investment, 367; human development index, 25; income

About the Book

THE FIFTH EDITION OF THIS CLASSIC READER RETAINS MANY OF THE ARTI-cles that have made the book a must-assign for classes on development and political economy, but has been updated with 14 new chapters that look even more deeply at long-term factors that help to explain the origins and current trends in the gap between rich and poor. An entirely new section focuses on natural resource and environmental issues, and the appendix of wealth and inequality indicators has been fully revised. The editors' short introduction to each selection, highlighting its significance, remains a key feature of the book.

Mitchell A. Seligson is Centennial Professor of political science at Vanderbilt University. **John T Passé-Smith** is professor of political science at the University of Central Arkansas.